Alfred Rambaud, Leonora Blanche Lang, Nathan Haskell Dole

History of Russia

From the Earliest Times to 1882 - Vol. III

Alfred Rambaud, Leonora Blanche Lang, Nathan Haskell Dole

History of Russia
From the Earliest Times to 1882 - Vol. III

ISBN/EAN: 9783743422315

Manufactured in Europe, USA, Canada, Australia, Japa

Cover: Foto ©ninafisch / pixelio.de

Manufactured and distributed by brebook publishing software (www.brebook.com)

Alfred Rambaud, Leonora Blanche Lang, Nathan Haskell Dole

History of Russia

A POPULAR

HISTORY OF RUSSIA,

From the Earliest Times to 1882.

BY

ALFRED RAMBAUD,

CHIEF OF THE CABINET OF THE MINISTER OF PUBLIC INSTRUCTION AND FINE ARTS, AT PARIS;
CORRESPONDING MEMBER OF THE ACADEMY OF SCIENCES OF
ST. PETERSBURG; ETC., ETC.

THIS WORK HAS BEEN CROWNED BY THE FRENCH ACADEMY.

TRANSLATED BY L. B. LANG.

NICHOLAS THE FIRST

History of Russia,

From the Earliest Times to 1882.

BY

Alfred Rambaud,

CHIEF OF THE CABINET OF THE MINISTER OF PUBLIC INSTRUCTION AND FINE ARTS, AT PARIS;
CORRESPONDING MEMBER OF THE ACADEMY OF SCIENCES OF
ST. PETERSBURG; ETC., ETC.

THIS WORK HAS BEEN CROWNED BY THE FRENCH ACADEMY.

TRANSLATED BY L. B. LANG.

EDITED AND ENLARGED BY NATHAN HASKELL DOLE.

INCLUDING

A HISTORY OF THE TURKO-RUSSIAN WAR OF 1877-78,
FROM THE BEST AUTHORITIES, BY THE EDITOR.

IN THREE VOLUMES.

Vol. III.

BOSTON:
ESTES AND LAURIAT,
301-305 WASHINGTON STREET.

CONTENTS.

CHAPTER I.
NICHOLAS THE FIRST.
1825-1855.

The December Insurrection. — Administration and Reforms. — Literature . 13 – 35

CHAPTER II.
AFFAIRS IN ASIA AND THE POLISH INSURRECTION.
1825-1855.

Persian War (1826 – 1828). — First Turkish War; Liberation of Greece (1826 – 1829). — The Russians and English in Asia. — The Polish Insurrection (1831) 36 – 71

CHAPTER III.
NICHOLAS THE FIRST: FOREIGN RELATIONS.
1825-1855.

Hostility against France: the Eastern Question. — Revolution of Eighteen Hundred and Forty-eight. — Intervention in Hungary . . . . . . 72 – 84

CHAPTER IV.
THE CRIMEAN WAR.
1853-1855.

Louis Napoleon. — Change in the English Cabinet. — Ministry of Lord Aberdeen. — The Holy Sites. — Conversations between the Emperor Nicholas and Sir George Hamilton Seymour . . . . 85 – 100

CHAPTER V.
THE CRIMEAN WAR.
1853-1855.

Prince Menshikof at Constantinople. — Lord Stratford de Redcliffe. — Colonel Rose. — M. Benedetti. — The French Fleet at Salamis. — Threatening Demands of Prince Menshikof. — Resistance of the Porte. — The Prince's Departure. — The French and English Squadrons at Besika. — Diplomatic Conflict. — Official Mediation of Austria. — The Russians cross the Pruth. — The Vienna Note. — Turkish Modifications. — Warlike Feelings. — Napoleon the Third. — Interviews at Olmütz and Warsaw. — The Porte declares War . . . 101 – 126

CONTENTS.

CHAPTER VI.
THE CRIMEAN WAR.
1853-1855.

Campaign of the Danube. — Austrian Interests. — Final Diplomatic Efforts. — Affair of Sinope. — The French and English Fleets in the Black Sea. — Diplomatic Rupture. — Count Orlof at Vienna. — Letters of Napoleon the Third and the Emperor Nicholas. — Austria and Prussia agree with France and England to maintain the Turkish Empire 127-144

CHAPTER VII.
THE CRIMEAN WAR.
1853-1855.

Military Arrangements of France and England. — The Allied Armies at Gallipoli and Varna. — Siege of Silistria. — Bombardment of Odessa. — Expedition into the Dobrudsha: the Cholera. — The Crimea. — Battle of the Alma. — Sevastopol 145-173

CHAPTER VIII.
THE CRIMEAN WAR.
1855-1856.

Accession of Alexander. — End of the Crimean War. — Treaty of Paris . . 174-206

CHAPTER IX.
ALEXANDER THE SECOND AND THE REFORMS.
1856-1877.

Imperial Manifestoes and Decrees. — The Act of the Nineteenth of February, Eighteen Hundred and Sixty-one: Judicial Reforms; Local Self-government. — The Polish Insurrection. — Intellectual Movement: Material Progress: Education . 207-256

CHAPTER X.
LITERATURE AND ART DURING THE REIGN OF ALEXANDER THE SECOND.
1856-1880.

The Natural and Realistic Schools. — Influence of the French Novelists. — The Historical Drama and Novel. — History. — Periodicals. — The Artistic and Scientific Movement 257-281

CHAPTER XI.
ALEXANDER THE SECOND.
1856-1880.

The Advance of Russian Power beyond the Caucasus. — Gortchakof's Circular Note. — Shamil and the Circassians. — Central Asia. — The Khanates. — The Khivan Expeditions. — Relations with China, Japan, and the United States . 282-308

CHAPTER XII.

ALEXANDER THE SECOND.
European Relations from 1856 until 1877.

Austria and Italy. — Prussia and Denmark. — Imperial Interviews; the Franco-Prussian War. — The Prussian Alliance. — Gortchakof's Circular Note of Eighteen Hundred and Seventy-one. — Reorganization of the Army . 309 – 324

CHAPTER XIII.

THE EASTERN QUESTION.
1875 - 1877.

The Herzegovinian and Bosnian Insurrection. — Count Andrassy's Note. — The Turkish Massacres. — Diplomatic Measures. — The Berlin Memorandum. — Events at Constantinople. — The Serbian War . . . . 325 – 346

CHAPTER XIV.

THE TURKO-RUSSIAN WAR.
1877.

Russia's Declaration of War. — The Passage of the Danube. — The Advance across the Balkans; Shipka Pass. — Capture of Nikopolis. — Repulse at Plevna. — Battle of Shipka Pass. — Operations on the Lom. — Third Battle of Plevna 347 – 368

CHAPTER XV.

THE TURKO-RUSSIAN WAR.
1877.

The Campaign in Asia. — Reverses. — Battle of Aladja-Dagh. — Storming of Kars. — Passage of the Balkans. — Advance upon Constantinople. — End of the War 369 – 381

CHAPTER XVI.

ASSASSINATION OF THE EMPEROR.
1881.

Popular Discontent. — Assassination of the Emperor . . . . . 382 – 388

INDEX 389

HISTORY OF RUSSIA.

CHAPTER I.

NICHOLAS THE FIRST.

1825–1855.

THE DECEMBER INSURRECTION. — ADMINISTRATION AND REFORMS. — LITERATURE.

THE DECEMBER INSURRECTION.

ACCORDING to the law of primogeniture, Alexander's successor should have been Konstantin Pavlovitch, who in eighteen hundred and twenty had been divorced from his wife Anna Feodorovna, in order to marry the Polish Countess Ioanna Grudzinska, afterwards created Princess Lovitch. An official manifesto issued at the same time formulated the principle that the right of succession to the throne could not be imparted to the children of any member of the Imperial family who married out of a royal house. Konstantin, two years later, addressed a letter to Alexander renouncing the crown in these words: "Being conscious that I have neither the genius, talents, nor energy necessary for my elevation to the sovereign dignity to which my birth might entitle me, I beg your Imperial Majesty to transfer this right to him to whom it falls next in succession, and thus establish forever a firm basis for the empire." Alexander immediately accepted his renunciation, and ordered Philaret, Archbishop and subsequently Metropolitan of Moscow, to draw up a manifesto which sanctioned the resolution taken by Konstantin and acknowledged his second brother, the Grand Duke Nikolaï, or Nicholas, as his successor. This document, signed at Tsarskoé-Selo on the twenty-eighth of August, eighteen hundred and twenty-three, was deposited in the Uspienski Sobor, or Cathedral of the Assumption, in Moscow, but was kept a profound secret even from Nicholas himself.

The news of Alexander's death was received in Warsaw some time before it reached Saint Petersburg, and Konstantin hastened to write a formal confirmation of the act of eighteen hundred and twenty-two, which he sent to Nicholas by his brother Mikhail. Nicholas, on the other hand, as soon as he learned of his brother's death, took the oath of allegiance to Konstantin, and obliged the army and the councillors of the empire to do the same. He also despatched a letter to Warsaw urging the new Emperor to come immediately to Saint Petersburg. The Tsesarévitch replied that his determination, which had been consecrated by Alexander, was immovable, and that everything must be arranged in accordance with Alexander's will. It was only on the twenty-fourth of December that the despatch from Konstantin, reiterating his formal renunciation of the throne, reached Nicholas and put an end to his indecision. He then published a manifesto, setting forth the circumstances which led to his unexpected accession, and claiming the allegiance of his subjects.

This contest of generosity, if generosity it was, contrasting so strongly with the ambitious habits and the political revolutions of the eighteenth century, cost the empire dear. During the three weeks' interregnum the minds of the people became troubled and uncertain; they did not know whom to obey. Such a crisis offered an opportunity for those who were inclined to revolutionary measures.

Had Colonel Pavel Pestel been at the head of the Society of the North, and possessed the full confidence of his associates, this perplexity of public opinion could have been used to terrible advantage. Pestel was an ardent revolutionist, but he saw clearly that it would take years to reorganize society upon a new and republican basis. He was convinced that first of all the Imperial family must be put out of the way, and that the land must be divided among the people. The associates of the North distrusted Pestel, they feared his ambition; it was said that he was a Napoleon rather than a Washington. In eighteen hundred and twenty-four Pestel himself went to Saint Petersburg and tried to unite the various political societies. He showed them that they must begin with a complete overturn of existing institutions; that the Emperor and his whole family should be put to death, and that the Senate and Holy Synod should be obliged to proclaim the new form of government. Pestel did not, however, succeed in persuading them to adopt his plans. When he returned to his regiment, he found it difficult to restrain the turbulent young officers who were additionally excited by the removal of Colonel Shveïkovski from his regiment. Moreover, the members belonging to the Society of the South and the United Slavs were becoming unwieldy, and though there was as yet no system of secret government police, still the danger of detection was imminent.

The Society of the North, existing partly in Saint Petersburg and partly in Moscow, was composed in large measure of government officials and members of the aristocracy. Everything that was done in the palace was immediately announced to the conspirators. It was known that the senators were to take the oath of allegiance to Nicholas on the twenty-sixth of December. The Society of the North resolved to act.

When, on the morning of the fatal day, the oath was administered to the troops, the Chevalier Guard, the Préobrazhenski, the Semenovski, and several other regiments offered no objection, but some of the officers belonging to the regiments of Moscow prevailed upon their men not to swear allegiance to

Nicholas, representing to them that the news of Konstantin's resignation was false, that the Tsesarévitch was a prisoner in chains, and that this second oath exacted of them was a sacrilege. Alexander Bestuzhef, one of the most active of the revolutionary society, who chanced to be present, assured them that he had been sent from Warsaw with orders to prevent the troops from taking the oath to Nicholas. The conspirators further inflamed the passions of the soldiery by telling them that the Tsar Konstantin considered them his favorite regiment, and was going to increase their pay. They were ordered to resist any one who was unfaithful to Konstantin, and to load their muskets with ball.

General Fridericks, attempting to approach his regiment, was severely wounded by Prince Shtchépin, who seized the colors, and shouting, "Hurrah for the Emperor Konstantin!" led the way to the Place of the Senate. Some of the conspirators raised the cry, "Long live the Constitution!" but this idea was meaningless to the masses; and, according to the monarchical historians, the ignorant soldiers believed that Konstitutsia was the name of Konstantin's wife.

The Emperor was informed that the Moscow regiment was in complete insurrection, and that General Fridericks and General Shenshin had been wounded while attempting to oppose the movement. He saw that the time had come for him to act without a moment's hesitation. Without stopping to put on his cloak, he placed himself at the head of a company of the Finland Life Guards which was on duty at the Winter Palace, and marched to the principal gateway, where a large crowd had collected. Here Nicholas, in order to give the battalions time to form, read in a slow and deliberate voice the manifesto which announced his accession. Then, claiming the loyalty and good-will of the people, he persuaded them to disperse. The military insurgents thus found themselves deprived of assistance from the masses, who, when they learned from the Emperor's own lips the true state of affairs, readily fell into their old habits of passive obedience.

The other regiments of the guard and nearly all the garrison, in spite of the efforts which had been made to tamper with their fidelity, remained unaffected, and the Préobrazhenski regiment, forming with great rapidity, hastened to the palace, where they were harangued by the Emperor, and in return promised to be faithful to the death.

The rebels, occupying the Place of the Senate with serried ranks, allowed no one to pass unchallenged. Miloradovitch, Governor-General of the city, attempted to reason with them. He showed them a sword which Konstantin had presented to him, and he argued that it was impossible for him to be a traitor to his old friend the Grand Duke. This speech and the sight of the brave old hero of fifty battles began to move the soldiers, when Kakhovski, suddenly approaching, shot him in the side and mortally wounded him. Several shots were also fired at General Voïnof, who attempted to address the insurgents. About the same time the marines of the guard, seduced by their officers, joined the mutinous Moscow regiment. The Emperor was obliged to send for reinforcements. He was even shot at as he attempted to reconnoitre. Prince Orlof was then commanded to charge with the cavalry; but as the rebels were in a dense mass, they easily repulsed the attack. Several of the foreign ministers begged leave to join the Emperor's suite in order to show the people that the legality of his claim was countenanced by them, but Nicholas sent back word that this was merely a family affair in which Europe had no concern. A portion of the grenadiers of the Life Guard, upon hearing the noise of the musket-shots, were induced by their officers to pass over to the side of Konstantin, and Lieutenant Panof was only by an accident prevented from getting possession of the Winter Palace. The insurgents, still more emboldened by their continual reinforcements coming to them, kept up an irregular but violent firing, and refused to listen to the intercession of the Grand Duke Mikhail, who rode up to them at the risk of his life, and begged of them to follow his example and take the oath to his brother the Emperor. One last measure of peace remained. Seraphim, Metropolitan of Saint Petersburg, and Evgeni, Metropolitan of Kief, were at the Winter Palace, in order to perform the Te Deum which had been appointed for that day. The Emperor resolved to try the influence of the Church upon the rebels, and sent for the prelate to appeal to their religious sentiments. Although Colonel Stürler fell at his very feet by the pistol of Kakhovski, the murderer of Miloradovitch, the venerable metropolitan, undaunted, advanced toward the rebels and tried to bring them to reason by calling upon God to witness the truth of his words. The leaders of the revolt interrupted him with cries that Konstantin was their lawful Tsar, and that this was not the affair of a churchman who could perjure himself by taking an oath to two different Emperors in one week. Shots were fired at the metropolitan in spite of his sacerdotal robes, and he received four balls in his mitre. His efforts remained fruitless; he was obliged to retire to save his life.

It was now three o'clock in the afternoon, and the short wintry day was fast drawing to a close. Nicholas sent General Sukhozanet once more to promise full pardon to all but the ringleaders if they would lay down their arms, but this last appeal was rejected. All attempts at conciliation having been in vain, the Emperor ordered the soldiers to direct the cannon against the barricades which had been hastily raised. A few rounds sufficed to scatter the crowd. The Senate Square was cleared. The revolt was crushed. The Préobrazhenski and Semenovski regiments immediately started in pursuit of the fugitives. Five hundred were taken prisoners, and during the night many more surrendered at discretion. Prince Trubetskoï who was the nominal head of the conspiracy, but had not appeared during the eventful day, was taken at the house of his brother-in-law, and all his papers, compromising many members of the Society, were seized by Count Nesselrode.

At seven in the morning, Nicholas returned victorious to his palace. Alexander Herzen says: "The conspirators did not succeed; that is all that can be said; but success was not out of the range of possibility. How would it have been if the conspirators had assembled the soldiers, not on the morning of the twenty-sixth, but at midnight, and if they had used the forces at their disposition in order to surround the Winter Palace, when there was no suspicion of any trouble? What would have been the result if the conspirators, instead of forming in a square, had attacked the troops guarding the palace, who were as yet undecided and irresolute?"

The same night Pavel Pestel, two Muravief brothers, and ten other members of the Society of the South were arrested by General Dibitch and General Tchernichef, who were with Alexander when De Witt brought the confirmation of the conspiracy. When the officers of the United Slavs heard this news they immediately collected several companies of soldiers and proceeded to liberate the prisoners. Pestel had been removed, but they set the others free. Sergi Muravief and Bestuzhef-Riumin put themselves at the head of the soldiers, and with the assistance of part of the regiment of Tchernigof occupied Vasilkof and marched against Kief; but at the village of Ustinovka they encountered General Geismar, who received them with a discharge of grape-shot. Sergi Muravief was severely wounded. A cavalry charge put the revolted companies to flight. Seven hundred men laid down their arms, and nearly all the leaders were made prisoners.

Nicholas granted a disdainful pardon to Prince Trubetskoï, who had caused the failure of the conspiracy by his cowardice and his fickle policy. He showed a certain clemency to the majority of the insurgents, but a hundred and twenty-one, "the élite of all that was civilized and truly noble in Russia," were brought before a commission consisting of Alexander Tatishtchef, the minister of war, the Grand Duke Mikhail, Prince Galitsuin, Kutusof, military governor of Saint Petersburg, Alexander Tchernichef, and several others. The poet Konrad Ruileef, the real head of the conspiracy, on being brought before this commission, said: "It was in my power to arrest the whole conspiracy, but I urged immediate action. I am the chief author of the events of December twenty-sixth. If any one deserves death for this day, it is I." A minute inquiry and many confessions enabled Nicholas to find the threads of the plot. The "traitors," as they were called, not having succeeded, were punished more or less severely. Five of them, Pestel, Ruileef, Sergi Muravief-Apostol, Bestuzhef-Riumin, and Kakhovski, the assassin of Miloradovitch, were condemned to be hanged. They did honor to their cause by the courage with which they faced an ignominious penalty, made doubly cruel by the awkwardness of their executioners. Ruileef said, after his condemnation, "The zeal of my patriotism and my love for my country may have deceived me, but as my actions have been guided by no personal interest or ambition, I die without fear." Pestel, the energetic dictator of the South, valued his life as of small consequence in comparison with the safety of his Russian Code. "I am certain," he said, "that, sooner or later, Russia will find in this book a refuge against violent commotions. My greatest error is that I tried to gather the harvest before sowing the seed."

Many of the ideas to which these generous-souled men became martyrs were indeed premature in a country like Russia, but some were destined to survive their originators, and to be carried into execution by the very power which they defied. They demanded the abolition of serfdom, the absolute independence of the peasants, greater equality of rights, more stability in the law. In spite of their mistakes, which they expiated with their lives, they proved that there existed in Russia men capable of dying for liberty. "I knew beforehand," said Ruileef, "that this enterprise would be my destruction, but I could not any longer endure the sight of my country under the yoke of despotism : the seed which I have sown will germinate erelong, and bring forth fruit."

This abortive conspiracy was in certain respects the beginning of regeneration. Many of the old dekabrists, or men of December, were, in letters, arts, and political philosophy, the glory of their country, and were able to advance as far as it was practicable by other means the work which they at that time began. The revolution of eighteen hundred and twenty-five gave an impetus to the country that the thirty years' reign of Nicholas could not destroy.

ADMINISTRATION AND REFORMS.

Nicholas, whose reign was thus inaugurated by the suppression of a wide-spread revolution, was to be throughout his life the indomitable enemy of all that was likely to favor the growth of popular liberty. In Europe as well as in Russia he stood forth as the champion of conservative principles. If he carried on the work of his brother Alexander, it was the Alexander of later years, when the grand ideas of innovation which had possessed his soul in eighteen hundred and one were all extinguished, when his liberal sympathies and his humane scruples were long ago forgotten. Nicholas, with his colossal stature, his imposing presence, his mystic pride, his infatuation for the role of a pontiff-king, his iron will, his power of work, his taste for even the petty details of government, his passion for military minutiæ, was a terrible incarnation of autocracy. Always buttoned tight in his uniform and playing his part before the people, Nicholas, the "crowned Sergeant!" held in check the mighty forces which would have advanced Russia far on the path of modern civilization. As it was, his reign was a constant protest against the progress of the world. He kept up a perpetual struggle to repress the living forces of humanity, to overcome the unrestrainable, invincible advance of the mind. He could not be an absolute obstacle to progress. He could act only as a drag upon the wheels. When his power broke, under its ruins was seen a new world which had grown to maturity without his knowledge.

One of the first cares of Nicholas was to take up the work of codifying the Russian laws, which had been so often begun by his predecessors: by Peter the Great with the help of the Germanic laws; by Catherine the Second with her great legislative commission; by Alexander with Speranski's almost Napoleonic project. Nicholas himself could only collect the materials, for it was an impossibility that the Russian laws should be codified until society, regenerated by the emancipation, became established in its final form.

In eighteen hundred and thirty appeared the "Complete Collection of the Laws of the Russian Empire," of which the Ulozhenié of Alexis Mikhaïlovitch formed the basis. This was followed in eighteen hundred and thirty-eight by the "Collection of Existing Laws," compiled after a systematic scheme which was intended provisionally to make legislation more consistent, and introduce greater rapidity into the action of the courts. It was time, for two million eight hundred and fifty thousand causes were declared to be pending, and one hundred and twenty-seven thousand persons, committed for trial, were still waiting judgment. In eighteen hundred and forty-nine was published the Code for the trial of crimes and misdemeanors. Tribunals of trade were established in order that commercial affairs might be more promptly despatched.

In the reign of Peter the Great the English law of entail was borrowed, with certain modifications. Anna Ivanovna suppressed it on the ground that it was opposed to Russian customs. Nicholas partially re-established it by granting permission to the father of the family to make use of it if he pleased. The practice of the praviozh, or forcible distraining for debt, still existed among the Don Cossacks; it was now abolished. Merchants, anxious to get into the ranks of the nobility, thronged to secure office in the public service; Nicholas, to turn their ambition into a different channel and at the same time to give them equal advantages, created a new subdivision in the class inhabiting the towns, — that of the chief citizens, who enjoyed the following prerogatives: exemption from the poll tax, conscription, and corporal punishment; the right to take part in the assessment of the landed property of the town, and the right of being elected to the communal offices of the same rank as those open to the merchants of the first guilds. All might be admitted among the chief citizens who had a certificate of secondary studies, a student's diploma, or that of a university student eligible for the degree of Master of Arts, or who were free artists having a certificate from the Academy of Fine Arts. Nicholas here revived one of the traditions of Catherine the Second, who attempted to constitute a third estate at the same time with a new nobility. He tried to regulate the mode of procedure used by the assemblies of peasants in the rural communes, and introduce the custom of voting with white and black balls. The autocratic Tsar was one of the first to countenance universal suffrage in Russia.

The vital question of emancipation slumbered during this reign. Nicholas contented himself with giving his approval to the great nobles who set their serfs at liberty. The Princess Orlof-Tchesmenski freed five thousand five hundred and eighteen. The class of free cultivators increased very slowly; in eighteen hundred and thirty-eight it numbered only seventy-two thousand eight hundred and forty-four husbandmen. The edict of eighteen hundred and forty-two, by which an attempt was made to fix the conditions of these contracts of emancipation, made the nobles anxious about the effect it would have upon their serfs. The government hastened to reassure them by affirming that the liberation of the peasants was not under consideration, and by ordering the arrest of individuals who propagated false news. They were authorized to use force, if necessary, in recalling refractory serfs to their obedience.

Nicholas established in the Court of the Holy Synod his aide-de-camp Pratasof, a general of hussars, who for twenty years governed the national church in a military fashion, and had no scruples about disciplining and dragooning the dissenters of White Russia.

Nicholas continued the work of joining the Don and the Volga by means of a canal, and undertook to improve the navigation of the Dnieper. In the reign of this champion of conservatism the first railways were created. He traced in a straight line with a ruler the railway between Saint Petersburg and Moscow, without allowing it to turn aside so as to pass through any towns of importance. A small branch joined Tsarskoć-Selo to the capital. Russia was still far behind in following the new European enterprises; no iron road as yet united the East and the West. The annoyances of the police, the censorship of the press, the custom-house dues, all contributed to its isolation from Europe. Its autocrat kept the rest of Europe in a kind of political quarantine. While speaking of public works, we must mention the reconstruction in fifteen months of the Winter Palace, which was destroyed by the fire of eighteen hundred and thirty-seven.

Nicholas created a "professorial institute"—a sort of normal school for the higher education—to recruit the ranks of public schoolmasters, and a "principal pedagogic institute" for the secondary course of instruction. His object was to remove the Russian youth from the influence of foreign masters. There were restrictions as to the employment of tutors and governesses in private houses. Their capacity and their morality, under the head of which were included their political opinions, were to be certified by one of the universities of the empire, under the penalty of a fine of two hundred and fifty rubles and of banishment. It was forbidden to send young men to study in Western universities, save in some exceptional cases, for which a special permission was required. In the government schools, at the expense of foreign languages and literature, a greater development was given to the Russian language, literature, statistics, and history, which were considered less dangerous. Other obstacles were imposed on freedom of foreign travel and residence; the term of absence attested by legal passports was fixed at five years for the nobles, and three for other Russian subjects. The University of Saint Vladimir was founded at Kief, to replace that of Vilna, which was suppressed after the Polish insurrection. The scholastic reaction, the mistrust of German philosophy, went so far that philosophy was finally forbidden to be taught in the universities, and was put under the exclusive care of ecclesiastics.

Nicholas bestowed especial attention on the establishments for military instruction, the corps of cadets, and the Academy of War. He created, however, a law school and a technological institute. The scientific publications of the government and those of the archæological commission established in eighteen hundred and thirty-four, of which Stroef, Korkunof, and Berednikof were important members, furnished, with the "Complete Collection of Russian Laws," new materials for the study of the national history.

The imperial library at Saint Petersburg was enriched by Pogodin's cabinet of antiquities, and to the liberality of Count Rumiantsof Moscow owes the museum and library which bear his name.

LITERATURE.

The most important historical work of this period was the "History of Russia," by Ustrialof, "written in an elevated style, but in reality scarcely more than a résumé of Karamsin." The "History of the Russian People," by Nikolaï Polévoï, is also worthy of notice, though it fails in being uncritical and superficial. Solovief, who is called the Augustin Thierry of Russia, began his enormous historical work, which was never finished. "The formation of the political unity of the country is explained with the hand of a master. He understood also how to describe in a clear and attractive manner the peculiarities of the principal characters as well as the customs of each epoch."

The censorship weighed heavily on the development of the national press. Until eighteen hundred and twenty-five there was really no newspaper worthy of the name, unless, perhaps, the Saint Petersburg News founded in the reign of Peter the Great. Gretch, with the assistance of Bulgarin, called the Russian Vidocq, established during the first year of Nicholas's reign a daily journal, the Northern Bee, which aimed at being a popular and literary newspaper. The struggle between the partisans of the romantic and classic schools was carried on with great vigor. The classicists, supported by the respectability of antiquity, founded many organs; while, on the other hand, the romanticists were at first limited to almanacs or pamphlets, though they occasionally made use of the columns of the Son of the Fatherland, which shared with the Northern Bee the dubious honor of carrying on a desperate war against everything foreign, especially everything French, as well as against liberty of thought."

Polévoï began his career by making common cause with Professor Katchenovski, the editor of the *Viestnik Evropui,* or "European Messenger," which was the champion of the classic school. He soon found reason, however, to change his views, and after a short and unsatisfactory engagement with

Bulgarin, he obtained permission in eighteen hundred and twenty-four to establish a new review which he called the Telegraph. He gathered about him as associates men of ability, such as Maximovitch and Krasovski, who wrote on scientific subjects, the witty and liberal Princes Viasemski and Odoïevski, and afterwards the poet Pushkin. He himself kept in the current of all that was new in the intellectual life of Europe. Nothing escaped his attention. The Telegraph soon became extremely popular. "Polévoï was acknowledged to be the judge of good literary taste, and the father of true Russian criticism." He was too independent not to win hosts of enemies who were envious of his success. After the revolution of eighteen hundred and twenty-five, and the events which took place in Europe five years later, liberality was looked upon with little favor by the censure. The Telegraph, which showed itself a partisan of the economical ideas of Adam Smith, was regarded as a dangerous sheet. Its enemies were on the watch to ruin it, and finally their opportunity came. A severe criticism of a wretched political drama by Kukolnik led to the arrest of the editor-in-chief and the suppression of the journal. The principal opponent of Polévoï was Nadezhdin, a celebrated professor of the University of Moscow, who in the Telescope developed the ideas of Schelling. Nadezhdin exposed relentlessly the poverty of Russian literature. One of his pupils was Biélinski, the prince of critics. He was the son of a country physician, and was educated at the University of Moscow, which was then at the height of its prosperity. He was not considered a remarkable scholar, but he soon joined the literary circle of which the ruling spirit was Stankiévitch, a man who exercised a great influence over his associates, and was endeavoring to introduce the ideas of Hegel, in contradistinction to those of Schelling. Biélinski first attracted attention by his article entitled "Literary Reveries," in which he went even further than his master, and denied that there was any Russian literature at all. He afterwards, in eighteen hundred and thirty-eight, took Shevuiref's place as director of the Observer, started by Stepanof in Moscow. This review, which was too exclusive and monotonous, soon ceased to exist, and Biélinski accepted a position as associate on Kraïevskiz's "Annals of the Country," in which he published brilliant criticisms of Russian literature and poetry, and articles on Lermontof and Pushkin. Several years later he was invited to edit the Contemporary, a review founded by Nekrasof and Panaïef. He died in eighteen hundred and forty-eight, an ardent advocate of Occidentalism. Pogodin called him "an atheist, a socialist, a propagandist"; his fickleness and the changes which his opinion underwent were his weak side, but the Slavophiles, who attacked him in the Epoch, the Times, the Citizen, and the Muscovite, could not appreciate his really brilliant qualities.

The principal representatives of the Slavophiles were Pogodin, Shevuiref, Aksakof, and Kirievski; they discussed questions relative to the unity of the Slav races, the nationality of the Russian people; they had only the greatest contempt for Western Europe; the natural school, including Gogol and Turgénief, they accused of plagiarism; they thought that "Ivan the Third was superior to Peter the Great, and that Russia before this great reformer was better than afterwards."

This period of the nineteenth century was as fertile in Russian as in French and English literature. To the names of Lamartine, Victor Hugo, Alfred de Musset, to the names of Byron, Shelley, Wordsworth, correspond those of Pushkin, Lermontof, Koltsof, Griboïédof, and Gogol.

Alexander Pushkin, the greatest Russian poet, and one of the first of modern times, was born in seventeen hundred and ninety-nine, at Moscow. His mother was of African origin. He was early initiated by an old nurse into the customs and legends of the people. His father had been educated in

France, and owned a large library consisting mostly of French authors. The young Pushkin learned French as his mother-tongue. When he entered the lyceum of Tsarskoé-Selo, at the age of twelve, he found French ideas predominant, and instead of studying, he spent his time in desultory reading, writing poems, and in all sorts of dissipation. He afterwards entered the civil service, and spent some years in the Caucasus and in Odessa. He resigned in eighteen hundred and twenty-four, and after the revolt lived quietly at Saint Petersburg and on his estate of Mikhaïlovsk, where he composed his poetical tales. He was killed in eighteen hundred and thirty-seven, in a duel with Baron George Heckeren-Dantes. Pushkin owes his inspiration partly to Lord Byron, though his muse is not so gloomy and misanthropical as that of the English poet. The first poem of Pushkin which attracted attention was " Ruslan and Liudmila," a tale in which are blended beautiful descriptions of scenery, interesting sketches of character, Russian legends, and Italian fancies. It is written in sonorous and musical verse. Afterwards followed the tales inspired by his numerous visits to the Caucasus. Perhaps his greatest work is the tragedy of Boris Godunof, which, in the opinion of Konstantin Petrof, recalls the genius of Shakspere. Pushkin wrote also several novels which are distinguished for their grace and beauty, although the characters are not always natural.

Mikhail Lermontof was born at Moscow in eighteen hundred and fourteen. Polévoï says that he lost his mother when he was two years old, and that nothing is known of his father except that he was of noble origin. His grandmother, Madame Arsenief, undertook his early education. He afterwards regretted that his training had been under foreign influences. "How unfortunate," he says, "that my nurse was German and not Russian. I failed to hear our popular folk-stories. In these there is certainly more poetry than in all French literature." At the age of ten his grandmother took him to the Caucasus, where Polévoï says that "he fell seriously in love with some blond-haired, blue-eyed maiden of nine." He afterwards studied at the University of Moscow, but in consequence of a youthful escapade was expelled. He then became a cavalry officer, and lived a gay and rather dissipated life. His first poem which attracted universal attention was the ode upon Pushkin's death, "in which he expressed his admiration for the poet, and his sorrow at his untimely death, and at the same time poured forth all the vials of his bitterness upon that coterie which was so incapable of appreciating Pushkin." This attack upon Pushkin's critics led to his banishment to the Caucasus, where the wild and beautiful scenery exercised a great influence over his genius. He returned to Saint Petersburg before the expiration of a year, and published his great poem "The Demon," in which are painted the remembrances of his youth, his dreams of love and happiness, his worship of beauty. "The Demon, driven from heaven, wanders through the world, takes pleasure in doing ill, contemplates the sublimity of the Caucasus with haughty and disdainful glance. He becomes melancholy as he thinks of the happy days of the past when his soul was full of love and faith. He wearies of wrong-doing, for he nowhere meets with resistance." He then sees the beautiful Tamara, and in the love of the pure mortal his thoughts gradually become pure and noble again.

Lermontof's life was abruptly ended by a self-sought duel. Being banished for the third time to the Caucasus, he quarrelled with a comrade named Martuinof, and was killed in eighteen hundred and forty-one. His tendency to doubt and his Byronic admiration of solitude are shown in his other poems, especially in "Valerika's Dream." He expresses his views of society in his celebrated novel "The Hero of our Time." "It is a vivid picture of the struggle of genius against the crushing and killing atmosphere which at that time weighed down free and independent minds. Biélinski says of him: "Lermontof wrote little, infinitely little, in comparison with the possibilities of his colossal talent. His indolent disposition, his fiery youth, so eager to receive new impressions, his peculiar manner of life, withdrew him from the peaceful occupations of the study, and from solitary meditation, the delight of the Muses. But already his impetuous nature was beginning to calm down, in his soul was growing the thirst for work and activity, and his eagle eye began peacefully to sound the depths of life."

Koltsof was one of the most distinguished poets of Pushkin's time. He reproduced the life of the people with much sentiment, basing his poems upon the Russian folk-song, in which love and the heavy yoke of slavery are thrown into vivid contrast. His best tales are "The Flight" and the "Song of the Brigand," in which many Cossack dumki are introduced. Koltsof lived a life of trial and privation, and died in eighteen hundred and forty-two, at the age of thirty-three.

Alexander Griboïédof is remembered chiefly for his celebrated comedy in four acts, *Horé ot Uma*, "Too Clever by Half," or, more literally, the "Misfortune of Sense," in which is given a remarkable picture of the society of Moscow during the first quarter of this century. The hero is filled with modern ideas, and despises the ancient régime. The dialogue is monotonous and inartistic, but the characters are vividly presented and well sustained. The author, who was killed in eighteen hundred and twenty-nine by the excited populace of Teheran, did not see the piece put on the stage. At first the play was not even allowed to be printed. Since his death it has occasionally been presented.

One of the most remarkable of the writers of this reign was Nikolaï Gogol-Ianovski, who was born in eighteen hundred and nine, in a little village near Poltava. His father was a learned man of some importance, and undertook his education until he was twelve years old, when he was sent to the Gymnasium of Niézhin. He detested German, and was not much more fond of the dead languages, but an excellent memory assisted him, and he soon won a local reputation as a writer and an actor. He edited a little paper called the Star. After he left the gymnasium he went to Saint Petersburg, where he gained a precarious livelihood under the protection of Zhukovski and Pushkin, by whose aid he published some Little Russian tales and an epic novel entitled "Taras-Bulba," "borrowed from the time when the Cossacks were still independent. Taras-Bulba is the true type of those Cossack chiefs, always ready to mount and give battle. War is his element." Gogol paints the beauties of the Ukraina with a loving hand. Biélinski was the first to give a definite position to Gogol. In eighteen hundred and thirty-five appeared his comedy "The Revisor," which was very successful, and stands next to Griboïedof's *Horé ot Uma*. Shortly afterwards he went to Italy to recruit his health. He then wrote *Mertvuia Dushi*, or, "Dead Souls," of which the subject is borrowed from the life of the provincial proprietors and serfs. The male serfs are reckoned by *souls*, and as the registration was infrequent the proprietors were often obliged to pay a tax on peasants who had died. This powerful novel revealed the plague-spots in Russian administration and society. Gogol's other works are "The Portrait," "Nevski Prospekt," "The Nose," "The Cloak," and "The Memoirs of a Madman," in all of which, abandoning the steppes, he took his scenes from Saint Petersburg and the life of the middle classes. Toward the latter part of his career Gogol's mind became affected by a species of religious insanity. He tore up at night what he had written during the day, and sent strange letters to his friends. He died at Moscow in March, eighteen hundred and fifty-two.

This was the golden age of translations. Zhukovski made Russian versions of Gray's Elegy and many German ballads in which sentimentality and romanticism were the ruling motives. Zhukovski was born in seventeen hundred and eighty-four at Biélef, near Tula. He studied in Moscow, then returned to his native village, where he spent twelve years in solitude and dreams of love and friendship. At the time of the Napoleonic invasion he served in the army and wrote "The Bard in the Camp of the Russian Warriors," which brought him to the attention of the Court. He was appointed tutor to Alexander Nikolaiévitch. He translated Schiller for the Grand Duchess Alexandra, and then turned his attention to Indian and Persian literature. His masterpiece is the Russian version of the Odyssey. He had never seen the original. It is not literal, and is too much colored with his romantic melancholy, but it is a remarkable poem. Zhukovski died at Baden-Baden in eighteen hundred and fifty-two.

Schiller, Hoffman, Walter Scott, Shakspere, George Sand, were either translated or imitated. Polévoï wrote his "Oath at the Tomb of our Savior," "The Deserted One," "Hamlet," and "Ugolin"; Marlinski continued the romantic movement with his "Terrible Prediction" and "The Proscribed." Byron was forgotten. From eighteen hundred and forty until the Crimean War there is nothing of very great importance in the domain of literature. It was a period of change and transition. The iron censure weighed heavily upon all original production. Turgénief says in his "Memoirs of Biélinski": "Life was very painful at this time, and the young people of to-day have to undergo no such experiences. In the morning your proof returned from the censure full of erasures, covered with words written in red ink, as it were stained with blood. Sometimes it was necessary to present one's self before the censor, offer him useless or humiliating explanations and apologies, and listen to judgments which had no appeal and were often ironical. On the street you would meet a general or an office-holder who overwhelmed you with nonsense or with compliments, which was still worse. Looking about, you saw venality in full feather, serfdom crushing the people down like a rock, barracks in every direction; there was no justice, threats were made of closing the universities, foreign travel was out of the question, it was impossible to procure a serious book, a gloomy cloud hung heavily over what was called the administration of literature and the sciences. Informers were lurking everywhere. Among the young there was no common bond, no general interest. Fear and flattery were universal."

And yet it cannot be called a barren epoch. Herzen, under the name of "Iskander," wrote his principal novel, "Whose Fault is it?" which showed great originality, and a tendency toward socialism; Ivan Turgénief struck the prelude to a world-wide reputation in his "Memoirs of a Huntsman," in regard to which he says: "I could no longer breathe the same air nor live with the thing that I detested; I had not sufficient force of character for that. I was obliged to recoil from my enemy, that I might fall upon him with greater violence. This enemy of mine had a fixed form, bore a well-known name, — it was serfdom. I resolved to fight it to the death; I vowed never to become reconciled. This was my Hannibal's oath."

Grigorovitch made use of the same sort of material as Turgénief, but with less success. His novels, "The Emigrants," "The Fishers," paint rather superficially the life of the peasants. Pisemski showed independence and originality in freeing himself from the influence of Gogol, and produced "The Liéshi, or Were-wolf," and "The Petersburgher," which depict the muzhik in less poetical and more natural colors than Grigorovitch. Dostoievski was at first also a partisan of the romantic school, and a follower of Gogol. He wrote several short stories and two novels, "The Poor" and "Sosia." His faults are monotony and vagueness. Dahl, who wrote under the name of "The Cossack of Lugan," made literary studies of the Russian people based upon his wide knowledge of their popular tales and proverbs. His Physiological Sketches made his reputation. Dahl is not only a conscientious observer, but also a literary artist. The stage also had its great writer in Ostrovski, whose comedies are taken from the life of the merchant class. Glinka began to write his operas. Russian poetry at this time is represented by Iazuikof and Khomiakof, who are not dissimilar in their treatment of historical subjects. The former wrote his two tragedies, "Iermak" and "The False Dmitri." Ogaref followed in the steps of Lermontof, and pictured misery, sorrow, and death with exaggerated emphasis. Markof, Fet, and Shtchervin described the beauties of nature. Aksakof wrote a historical drama entitled "The Deliverance of Moscow in eighteen hundred and twelve," which is conceived in strict conformity with actual events.

Throughout this period the Russian intellect, in spite of all obstacles, spread its wings and tried unknown flights, created new openings for itself, and nobly gave the lie to theories of a rigid conservatism. Russia, isolated though it was from Europe, nevertheless took its place among the great European nations.

CHAPTER II.

AFFAIRS IN ASIA AND THE POLISH INSURRECTION.

1825 – 1855.

PERSIAN WAR (1826 – 1828). — FIRST TURKISH WAR; LIBERATION OF GREECE (1826 – 1829). — THE RUSSIANS AND ENGLISH IN ASIA. — THE POLISH INSURRECTION (1831).

PERSIAN WAR; FIRST TURKISH WAR; LIBERATION OF GREECE.

AFTER the treaty of Gulistan, the Russian and Persian governments were continually quarrelling on the subject of the frontiers and the vassal tribes. The Shah continued to receive tribute from the khans of Karabagh and Gandja, but in his turn complained of the encroachments of Russia, the occupation of the district of Gokcha, and of the arrogance of Iermolof, Governor-General of the Caucasus. Soon the Russians learnt that the Mollahs were preaching on all sides a holy war, that English officers had entered the service of the Shah, and that Abbas-Mirza, Prince Royal of Persia, was beginning to cross the Araxes at the head of thirty-five thousand men, and to raise the tributary khanates. Nicholas at once despatched General Paskiévitch to join Iermolof. The Prince Royal was in full march on Tiflis, but he was held in check for six weeks by the heroic resistance of the fortress of Shusha. The Russians thus had time to concentrate their forces. Near Elisavetpol they defeated the Persian vanguard, eighteen thousand strong; on the Djćham, in eighteen hundred and twenty-six, Paskiévitch, with less than ten thousand men, dispersed the whole royal army, forty-four thousand strong, and obliged the remnant to retreat beyond the Araxes.

By the treaty of Teheran, signed in eighteen hundred and fourteen, England promised Persia, in case of invasion, assistance with troops and a subsidy of five millions. But now the English government affected that Persia had begun the quarrel and refused the promised aid, although Paskiévitch, appointed general-in-chief in eighteen hundred and twenty-seven, forced the defiles of the mountains and crossed the Araxes. He then captured ten thousand of the Prince Royal's men, took Erivan, the bulwark of Persia, by assault, entered Tauris, the second city of the kingdom, in triumph, and began his march to Teheran. The king, Fet-Aly-Shah, in alarm signed the Peace of Turkmantchaï on the twenty-second of February, eighteen hundred and twenty-eight, by which he agreed to cede to Russia the provinces of Erivan and Nakhitchevan, and pay an indemnity of twenty million rubles. He also promised important commercial advantages to Russian subjects. The Araxes became the frontier of the two empires, and Paskiévitch received the title of Erivanski. The peace was all but broken in eighteen hundred and twenty-nine by the massacre of the Russian legation at Teheran, in which the poet Griboïédof, the Russian minister, perished. The Court of Teheran disavowed the crime of the people, and, although Russia was then occupied in a war with Turkey, the Prince Royal came to Saint Petersburg to offer the most complete satisfaction. Persia became day by day more subject to Russian influence, to the great disgust of England.

With regard to Turkey, Nicholas took a more decided attitude than Alexander. The enemy of revolutions sympathized with the regeneration of Greece. He made two demands of the Sultan: in concert with the other powers, he insisted that an end should be put to the extermination of the Greeks, and in his own name he demanded satisfaction for the bloody outrages inflicted on the orthodox Christians since the massacre of Constantinople, and for the insults offered to his ambassador. On one side he, like the rest of Europe, invoked the rights of humanity; on the other, he claimed his rights as protector of the members of the orthodox Church, guaranteed by the treaties of Kaïnardji and Bukarest. Sometimes he acted in unison with Europe, sometimes he stood aloof, in order to act separately and more energetically.

In March, eighteen hundred and twenty-six, Nicholas presented his ultimatum to the Divan. His conditions were: The evacuation of the Danubian principalities, which the Turks had occupied under the pretext of the insurrection of eighteen hundred and twenty-one, and the re-establishment of affairs on the basis of existing treaties; the execution of the clauses of the Treaty of Bukarest, relating to the autonomy of Serbia and the liberation of the Serbian deputies who were detained in Constantinople; finally, satisfaction on all points under dispute and the appointment of an Ottoman plenipotentiary.

The Porte tried to resist, but the European powers persuaded the Sultan to yield, and on the eighth of October the Convention of Akkerman was concluded on the following conditions: The confirmation of the Treaty of Bukarest; the autonomy of Moldavia and Valakhia, under a hospodar elected for seven years in an assembly of nobles, who could be deposed only with the consent of Russia; the final cession to Russia of the disputed territories on the Asiatic frontier; seven years' delay to enable the Porte to organize Serbia in accordance with the Treaty of Bukarest; fair satisfaction to the Russian subjects who were creditors of the Turkish Government; free passage for Russian vessels from the Black Sea to the Mediterranean.

The Greek question still remained. The Duke of Wellington and Count Nesselrode had come to an agreement in the Saint Petersburg conferences. The Anglo-Russian protocol of the twenty-sixth of March, eighteen hundred and twenty-six, energetically supported by the French ambassador, was presented to the Porte by the representatives of the three powers. Greece was to be an autonomous dependency of Turkey, was to pay an annual tribute to the Sultan, to be governed by authorities elected by its own people, but over the nomination of whom the Porte was to exercise a certain influence. The Turks settled in Greece were to emigrate, and to receive an equivalent for their fixtures. The Divan rejected these propositions as "violating the passive obedience owed by subjects to their legitimate sovereign." France, England, and Russia signed the Treaty of London in June, eighteen hundred and twenty-seven, by virtue of which they imposed their mediation on the belligerents, Turkey and Greece. The Porte, when informed of this, replied by disembarking a Turco-Egyptian army in the Morea, under the command of Ibrahim. The three Western squadrons, commanded by Admirals de Rigny, Heiden, and Codrington, received orders to hinder, even by force, the prolongation of hostilities in the Peninsula. The Turkish fleet was then annihilated in the battle of Navarino, on the twentieth of October, eighteen hundred and twenty-seven. Nicholas addressed flattering letters to the French and English admirals, with the Order of Saint Alexander Nevski for M. de Rigny, and that of Saint George for Codrington.

The disaster of Navarino only exasperated Sultan Mahmud. He sent the three powers a note in which he demanded that prior to any negotiation he should receive a formal declaration that they would renounce all interference in the affairs of Turkey and Greece, make public and solemn reparation for the insult offered to the Ottoman flag, and pay an indemnity to the Porte for the injuries which it had suffered. In the mosques a holy war was proclaimed, and a general levy. At Constantinople such a phantom of a national representation as we have again seen recently was convoked.

England was already beginning to regret the destruction of the Turkish fleet; but France, in order to give the force of law to the decisions of the powers, disembarked a body of troops in the Morea under General Maison, who expelled the Turco-Egyptians from the Peninsula. Nicholas, joining his private grievances to the claims of Europe, declared war on Turkey, and ordered Field-Marshal Wittgenstein to cross the Pruth, while Paskiévitch entered Asia Minor. In Europe the Russians occupied Valakhia and Moldavia, passed the Danube in the presence of their Emperor, and took Brailof and Varna. In Asia they carried by assault the ancient fortress of Kars, defeated the Turks under the walls of Akhaltsuikh, and captured the town after a bloody action.

England began to be uneasy, and Austria made advances toward an alliance against Russia. Charles the Tenth of France openly said, "If the Emperor Nicholas attacks Austria, I will hold myself in reserve, and regulate my conduct according to circumstances; but if the Austrians begin the attack, I will instantly march against them." The Restoration hoped to find in the struggle in the East a revenge for the treaties of eighteen hundred and fifteen. The reunion to France of the left bank of the Rhine or of Belgium was discussed in the king's council in September, eighteen hundred and twenty-nine; and the co-operation of Russia was counted on, in exchange for the aid which France was giving it on the Danube. In a word, according to the expression of M. Nettement, the two powers were then closely united, "France against the European *statu quo*, Russia against the Oriental *statu quo*."

Nicholas was therefore free for the campaign of eighteen hundred and twenty-nine. In Asia, Count Paskiévitch defeated two Turkish armies and captured Erzerum; in Europe, Dibitch, successor to Wittgenstein, defeated the Grand Vizier at Kulevtcha, near Pravadui, and threw him back in disorder on the fortified camp of Shumla, after having killed five thousand men and taken forty-three guns. After the capitulation of Silistria he blockaded Shumla, boldly crossed the Balkans, and entered Adrianople, the second city of the Ottoman Empire. At sea the frigate Mercury fought a heroic battle with two Turkish ships; her crew had sworn either to conquer or to blow themselves up.

At last the Porte yielded. Mahmud had destroyed the Janissaries, and no regular army was as yet constituted. Persia refused to undertake a new war against Russia. At Adrianople the Porte concluded two treaties, — one with the European powers, and the other with Russia. In the first it agreed to adhere to the treaty of eighteen hundred and twenty-seven, and recognized the independence of Greece. By the second it surrendered to Russia the isles of the Danubian delta in Europe, and the fortresses and districts of Anapa, Poti, Akhaltsuikh, and Akhalkalaki, in Asia; it paid an indemnity of one hundred and nineteen million francs, equivalent to nearly twenty-four million dollars, and another of one million five hundred thousand ducats to the Russian merchants. The immunities formerly granted to Moldavia, Valakhia, and Serbia were guaranteed, and the Bosphorus and Dardanelles declared free and open to all the powers at peace with the Porte. Russian commerce had full and free access to the Black Sea. Thus this first alliance with France had secured the independence of Greece, and prepared for that of the Rumanians and Serbians.

From eighteen hundred and forty to eighteen hundred and forty-one England was occupied with the famous opium war in China. The Russians had previously obtained, with less trouble, a far more advantageous footing in the Celestial Empire. By the treaty of eighteen hundred and twenty-seven they acquired the right to establish at Pekin a place of education where young men might study the language and customs of China. Nicholas had carefully avoided clashing with the Court of Pekin on the subject of opium; and when he heard of the prohibition he forbade his subjects to introduce this commodity across the Russian frontier. In eighteen hundred and fifty-two a new commercial treaty was made, which opened a market on the Irtuish. This Western market, so called in opposition to the Eastern market of Kiakhta, afforded the Russian agents an opportunity to make closer observations of Bokhara. In spite of these cordial relations, the Russian outposts daily and noiselessly encroached on the Chinese territory; and in eighteen hundred and fifty-four Europe was astonished to find them established on the Amur. Thus, from one end of Asia to the other, Russia and England found themselves face to face. In their attempts to push back their frontiers and to extend their influence, both hastened the inevitable moment when they would be in direct conflict.

By the acquisition of Mingrelia, Imeritia, and Georgia, the Shirvan, and the Persian and Turkish provinces, Russia had possession of the whole southern slope of the Caucasus; by the acquisition of Daghestan it had acquired a foothold on the northern side, and thus completely surrounded the vast mountainous regions which constitute Circassia and Abkhasia. Numerous forts occupied the openings of the valleys. The warlike Tcherkesui and Abkhasui, however, bravely defended their independence. The road from Anapa to Poti was very unsafe, notwithstanding the number of fortified posts. Nicholas felt the necessity of securing communications with Southern Asia by both extremities of the Caucasus and by intermediate passes, and of making this enormous chain the impregnable citadel from the height of which he was to rule the East. This war with the mountain tribes, fertile in surprises and ambuscades, was a mingled success and failure. It took a more formidable development when Moslem fanaticism, awakened by the sectarian professors of Mirditism, embodied itself in Shamyl, the soldier priest, who gave to these rival races religious unity, and who for twenty-five years held the best in Shamyl, the soldier priest, who gave to these rival races religious unity, and who for twenty-five years held the best Russian generals in check. In eighteen hundred and forty-four the insurrection became so great that it was found necessary to post two hundred thousand men in the Caucasus under the brave and able Vorontsof. The English furtively favored the mountaineers, and the seizure, in eighteen hundred and thirty-seven, of the British schooner Vixen, as she was unloading arms on the coast of Abkhasia, made some noise. An Englishman named Bell was at the head of the Georgians in their short revolt.

Persia, where Fet-Aly-Shah, the ally of Napoleon the First, had been succeeded by his grandson Mohammed, was completely under Russian influence. In eighteen hundred and thirty-seven and eighteen hundred and thirty-eight Mohammed laid siege to Herat, which commanded one of the routes to India. The English obliged him to raise the siege by creating a diversion in the Persian Gulf. They followed up this by another in eighteen hundred and fifty-six, and secured the Isle of Karrack and the Port of Bushir. Three years after the siege of Herat the English themselves failed to capture Cabul.

Nicholas, in search for an opening in another direction, declared war against the Khan of Khiva under the pretext of putting an end to the exactions and robberies practised against the caravans. In eighteen hundred and twenty-five a caravan escorted by six hundred and twenty-five men was attacked at the crossing of the Iani River, and after defending themselves for three days, they were obliged to retire with a loss of more than half a million rubles' worth of merchandise. It was reckoned that every year two hundred Russians were kidnapped in the steppe or on the Caspian, and sold in the markets of Khiva, often with the connivance of the Khan. In eighteen hundred and thirty-five as many as a thousand Russian captives were waiting to be ransomed. The following year, after the great fair at Nijni-Novgorod, all the Khivan merchants were arrested with their goods, and the Khan was informed that they would not be allowed to return to Orenburg and Astrakhan until the Russians held captive in Khiva were set free. Although this inflicted a severe blow upon the Khan's commercial interests, he did not yield. It was then determined to send a military expedition to Khiva under command of General Perovski, which should have for its object the increase of Russian influence in Central Asia. Extensive preparations were made during the summer of eighteen hundred and forty. An army of over four thousand men, with two thousand horses and ten thousand camels, started in November across the sandy steppes of Turkestan. The weather soon became severely cold, fuel was lacking, many of the camels were found to be unfit for service, the supplies of provisions which were ordered to be forwarded to Novo Aleksandrovsk failed to reach their destination, the snow was so deep as to be almost impassable, and the Kirgiz camel-drivers were mutinous. Perovski's situation became hazardous in the extreme. Before he reached half-way to Khiva half of his camels perished. It was clearly impossible to continue the advance. Perovski wrote to the Minister of War: "Our retreat will be no less arduous than our advance; the four months' provisions stored at Emba are sufficient of themselves to assure the existence of the troops, but the lack of wood and forage, the deep snows and continual sharp frosts, have an undoubtedly injurious effect upon the men and the cattle; moreover, on account of the insufficiency of camels, the majority of the division will be obliged to remain at Emba until next spring." Near the middle of June the little army reached Orenburg after a disastrous eight months spent in the steppe. More than a thousand men died during this time. In spite of this failure another expedition was planned, but the Khan, who saw that things began to wear a serious aspect, offered satisfaction. He returned four hundred and eighteen Russian captives, and issued a firman decreeing the penalty of death against any Khivan who should dare to attempt the life or liberty of a Russian subject. It was clear, however, that a serious attempt against Khiva would not be practicable till the enormous distance of two hundred leagues, which separated this oasis from the Russian frontiers, should be made easier by the establishment of a line of fortified posts, by the more complete subjection of the savage hordes, and by the construction of a fleet on the Sea of Aral.

The navigation of the Sea of Aral was initiated in eighteen hundred and forty-seven. Lieutenant Butakof began a complete survey of it on the steamer Konstantin. In eighteen hundred and fifty-three General Perovski occupied Ak Meshet, the principal fort of the Kokanese. A year later the Khan of Khiva became a kind of vassal of the Tsar, and was kept under strict surveillance by the resident Russian ambassador.

THE POLISH INSURRECTION.

Towards the year eighteen hundred and thirty Russia found itself in a singular state of uneasiness. The cholera was just making its appearance; fierce revolts had broken out at Staaïra Rusa, Sevastopol, and Novgorod. The peasants, who were chiefly attacked by this dreadful scourge, thought that it was in consequence of a plot made by the upper classes against them; they broke into the hospitals, killed the doctors, and removed the patients by violence. They also hung and tortured the officers of the military colonies, and committed the most horrible atrocities. The suffering and disorder among the lower classes was relieved by the noble generosity of many wealthy citizens, who established hospitals and gave largely to the poor. The Emperor seemed agitated by gloomy presentiments. In France the conservative ministry published a body of ordinances which entirely altered the constitution of the country, and destroyed the freedom of the press. This measure led to the insurrection of July. The French government proved to be powerless to crush it, and after the streets of Paris had run with blood for three days, the city was left to the mercy of the mob. Charles the Tenth abdicated in favor of his grandson, and took refuge in England. It seemed likely that a ministry of the Left would come into power, and that a continental war would be the result.

Nicholas, at the first news of this uprising of the French, was unable to control his indignation. He immediately ordered the army in Poland to be put on a war-footing. He would gladly have headed a coalition to march against France and re-establish the ancient order of things. He was still more shocked by the Belgian and Italian revolutions which immediately followed. The moral epidemic which led the people of Europe to think of freedom was something to be more dreaded than the Asiatic cholera.

The tricolor flag, the flag of seventeen hundred and ninety-nine and eighteen hundred and twelve, which replaced the white flag of royalty upon the French Consulate at Warsaw, hastened the explosion of the Polish revolution.

The time was already far in the past when Alexander, while opening the Diet of eighteen hundred and eighteen, boasted of "those liberal institutions which had not ceased to be the object of his watchful care," and which allowed him to show Russia itself "what he had been for so many years preparing for it." It was a long day since he congratulated the Polish deputies on having rejected the proposed law regulating divorce, since he proclaimed to them "that, having been freely elected, they must freely vote."

There was no question that the material prosperity of the kingdom was increasing. Commerce and manufactures were becoming more and more widely developed; the finances were in a satisfactory state, and from the remnant of the Napoleonic legions the Grand Duke Konstantin had formed an excellent army of sixty thousand men. Unhappily, it was very difficult for Alexander, who in the latter years of his life had become more and more autocratic in Russia, to accommodate himself in Poland to the liberty of a representative government. The Diet of eighteen hundred and twenty irritated him profoundly by its attack on the ministers, and its rejection of certain projects of law. He looked on these ordinary incidents of parliamentary practice as an attempt to attack and undermine his authority. He lent an ear to the counsels of Karamsin and Araktchéef. He put forth an "additional act of the constitution" which forbade the sittings of the Diet to be open to the public. After the session of eighteen hundred and twenty-two the convocation of the Estates was adjourned indefinitely. The liberty of the press was restrained, and the police became more vexatious. The soldiers complained of the severity, and sometimes of the brutality, of the Grand Duke Konstantin, who was full of good intentions, who loved Poland, and had given proof of it by sacrificing the crown of Russia for a Polish lady, but who could never control his impetuous and eccentric character. The officers who had served under Dombrovski, Poniatovski, and Napoleon found it almost impossible to accommodate themselves to the Muscovite discipline. Ancient jealousies and national hate, revived by the events of eighteen hundred and twelve, were on the point of breaking out between the two peoples. Besides the Polish malcontents who grumbled at the violations of the Constitution of eighteen hundred and fifteen, and were enraged at the Emperor for not having restored to the kingdom the palatinates of White Russia, there was the party which dreamed of the Constitution of the third of May, seventeen hundred and ninety-one, or of a republic, and which desired to re-establish Poland in its ancient independence, and within its ancient limits. The secret associations of the Templars and the Patriotic Society were formed. The trial of the Russian dekabrists had revealed an understanding between the conspirators of the two nations.

Konstantin made another mistake, that of persuading the Emperor Nicholas that the Polish army should not be employed against the Turks. He loved this army after his own fashion, and his saying has been quoted, "I detest war; it spoils an army." Victories gained in common over the ancient enemy of the two peoples might have created a bond of military fraternity between the Russian and Polish armies, given an opening to the warlike ardor of the Polish youth, and crowned with glory the union of the two nations. Konstantin's unpopularity increased in consequence of this error. Nothing, however, was as yet imperilled. When the Emperor Nicholas came to open the Diet of May, eighteen hundred and thirty, in person, his presence in Warsaw excited some hopes. In spite of the reserve which the deputies had imposed on themselves, they could not refrain from rejecting the unhappy scheme of the law of divorce, from lodging complaints against the ministers, and uttering a wish for the reunion of the Lithuanian provinces with Poland. This wish could not, of course, be granted by Nicholas without deeply wounding the patriotism and the rights of Russia. The "King of Poland" and his subjects separated with discontent on both sides; the secret societies became more active than ever in their conspiracies, and the news from Paris found all the elements of a revolution already prepared.

Zalivski, one of the leading members of the secret societies, on receiving the first news of the July revolution, called a meeting of the sub-lieutenant Vysotski and his confidants, in order to decide upon taking action. Finding their strength as yet insufficient, another meeting was held about the middle of August by some twenty active men who were united in their desire to strike a decided blow, but who were at odds regarding the time. Zalivski was in favor of postponing action until February, and in this he was supported by

Ostrovski, Urbanski, and others who felt that a military insurrection without the support of the people would be unsuccessful. They also felt the need of an efficient director. Some of the old generals, Shembek, Stanislas, Pototski, Khlopitski, were brought to take the lead, but they all felt that it was a fool-hardy undertaking to try to incite the provinces into a triple war with Russia, Prussia, and Austria. The young enthusiasts were not discouraged by this opposition. Vysotski, Schlegel, and others soon formed an organization which spread rapidly in all the Polish regiments stationed in Warsaw. They sent out emissaries into the provinces of Lithuania, Podolia, and Volhynia, in order to win over soldiers and citizens to the patriotic cause; while the students of the universities and the cadets belonging to the School of the Standard-bearers entered into the conspiracy with all zeal, the older officers of the army, Pats, Zymirski, Skrzynetski, and others refused their co-operation, though they had keen sympathy with the patriotic motives which stimulated the revolutionary party.

The explosion of the revolution was hastened by the appearance of the Emperor's manifesto at the end of October, which seemed to threaten still greater diminution of the Polish liberties. Zalivski was informed that Nicholas designed either to force France to join the Russian Coalition or to incorporate the whole of Poland into his dominion at the expense of Prussia and Austria. It therefore appeared to these young men a noble thing to prevent Poland on the one hand from falling a prey to Russia, and on the other to prevent its being ranged against the European movement for popular freedom as manifested in Paris and Brussels.

Besides these patriotic motives for decisive action, there doubtless existed others which had a great weight: the rapid growth of the association, and the large numbers interested in the movement, gave constantly increasing chances that the police would detect it, in spite of the careful arrangements made by Zalivski, who was kept informed of every step taken by all of the initiated. Nevertheless, signs of the approaching storm occasionally cropped out; the vice-president, Liubovitski, was beaten in the street; a letter was nailed upon the wall of Konstantin's villa, Belvedere, warning him of the new year. The Grand Duke was warned by Liubovitski of the conspiracy. Novosiltsof knew of the league between the students and the cadets. One of the cadets played the part of informer; double watch was kept upon the school by General Trembetski, who forbade them to have any intercourse with the city. A commission of investigation was established, and Urbanski, one of the original conspirators, was arrested. Vysotski himself was put under examination, but as nothing was proved against him, he was set at liberty.

There was evidently no time to lose, and as the conspirators counted upon having forty thousand men under arms, small doubts were entertained that the whole nation would not follow so brave a leading. Zalivski and Vysotski, the leaders of the movement, decided to appoint the night of November twenty-nine for the outbreak, as they knew that the city would be guarded entirely by Poles.

The evening before, the officers of all the Polish regiments were summoned to the house of sub-Lieutenant Barkiévitch, where the plan of action was disclosed to them. It was resolved to begin by surprising Belvedere, seizing or killing the Grand Duke, and putting to death the hated instruments of Russian oppression as well as those Polish officers who set themselves in opposition to the conspiracy.

The Grand Duke, in spite of the warnings which he had received and his conviction that the Poles were ready to embrace the opportunity of showing themselves unfriendly, remained in apparent heedlessness. He was loath to entertain doubts of his army, and Liubetski, in his report, said that the plot was being undertaken by "lawyers without clients, physicians without patients, and young officers unwilling to occupy subordinate positions." He felt that he had little to fear from a mob, as Vićlopolski called it, composed of the refuse of all classes, — faithless monks, dissipated nobles, dishonest officials, young demagogues and corporals, ruined proprietors, bankrupt debtors, and a rabble with communistic tendencies. In case of such an outbreak he would withdraw from the city a day or two until order was restored.

The Russian force stationed in Warsaw amounted to about eight thousand men scattered in different parts of the city; only in the matter of cavalry were they superior to the Polish garrison. Zalivski drew up an admirable plan of attack, which failed to be carried out, owing to the carelessness of those who had charge of the details.

General Stanislas Pototski was to have the supervision of all the operations. A portion of the infantry, together with the cadets led by Vysotski, under Sieravski, were to surround and disarm the three Russian regiments stationed in the barracks of the Shulets quarter; the Polish guard under General Zymirski were to disarm the Russian grenadier-guard in the northern portion of the city; other troops were ordered to seize the arsenal, to protect the bank, to occupy Praga and the bridge over the Vistula, and to take the powder-magazine. The Russian generals were to be captured as they attempted to join their regiments. Bronikovski had charge of the popular revolt. All the Russian garrisons in the vicinity of Warsaw were also to be surprised, and the insurrection was to be carried into the provinces.

Unfortunately Sieravski was absent on the eventful day. Pototski knew nothing of the fact that he had been appointed generalissimo. Vysotski failed to inform the Polish guard of the time set for them to take arms; the Polish regiment of mounted sharp-shooters were opposed to the insurrection. Only three of the leaders — Zalivski, Vysotski, and Urbanski — were found at their posts.

It was decided to give the signal about six o'clock by setting on fire a brewery near the barracks in the Shulets quarter. The party of students and citizens under command of Nabiélak and the poet Gostchinski, which had been detailed to secure the Grand Duke's person, assembled in Lazienski Park and waited for the light of the signal. The fire-bells gave them the first intimation that the beacon had been lighted, and, a tumult ensuing, this band scattered without accomplishing its object. Nabiélak hastened to the School of Ensigns, where all was quiet. On his way back he met Vysotski and a few followers, who summoned the cadets to arms. They demanded cartridges. "Cartridges!" cried Vysotski, "you will find them in the boxes of the Russians."

Nabiélak, taking a handful of the cadets, rushed to the palace of the Belvedere, where they forced their way through barricaded doors, but failed to find the Grand Duke. Konstantin, with the Prussian ambassador Schmidt, had just time to escape to a small cottage in the vicinity. The party found only Liubovitski, the director of the police, and General Zander, whom they mistook for Konstantin. Both of these officers they left for dead.

The rest of the cadets, one hundred and sixty in number, who hastened to surprise and disarm the Russian cavalry at the barracks, failed of their purpose as completely as those who attempted to seize the Grand Duke. When they arrived at the barracks, under command of Vysotski, Schlegel, and Dombrovski, they looked about for the reinforcements which were to meet them there. Being conscious of their weakness in numbers, they neglected to secure the drawbridges defending the barracks, and withdrew to the alder grove and the Sobieski bridge, where the band from the Belvedere joined them.

Zalivski, who had been vainly waiting for several hours for the signal, at last took it upon himself to set on fire a small wooden house near the arsenal. In a short time all the Polish troops, the infantry, a battalion of sappers, the horse artillery, and a regiment of grenadiers hastened to this point, seized a quantity of arms, and distributed forty thousand muskets among the people. The fire near the arsenal alarmed the Russian troops in the other parts of the city, as well as the Polish regiments. Had not the guards been composed of national troops, the revolution would have been immediately crushed. It was now about the arsenal that the revolt grouped itself. Zalivski held the approaches with two companies of grenadiers, and managed to capture the generals of the Volhynian and Lithuanian regiments, Engelmann and Iesakof. The Polish General Blumer attempted to resist, ordered his men to fire, and was himself killed. Stanislas Pototski was put to death by the angry populace because he refused to take the command of the army. The war minister Hauke, Colonel Mietsishevski, Colonel Sass, and Trembetski, the head of the School of Ensigns, also fell victims to the indignation of the people. The brave General Novitski, who was mistaken for Mayor Levitski, suffered the same fate.

The Grand Duke, who was entirely confused by the attack upon the Belvedere, instead of resolutely grappling with the insurgents, determined to evacuate the city. He pitched his camp in a little village a mile from Warsaw. The Russian generals were in favor of decisive and immediate action, but his Polish followers advised him to discontinue hostilities. He was unable to come to any decision, and thus he wasted two precious days, in which the revolution had time to spread. One regiment after another joined the patriotic cause. While Konstantin waited for reinforcements from the provinces he expressed a wish to listen to the desires of the Poles, and a deputation consisting of Princes Tchartoruiski and Ostrovski, Liubetski and Lélével, the celebrated professor and historian, conferred with him on December second. The Princess Lovitch was present, and did not hesitate to heap scorn upon Liubetski and to designate Lélével as the cause of the mischief. The deputation demanded surety for the inviolability of the constitution, and the accomplishment of the union with the Lithuanian provinces. The Grand Duke could make only vague replies, and contented himself with suggesting an exchange of prisoners, and promising not to attack the city without two days' notice.

The Grand Duke flattered himself that the larger part of the Polish troops had remained faithful to him, but Lélével looked at his watch and said, " They are so no longer"; and, indeed, at that very moment General Shembek was being unwillingly carried away by the enthusiasm of the younger officers, and joined the insurgents. His defection gave the signal to the rest. The Grand Duke, still trusting in his army, gave permission to all the Poles who had remained faithful to him to return to Warsaw, and his grief was keen when, without exception, they renounced their allegiance and joined their compatriots.

The Grand Duke now saw that his position was untenable, and, breaking up his camp at Mokotof, he proceeded by short stages to evacuate the country. His troops, who marched without discipline and were ill supplied with provisions, committed the most terrible excesses upon the proprietors and peasants whom they met. But no steps were taken to interrupt him in his retreat, or to liberate General Lukasinski, who was carried off in chains. The historians of the Polish insurrection consider that this studied policy of allowing the eight thousand troops of the enemy to leave the country was the fatal mistake of the conspirators. Had an attempt been made to annihilate or take them prisoners, the Grand Duke would have been prevented from bringing to the frontier the nucleus of a strong army well provided with arms and ammunition, and the Lithuanians would have been incited to emulate their example. Konstantin crossed the Vistula at Pulavy on December sixth, and a week later he reached the Bug, where he halted and immediately began to weed out from his troops the revolutionary element, by distributing among distant regiments those officers who were suspected of favoring the revolt.

At the very beginning of the trouble Prince Liubetski, assured of his popularity among the people and his influence with the Emperor, had hastened to convoke the council of administration, to which he added a certain number of the more popular citizens who were opposed to the revolution. He desired to bring about a reconciliation with the Emperor before matters had proceeded too far. He thought if a restoration of the constitution should be granted, that the majority of the people would be satisfied, without paying attention to Zalivski's threatening demands.

General Pats, who temporarily filled the office of generalissimo, like the other older officers was alarmed and full of disquiet. When, finally, Khlopitski accepted the office, it was only on condition that it was in the name of the Emperor. Many of the most patriotic citizens felt that it was a ruinous plan to carry the revolt further, and the council issued a proclamation entreating the people "to end all their agitation with the night which had covered them with her mantle," and assuring them that the Grand Duke had forbidden the Russian soldiery to interfere.

This proclamation was distasteful to the original supporters of the revolution, who saw plainly enough that to be successful there must be no chance for reconciliation, that the split between government and people must be so wide that a sort of despair would nerve their hearts to bravest resistance. It was to them, therefore, a cruel mistake that the Grand Duke was allowed to escape imprisonment or assassination.

They felt that their only hope of success against the great army which they knew would be led into Poland in a few days would be to unite with the Lithuanian troops and make of it a national war, establish the independence of Poland, and bar the Russians from entering Europe. These enthusiasts wanted to be led by their old and favorite generals in this desperate but glorious contest, and their disappointment was indeed bitter when they found them inclined to half-measures and unwilling to run the risks which they themselves gladly ran. Zalivski could not be consoled when Vysotski wrote an article for a Polish newspaper in which he said that the plot was the work of a few youths, and had not the sympathy of the whole nation.

Two parties, therefore, were organized in the bosom of the State, opposed in all their interests: the aristocratic, conservative party, who wished to mend the link which had been broken with the legal government by soliciting, at the most, a reform of the constitution and the annexation of the Lithuanian palatinates; and, on the other hand, the party of the radicals or democrats, who insisted on the abdication of the Romanofs, the restoration to the country of its independence, and the recovery by arms, if necessary, of the lost provinces.

The failure of the revolution was due to this lack of unity. From the second day of the outbreak they began to measure their strength, and to try each to supplant the other in the direction of affairs.

The young revolutionists, angered at the management of the administrative council and by Khlopitski's actions, under the auspices of Lélével opened a Patriotic club, which was far from being select in its choice of members. Open meetings were held; a daily paper was published; the object of this society was "to watch over all the departments of the administration, to see that the measures adopted were congenial to the wishes of the people and in the spirit of the revolution, and to promote fraternity and union throughout the nation."

The day after the formation of the Patriotic club, Khlopitski, the generalissimo, caused the arrest of Zalivski and Urbanski as disturbers of the peace. They were set free almost immediately, and brought before Liubetski, who apologized for the action. Liubetski, gradually yielding to the pressure of the revolutionary element, appointed an executive council supplementary to the council of administration, so that now, side by side with the aristocratic Radzivil, Khlopitski, and Kokhanovski, sat the most impetuous of the patriots, Gustaf Malakhovski, Dembovski, Ostrovski, and Lélével.

When the Patriotic club learned the failure of the negotiations with the Grand Duke, they sent a deputation to the council of administration, demanding that the Russians should be disarmed, that the revolution should be organized in the provinces, and that measures of offensive and defensive warfare be immediately undertaken; they added the threat, that, if these demands were not acceded to before morning, a change would be made in the council. The action of General Shembek's regiment decided Liubetski, and he added to the council four of the most advanced radicals of the club. On the same day he appointed in place of the executive council a provisory revolutionary government, from which he took pains to exclude himself and the four members of the club, as well as Radzivil. This government consisted of seven men, Tchartoruiski, Kokhanovski, Lélével, Pats, Dembovski, Niemtsévitch, and Ostrovski, who admitted into their sittings some members of the Patriotic club. Mokhnatski, one of the leaders of the revolt, seized the opportunity to condemn as treachery the action of the provisional government in regard to Russia. This attack aroused all the opposition in Khlopitski's fiery nature. Khlopitski was a brave soldier of sixty years of age. He had served with distinction in Italy under Dombrovski and Napoleon, and had won laurels in Spain with the Duke of Albuera. By his opposition to the Grand Duke's military measures he had become extremely popular with the whole nation; but he saw no hope for Poland now, save in a prompt reconciliation with the Emperor. The revolutionary plans of the young radicals were absolutely distasteful to this stiff-necked believer in law and discipline. He did not try to dissimulate his feelings; he continued to wear his Russian orders; he declared his unwillingness to waste powder in order to join the palatinates to Poland. He believed that the blame of the insurrection might in large measure be laid upon the Grand Duke's followers, who had made a real union between Poles and Russians impossible. He felt that the only chance for the Poles was in some one man who should possess their entire confidence, or who could force them to absolute submission to his will; and he had no choice between resigning his position as generalissimo and being, on the other hand, placed in complete command. Mokhnatski's attack so incensed him that he decided upon the former alternative; and Tchartoruiski and Niemtsévitch in vain implored him to retain his place. The Patriotic club was divided by this action. The academical students who had been organized into a crack regiment openly renounced Mokhnatski, and an opposition club was started by Marquis Viélopolski, which had leanings towards the aristocratic principles. The Septemvirate, also divided against itself, now offered Khlopitski the dictatorship instead of the office which he had laid down. Khlopitski, entirely scorning this offer, declared that in such times of peril the civil and military power ought to be in the hands of one man, and that by reason of his long services he felt himself entitled to claim the post of dictator, which he should retain until the assemblage of the Diet, which was appointed for the eighteenth of September. The people in general had no inkling of Khlopitski's true designs. The glamour of his previous reputation and his eminent character deceived his countrymen. The army had more confidence in him than in the revolutionary officers who opposed his designs. The aristocratic party triumphed when they saw the power firmly vested in Khlopitski.

The Dictator now proceeded to adopt the measures in which he conceived lay safety for the country. The provisional government was reinstated with the exception of Lélével; but its duties were confined to internal affairs. The clubs were suppressed. The Lithuanians, Gallicians, and Prussians who were flocking to the assistance of the revolutionists were directed to return home. The Emperor's name was mentioned in the church service. He despatched Count Iezierski and Prince Liubetski to Saint Petersburg to bring to the Emperor the complaints of the Poles against the Grand Duke's management, and to ask only that the promises which had been made might be fulfilled. The desires of his Polish subjects did not go beyond the carrying out of the constitution, the removal of the Russian garrisons, and the union of the Lithuanian provinces. Khlopitski wrote a letter to the Emperor, assuring him of the loyalty of the country, and explaining the position which he assumed in order to put an end to anarchy in Poland.

The day before the Diet opened, a deputation headed by Tchartoruiski visited the Dictator for the purpose of sounding his intentions. They spoke to him in favor of an offensive war and an invasion of Lithuania, but Khlopitski would not yield, and declared that he had sworn to remain faithful to Russia. When one of the deputies answered that the revolution had not been begun with the simple design of protecting the constitution, and preserving the boundaries granted by the Vienna Congress, Khlopitski left the room, saying that " he was not there to contend with provincial deputies." So great was their fear lest they should lose the confidence of the army, that they agreed among themselves not to make public the manner in which the Dictator had received their advances, and even Lélével kept his promise.

The very first act of the Diet, however, raised the expectations of the revolutionary party. The Chamber of Deputies elected Count Ladislas Ostrovski marshal, and proceeded to sanction the revolution. The Senate with Tchartoruiski as president supported this action, which so angered Khlopitski that he again sent in his resignation; and only on condition that the Diet should adjourn was he persuaded by

Tchartoruiski, Ostrovski, and Niemtsévitch to retain the dictatorship. The Diet consented to this condition, but before the adjournment it appointed a committee to draw up a manifesto and a delegation of inspection consisting of fifteen members to support the Dictator, and gifted with the power to remove him for cause. Khlopitski immediately prorogued the assembly, and formed a ministry and a council of five members, — Tchartoruiski, Radzivil, Barzikovski, Dembovski, and Ostrovski. He put Lélével and Niémoïevski into the ministry in order to weaken their influence. Khlopitski seemed to have played his game well. He had concentrated in his own hands all the power, and the conflicting interests were balanced in the council.

Nevertheless, Khlopitski's popularity was beginning to wane. The bitter attacks upon him in the press began to have their effect upon the people, and the party divisions became more and more clearly marked. Gervinus says of this period: "The patriarchal good nature of the Poles spread over these circumstances a veil of illusion which allowed no real quarrel to arise between the extremes of indifference and exaltation which divided society through and through. Far from feeling the bitter earnestness which in similar times lay hold upon the merriest-hearted of the merry-hearted French, the Poles assembled in coffee-house and drawing-room as for a joyous holiday. They discussed, drank, danced, and after the dance took up the thread of the discussion where they had dropped it. Then the ladies in their enthusiasm stopped quarrels and hatred, or a favorite proverb or the magic word 'Fatherland' would do service of reconciliation, and punch and the mazurka end the day."

But the impatience at the delay began to grow more serious; the minority worked assiduously to spread their ideas among the people by violent articles in the papers, by bribery, by any means, fair or foul, which occurred to them. The leader of this party was Lélével. "He was forty years of age," says Gervinus, "pale, thin, with sunken eyes, unaccustomed to deal with men, an extremist by reason of his theories, and still more so by reason of his ambition, which in men of this stamp grows the more lofty the less they are capable of mingling in affairs. The Russians saw in him a Robespierre, and in the fiery Mokhnatski his Saint Just."

Lélével was particularly uncongenial to the Dictator; in every respect he was his opposite. He was of the opinion that the Poles ought to take the offensive, throw themselves into Lithuania and Volhynia, arm the peasants and raise a general levy. He declared that if the insurrection did not spread, it was certain to fail. He used his position in the ministry to undermine Khlopitski; he did not hesitate to plot against his life. The revolutionary ideas now began to permeate the militia, which was Khlopitski's chief support. The Dictator learned at the same time of the plot against his life, and he had Lélével, Bronikovski, and Ostrovski arrested. This step created such a feeling, however, that he was obliged to liberate the prisoners. The popular feeling against the Dictator arose still higher when it was found that the Vice-President Liubovitski, whom the people were waiting to hang, had escaped and taken refuge in Prussia.

The news of the Emperor's proclamation of December seventeen was the final blow which led to Khlopitski's fall. Nicholas repelled all efforts to treat which were not preceded by an immediate and unconditional submission. He characterized the rebellion as infamous. He gave orders to put an end to all illegal armaments, and to restore the administrative council. The insurgents saw that there was no hope of their "obtaining concessions as the reward of their crimes."

From this time the war party at Warsaw triumphed over the peace-party. The committee from the Diet had the manifesto printed and distributed without Khlopitski's knowledge. The wrongs of Poland were thus publicly brought before the notice of Europe. The language used was not extravagant, but the disgraceful things which had been done were handled in plain speech which could not fail to be distasteful to the Emperor; it showed that the union of the constitutional kingdom with an autocratic form of government was impossible; it complained that the provinces were still unannexed; it was a direct challenge to the Emperor offered in the face of all Europe.

Count Iezierski now returned from Saint Petersburg and announced that the Emperor was inclined to be reconciled, only he would hear nothing of any concessions. Viélezinski, another of Khlopitski's messengers to the Emperor, also returned bringing letters from Grabovski, the Polish Secretary of State, advising him to give up entirely the cause of the revolutionists. Viélezinski reported General Dibitch as saying to the envoys: "Well, Gentlemen of Poland, your revolution has not even the merit of being well timed. You have risen at the moment when the whole force of the empire was on the march toward your frontiers, to reduce to order the revolutionary spirits of France and Belgium."

Khlopitski summoned the Diet to meet on the nineteenth of January, and he then declared that, as he saw the impossibility of carrying on a war with Russia, he was unwilling to take upon himself the responsibility of a rupture, and would not retain the dictatorship unless unlimited powers were given him to bring about an understanding with the Emperor. This was not granted. "Well, then," said Khlopitski, impatiently, to Lélével, "make war with your reapers, yourself,"—and he for the third time resigned his command. From this moment his popularity vanished; the army declared for the national party; the government was entrusted to the Senate under the presidency of Prince Tchartoruiski, and the command of the army was given to Prince Mikhail Radzivil, an inefficient man without military talent, but connected by family with the King of Prussia. His election was hailed by cries of "To Lithuania! to Lithuania!" Khlopitski took a subordinate place in the suite of the generalissimo, and became a member of the council for the administration of military affairs.

The Diet now began its sittings. On the very first day Ostrovski proposed to declare the independence of Poland. On the twentieth of January Roman Soltuik brought in a motion to depose the Romanof family, to free the provinces from their oath of allegiance, and to proclaim their separation from Russia. Tchartoruiski and his aristocratic following strained every nerve to induce Soltuik to withdraw his motion, but the patriots of the club, who were no longer embarrassed by Khlopitski, kept up an increasing activity in circulating extreme ideas: promises of material aid from France, and moral sympathy from the rest of the world, fanned their enthusiasm to the highest glow. It was known that General Lamarque had proposed, for the protection of the Polish insurrectionists, that a Franco-English fleet should threaten Constantinople; that Sweden should interfere in favor of Finland; that Austria and Prussia should be held in check by advances in Italy and on the Rhine. All these rumors excited the Poles to a fever of enthusiasm; they forgot the old proverb that God is too high, and France too far, to help them. They scorned the warning of the French Consul in Warsaw, who told them not to depend upon French interference. They told the Duc de Montemart, who was sent by Louis Philippe to the Court of Saint Petersburg, that their reliance was firm in Lafayette, that the die was cast, and they should gain all or nothing; and his unfavorable reply had no power to influence them. Khlopitski's letter to the Emperor and the answer were brought before the Diet, and the popular feeling was still further imbittered by the proclamations issued by Dibitch Zabalkanski, in which he threatened the rebels with the utmost rigor, and told them that they had to choose between the benefits coming from unqualified submission and the evils arising from a hopeless conflict.

In the session of the twenty-fifth of January, Count Iezierski was requested publicly to give an account of the negotiations with Nicholas. The Emperor's replies did not give any more ground for hope than his proclamation of the seventeenth of December. He refused to parley with rebel subjects. He at once rejected the idea of despoiling Russia of the Lithuanian provinces for the benefit of Poland. He considered it a sacred duty to stifle the insurrection and punish the guilty, adding that if the nation took up arms against him, Poland would be crushed by Polish guns. At the mention of Polish guns, Ledokhovski shouted "Down with Nicholas!" and the deputies overwhelmed Iezierski with reproaches at his weakness, while he retorted that it was one thing to speak in Warsaw of the Emperor, and another to speak before the Emperor in Saint Petersburg. The indignation against Liubetski and the conservative leaders grew rapidly, and Ostrovski, profiting by the tumult, again motioned to depose the Romanofs from the throne, and the motion was carried by acclamation.

The revolutionists hoped by this step to engage the sympathy of the Western courts, but in reality it rendered all attempts at pacific mediation impossible, — the Poles having abandoned the ground of the treaties of eighteen hundred and fifteen, the only ones to which European diplomacy could appeal. As to an armed intervention in the presence of the hostility of the German Powers, neither England nor France could dream of such a thing. In vain the population of Paris made energetic manifestations of its sympathies; in vain the chambers resounded with warlike addresses, — all these demonstrations had no effect. On the twenty-ninth of January the Diet instituted a provisional government composed of five members, — Adam Tchartoruiski (president), Barzikovski, Nićmoïevski, Moravski, and Lélével. All parties were thus represented, from the extreme democratic tendencies of Lélével to the natural aristocratic feelings of Tchartoruiski, who was by family interests and precedent bound to the imperial régime, but who now accepted the situation and yielded to the will of the people. A proclamation announced to the world that Poland was henceforth an independent constitutional monarchy.

Although the Grand Duke had long ago evacuated the kingdom, comparatively little had been done toward putting the strongholds in a posture of defence. The fortresses were all in the hands of the rebels, but no works of importance had been erected except at Praga, Zamosts, and Modlin. The country was left open to the approach of the enemy, but they threw up a formidable work to cover the bridge on the east of Warsaw. The Polish forces with the new levies amounted to somewhere between seventy and ninety thousand men, with more than a hundred pieces of artillery.

Early in February, eighteen hundred and thirty-one, in a season of severe cold, an army of one hundred and twenty thousand Russians with four hundred cannon, under the command of Count Dibitch Zabalkanski, the hero of the Balkans, entered Poland at four distinct points. According as the different army corps converged upon Warsaw, the Poles, prudently avoiding a general engagement, fell back toward the capital. The insurgent General Dvernitski gained an advantage at the skirmish at Stotchek, and several other minor victories encouraged the Poles. On the nineteenth and twentieth of February a bloody battle was fought at Grokhof, and though the Polish troops won imperishable glory for their bravery, they did not hinder the Russians from approaching Warsaw. The Russian general, having received reinforcements, carried the village of Bialenska on February twenty-four, and the following day he attacked and took a grove in front of Praga. The battle lasted two hours, and the Poles finally retired in good order to the fortifications of Praga. Prince Radzivil, acknowledging that he was incapable of retaining his office of generalissimo, now resigned and was succeeded by General Ian Skrzynetski, who by his bravery and ability had risen rapidly into note. The main body of the Russian army, abandoning the bank of the Vistula and retiring to Plotsk, was waiting for reinforcements; only three strong divisions — that of Rosen at Dembévilkić, that of Geismar at Vavr, and a third opposite Praga — were left to watch Warsaw. The Polish general used the respite which the inactivity of Marshal Dibitch gave him to strengthen his army and fortify the capital. He also took the offensive. On the night of March thirty, with a force of twenty-five thousand men, he surprised Geismar at Vavr and Rosen at Dembévilkić. General Rosen abandoned Minsk, and was again defeated at Igani. Some of the Polish troops even crossed the Bug and approached the vicinity of Dibitch.

Up to this time fifteen battles had been fought, and the advantage seemed to be with the insurgents; but fortune began to change. After the victories of March and April, General Sieravski advanced southward to join Dvernitski, who was trying to raise Volhynia. At first their operations were successful; they swept the right bank of the Vistula, but unfortunately they kept too far apart, and on the seventeenth of April Sieravski was defeated by General Kreutz, and General Dvernitski was completely surrounded by the Russian forces of Rudiger. In order to escape a fatal battle, he took refuge on Austrian soil, when his troops were disarmed by the authorities. General Khrzanovski was sent into Volhynia to take his place, but the expedition failed completely.

The troops which were sent to the assistance of the Lithuanian insurrection met with disaster in the vicinity of Vilna; the Poles were obliged to cross the Prussian frontier, when they were disarmed, and only one division, through the skill and bravery of General Dembinski, succeeded in re-entering Warsaw. In the meantime Skrzynetski attacked the right wing of the Russians at Ostrolenka on the Narova, and after a severe fight was forced back to the other side of the river. He retreated to Praga, and for the greater part of June devoted himself to repairing his losses.

The cholera was now raging in both armies. This disease appeared in Moscow in eighteen hundred and thirty, and the following year it spread throughout the empire and a large portion of Europe. It was communicated to the Polish troops by the Russians immediately after the battle of Igani. Marshal Dibitch fell a victim to it on the tenth of June, and seventeen days afterwards the Grand Duke Konstantin died of it at Vitepsk.

Paskiévitch-Erivanski was appointed Dibitch's successor, and immediately began his operations against Warsaw. Warsaw was prepared for a siege; the inhabitants worked night and day digging intrenchments and raising barricades. But political divisions now, as always, ruined Poland. According as the crisis approached, harmony and confidence became shaken. The disasters which succeeded the battle of Ostrolenka, the abandonment of Poland by the Western powers, the failure of the insurrections in the neighboring provinces, and the defeats in Volhynia and Lithuania had aroused the suspicions of the people. It was whispered about that it was due to treason; the capacity of the generals was doubted. Discontent began to enfeeble enthusiasm. A plot to surrender the city, instigated by certain Polish generals in conjunction with some of the Russian prisoners of war, was discovered, and it was proposed and almost decided in the chamber of deputies to substitute a new dictatorship for the provisional government. General Skrzynetski refused to communicate to a commission of inquiry the plans of his future operations, and after some violent scenes he resigned his position and was replaced by Dembinski, whose bold retreat from Lithuania had won for him golden opinions. But Dembinski was soon removed to give place to Malakhovski. The more violent members of the clubs proposed to court-martial Skrzynetski, and the government weakly consented; but this did not appease their passions. A revolt broke out on the fifteenth and sixteenth of August. The royal castle was sacked, and many state prisoners were massacred. The streets of Warsaw ran with blood. The prisons were broken into, and innocent and guilty perished indiscriminately. The governor of the city was entirely unable to restore order. The moderate party took flight; Tchartoruiski fled in disguise. The provisional government resigned its power into the hands of the Diet, who invested General Krukovietski with the office of dictator. He had some of the mutineers executed, but was not able to re-establish order. Meantime Paskiévitch-Erivanski, taking advantage of the anarchy which reigned at Warsaw, and strengthened by the benevolent help of Prussia, which had thrown open to him its arsenals and magazines of Dantzig and Königsberg, crossed the Vistula at Plotsk without opposition, and transported the theatre of war to the left bank. He intended to attack the capital, not from the side of Praga, as Suvorof had done, but from the side of Vola and the Tchysté quarter. He had an army of about a hundred thousand men which invested the city. Two semicircles of concentric intrenchments corresponded to these two quarters, but the Russians had no longer, as on the Praga side, to overcome the obstacle of the deep and rapid Vistula.

On the sixth of September the Russians began the attack upon Vola. Both sides fought with equal bravery. General Sovinski, who had lost a leg at the Moskova, and Vysotski, who began the revolution, were killed. But at night the Russians remained masters of Vola. The same night Paskiévitch cannonaded the town. The capital was at his mercy. The next morning Krukovietski asked permission to capitulate. Paskiévitch exacted the unconditional submission of the army and the people, the immediate surrender of Warsaw, the reconstruction of the bridge of Praga, and the retreat of the troops on Plotsk. The Diet having allowed the time fixed for a reply to pass, Paskiévitch began the attack. Krukovietski had accepted his terms, but he had been replaced in the interval by Nićmoïevski. The brave French General Ramorino had been sent, with twenty thousand men, into Podlakhia after provisions. His return was momentarily expected, and the Poles delayed as long as possible sending their answer to Paskiévitch. The Russians carried Tchysté, which was now in flames, and were scaling the ramparts, when the Poles capitulated.

"Sire, Warsaw is at your feet," wrote Paskiévitch to the Emperor. "The submission is general and complete."

"Order reigns at Warsaw," — such was the funeral oration pronounced by official Europe over the insurrection. The Polish army retired to Plotsk, and twenty thousand laid down their arms. A few brave generals, among whom was Ramorino, made one more attempt to arouse the people, but they were soon surrounded; and some of them, preferring exile to submission, took refuge in Prussia and Austria. Paskiévitch was created a prince, Varshavski, and made governor-general of Poland.

At the end of a month, not only Warsaw but Poland itself lay at the feet of Nicholas. He felt that he was bound to make a severe example in order to intimidate the European revolution. On the thirteenth of November he published a decree of amnesty in which he deplored the necessity "of employing other means than persuasion, in order to bring his misguided subjects back to their duty," and distinguished between those who were responsible for the insurrection and those who were weak enough to be led into it. A "complete amnesty" was then granted to all of his subjects belonging to the kingdom of Poland, except "the authors of the bloody revolt," and the men who attacked the life of the Grand Duke Konstantin and the other Russian and Polish officers; the chief members of the illegal governments; the deputies to the Diet who proposed and accepted the act of deposition of January the twenty-fifth; the officers of the forces commanded by Ramorino, Rozitski, Kaminski, and Ribinski. Sequestrations, confiscations, imprisonments, and banishments to Siberia served as commentaries on the amnesty. Five thousand Polish families were transported to the Caucasus; the total of the confiscated property was estimated at three hundred and thirty-seven million francs. The constitution granted by Alexander was annulled; the public offices were abolished and replaced by mere commissions emanating from the public offices of Russia; the directors of these commissions formed, under the management of the namiestnik, the council of government. There were to be no more diets; Poland was administered by the officials of the Tsar. The Polish army no longer existed; it was lost in the imperial army. The national orders were preserved only as Russian orders, distributed among the most zealous servants of the government. The Russian systems of taxes, justice, and coinage were successively introduced into the kingdom. The metric system of weights and measures was changed to the Russian; the Julian calendar supplanted the calendar in use all over the world. The Polish language was prohibited to be taught in schools; the University of Warsaw was suppressed, and its library taken to Saint Petersburg. The ancient historical palatinates gave way to Russian provinces; the ancient divisions were modified. These governments amounted to five after eighteen hundred and forty-four: Warsaw, Radom, Lublin, Plotsk, and Modlin. Thus were matters ordered in Poland proper.

In Lithuania and White Russia the Polish element was more narrowly watched. The germs of nationality left by Tchartoruiski's educational policy were stifled. As a punishment for the Lithuanian insurrection, the University of Vilna was suppressed, and the Russian language drove the Polish from the schools. In order to attach the southwest provinces more closely to Russia, Nicholas, assisted by Bishop Joseph Siémashko, abolished the Uniate Church, which since fifteen hundred and ninety-six had been the strongest factor of nationality. Severe laws were passed in regard to mass, to

Roman Catholic instruction, and to baptism. Indemnity and pardon was offered to Roman Catholic criminals on condition of recantation. In eighteen hundred and thirty-nine the Uniate bishops and clergy, overcome by a long series of legislative oppressions and bribes, signed the act of Polotsk, by which they entreated to be admitted into the bosom of the national orthodox church, and asked pardon both of the Emperor and of God for their sins of obstinacy and blindness. The Holy Synod hastened to gratify their request, and announced that this happy union was brought about by mildness and persuasion. Some of the monks and the faithful resisted. Siemashko, now made metropolitan as the reward for his services, was particularly eager in his professions of orthodoxy, and organized missions in which an amount of violence and zeal was used to destroy the old schism, equal to that which the Jesuit party of the seventeenth century had employed to cement it. Siemashko's attempt to convert the Basilian nuns of Minsk made a special scandal. When the arts of persuasion had been exhausted, and they refused to leave the communion of Rome, they were once more offered their choice between the orthodox religion and hard labor in Siberia. They rejected the offer of recantation, and were marched in irons seven days' journey to Vitepsk, where they were obliged to perform the most degrading tasks under the lash. Several were killed by violent treatment. Their obstinacy under persecution became more confirmed, and finally such tortures were employed as recalled the worst days of the Spanish Inquisition.

The orthodox peasants profited, however, by this revolution. In order to protect them against the ill-will of their masters who remained Catholics or Uniates, the authorities of White Russia and Lithuania were required to make "inventories" which would exactly determine the amount of their rents and the sum of their dues. The inventories put an end to the despotism of the nobles.

CHAPTER III.

NICHOLAS THE FIRST: FOREIGN RELATIONS.

1825 – 1855.

Hostility against France: the Eastern Question.—Revolution of Eighteen Hundred and Forty-eight.—Intervention in Hungary.

HOSTILITY AGAINST FRANCE: THE EASTERN QUESTION.

THE Polish insurrection had resulted, as to general European policy, in a more intimate union between the three powers of the North, which bound themselves by a treaty to deliver up each other's rebel subjects, and in a kind of rupture between Russia and those Western powers which had given especial evidences of their sympathy for the Polish cause. Nicholas the First, the chief representative of conservatism in Europe, looked upon France as the hot-bed of perpetually recurring revolutions. He wished the world to remain immovable; but Paris periodically overturned the established order of things, and shook the thrones of Europe with its "days." The insurrection of eighteen hundred and thirty overthrew his ally, Charles the Tenth, caused Belgium and Central Italy to break the bonds of their allegiance, and the direct consequence of it was the long and bloody struggle with the revolutionists of Poland. The sympathies of the French for Poland were strongly manifested. Riots took place in the streets of Paris, and windows were broken at the Russian Embassy; addresses were presented in the Chambers at each new session, and the more extravagant sympathizers promised the co-operation of the French army. When the revolution was crushed, the proscribed Poles nowhere received a warmer welcome than in Paris, and Polish schools were provided for their children. Under the protection of France, the revolution which was sweeping over Europe made use of the Polish emigrants as fast allies in the cause of freedom. In Hungary, in Turkey, in the Caucasus, everywhere Nicholas was to find these exiles, these guests of France, arrayed against him.

But Nicholas did not wait for these acts of hostility, to declare himself against the French. His relations with Louis Philippe, the July king, were a long series of frets, of annoyances, of scarcely disguised insults. In his reply to the notification of the accession of the new sovereign, he had designated the revolution which had given Louis Philippe his crown as an "event forever to be deplored." He affected a polite impertinence towards the representatives of France, or gave them to understand that the respect he paid them was a tribute merely to their personal merit, and not to their diplomatic quality. MM. de Bourgoing, de Barante, Marshal Maison, and Casimir Périer the younger, were placed one after the other in this false position.

The ill-will of Nicholas was shown by acts of a graver kind, — by threatening manifestations and displays of military force, by meetings of sovereigns which seemed ominous of the reconstitution of the Holy Alliance, by attempts at coalition, and even by flagrant violations of treaties. Nicholas was one day to expiate cruelly the dangerous satisfaction to his pride which he derived from these vain provocations to France and the new ideas. This situation of king of kings, of head of the monarchical governments, of arbiter of Europe, which he was allowed to hold by the complaisance of Austria and Prussia, was more apparent than real, and had more prestige than force. Once more the so-called policy of principles was to bring misfortune to Russia.

In eighteen hundred and thirty-two Mehemet Ali, the Khedive of Egypt, quarreled with Abdullah Pasha, the Governor of Saint-Jean-d'Acre, about some real or imaginary grievance. Mehemet's adopted son, Ibrahim, at the head of a powerful army, entered Syria, without consulting the Turkish Sultan. Mahmud commanded peace between the belligerents, and ordered Ibrahim to return to Egypt. Ibrahim disobeyed, and captured the Syrian forts, Gaza, Jaffa, and Caiffa. In May he reduced Acre to a heap of ruins, and finally starved it into submission. He now determined to conquer all Syria; and the capture of Damascus, together with a great victory on the banks of the Orontes, enabled him to advance as far as Antioch. There again he routed the Turkish army, and opened the road to Constantinople. The Sultan made one more effort, and sent out a force of sixty thousand men under Redshid Pasha, who was entirely defeated at Konieh on the twenty-first of December. Turkey then appealed to the European powers, and the Russian General Muravief was sent to Alexandria to co-operate with the Austrian consul in persuading the Khedive to put an end to hostilities. He consented; but, nevertheless, Ibrahim continued to threaten Constantinople, and in February the Sultan sent to Russia for assistance. A fleet from Sevastopol anchored at the mouth of the Bosphorus, ten thousand men disembarked on the coast of Asia, and an army of twenty-four thousand men was caused to advance to the Pruth. France and England protested through Admiral Ronsin and Lord Ponsonby, and obtained the withdrawal of the Russian forces, the retreat of the Egyptian army, and the treaty of Kutaieh, by which the Sultan guaranteed the Khedive the possession of his Syrian conquests.

All seemed to have ended quietly, when a rumor spread that Count Orlof had concluded with the Porte the treaty of Unkiar-Skelessi. This treaty, which was signed on the eighth of June, eighteen hundred and thirty-three, under the appearance of an offensive and defensive alliance, established the dependence of Turkey on Russia. Each of the two contracting parties engaged to furnish the other the aid necessary "to secure the tranquillity of its states." This latter stipulation might, in such a distracted country as Turkey, involve a permanent occupation by the Russian forces.

The true significance of the treaty was contained in an additional secret article by which the Sultan undertook, in case Russia were attacked, to close the Dardanelles, and to permit no foreign ships of war, on any pretext whatever, to pass through them; while on the other hand the Tsar agreed to spare his ally the trouble and expense of giving him military aid. England and France protested loudly, but subsequent events prevented the execution of this treaty.

The Khedive of Egypt had been left in full possession of his Syrian conquests, and the threats of the Russian Emperor did not prevent his renewing his hostilities in eighteen hundred and thirty-nine. Sultan Mahmud was succeeded by his son, Abdul-Medjid, who was soon reduced to such straits that finally France and England signed a note placing the Ottoman Empire under the common protection of the five great powers. Mehemet Ali demanded only recognition as independent and hereditary ruler of Egypt, and a confirmation of his right to the possession of Syria and Adana. Nicholas took advantage of the lively sympathy shown by France for the Viceroy to put it in a state of complete isolation from the other powers. England, which entirely discountenanced the Viceroy's pretensions, and was always anxious to maintain the integrity of the Ottoman Empire, separated from France, and was glad to take part in the conspiracy, the aim of which was to exclude the French from the assembly of European powers. A convention was concluded at London, on July fifteenth, eighteen hundred and forty, between Great Britain, Russia, Austria, and Prussia, whereby this ultimatum was offered to Mehemet Ali: He was to have the hereditary sovereignty of Egypt and the possession of the pashalic of Saint-Jean-d'Acre for life. If he did not accept these terms within ten days, the Sultan should offer him

Egypt only, and if he still persisted in his obstinacy, the four powers threatened to use force in order to compel him to yield.

This treaty was made known in France two days after it had been signed, and was received with a burst of indignation. The excitement reached a fever height, additional levies were made for the army and navy, inflammatory pamphlets were published, calling for war and reiterating every quarrel which France and England had known for centuries. Measures were taken to fortify Paris as a reply to the concealed menaces of the quadruple alliance. A French journal declared: "We have trusted for ten years in the alliance of England; we trust in it no more. We stand alone, and are ready to maintain alone, if need be, the balance of power and independence of Europe." The king, however, was firm in his desire for peace, and soon came in collision with Thiers and his colleagues who wished to announce the additional levy of one hundred and fifty thousand troops, and were full of the most warlike spirit.

Mehemet Ali, having made all preparations to resist compulsory measures with force, before he returned an answer to the ultimatum tried to patch up a peace with the Sultan. But his proposals were not deemed satisfactory, and Abdul-Medjid immediately sent a firman to Alexandria announcing the formal deposition of the Khedive from the head of Egyptian affairs. Although this extreme step was not approved of by the four powers, they resolved to declare that the ports of Egypt and Syria were in a state of blockade. Admiral Stopford appeared off Beyroot on the ninth of September, and after a week's siege compelled the governor to withdraw his troops. Commodore Napier, with a body of British, Austrian, and Turkish infantry, dispersed Ibrahim Pasha's army. In October the almost impregnable fortress of Acre was bombarded and reduced to subjection by Admiral Stopford. These successes of the allies quickly subdued the Khedive. Ibrahim Pasha's army had dwindled from seventy-five thousand to twenty thousand men. Napier then made a convention with Mehemet Ali, by virtue of which the Viceroy should be confirmed in his sovereignty of Egypt as soon as he withdrew Ibrahim from Syria and restored the Turkish fleet. The Porte considered that Napier had exceeded his instructions, and refused to acknowledge Mehemet; but the authority of the four powers was brought to bear, and, after some trifling on the part of the Sultan, the hereditary succession to the throne of Egypt was guaranteed to the Khedive without any annoying restrictions.

England, which had forsaken France to defend Turkey against Egypt, soon felt the necessity of returning to its first allegiance, in order to guarantee Constantinople against the protectorate of Russia. On the occasion of the "Convention of the Straits," signed July thirteen, eighteen hundred and forty-one, France emerged from its state of isolation, and regained its position in the European concert.

Nicholas had played the singular part of protector of the Ottoman integrity. He had allied himself with England, his natural enemy and rival; but, at the price of these inconsistencies, he had given himself the pleasure of humiliating the government of Louis Philippe; he had seen with intense satisfaction the affront offered to France by the treaty of London, the irritation caused at Paris by the intervention of the allies in Syria, the embarrassment into which the French were thrown by the warlike policy of Thiers's cabinet, and the imminence of a general conflict, where, for such a poor stake, they would have had a coalition of all the great powers arrayed against them.

During all this period he redoubled his ill offices toward France. In eighteen hundred and thirty-three he convoked the Congress of Münchengrätz, where the sovereigns of Russia, Austria, and Prussia, together with their principal ministers, assembled. In eighteen hundred and thirty-five, at the manoeuvres of Kalish, he reviewed an army of ninety thousand men in the presence of the King of Prussia, the Austrian archdukes, and a multitude of princes. The same year he held a congress at Töplitz with the two German sovereigns. On the death of Charles the Tenth he ordered a court mourning of twenty-four days.

At the third partition of Poland, in seventeen hundred and ninety-five, Krakof was submitted to Austria. Fourteen years later it was united to the Duchy of Warsaw; but after Napoleon's fall it was made a free, independent, and neutral city, under the mutual protection of the three northern powers. Both Austria and Russia had made use of this territory at various times — in eighteen hundred and thirty-one and again in eighteen hundred and thirty-six — as a fulcrum where they might bring pressure to bear upon their rebellious subjects. In eighteen hundred and forty-six troubles broke out in Austrian Galicia. The upper classes made great preparations for a rising against Austria. The insurrection began at Pilsno, near Tarnof. A provisional government was established at Krakof, which formulated communistic principles. "Let us endeavor," said its manifesto, "to establish a community where every one will enjoy the fruits of the earth according to his merits and capacity; let all privileges cease; let those who are inferior by birth, education, or physical strength obtain without shame the full assistance of communism, which will divide among all men the absolute ownership of the soil, now enjoyed by a small minority; let all taxes cease, whether they be paid in money or labor; and let all who have fought for their country have an indemnity in land taken from the national domain." The Austrian troops at first evacuated Krakof, and Count Patelski entered at the head of a small body of peasants armed with scythes. The first success of the insurgents inspired the people with hopes that the whole of Poland might be set free.

But the Galician peasantry, taking advantage of their power, turned against the nobility, whom a long series of oppressions had caused them cordially to hate; and they now began to wreak their vengeance by burning and pillaging the property of the nobles, and indulging in a general massacre, in which they were encouraged by the Austrian authorities. The insurrection having thus failed by internal dissensions, the Austrians surrounded Krakof, and threatened immediate bombardment unless the insurgents surrendered and gave hostages to guarantee peaceable admission of the troops into the city. The dictator, Vishievski, at first resisted, and ordered barricades to be erected in the streets; but the chief inhabitants opposed this step, and sent a deputation to treat with General Collin. While the negotiations were going on a battalion of Russian infantry entered the city, followed by a Prussian army, and the insurrectionists surrendered at discretion.

Nicholas, in his character of queller of insurrections, was here in his element. His troops were the first to enter Krakof. The fall of this free city roused much interest in France and England. Palmerston said: "I have too high an opinion of the sentiments which must animate the three powers, to doubt of their acting toward Krakof in any other spirit than that of the treaty of Vienna. Those governments are too intelligent not to perceive that the treaty of Vienna must be considered in its integrity, and that no government is permitted to make a choice of those articles which it may wish to preserve or violate. I must add that if there are any powers who have signed the treaty of Vienna who are specially interested in its faithful execution, they are the German powers; and I am sure that it cannot have escaped the perspicacity of those powers that, if the treaty of Vienna is not good on the Vistula, it must be equally bad on the Rhine and the Po." Guizot, then minister of foreign affairs, protested also against this violation of the treaties of eighteen hundred and fifteen. Notwithstanding these protests, the republic of Krakof was suppressed, and the city itself was annexed to Austria on the eleventh of November, eighteen hundred and forty-six.

THE REVOLUTION OF EIGHTEEN HUNDRED AND FORTY-EIGHT.

The Revolution of eighteen hundred and forty-eight shook Europe with a violence which had been hitherto unfelt. Not only all Italy and Western Germany shared in the movement, but countries which till now had seemed opposed to the new ideas, and which had been the very bulwark of monarchical Europe against the revolutionary spirit, caught the infection, and the excitement spread even to the frontiers of Russia. The Germanic constitution was overthrown; the Germans called a Parliament at Frankfort, at which the principle of German unity was laid down in a way which threatened the dissolution of the Austrian State. "Germany," it was said, "exists wherever German is spoken"; the Slavs held a congress at Prague, and discussed the formation of a Slavic republic. The Emperor Ferdinand was driven from Vienna, and signed the act of abdication in favor of his nephew Francis-Joseph. At Berlin Frederick-William the Fourth saluted the corpses which were publicly displayed by the revolutionists. Hungary rose at the voice of the great patriot, Louis Kossuth, and on the fourteenth of April, eighteen hundred and forty-nine, declared itself free and independent. Even the Danubian principalities, influenced by the party of Rumanian unity, dethroned the Hospodar Bibesco in Valakhia and the Hospodar Sturdza in Moldavia. Where would the movement stop? Plots were discovered in Russia; Poland, whose national banner the Parisian workmen waved in their tumultuous processions, quivered with excitement.

The Emperor Nicholas planted himself in the face of revolutionary Europe. He first acted in the countries nearest to him. He used the might of his influence to prevent the King of Prussia from accepting the imperial crown of Germany. He sent an army to the principalities, on the pretext that he felt it his duty to defeat any effort that might be made to impair the integrity of the Ottoman Empire, now more than ever essential to the maintenance of general peace. He seized the moment when the successful Hungarian insurrection had received a shock from the counter Kroat insurrection to violate the law of nations, and send an army to the assistance of the young Emperor Francis-Joseph. In spite of the protests of the Hungarian emissaries at Paris and London, neither France nor England was willing to take any official steps to prevent the intervention of the Tsar. Lord Palmerston refused to recognize Hungary, except as an integral portion of the Austrian Empire; and when Count Nesselrode in a circular note dated February the ninth announced the entrance of the Russian troops into Transylvania, solely with a humanitarian view and to protect two cities against the pillage and massacres of the Hungarians, he did not feel himself authorized to make any reply.

Buda was in the hands of the Hungarians. The Austrian army was defeated at all points. Had England and France acknowledged its declaration of independence, the Tsar would not have ventured to cross the boundary. But the silence of the two courts virtually gave him a safeguard; and he, as the universal restorer of European order, could not see a free state established at his very doors, to encourage the already too susceptible Poles in their desires for liberty. Moreover, the Hungarians had shown special sympathy for the Polish revolution of eighteen hundred and thirty-one, and he was glad of the opportunity to teach his subjects a new lesson by helping to crush the malcontents of a neighboring state.

On the first of May it was officially announced in Vienna that the Emperor of Austria having asked for the armed assistance of Russia, the Tsar had immediately granted it, "with the most generous zeal and in the most liberal manner." And the Saint Petersburg Gazette during the same month published a manifesto, by which the Emperor of all the Russias gave notice that, at the request of the Austrian Emperor, he was about to send his armies to crush the revolution in Hungary, "where the Polish traitors of eighteen hundred and thirty-one, together with refugees and exiles from other nations, were usurping the power." This fact of foreign influence at work in Hungary was made especially prominent as a sort of justification; yet, while the Hungarian army amounted to nearly two hundred thousand, the number of foreigners who took service was estimated not to exceed five thousand, only three fifths of whom were Poles, and the majority of those, Galicians.

Paskiévitch was charged to complete in the plains of Hungary his victory over Poland. Having made all the arrangements of a prudent general, he entered Hungary in the north, at the head of an army of one hundred and thirty thousand men. On June the nineteenth General Lüders also invaded Transylvania with more than fifty thousand men. The total force of Russian troops destined to co-operate with the Austrian troops was upwards of one hundred and ninety thousand men. To oppose to this immense army, which, with the Austrians, amounted to three hundred thousand men, the government of Kossuth could furnish only about one hundred and fifty thousand. The Polish general, Vysotski, had taken, in the north, the place of Dembinski, who had been forced to resign by the machinations of General Görgey. Paskiévitch defeated the Hungarian army at many points, occupied all Transylvania, and on the twelfth of August, eighteen hundred and forty-nine, received the traitorous capitulation of the generalissimo, Görgey, at Világos. General Bem retreated to Transylvania, and met the Russians at Déva. He obtained an armistice of twenty-four hours; but, finding that he could not control his men, he resigned his command, and with Guyon, Stein, and a few others, escaped to Turkish soil.

The emperors of Austria and Russia demanded the extradition of the refugees; but the Sultan, feeling that it was a question of honor with him not to violate the right of asylum, addressed a note to the representatives of France and England, asking, if the question of the refugees should lead to war between the allied emperors and the Sultan, whether Turkey could be assured of the support of the Western powers. The representatives replied in the affirmative, and Sir Stratford Canning summoned the English fleet to approach Constantinople. Turkey therefore absolutely refused to submit to the wishes of the two emperors; Russia and Austria, foreseeing complications, consented that their rebellious subjects should be simply expelled or sent into the interior. General Bem and several hundred of his companions abjured Christianity and became Mussulmans, hoping that they would thus have the chance to avenge themselves on the enemies of their country. Notwithstanding the protection afforded them by Turkey, these unfortunate refugees underwent terrible sufferings; from exposure and lack of food nearly four hundred died in less than two months. The Austrian government, fearing that they would form the nucleus of an army, offered certain conditions for their return, and about three thousand of them accepted. Of those who remained, the converts were isolated at Alep; the others, including Kossuth, Batthyány, Mészáros, and Vysotski, were sent to Kutahia, in Asia Minor. But, owing to the sympathy of Europe, their captivity lasted only till eighteen hundred and fifty-one. The United States government sent a frigate to convey the heroes to its hospitable shores. Before they departed General Bem, "the hero of Hungary and Poland," died at Alep. " Hungary is at the feet of your majesty," Paskiévitch had written to Nicholas. The capitulation of Világos, the surrender of Bem and Kazinczy, the fall of Arad and Munkács, the flight of Kossuth and the government, assured the stability of the victory. Two points, however, still remained unconquered. Over the fortresses of Peterwárad and Komáron still floated the flag of Hungarian independence. General Klapka, with about eighteen thousand men, still hoped to make a firm resistance. It was only after the news of the successive victories gained by the Russians and the surrender of Petervárad that Klapka decided to give up the vain struggle. On October the fifth the Austrian flag replaced the tricolor.

On the second anniversary of the death of the Austrian minister, Latour, began the work of vengeance. The chiefs of the national defence were put to death by order of Francis-Joseph. Louis Batthyány was the first victim; on the same day thirteen other patriots were executed at Arad. Not only for days and months, but for years, the punishments inaugurated by General Haynau were carried out in all rigor. Francis-Joseph treated Hungary more cruelly than Nicholas had treated Poland. All the germs of nationality were destroyed. The general constitution was abolished; the national diets, the ministry, the separate administration, the communal system, — all was destroyed. The paper money issued by the national government was burned, and, in addition to the distress thus caused, new and heavy taxes were imposed. The national language, church, and institutions were crushed. Thus cruelly resulted Russian intervention in Hungary.

But the Tsar's interference with the Danish question had happy consequences. He sent a fleet to support the demands of the Danish government; and on the tenth of July a treaty was signed at Berlin granting a six months' armistice, and obliging the Prussian and German troops to evacuate the duchies which were to have a separate administration. Thus the rights of Denmark upon the Baltic and North Seas were secured against the unjust pretensions of Germany, and the revolted Holsteiners were deprived of foreign support. On the eighth of May, eighteen hundred and fifty-two, Nicholas joined the other powers in causing the integrity of the Danish monarchy to be recognized at the treaty of London.

Nicholas's power blazed forth for the last time when, on the fifteenth of May, eighteen hundred and fifty-two, he reviewed the Austrian army on the slopes of Vienna, and pressed to his heart that Austrian sovereign "whose ingratitude was to astonish Europe."

CHAPTER IV.

THE CRIMEAN WAR.

1853–1855.

Louis Napoleon. — Change in the English Cabinet. — Ministry of Lord Aberdeen. — The Holy Sites. — Conversations between the Emperor Nicholas and Sir George Hamilton Seymour.

AT the other extremity of Europe arose a man who seemed to co-operate with Nicholas in his attempts to put an end to the European revolution. On his advancing path toward the empire, Louis Napoleon, by his subservience to the Church of Rome, won the special approbation of the Pope; by the expedition to Rome he extinguished the Italian republic; by the December coup-d'état he raised himself above the ruins of the French republic. Nicholas, almost reconciled to the hated name of Bonaparte, and to the imminent restoration of the Napoleonic dynasty, remarked, "France has been setting an evil example; it will now set a good one. I have faith in the wisdom of Louis Napoleon."

The Second Empire, however, was to make him suffer in return for his hostile and impolitic conduct toward the July monarchy and the republic of eighteen hundred and forty-eight. His desire for the coup-d'état was gratified, but to his own hurt.

The new French government espoused the cause of the Latin monks in their quarrel with the Greek monks about the places which tradition assigned as the scenes of the birth and sufferings of Jesus Christ. The chief bone of contention was the possession of the key to the great door of the church at

Bethlehem and the right to place a silver star in the sacred grotto where it was claimed Christ was born. This petty quarrel covered deeper political complications. Religious fanaticism, wakened by the discussion, was fanned by the French Emperor into a flame of enthusiasm; he knew that Russia was unlikely to yield the point, and that if he allowed himself to be humiliated by the Tsar, his influence would be destroyed. The unforgotten retreat from Moscow, the presence of the Russian army in Paris, the partition of Poland, the attitude of Nicholas since the flight of Charles the Tenth, all served to irritate the French people, and Napoleon craftily calculated upon their support in his struggle with the Tsar.

Toward the end of the year eighteen hundred and fifty-two, almost immediately after the proclamation of the Empire in France, a vote passed by the English House of Commons upon Disraeli's "clever and elaborate system of finance" led to the resignation of Earl Derby's Tory ministry, which, as was well known, was inclined to the French alliance. A coalition cabinet was immediately formed by the Earl of Aberdeen. Several members of the new government were so opposed to the French Empire that they did not hesitate to give public expression to this hostility. The majority did not declare themselves, but there was only one decided partisan of the Napoleonic régime. To be sure, this single adherent was none other than Lord Palmerston; but while it seemed that the natural place for this statesman was in the Foreign Office, it was seen that he was transferred to the Department of the Interior, and the provisional direction of foreign affairs was entrusted to Lord John Russell until the arrival of the Earl of Clarendon. This unexpected disposition of the secretaryships made a sensation. At London and throughout Europe it was interpreted as an evidence of coolness between England and France. Nowhere was the news more joyfully received than at Saint Petersburg.

The Turkish government, obliged on the one hand to yield to the demands of the Tsar, and on the other terrified at the French threat of an appeal to arms, had failed to make good its promises in regard to the Holy sites. The concessions which were made by the court of Constantinople were not carried out at Jerusalem; and the Tsar, on the watch for his opportunity, did not fail to proclaim this lack of good faith and denounce it as an insult to his own person. If he should succeed in persuading England to recognize his grievances, to share his views, and to assist in his plans, it was over with the Turkish Empire. The enterprise was delicate, difficult, possibly risky; but should he succeed, what a triumph it would be! The authority of his person and his name, the ascendency which he enjoyed throughout the world, the eight-and-twenty years of a reign second to none, his steadfastness in a well-tried policy, the order and peace which he had done most to maintain throughout Europe, did not stand in the way of his sacrifice, if it was necessary. But, in playing so dangerous a game, he determined to trust no one but himself. Never before in the history of the world did a monarch so absolutely and directly take upon himself a responsibility.

On the ninth of January, eighteen hundred and fifty-three, at a reception given by the Grand Duchess Helena, the Emperor Nicholas approached the British ambassador, Sir George Hamilton Seymour, spoke to him graciously of the new ministry which had just been formed in London, and sent his especial congratulations to Lord Aberdeen, with whom he had been acquainted for nearly forty years. He added: "You know my sentiments in regard to England; it is essential for the two governments — that is, for England and me — to be on the best terms. Never was the necessity of it greater than at present. I beg of you to transmit these words to Lord John Russell. If we agree, I have no solicitude about Western Europe; what others may think is in reality of little consequence. As to Turkey, that is another question. That country is in a critical state, and may easily give us much embarrassment."

Thereupon, without any further explanation, the Tsar was in the act of turning from the English minister, when the latter, finding the conversation interesting, but incomplete, and fearing that an opportunity to renew it would not soon occur, ventured to ask the Emperor for a few words in regard to the Ottoman Empire more assuring than those he had just uttered. The Tsar hesitated at first, and seemed disinclined to go beyond generalities; then, suddenly, like a person about to commit himself, "Well," said he, "we have on our hands a sick man, a very sick man. I tell you frankly it would be a great misfortune if he should give us the slip some of these days, especially if it happened before all the necessary arrangements were made. But this is not the fitting time to speak to you of these things."

Five days afterwards, on the fourteenth of January, Sir George Hamilton Seymour was informed by the chancellor, Count Nesselrode, that the Tsar wished to have an interview with him. He immediately repaired to the palace. The Tsar was alone, and ready to take up the conversation, the prologue to which at the Grand Duchess's reception had been so interesting, but so short and mysterious. Though couched in a courteous and familiar form, the discourse which the Emperor delivered before his auditor was methodical and carefully composed. "You know the dreams and plans in which the Empress Catherine was in the habit of indulging; they have been handed down to our day; but while I inherited immense territorial possessions, I did not inherit those visions, or those intentions, if you prefer the name. My country is so vast, so happily circumstanced in every way, that it would be unreasonable in me to desire more territory or more power than I possess. On the contrary, I am the first to tell you that our great, perhaps our only danger, is that which would arise from an extension given to an empire already too large.

"Very near us lies Turkey, and, in our present situation, nothing better for our interests can be desired; the time has gone by when we had anything to fear from the fanatical spirit or the military enterprise of the Turks. That country is strong enough, or has hitherto been strong enough, to preserve its independence and to insure respectful treatment from other countries.

"Now, in that empire there are several millions of Christians, whose interests I am called upon to watch over. Moreover, the right of doing so is secured to me by treaty. I may truly say that I make a moderate and sparing use of my right, and I will even confess frankly that it is attended with obligations which are occasionally trying; but I cannot withdraw from the discharge of a distinct duty. Our religion, as established in this country, came to us from the East, and there are feelings and obligations which must never be lost from view.

"But Turkey, placed as it is, has by degrees fallen into such a state of decrepitude, that, as I said the other evening, however anxious we all may be to prolong the sick man's existence, — and I beg you to believe that I am as desirous as you can be for his continued existence, — he may suddenly die upon our hands. We cannot bring the dead to life again: if the Turkish Empire falls, it falls to rise no more; and I put it to you, therefore, whether it is not better to be provided beforehand for such a contingency than to run the risk of the chaos, the confusion, the certainty of a European war, all of which would attend the catastrophe, if it should occur unexpectedly and before some ulterior system has been sketched. This is the point on which I am desirous that you should call the attention of your government."

The English diplomatist answered, in substance, that Turkey had more than once emerged from crises in which it had been believed that the end had come, that England was not as a general thing inclined to make these provisional engagements, and that in fact it would be very loath to anticipate the succession of an old friend and ally.

"The principle is excellent," replied the Emperor, "especially in times of uncertainty and change like the present. Nevertheless, it is of the highest importance that we should understand one another, and not allow ourselves to be taken by surprise. Now I want to speak with you as a friend and as a gentleman : if England and I come to an understanding in regard to this matter, everything else is indifferent to me, no matter what the others think and do. So I tell you, without reservation, that if England expects to get a foothold some time in Constantinople, I will not allow it. Not that I ascribe that intention to you, but it is better to speak frankly. As for my part, I am equally willing to engage not to establish myself there, — that is, as a proprietor, I do not say as a guardian. If no precautions are taken, if everything is left to chance, I may be obliged by circumstances to occupy Constantinople."

However startling to Sir Hamilton Seymour the Emperor's overtures may have been, they were not new to the British government; for when Nicholas visited England in June, eighteen hundred and forty-four, he held long conversations upon the Eastern question with the Duke of Wellington, Lord Aberdeen, and Sir Robert Peel. His propositions, or rather his ideas, of uniting the two governments in a special agreement upon this question were committed to a memorandum by Count Nesselrode, which was sent to London, and deposited in the secret archives of the Foreign Office.

This conversation having been fully reported to the English government, Lord John Russell replied on the ninth of February, congratulating the Emperor on his moderation, frankness, and friendly disposition, asserting that an agreement to divide the Sultan's provinces before the dissolution of the

Turkish Empire would tend to hasten the very contingency. Lord John Russell's note also insinuated that no policy more wise, disinterested, and beneficent could be followed by the Russian Empire than that "which his Imperial Majesty has so long followed and which will render his name more illustrious than that of the most famous sovereigns who have sought immortality by unprovoked conquest and ephemeral glory." The greatest forbearance towards Turkey was advised, and friendly negotiations rather than peremptory demands were to be the remedies for grievances. Thus the English government and the Tsar held views diametrically opposed to each other, — the former being unwilling to enter into any secret stipulation, and not recognizing the probability of Turkish dissolution.

On the twentieth of February Sir Hamilton Seymour, after communicating Lord John Russell's despatch to Count Nesselrode, announced his intention of sending a copy to the Tsar the following day. The same evening, at the reception, he met the Tsar, who said, "I hear that you have received your answer and are to bring it to me to-morrow?" "Sire, I am to have that honor," was his reply, "but your Majesty is aware that the answer is precisely what I had led you to expect."

"So I was sorry to hear; but I think your government does not understand my object. I am not so anxious to know what shall be done when the sick man dies, as to determine with England what shall not be done."

And when Sir George Hamilton Seymour protested that Turkey was not dying, but would exist for many years unless the event were hastened by the rash action of Russia, the Tsar answered with some asperity: "I will tell you that if your government has been led to believe that Turkey retains any elements of existence, it must have received incorrect information. I repeat it to you: the sick man is dying, and we can never allow such an event to take us by surprise. We must come to some understanding; and this we should do, I am sure, if I could hold but ten minutes' conversation with your ministers; with Lord Aberdeen, for example, who knows me so well, who has full confidence in me, as I have in him. And remember, I do not ask for a treaty or a protocol; a general understanding is all I require; between gentlemen, that is sufficient."

It did not require very deep discernment on Sir George Seymour's part to penetrate the designs of the Emperor. That very day he drew the following conclusion from the hasty skirmish which he had with him: "There is no room for doubt that a sovereign who insists so strenuously upon the imminent downfall of a neighboring state has decided in his own mind that the hour has come, not to expect its dissolution, but to hasten it. The Emperor's aim would be to induce the Queen's government, in accord with the cabinets of Saint Petersburg and Vienna, to engage in a plan of dividing Turkey, and excluding France from such an arrangement."

On the following day Sir George Seymour read Lord Russell's despatch to the Emperor, who made comments as he proceeded. The Emperor regretted that the English government had not directly answered the question as to what ought not to be permitted in case of the sudden downfall of Turkey. The ambassador replied, "Perhaps your Majesty would be good enough to explain your own ideas upon this negative policy." This for some time the Emperor refused to do; but in his efforts to draw his prudent adversary upon his own ground, he himself had gone too far to beat an honorable retreat. "Well," he said at last, "there are several things which I will never allow; and, in the first place, as regards ourselves: I do not desire the permanent occupation of Constantinople by the Russians; but, on the other hand, having said this, I will say that it shall never be held by the English, nor by the French, nor by any other of the great powers. Again, I will never permit an attempt to reconstruct a Byzantine Empire, or such an extension of Greece as would render it a powerful state. Still less would I permit the partition of Turkey into little republics, ready-made asylums for the Kossuths, the Mazzinis, and the other revolutionists of Europe. Rather than submit to any of these arrangements, I would go to war, and carry it on as long as I have a man and a musket left."

The English ambassador, in his turn somewhat aroused, took refuge in the strong position which he occupied from the very first, — Why should they continue to discuss the downfall of the Turkish Empire and the arrangements to be made, when it would be far better to bring the sick man to health? The Tsar then spoke of France, and hinted that the French, in their designs upon Tunis, were trying to embroil matters in Constantinople and Montenegro. He had offered the Sultan the support of Russia in case France resorted to threats. Sir George Hamilton Seymour replied that the English government would not tolerate the presence of the French at Constantinople; and, in order to find out whether there was any understanding between the cabinets of Saint Petersburg and Vienna, he added, "But your Majesty has forgotten Austria. All these Eastern questions are of great importance to her. She would naturally expect to be consulted." "You must understand," replied the Emperor without a moment's hesitation, "that when I speak of Russia, I speak of Austria as well. What suits the one suits the other. Our interests, as regards Turkey, are perfectly identical."

Sir Hamilton Seymour, then making some allusion to the ambition of the Russian people, who for many years had harbored designs against Turkey, the Tsar replied that the Empress Catherine had indulged in dreams of conquest, but they had not been shared by her descendants. "You see how I am treating the Sultan. He breaks his word, and acts towards me in a singularly vexatious manner; yet I am satisfied to despatch an ambassador to Constantinople to demand reparation. I should certainly be justified in sending an army, if I so pleased, which nothing could stop; but I content myself with a simple demonstration, to prove that I do not mean to be trifled with." The English minister, who at that time had no reason to distrust the Tsar's moderation, offered him his sincere congratulations, and the conversation then came back to the dissolution of the Turkish Empire. Without paying the slightest heed to what he had said a few moments before, the Emperor began boldly to discuss a plan of partition in the event of the dissolution of the Ottoman Empire. "The Principalities," he said, "are, in fact, an independent state under my protection; this might so continue. Serbia might receive a similar form of government, Bulgaria the same. There is no reason, so far as I know, why this province should not form an independent State. As to Egypt, I quite understand the importance to England of that territory. All that I can say is that, in case of a distribution of the Ottoman domain upon the fall of the empire, if you should take possession of Egypt, I should have no objections to offer. I would say the same thing of Candia; that island might suit you, and I do not see why it should not become an English possession." Here the ambassador felt called upon to answer coldly that the designs of England upon Egypt did not go beyond the point of securing a safe and ready communication between British India and the mother country.

The Tsar, who was not satisfied with the first reception of his overtures, commanded Sir George Seymour to engage his government to write with the fullest confidence and detail about this matter. "It is not an engagement, a treaty, which I ask for, but a free interchange of ideas, and, if necessary, the word of a gentleman. Between us that is enough." In this interview the Tsar, without doubt, exposed his position more completely than he intended, or than was well for the success of his tactics. He had unmasked his batteries prematurely. So for the first time since the beginning of this extraordinary negotiation, the Chancellor of the empire, the consummate diplomatist, Count Nesselrode, was brought, like a reserve, into the action. Apparently as an official answer to the official despatch of Lord John Russell, on March the seventh he gave Sir George Hamilton Seymour a memorandum, dated February the twenty-first, as though it had been written immediately after the conversation with the Emperor. The Tsar's principal arguments were reproduced in it; but revised, corrected, and freed from all imprudent and exaggerated developments.

The Russian chancellor took especial pains to explain the project of partition, which the Emperor had been rash enough to develop before the English ambassador. "In conversing familiarly with the British envoy," the memorandum ran, "upon the causes which from one day to another may bring about the fall of the Ottoman Empire, it had by no means entered into the Emperor's thoughts to propose for this contingency either a plan or a system entirely arranged by which Russia and England should dispose beforehand of the provinces ruled by the Sultan; still less a formal agreement to be concluded between the two cabinets. It was purely and simply the Emperor's notion that each party should confidentially state to the other less what it wishes than what it does not wish,—what would be contrary to English interests, what would be contrary to Russian interests,— in order that, the case occurring, they might avoid acting in opposition to each other. There is in this neither plan of partition nor a convention to be binding on the other courts. It is merely an interchange of opinions, and the Emperor sees no necessity of talking about it before the time. It is precisely for this reason that he took especial care not to make it the object of an official communication from one cabinet to the other, being desirous that the result, whatsoever it might be, of these communications should remain a secret between the two sovereigns. Consequently, there is an end to the objections which Lord John Russell raises to any concealment as regards the other powers, in the event of a formal agreement being avowed,—of which, at present, there is no question.

"In short, the Emperor cannot but congratulate himself upon having given occasion for this intimate interchange of confidential communications between her Majesty and himself. The two sovereigns have frankly explained to each other what, in the extreme hypothesis of which they have been treating, their respective interests cannot tolerate. England understands that Russia will not suffer the establishment at Constantinople of a Christian power strong enough to control and trouble it. She declares that, for herself, she renounces any intention or desire to possess Constantinople. The Emperor equally disclaims any wish or design of establishing himself there. England promises that she will enter into no arrangement for determining the measures to be taken, in the event of the fall of the Turkish Empire, without a previous understanding with the Emperor. The Emperor, on his side, willingly binds himself to the same engagement." This document, thus worded, would have seemed sufficiently reassuring and satisfactory to Sir Hamilton, if he had not remembered the more significant remarks of the Tsar, and if, besides the engagement agreed upon by Russia not to establish itself at Constantinople, he had found a formal guarantee or protest against the idea of even a temporary occupation.

Just at this juncture, on the twenty-first of February, Earl Clarendon took possession of the Foreign Office at London. His attitude and language corresponded perfectly with Lord John Russell's; a like approval of Sir George H. Seymour's judgment and discretion in his interviews with the Tsar, a like opinion as to the necessity of preserving in Europe the balance of power and general peace by the maintenance of the Ottoman Empire. On the twenty-third of March Earl

Clarendon wrote to Sir Hamilton Seymour as follows: "Her Majesty's government persevere in their belief that Turkey still possesses the elements of existence. They have learned, with sincere satisfaction, that the Emperor considers himself even more interested than England in preventing a catastrophe in Turkey, because they are convinced that upon the policy pursued by his Imperial Majesty towards Turkey will depend the hastening or the indefinite postponement of an event which every power in Europe is concerned in averting. Her Majesty's government are convinced that nothing is more calculated to precipitate that event than the constant prediction of its being near at hand; that nothing can be more fatal to the vitality of Turkey than the assumption of its rapid and inevitable decay, and that, if the opinion of the Emperor that the days of the Turkish Empire are numbered become notorious, its downfall must occur even sooner than his Imperial Majesty now appears to expect." The English minister agreed entirely with the Tsar that, should the crisis occur, the occupation of Constantinople by either of the great powers was incompatible with the true interests of Europe; that a reconstruction of a Byzantine empire was impossible, and that the systematic misrule of Greece precluded an increase of its dominion; but his language in regard to an exclusive understanding between England and Russia upon sharing the rich spoils of Turkey was clear and to the point: "England desires no territorial aggrandizement, and could be no party to a previous arrangement from which she was to derive any such benefit. England could be no party to any understanding, however general, that was to be kept secret from the other powers." Lord Clarendon then went on to declare how important it seemed to avert any catastrophe, on the ground that the first cannon-shot would be "the signal for a state of things more disastrous even than those calamities which war inevitably brings in its train," and asking for Turkey "that friendly support which, among states as well as among individuals, the weak have a right to expect from the strong."

When Lord Clarendon wrote this remarkable despatch he had not as yet received the memorandum dated February twenty-first, but it contained so complete an answer, in advance, that, when Count Nesselrode's document finally reached him, he judged that it was unnecessary to write a special reply, and that it was best to put an end, as quick as possible, to these singular negotiations. By a remarkable coincidence, Count Nesselrode was equally desirous to finish the matter. "These things," he said to the English envoy, with the satisfaction of a man freed from a great responsibility, — "these things are so delicate that it is always troublesome to discuss them"; and as a finishing stroke to the discussion, he gave Sir Hamilton, on the fifteenth of April, a document which agreed in the main with the English opinions. After expressing his satisfaction at the result of the discussion, and expressing some doubt whether the English government had been correctly informed about the treatment of the Christian subjects of the Porte, the document said: "The Emperor will readily agree that the best means of upholding the Turkish government is: not to harass it by overbearing demands supported in a manner humiliating to its independence and its dignity. His Majesty is disposed, as he has ever been, to act upon this system, with the clear understanding, however, that the same rule of conduct shall be observed, without distinction and unanimously, by all the great powers, and that none of them shall take advantage of the weakness of the Porte to obtain from it concessions which might turn to the injury of the others. This principle being laid down, the Emperor declares that he is ready to labor in concert with England to prolong the existence of Turkey, setting aside all cause of alarm on the subject of its dissolution."

The Tsar, however, to Count Nesselrode's great annoyance, was not inclined to allow his wise councillor the honor and advantage of the last word. Three days after the despatch of this memorandum he added an entirely personal epilogue. On the eighteenth of April, Sir Hamilton Seymour being at dinner at the palace, the Tsar took for a pretext the quarrel about the Holy Shrines, in which he claimed that he had been personally aggrieved by the bad faith of the Sultan. He finally declared that, though as yet he had not moved a ship nor a battalion, he did not intend to be trifled with, and, unless the Turks yielded to reason, they would be brought to yield by the imminence of danger.

Thus terminated, with this vague and threatening avowal, the strangest series of negotiations known among the archives of diplomacy. The secret was loyally and religiously kept by the English government until a year had elapsed, when an imprudent provocation on the part of the Russian government led to the public being initiated.

In reply to a speech made in the House of Commons by Lord John Russell, on the seventeenth of February, eighteen hundred and fifty-four, the Imperial chancelry caused to be printed in the Journal of Saint Petersburg, of March second, an article in which the secret negotiations of the preceding year were divulged and brought forward as proof that the Tsar had never failed in frankness toward the English government, and that if France had a certain justification for distrust, England, at least, had none at all. "The British government ought to be the very last to indulge in such suspicions," said the Russian journal, "for it has possession of written proof that they rest on no foundation."

In consequence of this sort of challenge, the Foreign Office published all the correspondence which had passed between the two cabinets, and which showed so clearly the good faith and political wisdom of England. By the sudden light of this startling revelation many obscure points were explained. The year eighteen hundred and fifty-three, the diplomatic year par excellence, was illuminated to its most secret recesses.

The motives which worked upon England and France, at the beginning of the crisis, were laid open. England was seen to be far-seeing, wise, and happily preserved from the peril of temptations and false confidences; France, hesitating, wary, at once distrustful and confiding, under the influence of a sovereign who was bound to woo and win.

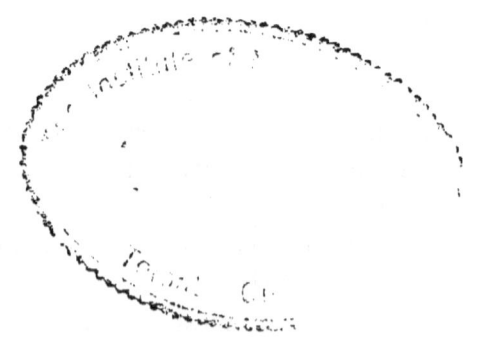

CHAPTER V.

THE CRIMEAN WAR.

1853-1855.

PRINCE MENSHIKOF AT CONSTANTINOPLE. — LORD STRATFORD DE REDCLIFFE. — COLONEL ROSE. — M. BENEDETTI. — THE FRENCH FLEET AT SALAMIS. — THREATENING DEMANDS OF PRINCE MENSHIKOF. — RESISTANCE OF THE PORTE. — THE PRINCE'S DEPARTURE. — THE FRENCH AND ENGLISH SQUADRONS AT BESIKA. — DIPLOMATIC CONFLICT. — OFFICIAL MEDIATION OF AUSTRIA. — THE RUSSIANS CROSS THE PRUTH. — THE VIENNA NOTE. — TURKISH MODIFICATIONS. — WARLIKE FEELINGS. — NAPOLEON THE THIRD. — INTERVIEWS AT OLMÜTZ AND WARSAW. — THE PORTE DECLARES WAR.

WHILE the attempt at seduction which we have seen developed behind the scenes was resulting in the discomfiture of the tempter, a brilliant and exciting display held the attention of the public on the stage. And this is scarcely a metaphor; the details, the theatrical effects, — everything was calculated to insure the triumph of the Russian policy at Constantinople, as though it were a drama. In the extraordinary embassy which the Tsar sent to the Sultan all was expressly and designedly theatrical. What could have been more so than the very choice of the ambassador? On the fourth of February, eighteen hundred and fifty-three, Count Nesselrode informed Sir Hamilton Seymour that the Emperor Nicholas had determined to send to Constantinople one of the high dignitaries of the empire, the Minister of the Marine, the Governor of Finland, Prince Menshikof; and four days later the Tsar's envoy in Paris made it known to the Minister of Foreign Affairs, M. Drouyn de Lhuys. The choice of such an ambassador was alarming. So exalted a personage would scarcely put himself out for a mere trifle. Count Nesselrode, however, took pains to calm the apprehensions excited by the excessive disproportion of the negotiator to the object under negotiation. "The Prince's instructions are rather vague, he said, on the ninth of February, to the English envoy, for it is difficult to determine how far the rights promised to the Greeks last year have been violated."

On the tenth of February the Prince left Saint Petersburg. While Russian officers preceding him reached Constantinople and made much stir about the mission of their chief, and while the Russian legation, at the instigation of the others, caused unusual preparations to be hastily made, the Prince solemnly reviewed near Odessa the troops which were on their way to join the forces already collected in Bessarabia; then he paid a visit, also in great state, to the Black Sea fleet anchored in the harbor of Sevastopol. Finally, on the twenty-eighth of February, the steamboat on which he took passage was signalled at the mouth of the Bosphorus. A noisy throng gathered in the vicinity of the Russian legation: it was the Greek population, or rather the populace, of Constantinople, who saluted with their shouts of welcome the promised avenger of the orthodox faith. The legation had exacted from the Porte extraordinary honors for the reception of the extraordinary ambassador. It seemed as though he were to be received as a conqueror. His entrance was, in fact, rather that of a commander-in-chief than a diplomat. His suite was a staff on which men of eminence served: Vice-Admiral Kornilof, Prince Galitsuin, Count Dmitri Nesselrode, Imperial aides-de-camp and generals. The throng of military and naval officers was innumerable.

In accordance with the customs of diplomacy, it should have been the ambassador's first duty to visit the Grand-Vizier Mehemet Ali Pasha and the reïs-effendi Fuad, Minister of Foreign Affairs for the Ottoman Empire. On the second of March Prince Menshikof repaired, it is true, to the Porte, but in civilian's clothes, not in full dress. If anywhere in the world diplomatic etiquette is rigorously observed, it is at Constantinople. The ambassador's négligé created a scandal: it was conserved into a studied contempt of the simplest formalities. But this disagreeable surprise was small compared to that which the Tsar's representative reserved for the councillors of the Sultan. In the palace known officially by the name, "the Sublime Porte," the reïs-effendi's apartments were next those of the Grand Vizier. In both, equally magnificent arrangements had been made to receive the ambassador; a throng of officers was drawn up in line in the ante-rooms; Fuad-Effendi's secretaries were waiting at the door, ready to introduce the illustrious visitor. After a few moments' conversation the Prince leaves the Grand Vizier, passes by the apartments of the reïs-effendi, turns his back upon those who are waiting for him, crosses the vestibule, and goes out. The astonishment, the confusion of the officers, beggars description; they do not know what to believe; they do not dare even to think of this strange proceeding. Some indulge in the hope of an explanation, but no one ventures to demand it. The day passes, but no apology or excuse appears. The next day a note from the Prince informs the Grand Vizier that the ambassador of the Tsar had no intention of casting the least slur on the Sultan's authority by his action the evening before, but that it was impossible for him to treat with an untruthful minister.

There was no question about it, the ambassador of the Tsar had intended to inflict upon Fuad-Effendi a public and an official insult. In times gone by, even in the days of Mahmud, the Turkish government would have resented the insult as a state matter, and demanded immediate reparation, in default of which they would have incarcerated the offender in the Seven Towers, and declared war. But Turkey was no longer capable of such a bold stroke. Without going back to the great Sultans of the past, there was no comparison to be made between Mahmud and his son, Abdul-Medjid. In face of the immediate and mortal danger which threatened the Turkish Empire, Fuad-Effendi sacrificed his fortune to the safety of his prince and his country. He resigned his office. Rifaat Pasha succeeded him in the direction of foreign affairs. However noble or politic was the sacrifice of Fuad, the crisis which he averted was only postponed. A single victim was not sufficient to satisfy Prince Menshikof: by his first blow he had made a breach in the Turkish government; he expected by the second to bring it to terms. When he sent the Prince to Constantinople the Emperor Nicholas made choice of exactly the right time. The ambassador of the Tsar was not only assured against meeting among the Sultan's ministers an adversary of his stature, but not a person of equal importance and dignity could be found in any of the foreign legations. The English and French embassies at this time were both deprived of their chiefs. In their anxiety to remove every pretext for the complaints of Russia, to moderate England's distrust, and to assure Europe by the moderation of their attitude regarding the Eastern question, the government of the Emperor Napoleon the Third had recalled from Constantinople the Marquis de Lavalette, who was somewhat compromised by the extravagance of his demands in the matter of the Holy Places; and, while M. de Lacour was appointed his successor, pains were taken not to hasten the departure of the new ambassador. On the other hand, in order to show that indifferent neutrality at Constantinople which it was proposed to sustain in regard to the quarrel which involved France and Russia, the English government authorized, or rather invited, Sir Stratford Canning, the Queen's envoy, to take leave of absence and visit England. For more than twenty years this able diplomatist had been resident minister at the Turkish Court, and during this long term of office he had, by the clearness of his understanding, by the correctness of his judgment, and, above all, by the firmness of his character, gained at Constantinople, as well as at London, an incontestable and unequalled authority. In the Queen's Cabinet his despatches had the weight of law; in the Sultan's Council his opinions were held as oracles. It is clear, therefore, how such a rival would have served as a check upon Prince Menshikof; how fortunate it was for him not to have his presence to contend with, and how melancholy it was for the Turkish ministers not to be able to hide behind his powerful protection. Their confusion was complete; a perfect panic deprived them of their senses. England and France were then represented by chargés d'affaires; the former by M. Benedetti, the latter by Colonel Rose. The Grand Vizier went to consult both of them. He painted in vivid colors the danger which threatened the Turkish Empire; he already saw the fleet of Sevastopol bearing down upon the Golden Horn. He demanded the immediate summons of the French and English squadrons, at least as near as the waters of Smyrna. If the sudden fall of Fuad-Effendi had been only an isolated circumstance, Colonel Rose would not have probably been much concerned, for he was certainly prepared for it; but his personal observations and the information which he gathered caused him to believe that the fears of the Divan were not without foundation. At Constantinople, the attitude of Prince Menshikof was threatening and mysterious; on the Danube, the movements of the Russian forces were threatening and significant. Colonel Rose wrote to his government on the sixth of March that the Russians were advancing toward the Turkish territory, instead of withdrawing or remaining where they were, and that arrangements were being made in Moldavia and Valakhia to furnish them provisions, while as yet no declaration had been sent to the Porte of their grievances. Russia "is making other great military and naval preparations, with the evident intention of destroying the independence of Turkey or of making war upon her." At the same time Colonel Rose took the responsibility of giving a formal invitation to Vice-Admiral Dundas to bring the English squadron as soon as possible from the roadstead of Malta to the Archipelago. The French chargé d'affaires felt that he was not authorized to make the same appeal to the French fleet; he contented himself with informing his government in regard to all the circumstances by which Colonel Rose's determination had been influenced. The action of the two Cabinets — France and England — was precisely opposite to that of their respective agents at Constantinople. The English Minister, without expressly disavowing Colonel Rose, countermanded the invitation which he had given Admiral Dundas, and required the fleet to remain at Malta. Sir Stratford, now Lord Stratford de Redcliffe was hurried off to his post. While the French government likewise sent M. de Lacour to Constantinople, it commanded the Mediterranean fleet, which was at the islands of Hieres, to sail immediately to Salamis.

The difference between the actions of France and England could not fail to give rise to more or less favorable comments, which was the very thing which M. Drouyn de Lhuys wished to guard against. "The important thing, in my opinion," he wrote, on the sixth of March, to Count Walewski, the French envoy at London, "is, that no one in Europe should feel authorized to think that, if a crisis arose at Constantinople capable of compromising the existence of the Ottoman Empire, France and England would take contrary attitudes. Nothing would be more fatal than such a suspicion." M. Drouyn de Lhuys was not far wrong in feeling anxiety about this divergence between the views of the two principal naval powers of Europe. It had been noticed at Saint Petersburg and turned to account. Among the most interesting documents already produced by this diplomatic contest is the despatch addressed on the seventh of April by Count Nesselrode to Baron Brunof, the Tsar's envoy at London. "It is very agreeable to us," said the Chancellor of the Russian Empire, "to see that all the false rumors circulating in Constantinople about our intentions have caused no alarm or apprehension to the Cabinet of London, which must be convinced by the personal assurances of the Emperor that his Majesty desires and intends to respect the independence and integrity of the Turkish Empire, and that if his views undergo any change in this regard, our august master would be the first to inform the English government. Be kind enough to assure the ministers of the Queen, in the most positive terms, that the Emperor's intentions remain unchanged, and that all the vain rumors to which the arrival of Prince Menshikof in the Ottoman capital has given rise, the occupation of the principalities, increase of territory on our Asiatic frontiers, the claim to nominate the patriarch of Constantinople, the threatening and hostile language used by our ambassador to the Porte, are not only exaggerated but entirely groundless; that, in a word, the mission of Prince Menshikof has had and still has no other aim than that which your Excellency has been commissioned to communicate to the British government. The Emperor bids you take particular pains to thank Lord Aberdeen and Lord Clarendon, in his name, for the salutary turn which they have just given the decisions of the English Cabinet. By believing our assurances, by refusing to follow the example of France in taking a measure, if not hostile, at least full of distrust of us, England on the present occasion has given proof of a wise policy. Nothing would have been more to be regretted than to see the two maritime powers acting in concert, were it only for the moment and in appearance rather than in reality, upon the Eastern question as it now is. Although their views upon this differ absolutely, yet, as the European public is scarcely capable of making the distinction, their apparent identity must necessarily have seemed like a close alliance. The situation of all Europe would have been instantly put in a wrong light. The simultaneous appearance of the two fleets would have rendered the question insoluble at Constantinople. Since France has taken this step alone, the seriousness of it is largely, though not entirely, diminished; the Emperor does not take much notice of it, and sees no reason, as yet, for changing his former plans and purposes."

While the French government, feeling more alarmed by the news which came from Constantinople, and having kept a more watchful eye upon the movements of the Russians in Bessarabia, foresaw, after the twenty-second of March, their entrance into the Danubian principalities, and, with remarkable sagacity, gave M. de Lacour instructions appropriate to the gravity of the situation, at this very date the English minister, trusting the solemn assurances which were abundantly vouchsafed to him at Saint Petersburg, declared to the French envoy that he felt bound to believe, until it was disproved, that Prince Menshikof's mission did not threaten the independence and integrity of Turkey. At London, however, the commercial and financial world were far from sharing the thorough confidence felt by the government. The wind from Saint Petersburg was ominous for war; Constantinople news grew more threatening every day.

After his first triumph Prince Menshikof held himself a fortnight in such reserve as was calculated to excite the attention of the public; paying no heed to legations or the seraglio, he remained impenetrable. At last, on March seventeenth, the ambassador of the Tsar determined to make his official visit upon Rifaat Pasha. The sphynx had spoken; the first of his demands was that all that he had to communicate should be kept as an absolute secret, and the others, judging from the attitude of the Turkish ministers, were nothing less than excessive. Fear gave place to perfect dismay. This phase of terror lasted another fortnight. On the fifth of April Lord Stratford arrived at Constantinople, and a few days later, M. de Lacour. The ministers approached them, especially at first, as though they were protecting spirits. The constrained silence was broken; tongues were loosed; the whole story was not told, but, in spite of reticence and half-avowals, diplomatists as skilful as the French and English ambassadors were not slow in getting at the truth. It was evident that the affair of the Holy Places was not the only nor even the principal object of this mysterious negotiation. The proof was soon furnished. After the arrival of M. de Lacour, Prince Menshikof consented to examine with him the details of the quarrel, and an understanding was so easily and so quickly brought about that, in less than three weeks, a difficulty which for three years had kept European diplomacy on the strain was definitely settled to the common satisfaction of Turkey, Russia, and France. From the fourth of May, eighteen hundred and fifty-three, the question of the Holy Places was at rest.

It was thought that all trouble was at an end; it was only the beginning. One day, when Sir Hamilton Seymour asked Count Nesselrode whether there would be any cause of misunderstanding between Turkey and Russia if once the affair of the Holy Places were satisfactorily settled, the Chancellor of the empire replied: "Assuredly not; there will be only a few unimportant business details to regulate." Business details! Certainly diplomacy has great skill in the use of language, but this euphemism is of incomparable value. After he had used his full quiver of threats and promises to wrest from the terrified or corrupted ministers of the Sultan an appeal to the all-powerful and generous protection of the Tsar, Prince Menshikof, hopeless of bringing them to terms, found himself constrained to speak more frankly than he had at first wished, and his explanation was made with a sort of brutal decisiveness which showed clearly his deep scorn. In a note dated the nineteenth of April he said: "While the Emperor desires to forget the past and asks as reparation only for the dismissal of an untrustworthy minister and the prompt execution of solemn promises, he feels obliged to demand solid guarantees for the future. He desires that they be formal, positive, and calculated to assure the inviolability of the religion professed by the majority of the Christian subjects both of the Sublime Porte and of Russia, as well as by the Emperor himself. He will not be satisfied unless these guarantees are included in a treaty, or an act equivalent to a treaty, which shall secure them from the interpretations of an ill-advised and unscrupulous envoy." Thus it is seen that Count Nesselrode placed carelessly in the category of unimportant business details a treaty which would have given the Tsar the right of protecting the Christian subjects of the Sultan.

Encouraged by the presence and sustained by the moral support of the French and English ambassadors, Rifaat Pasha now gave up the systems of temporization behind which he at first sheltered himself. Prince Menshikof, also weary of dilatory measures, demanded a prompt and categorical answer. On the fifth of May, the day following the agreement about the Holy Places, the Prince submitted to the reïs-effendi a plan for a *sened*, or convention, together with a note which left no doubt or ambiguity as to the meaning attached to this step by the Tsar's representative. While inviolable guarantees were demanded with redoubled urgency under the form of a solemn engagement equivalent to a treaty, the ambassador insisted upon the most important point of his mission, the principal object of the Emperor's anxiety, and declared that if on the tenth of May, five days from date, his demands were not satisfied, " he should be obliged to consider a longer delay as a lack of respect toward his government, which would impose upon him the most painful obligations."

Russia dated its pretensions from the treaty of Kaïnardji, concluded in seventeen hundred and seventy-four, and confirmed in eighteen hundred and twenty-nine by the treaty of Adrianople. If, as the Tsar affirmed, these ancient stipulations had implicitly conferred upon him the rights of a protector over the Sultan's Christian subjects, and if, as he at the same time protested, he was not anxious to gain a wider extension to these pretended rights, what was the meaning of Prince Menshikof's mission, his demands, and his threats? And how, above all, could he justify this pressure, brought to bear upon Turkey by Russia alone, and this exclusive claim to meddle with the internal affairs of the Ottoman Empire, when the treaty of July thirteenth, eighteen hundred and forty-one, had introduced Turkey into what was called the European concert, and placed the independence and integrity of the Turkish dominions under the collective guarantee of the five great powers? Looking at it in this light, Lord Stratford de Redcliffe wrote an official and confidential letter to Prince Menshikof, in which he brought forward arguments designed to moderate his demands, which threatened virtually to transfer from the weakest to the strongest party, powers reserved in every country for the supreme authority of the State. "Such an extension of existing treaties," said the English Envoy, "would be liable to be regarded elsewhere as an innovation entirely disproportionate to the special question which brought about your embassy, and which is out of harmony with the spirit of legality unanimously sanctioned by the treaty of eighteen hundred and forty-one." Nothing came of this; Prince Menshikof still maintained all of his pretensions. On the day fixed he received from the reïs-effendi a note animated by the kindest feelings for the Sultan's Christian subjects, and promising to preserve their privileges in religious matters. "As to concluding with Russia a treaty on this subject, the note proceeded to say the Porte could never consent to it without compromising the fundamental principles of its sovereignty and independence. It is thus obliged to decline the proposition made by the Emperor of Russia to enter into a convention which would fetter it in this way. The Porte trusts to the public opinion of the whole world, which would never permit this violation of its independence and national rights, and appeals to the justice and fairness of the Emperor himself."

Although Prince Menshikof put the form of an ultimatum

upon his last communication, the declaration of a rupture which the Grand Vizier expected was forestalled by a request for an interview. The meeting was arranged for the thirteenth of May; great preparations were made at the Porte, as was the case on the second of March. When the hour passed a strange rumor disturbed the Grand Vizier and the reïs-effendi, who were already surprised at the delay. The envoy of the Tsar did not go to the Porte at all, but went straight to the Palace of Sheragan, to the Sultan himself, whom he knew to be overwhelmed with trouble and affliction, for he had just lost his mother. The impropriety of the step was punished by the humiliation which diplomatic etiquette administered. Not only was he not received, but by the Sultan's express orders he was referred to the ministers. The ministers, on their side, felt that they could no longer treat with him and retain their dignity. The insult of May thirteenth necessarily carried with it similar consequences to that of March second. Mehemet Ali and Rifaat Pasha followed Fuad-Effendi's example, and resigned. Mehemet Ali resumed the office of Seraskier, or Minister of War. Reshid Pasha took the direction of Foreign Affairs; with this new minister, more docile, as it was believed, to Russian influence, Prince Menshikof affected the most conciliating humor: he demanded neither treaty nor sened; he wanted a simple note which, though indeed dictated by himself, was to be copied, adopted, and signed by Reshid Pasha, and serve as the personal and official answer of the reïs-effendi to the ambassador of the Tsar. What could be more simple! It proved, however, that the concession of the Prince was only apparent, and that under a new form the matter was unchanged. Treaty, sened, or note, what he wished to conquer in open battle or gain by surprise was a genuine engagement, an onerous contract subscribed to by the Sultan for the Tsar's advantage. In spite of these manœuvres, Reshid Pasha was not deceived; like Fuad and Rifaat, he refused to put his name to the moral ruin of the Turkish government.

The Prince, who had already retired with the full Russian legation to Buyukdéré, addressed a note to Reshid on the eighteenth of May, in which he declared that his mission was ended, and that diplomatic relations between the Russian and Turkish empires were broken. Three days later the ambassador of the Tsar, worsted in the conflict, re-entered the Black Sea on the same ship from which three months before he had triumphantly disembarked at Constantinople. He now would carry back to Russia anger at his defeat, and demand vengeance.

The ultimatum of May fifth, known and published at London on the twentieth, had the effect of a thunder-bolt. Until this time public opinion had hesitated, hovering between the vague alarms which came from Constantinople and the confident declarations of the ministers; its force was now resistless. As for the cabinet, surprised in its optimistic dreams, dazed by this rude awakening, it was compelled instantly to change its language and its course. Instead of a petty squabble, as it was disdainfully called the evening before, they were obliged to recognize the danger of a catastrophe impending over the Turkish Empire; instead of indulging in jealousy or raillery of France, they were obliged to confess that France alone had had its eyes open and been on the watch. In a few days efforts were made to redeem the lost time; on the twenty-eighth of May Lord Clarendon in the House of Lords, and Lord John Russell in the House of Commons, declared that the government was resolved to lend a helping hand to Turkey in case of need, and a despatch to Lord Stratford de Redcliffe on June first placed at his disposal the fleet stationed at Malta. Nevertheless, a few of the ministers, Lord Aberdeen especially, retained at heart a trust in the word of the Tsar, as it were a relic of long-enduring confidence; they preferred to believe that Prince Menshikof had exceeded his authority, and they did not despair of seeing him disavowed. These loyal hearts again reckoned without their host; a telegram from Saint Petersburg dissipated their last illusion. Not only was Prince Menshikof's conduct fully approved by the Tsar, but his threats were promptly followed by the sanction of action. "In a few weeks," Count Nesselrode wrote to Reshid Pasha, "the Russian troops will receive the order to cross the boundaries of the empire, not for the purpose of making war, but in order to obtain material guarantees until such time as the Ottoman government, coming to more equitable sentiments, shall give Russia the moral sureties demanded in vain for two years by its representatives in Constantinople, and lastly by its ambassador. The draught of a note which Prince Menshikof has sent you is in your hands. Will your Excellency without delay, having obtained the consent of his Highness, the Sultan, sign this note without variations, and send it to our ambassador, who is still at Odessa?" This letter was dated the thirty-first of May: the telegram which brought the news came on the first day of June; on the second the English government, in perfect accord with France, gave orders directly to Vice-Admiral Dundas to set sail without awaiting Lord Stratford's summons to join the French fleet and co-operate with it. On the thirteenth and fourteenth the French and English flags, the one coming from Malta, the other from Salamis, floated above Turkish waters in the anchorage of Besika, between Tenedos and the coast of Asia, at the entrance of the Dardanelles.

This understanding between France and England, which the Tsar had never believed possible, was not the first nor perhaps the bitterest of his miscalculations: Russia saw Austria and Prussia fall away, — Prussia an old family alliance, Austria a client just rescued from the perils of the Hungarian insurrection. Neither Prince Menshikof at Constantinople, nor the Tsar at Saint Petersburg, nor his envoys at Berlin and Vienna, had found among the representatives or ministers of those two powers that support upon which Russian policy had a right, or supposed it had a right, to depend. On the contrary, in forms more or less cautious, the disavowal was universal. During the month of April Count Buol, the head of the Austrian ministry, said to the French ambassador, M. de Bourquency, that it was not the province of one nor of two cabinets privately to regulate affairs in which all Europe was interested, and which, in a word, ought to be treated by the five great powers. It was precisely this community of European interests which was the idea happily chosen and carried out by French policy. For diplomats formed by the school of the First Empire, full of memories of eighteen hundred and fifteen, what a surprising spectacle! They saw the heir of Napoleon using as an argument against Russia the obligation of treaties, and calling upon all Europe to maintain the equilibrium, and the heir of Alexander threatening the established order of things and aiming a mortal blow at the Holy Alliance. It was also an extraordinary novelty for the diplomatists of the old school, nourished in the tradition of silence and mystery, to see despatches, notes, and circulars, almost before they had gone the round of the cabinets, printed and published to all the world. It continued to be a war of chicanery, but in open daylight, and no longer in secret. Between Russia and its adversaries a power entirely modern but mighty, the power of public opinion, was called in as a judge and mediator. On both sides the weight of its influence was invoked as the law of a sovereign magistrate. In this great suit France had eloquent and able advocates. Inspired by M. Drouyn de Lhuys, and secondarily by M. Thouvenel, French diplomacy was enabled to speak in a lofty, decided, and moderate tone, without boast or bravado, with success the more glorious because it was won in contest with a stronger party. In controversy, as well as on the field of battle, Russia was always a terrible champion.

Count Nesselrode began the public discussion. A circular, addressed on the eleventh of June by the Chancellor of the empire to the representatives of Russia abroad, was printed in the "Journal of Saint Petersburg." The principal aim of this argument was to prove that Prince Menshikof confined himself strictly to the limits of his mission after the affair of the Holy Places had been settled, in demanding of the Turkish government guarantees implicitly contained in the treaties of Kaïnardji and Adrianople, and that he had asked nothing unusual or new, nothing indeed which exceeded the right which every state naturally possesses, of treating its private wrongs or interests with another. It was this claim to deprive the other powers of the examination of this question, which none of the great European cabinets could admit. Said M. Drouyn de Lhuys to Kisselef, the Russian envoy: "If you believe that the Porte is mistaken, if you think your claims are legitimate while the Porte finds them inadmissible, allow me to say that there exists a tribunal on purpose to settle the difficulty. A conference between the five powers took part in the treaty of eighteen hundred and forty-one. They can now determine whether the Divan does not exaggerate the importance of your demands, or whether you yourselves do not mistake their actual force."

England and France alike desired to unite the signers of the treaty of eighteen hundred and forty-one in the present interests of conciliation and peace. On principle, Austria was at one with them, but in reality the Emperor Francis Joseph had in mind to spare the dignity of Russia and the Tsar's pride. As he favored the idea of a direct transaction between the Porte and his formidable neighbor, he took pains to address himself with a mixture of tenderness and deference to the affectionate impulses of the Emperor Nicholas, and he commissioned one of his private aides-de-camp, Count Gyulai, to carry his letter to Saint Petersburg. On the twenty-fourth of June the Tsar received the touching appeal which a sentiment of gratitude had dictated to the young sovereign of Austria, but lately almost his ward. He answered it indirectly and unfortunately, two days afterwards, by an appeal to the faith of the Russian people. The occupation of the Principalities was ordered; but in case that were not sufficient to overcome the obstinacy of the Turks, then, the manifesto went on to say, "invoking God to aid us, we will leave to his care to decide our difference, and, placing our full hope in his all-powerful hand, we will march to the defence of the orthodox faith."

On the third of July the Russian columns crossed the Pruth; three days afterwards Prince Gortchakof entered Bukarest. At the same time Count Nesselrode issued a second explanatory circular, much less for the convenience of his diplomatic agents than for the use of the European public. The cleverness of this consisted in its putting the occupation of the Principalities as a reply to the movement of the combined squadrons of France and England, a military position compensating for the maritime occupation; in a word, as a simple question of maintaining the balance. M. Drouyn de Lhuys had already answered the circular of June eleventh. It was not then difficult for him to prove that this famous treaty of Kaïnardji, so often invoked by the Russians, had never contained all that they would be glad to find in it. It was just as easy for him now to refute the new circular of July second. If there had ever been any analogy between the respective situations, any equilibrium between the Russian forces on one side and the united squadrons on the other, it was at the time when the latter were anchored at Besika, and the former were watching the left bank of the Pruth; but since the Russians had entered the Turkish territory while the fleet had not moved from its anchorage, it was presuming too much upon the good nature of the public to speak of maintaining the equilibrium, of reversing the rôles and imputing to the others the initiation of threatening demonstrations. It was sufficient to array facts and dates against the ingenious subtleties of Count Nesselrode. The invasion of the Principalities, though effected on the third of July, had been announced by the Chancellor himself more than a month before, and it was only on the thirteenth of

June that the fleets began to show themselves in the Turkish waters. The rash statements made by the Russian government, and criticised by M. Drouyn de Lhuys, met with the same treatment at the hand of Lord Clarendon; but the French circular was given to the public, while Lord Clarendon was satisfied with announcing to the House of Lords, amid great applause, that England's answer was in complete conformity with the note published by the French government, and that all the measures taken in so important a crisis were likewise in accord.

The question whether the occupation of the Principalities was a warlike deed, justifying Turkey in the use of violence to repel violence, would be answered in the affirmative even if only international law and the acts which regulated the peculiar condition of the Principalities were consulted. It is safe to say that this was the general opinion in Europe, it was certainly the opinion of the French government; but in the English cabinet Lord Aberdeen and a few of his colleagues refused to consider the crossing of the Pruth as an event likely to lead to such weighty consequences. They advised patience at Paris, and hoped that the French government would join in advising it at Constantinople. France yielded; Turkey protested for form's sake, and diplomacy renewed its efforts at reconciliation. On the part of Austria, they had never ceased, nor had Russia formally declined its good offices. Things had not gone too far. The French ambassador at Saint Petersburg, long neglected, now found himself received with unwonted favor, and the opposite happened to the English minister; the Tsar's coldness seemed to have been transferred from General de Castelbajac to Sir Hamilton Seymour. During the early days of June the Tsar charged the General to transmit directly to Napoleon the most friendly expression of his sentiments and an invitation for a personal negotiation. Touched by these advances, the Emperor, Napoleon the Third, was easily persuaded to send a favorable reply;

but he did so warily, without imprudently isolating himself and separating from England. The draught of a note written by him, which was sent to London on June twenty-seventh, and approved, had been transmitted to General de Castelbajac, with instructions to place it in the hands of the Emperor Nicholas. At the same time, as it was important to keep on good terms with the Austrian Emperor, whose mediation the Tsar had just accepted, and who was exercising his ingenuity to form a basis of agreement, the draught was sent to Vienna, where it was received with favor; and Prussia also being invited to examine it, a sort of conference was naturally established between the four powers which, twelve years before, participated with Russia and the Porte in the transactions of eighteen hundred and forty-one. Austria was represented by Count Buol-Schauenstein, France by Baron de Bourqueney, England by Lord Westmoreland, and Prussia by Herr von Canitz.

In reply to Russia's first threats and claims to interfere with the internal affairs of the Ottoman Empire, England advised the Turkish government to furnish a solemn and public confirmation of the rights of their Christian subjects granted or acknowledged by the Sultans. In this spirit Reshid Pasha had endeavored to answer the note presented by Prince Menshikof. The draught sent by the Emperor Napoleon to Vienna was a compromise between the Prince's plan and the reïs-effendi's counter-plan. During the entire month of July the conference gave it the most careful and minute examination; modifications were proposed, — some offered by Austria more favorable to Russia, others by England more favorable to the Porte. At last the text, amended, corrected, reread, revised, and final, was unanimously adopted on the thirty-first of July. The Emperor Nicholas, to whom it had been communicated beforehand, sent a telegram on the third of August, declaring that he accepted the expedient devised at Vienna on condition that the Porte should make absolutely no observation or change in it.

The Tsar accepted; that was great news. It was a triumph of diplomacy; trade revived; a general increase of prices obtained; the congratulation was universal. Napoleon the Third, on the fifteenth of August, congratulated himself, in presence of the diplomatic corps, that the peace of Europe had been preserved, and on the twentieth the Queen's ministers gave Parliament reason to hope for the prompt conclusion of an honorable adjustment.

At Constantinople, however, the preparations for an armed resistance had not ceased for two months; the men of the *redif*, or reserve, were brought into activity, the regular lists of the *nizam* were filled to the full war quota, the Egyptian contingents were momentarily expected. These martial sights and announcements could not fail gradually to excite the passions of the Mussulmans. They were at a boiling point when, on the ninth of August, the Vienna note was dropped into the midst of the excitement. Two days later the quick consent given by the Tsar was known. After so many traps and toils had been brought to light, how was it possible not to suspect new snares? The Divan, at its first session, rejected the note; then, at the instance of Reshid Pasha, it was taken up again, examined, explained, and finally accepted in all but three passages, which allowed an interpretation unfavorable to the rights of the Sultan. The changes suggested by the Divan, and put in the form of a memorandum, were communicated to the representatives of the four powers on the twentieth of August. It was a great surprise. The angry disapproval of this step was universal. These Turks had the arrogance to carry their remonstrances to the bar of Europe, and when Europe lent them a helping hand, with unparalleled infatuation they insolently brought upon themselves the catastrophes they would avoid. How willingly they would have abandoned them to their foolish pride, if the equilibrium of the world had not been fatally involved in their wretched existence. At Vienna the conference, in ill humor, set themselves again to their work, the careful, irksome, trying work of comparing texts almost impalpably dissimilar. They sifted words, weighed syllables, discussed periods and commas; grammarians would not have made more stock out of it. Then, when the whole had been examined and proved by the microscope, they came to the common conclusion that the Turks had not the political sense, that their claims were impertinent, their fears ridiculous, and their corrections valueless.

While the four powers brought all weight to bear upon the Turks to make them yield, Austria used its influence with the Tsar in order to obtain his contemptuous assent to a few insignificant changes; but as he had declared beforehand that he would accept no change, it was impossible to persuade him to go back upon his word. Then still stronger efforts were made in Constantinople; the French government, which had the best right to claim the paternity of the Vienna note, was no less urgent than Austria and Prussia. From London also Lord Clarendon used equal insistance; but Lord Stratford de Redcliffe, on the spot, did not seem inclined to add the considerable weight of his own authority and personal influence to his official action. The reserve of this famous diplomat, however it may be explained, was the only and very feeble encouragement which the Porte found in its resistance; but as everything was destined to proceed by theatrical surprises in this strange episode, — perhaps the strangest in the history of diplomacy, — safety came to Turkey from a most unexpected quarter. In a very dignified and faultless note, dated September the seventh, Count Nesselrode informed the four powers that, as the Emperor of Russia on his part had renounced the right of changing a single word in a draught of the ultimatum made by them, he could not admit nor recognize as legitimate the exercise of the same right by the Porte. " Either the alterations which the Porte requires are important, in which case it is plain that we must refuse to accede to them; or they are unimportant, and then the question arises, Why should the

Porte unnecessarily make its acceptance dependent on them?" What answer could be found for this? Europe acquiesced, and Turkey was evidently lost, when, a few days after the despatch of this note, which seemed to leave nothing to be said, there appeared in a Berlin newspaper a circular addressed by Count Nesselrode to the Russian agents in the foreign courts. This document, the publication of which was no less astonishing than the audacity of its dangerous admissions, was entitled, "An Examination of the Modifications introduced by the Ottoman Porte into the Austrian Note." This commentary went to show that the changes insisted upon by the Divan were of the greatest importance, and that, if Russia had accepted the Vienna note without variation, it was because it contained an equivalent to all that Prince Menshikof's ultimatum had demanded.

Thus for three months European diplomacy exhausted its ingenuity for the Tsar's greatest gratification without the slightest suspicion, believing all the time it was doing the opposite. And this derisive gratification could not be restrained at the moment of its triumph. Imprudence answered to confusion. The heedlessness of the judges deserved no less a punishment than the rash indiscretion of Russian policy. It was not punished, thanks to Turkey, but an apology was due. It had to be confessed that "the sick man," to use the Emperor's expression, was wiser than his doctors, and that in his amendment to their decision, it being with him a question of life or death, he had most successfully taken advantage of a perfectly legitimate right.

This was the great crisis for all parties interested. In England the power passed decidedly from the peace party to their opponents; from Lord Aberdeen to Lord Palmerston. This was proved by the speeches made in public by several of the ministers, — Lord John Russell, Mr. Gladstone, Sir James Graham, and Lord Palmerston himself. In France the effect was similar, though not so pronounced. The Emperor, Napoleon the Third, had taken great delight in dreaming of a compromise initiated by himself and shedding its glory upon him; by the Vienna note he thought that his dream was about to be realized. When the miscalculation became apparent, he did not lose his usual sluggishness, since he, in common with the rest of Europe, had been deceived, and at least the advantage accruing from his good-will remained to him. The idea of a reconciliation still seemed desirable and possible, but it was not the only idea that came into his mind; war began to hover irresolutely in his conceptions. The double game of a policy of counter-currents was always more pleasing to him than any other; he came back to it as by a natural inclination. In internal as well as external affairs, Napoleon the Third almost always made this dualism a principle of his government, and it is by no means new to history; but between the great statesmen who have succeeded in spite of the falsity and immorality of this system, and Napoleon, who was brought by it to his ruin, there is all the difference that distinguishes quick, supple, inventive activity of a genius ready to conceive, and prompt to act, from the heavy, doubtful, hesitating, cumbersome sluggishness of a phlegmatic theorist. By a fortunate run of circumstances, the Eastern question, from the very beginning of his reign, came to him on the side most favorable to the peculiar turn of his character and mind. In fact, the Emperor Nicholas gave him a fair opportunity; during these long diplomatic debates Napoleon the Third had all the time that he needed to decide, and yet when, in March, eighteen hundred and fifty-four, he was obliged to take part in the war which for five months had been raging between Turkey and Russia, he had not begun to get ready.

Austria was better prepared than France, though it had much greater repugnance to war. Until the last moment it had done its utmost to prevent the outbreak of hostilities. The Emperor Francis Joseph established himself on the eighteenth of September at the camp of Olmütz, where great military manœuvres were on foot; the Emperor of Russia and the King of Prussia were expected to be present; foreign ministers, diplomats, and officers were likewise invited. The Emperor Nicholas arrived on the twenty-fourth of September. His coldness toward Lord Westmoreland, the English ambassador, was remarked, as well as his graciousness to the French military commission commanded by General de Goyon. When the review was concluded, the Tsar went straightway to Warsaw, where he was visited by the Emperor Francis Joseph; the King of Prussia, absent at the first meeting, was present at this. At Warsaw, as at Olmütz, Count Buol and Count Nesselrode held continual conferences; the design was to repair, if possible, the enormous blunder committed by the Russian chancellor in his unlucky commentary. After many combinations and endeavors, the skill of these statesmen succeeded in devising the following expedient: the text of the Vienna note should be preserved, but the four powers should unite to assure the Porte that Russia had neither the intention nor the desire to meddle with its concerns. This assurance was almost as serious as that contained in the famous letter of Ninon to La Châtre. Russia did not disavow any part of the commentary; it would have disavowed it, had the commentary been less fruitful of meaning. So England and France declined to recommend Count Buol's expedient to the Porte.

Meanwhile events at Constantinople were coming to a crisis. The Tsar's religious manifesto and his call to support the holy war had the natural result among the Turks. The Mussulman population was the more excitable because the festivities of the *beiram* were about to succeed the fast of *ramazan*. On the tenth of September a body of forty *softas*, or students of the Koran, presented themselves before the Sublime Porte, demanded to be heard by the Council, and produced a petition praying for war in the name of the Prophet. The petition was largely composed of quotations from the Koran enjoining war on the enemies of Islam, and it threatened violence if it were not granted. To the objections raised by some of the ministers they said: " Here are the words of the Koran; if you are Mussulmans you are bound to obey. You are now listening to foreign and infidel embassadors, who are the enemies of the Faith; we are the children of the Prophet. We have an army, and that army cries out with us for war to avenge the insults which the giaours have heaped upon us." In consequence of this manifestation the excitement grew rapidly in violence. The ministers were anxious; they feared some attack upon the Greeks of the city, upon the foreigners, upon the Sultan himself. The French and English ambassadors each summoned two steam frigates to Constantinople. The Austrian envoy, Herr von Brück, on the other hand, still persisted in advising the Divan to accept the Vienna note pure and simple. In order to do away with all further importunities, the Sultan held a council of his ministers on the twenty-fourth of September, at the palace of Tcheragan; the note, without the modifications proposed by Reshid Pasha, was once more unanimously judged unacceptable; at the end of the session the Sultan ordered for the next day a general reunion of the Great Council at the palace of the Sublime Porte. One hundred and sixty-three individuals, the leading men of the empire, assembled on the twenty-fifth; after a deliberation which extended far into the night, one hundred and sixty voices voted to advise the Sultan to substitute a state of actual war for illusory negotiations. For three days Abdul-Medjid suspended his final decision; on the twenty-ninth he gave it. An imperial *hat*, authorizing the result of the deliberations of the Great Council was sent to the Porte, and transmitted without the loss of a moment to the general-in-chief of the army of Rumelia. On the eighth of October the *Mushir* Omer Pasha, from his camp of Shumla, where he had just received his master's orders, summoned General Gortchakof to evacuate the Turkish territory within fifteen days. The existence of war having effectively annulled the stipulations which forbade foreign squadrons to enter the Sea of Marmora, Vice-Admiral Dundas and Vice-Admiral Hamelin, with instructions from London and Paris, left the Bay of Besika at the summons of the Sultan, crossed the Dardanelles, and with all their forces steamed by Constantinople and cast anchor in the harbor of Beïkos in the Bosphorus. The war with Russia was beginning for the Porte; for England and France it would soon begin.

CHAPTER VI.

THE CRIMEAN WAR.

1853–1855.

Campaign of the Danube. — Austrian Interests. — Final Diplomatic Efforts. — Affair of Sinope. — The French and English Fleets in the Black Sea. — Diplomatic Rupture. — Count Orlof at Vienna. — Letters of Napoleon the Third and the Emperor Nicholas. — Austria and Prussia agree with France and England to maintain the Turkish Empire.

CAMPAIGN OF THE DANUBE. — AUSTRIAN INTERESTS. — FINAL DIPLOMATIC EFFORTS. — AFFAIR OF SINOPE.

PRINCE GORTCHAKOF replied to Omer Pasha's summons simply that he had no power from the Emperor, his master, to treat either of peace or war or the evacuation of the Principalities. "This is our situation in brief," said Count Nesselrode to Sir Hamilton Seymour. "War is declared against us; we shall probably not publish any counter-declaration. We shall not attack Turkey; we shall remain with folded arms, resolved only to resist all aggression made against us either in the Principalities or on our Asiatic frontier. We shall thus pass the winter, ready to receive all the overtures of peace which Turkey will offer." At the two points indicated by Count Nesselrode, the first shots were fired at almost the same time. On the twenty-fifth of October a Russian fleet, composed of two steamboats and eight gunboats, ascending the Danube from Ismaïl to Galatch, lost a few men in passing under the fire of the Turkish batteries of Isaktcha. At the other extremity of the Black Sea the little garrison of

Fort Nikolaï, surprised during the night of October twenty-seventh by a Turkish detachment from Batum, was almost entirely captured after a heroic resistance. "It is painful to me," said Prince Vorontsof in his report, "to have to begin my communications regarding our hostilities with the Turks by an event so unfortunate for us; but we have hope for the future." In fact, the Ottoman forces of the army of Asia, ill-equipped, ill-organized, were not slow in paying dear for this first success. Beaten at Bayanduri by Prince Orbeliani on the fourteenth of November, on the twenty-sixth by Prince Andronikof near Akhaltsikh, on the first of December by Prince Bebutof at Bash-Kadiklar, they were driven back in the greatest confusion under the protecting cannon of the powerful fortress of Kars.

Things were not so favorable for the Russians on the banks of the Danube. The Kroat, Michael Lattas, formerly a cadet in the Austrian regiment of Ogulin, now general-in-chief of the Turkish forces, under the name of Omer Pasha was showing the resolute ability of a warrior. After he had drawn up the ninety or one hundred thousand men of the army of Rumelia under the walls of Adrianople, he carried the larger part of it into Bulgaria. Entire divisions or large detachments were placed along the great river in well-chosen positions. Viddin, Rahova, Nikopol, Sistova, Rustchuk, Turtukaï, Silistria, Rassova, watched the seventy thousand men of Prince Gortchakof, scattered at unequal posts on the other bank, while two strong reserves — one at Sofia behind Viddin, the other supported by the Balkans at Shumla behind Silistria — guarded the right and left flank of this long line, and at the same time covered the roads which might lead the Russians to Constantinople. Without departing from the defensive, which was the basis of his tactics, Omer allowed sudden attacks to enter into his plans, local and temporary skirmishes, which could not fail to astonish the enemy, prevent him from concentrating his forces, accustom his own troops to battle, and win for them the approval of watchful Europe. Thus from the twenty-eighth of October to the second of November the Turks crossed the river at four places at once. From Viddin they pushed on to Kalafat, from Rustchuk to Djurdjevo, from Turtukaï to Oltenitsa, and from Silistria to Kalarash. The attacks upon Kalarash and Djurdjevo were merely unimportant demonstrations; the other two were far more serious in their consequences.

Oltenitsa, occupied by Ismail Pasha, Omer's lieutenant, with a force of nine thousand men, was only three or four days' march from Bukarest, capital of Valakhia. On the fourth of November a desperate attempt was made by the Russians to dislodge him; but in less than forty-eight hours he succeeded in protecting himself by field-works and in erecting a battery in the quarantine building, or lazaretto, which was of solid construction with vaulted chambers. His line of defence, moreover, was flanked on the other side of the Danube by batteries placed east of Turtukaï on the slopes of the Bulgarian banks. The opposite shore was flat, marshy, unsuitable for manœuvres and rapid movements, and put the assailant at odds on all sides. Their cavalry and artillery stuck fast in the mire; their infantry was unable to force the redoubts. The Russians fell back with a loss of more than twelve hundred men. This was a great success for the Turks. Omer, like a prudent man, had no desire to compromise himself; but he took his time, and without putting himself to inconvenience, nor waiting to be driven back by the Russians, who were collecting in large numbers at Bukarest, he beat a calm and voluntary retreat after holding his position ten days.

While he evacuated Oltenitsa because he was unwilling to risk a general engagement to hold this fort, he fortified himself at the extreme left of his line in the position at Kalafat. He then constructed a vast battery well provided with cannon, and which could easily shelter fifteen thousand men; a pontoon bridge secured communication with Viddin. As the

Russians contented themselves with watching this formidable work from a distance, Omer determined, after two months had passed, to make a sortie and attack them himself. Three or four hours' march to the north of Kalafat, a brigade of Russian infantry with its field-pieces, a regiment of hussars and a few *sotnias* of Cossacks occupied several villages, the chief of which was Tchetat. After reconnoitring and skirmishing with the enemy on the thirty-first of December, Omer caused two columns, a week later, to advance, — one by a road which skirted the Danube, the other on the river itself, by means of boats hauled up the stream. The whole force, with artillery equal to that of the Russians, was superior to them in strength. They began the attack, and in spite of the energetic resistance of the enemy, by their numerical advantage they drove the Russians from post to post beyond Tchetat; but as reinforcements arrived from Kraïova, the Turks fell back from Tchetat, and while the river column retreated on the Bulgarian shore, the other took the direct road to Kalafat undisturbed. As the Turks had been obliged to leave two dismounted field-pieces, the Russians seized upon them as trophies; but it was not much to boast about, for though they had saved their honor, they had not gained the day; their acknowledged loss was more than two thousand men. On one of their batteries sixty-five men were killed or wounded out of seventy, and fifty-seven horses out of sixty. On the tenth of January Omer renewed his attacks with no pronounced success on either side; but the moral effect was in favor of the Turks, who kept on the offensive and were not molested in Kalafat by the Russians.

In attracting the brunt of hostilities in this direction, trenching upon Austria, Omer Pasha showed that he understood his game as well as the sharpest of politicians. In the eyes of Austria, contact with Russia on the side of Gallicia was certainly dangerous; by means of the Principalities it would be deadly. It was of little consequence whether the Principalities were more or less independent under the more or less effective suzerainty of the Sultan; the main point was that Russia should not control them. For Austria, the principle of the integrity of the Ottoman Empire, the fact of the real if not absolute autonomy of the Principalities, and the free navigation of the Danube were vital questions. "My policy in regard to the Eastern question? but it is written on the map," said Count Buol to his brother-in-law, Baron von Mayendorf, the Russian ambassador at Vienna; "I have changed it in no respect. My policy is that which Prince Metternich bequeathed to me." Could Baron von Mayendorf doubt what this was? "Beware," said the old Chancellor of the Austrian Empire to him one day, — "beware; from what I hear, I understand that your Emperor is anxious to come to extremes with Turkey; let him think long. Be sure that if he does not leave the East in peace, the face of things will change throughout Europe, and I would not be held responsible for anything." "I am sorry to tell you," was Baron von Mayendorf's reply, "that the Emperor sees things in quite another light; the instructions which he has given me oblige me to urge you to take a decided stand." "Very well," said Prince Metternich, "I warn you that my conscience will not allow me to hold my peace in such grave circumstances and I shall tell the Emperor, my master, of your designs. He will not follow you in the path where you wish to conduct him. He will not follow you, since he cannot, and your sovereign, believe me, will find himself alone in Europe." Now that the Russians had crossed the Pruth and invaded the Principalities, now that they had substituted the full authority of the Tsar for that of the Hospodars and the Sultan, and especially now that the heavy roar of the cannon of Kalafat could be heard on the frontier of Banat, the anticipations of Austria passed from distrust to the liveliest anxiety.

Was the Vienna Conference still in existence? According to the general opinion, it had received a death-blow from the war. But Count Buol, at a hint from the French government, hastened to bring it to life again, and to give it what it had not before possessed, — an official existence. The conference decided to offer its mediation between the belligerent parties, and its decision was embodied in the famous protocol of the fifth of December. Two principles were formulated, two obligations declared: first, that an end must be made to hostilities which could not be prolonged without affecting the interests of other states, and, secondly, that the integrity of the Ottoman Empire must be maintained. "The assurances given on several occasions by the Emperor of Russia preclude the idea that that august sovereign entertains any wish to interfere with the integrity of the Ottoman Empire. The existence of Turkey in the limits which treaties have assigned it has, in fact, become one of the necessary conditions of the European equilibrium; and the plenipotentiaries declare with satisfaction that the present war cannot in any case involve modifications in the territorial circumscriptions of the two empires calculated to alter the state of possession which time has consecrated in the East, and which is equally necessary for the tranquillity of all the other powers." And in a collective note the conference invited the Turkish government to inform it "on what conditions the Ottoman Empire would consent to negotiate a treaty of peace."

Meanwhile Lord Stratford de Redcliffe began at Constantinople to devise a similar proposition, and had come to an agreement with the Austrian and Prussian envoys, and with the new French ambassador, General Baraguey d'Hilliers, who now took M. de Lacour's place. Whether he was in the right or wrong, Lord Stratford, with a weakness natural to man, vastly preferred what he was doing in Constantinople to what others might do elsewhere. He was not always careful to obey his instructions from London; how should the Vienna conference — that resurrected conference, as he called it — expect to find him more docile? The famous August note had won from him only a cold support; when the note of the fifth of December came to him, he put it in his pocket and calmly advised his colleagues not to pay any attention to it. This proceeding was severely criticised and blamed at Vienna, but there was no other consequence, and as the Porte had the good-will to answer in the sense most favorable to the overtures which the representatives of the four powers at Constantinople had directly made, the conference had also the good-will to forget its wounded feelings and to ratify the amiable answer of the Turkish government as though it had been in reply to its own overtures. As to Russia, one would say that either it did not care at all for peace, or else that an unlucky influence acted as a dead weight upon its counsels. The advantage of the first note of Vienna had been ruined by a piece of stupidity; must the act which involved the Tsar not with Turkey alone, but with France and England, pass into history as a provocation or a blunder?

Toward the last of November an Ottoman squadron, consisting of seven frigates, three corvettes, and two small steamers, left the Bosphorus to cruise in the Black Sea. It carried provisions and a few reinforcements for the troops at Batum. It was not without anxiety that the French and English vice-admirals saw it sail away, for Turkish ships had recently met and even been attacked by Russian vessels, which proved that the fleet of Sevastopol was cruising about. Vigilance was extremely needful and the operation required the greatest despatch. Vice-Admiral Osman Pasha, however, met with foul weather, and put into the open roadstead of Sinope, or Sinub, situated in Anatolia, on the southern shore of the Black Sea, half-way between Constantinople and Trebizond. On the twenty-seventh two or three Russian sails appeared at the entrance of the bay as scouts. The Turkish fleet, though prevented from pursuing its course, could at least have regained the Bosphorus; it did nothing of the sort. After spending three days in strengthening his position, Osman saw six ships of the line, two frigates, and three steamers arrive, under command of Vice-Admiral Nakhimof. The frigate of the Turkish admiral began the fire at half past one. The Russian fleet replied. At five o'clock nothing remained of the Turkish fleet. One corvette remained at anchor, but crippled; the Russians endeavored to tow her off as a prize, but they soon set fire to her. The batteries built on the shore for the defence of the roadstead were dismounted and ruined; the city itself, which numbered about ten thousand inhabitants, suffered severely. The Turks lost more than four thousand men in this engagement. One steamboat alone, the Taïf, signalled by Osman Pasha at the beginning of the action, managed to gain the offing and escaped to Constantinople.

THE FRENCH AND ENGLISH FLEETS IN THE BLACK SEA. — DIPLOMATIC RUPTURE. — COUNT ORLOF AT VIENNA.

The news brought by the Taïf spread through all Europe like lightning. Everywhere the excitement was deep and violent; there was only one cry, — of indignation against Russia, and a curse upon the Russian fleet. To-day, so far removed by the course of time from the universal outburst which this event caused, it is allowable, it is a duty, for us to render a calmer judgment upon the affair of Sinope. Even if the Russians held themselves on the defensive, as it was affirmed they had promised to do, it was their right to cut off supplies of provisions, to intercept or destroy the convoys of their enemy. This right had already been exercised without any protest being raised against them. At Sinope the use made of this right was entirely legitimate; but, considering the state of affairs and opinions, it was imprudent and excessive. It was the disproportion of forces, the feebleness and the entire ruin of the enemy, — in a word, it was the enormity of the success which aroused against the conqueror the instinctive sense of justice implanted in the human heart; and it was at the very moment when diplomacy was endeavoring to regain an authority surely unsubstantial enough, that instead of allowing feeble efforts to be made and wasted, Russia gave neutral and hesitating states reason to fear that the Tsar was willing to discredit negotiations by an act of violence. As far as those were concerned who, like France and England, were already more than half enlightened, it seemed as though Russia had designedly hastened the decisive rupture between them; and such was the universal opinion in the two countries, and at first in the two fleets which, lying in the immediate scene of the action, saw in it a sort of provocation and, as it were, a challenge.

It was vain for Russia to protest against the wrongful imputation; the sincerity of its protestations was idle against the effect of its rashness. "The blow struck at Sinope was not against Turkey alone," said M. Drouyn de Lhuys on the thirteenth of December, and the next day he addressed a telegram to General Baraguey d'Hilliers, urging him to unite with the English envoy in despatching the combined fleets as soon as possible into the Black Sea. He wished to counteract the occupation of the Principalities by a genuine "maritime occupation." "Either the army commanded by Prince Gortchakof shall repass the Pruth," he wrote to Count Walewski, the French envoy at London, "or our vessels shall enter, as far as the season will admit, into the Euxine, and cut off all maritime communication between Russia and its Asiatic provinces. We shall thus keep the Black Sea as a pawn until the evacuation of the Principalities and the re-establishment of peace." Every Russian ship of war encountered at sea by the French or English cruisers was to be required to return to Sevastopol. The seriousness of the proposition at first startled the cabinet of St. James; nevertheless they yielded, and it may be said they contributed the harshness of the form in which the severity of the decision was couched. "It is essential," said Lord Clarendon in his depatch of the twenty-seventh of December to Sir Hamilton Seymour, — "it is essential that the combined fleets should have the command of the Black Sea. You will inform Count Nesselrode that, in order to prevent the recurrence of disasters such as that at Sinope, the combined fleet will require, and, if necessary, compel, Russian ships of war to return to Sevastopol or the nearest port."

On the third of January, eighteen hundred and fifty-four, Vice-Admirals Dundas and Hamelin left simultaneously the anchorage of Beïkos on their way from the Bosphorus into the Euxine. While one division of the fleet flying the French and English flags escorted a convoy of Ottoman transports to Batum, the rest of the ships cast anchor in the roadstead of Sinope. An English frigate, the Retribution, was sent to Sevastopol with a notification of the agreement between the powers. On the seventh of January, at daybreak, she came in through the channel, without having been signalled by the lookout-men, owing to the dense fog, and all of a sudden she appeared amid the mist, like a fantastic vision. The Russians could not believe their eyes; never before had a foreign flag floated over these forbidden waters. The military port was filled with confusion; signal-guns thundered from the neighboring batteries; an admiralty boat, however, accosted the audacious visitor, and refused to receive its despatches before it had retired beyond gunshot. The frigate turned slowly and steamed down the bay at her leisure; then, having reached the limits and declared her message, she disappeared in the direction of Sinope.

The resolutions taken by the cabinets of Paris and London were officially brought to the notice of Count Nesselrode on the twelfth of January by Sir Hamilton Seymour and General de Castelbajac. The Chancellor answered indirectly by demanding explanations through the Emperor's envoys at the courts of England and France. Two questions were laid before them: If the Russian fleet was no longer at liberty to attack the Ottoman flag and territory, would the Ottoman fleet be at liberty to attack the Russian flag and territory? And, secondly, if Turkish squadrons could sail with impunity from one port to another, would Russian squadrons, by the principle of just reciprocity, be guaranteed the same advantage? Lord Clarendon and M. Drouyn de Lhuys having each answered these questions in the negative, Russia, satisfied on the first point, but aggrieved on the second, took a decided step. On the fourth of February the formal suspension of diplomatic relations between Russia on one side and France and England on the other was declared at London and Paris by Baron Brunof and Mr. Kiselef. Three days later General de Castelbajac and Sir G. H. Seymour were instructed by their governments to withdraw from Saint Petersburg.

But while the Emperor Nicholas was breaking decidedly with France and England, he made desperate efforts to attach Austria and Prussia to his cause. He knew that in the month of September, or October, eighteen hundred and fifty-three, at the interviews of Olmütz and Warsaw, Austria, still in a state of hesitation, had proposed to Prussia that each should remain neutral, and he knew the surprising fact that it was Prussia which declined the propositions of Austria. To awaken these wishes for neutrality, to destroy the unanimity of the Vienna conference, and, while waiting for better things, to oppose to the martial ardor of the Western powers, the reserve and inaction of the German powers — such were the designs which the inflexible and domineering Tsar was still revolving in his mind. To bring these things to a surer fulfilment, he made choice of one of his most important statesmen, who most thoroughly sympathized with his policy. Toward the end of January, eighteen hundred and fifty-four, he sent Count Orlof to Vienna just as he had before sent Prince Menshikof to Constantinople. In these two missions there were the same tactics, the same affectation of mystery, the same dissatisfied and haughty demeanor. After several days of noticeable silence, Count Orlof asked, and was granted on the thirtieth of January, a private interview with the Emperor Francis Joseph. He gave him an autograph letter from his sovereign, in which the Tsar declared that he was ready to conclude an honorable peace, but meanwhile he demanded that the Austrian Emperor, in conjunction with the King of Prussia, should engage to preserve a strict neutrality. Before giving his answer, the Emperor Francis Joseph asked the envoy of the Tsar whether his master would confirm his engagement not to cross the Danube, to evacuate the Principalities after the war, and not to disturb the actual order and the territorial possessions of the Turkish Empire. As Count Orlof refused to undertake any such engagement in the name of the Russian Emperor, Francis Joseph also refused absolutely to make any promise to the Tsar; he even added that he should be faithful to the principles adopted by the four powers and should continue to regulate his conduct in conformity to the best interests as well as the dignity of his empire.

Dissatisfied, but not bluffed, the Tsar's confidant endeavored to play a better hand with Count Buol; in a far more explicit interview than the imperial audience had been, he subjected to the Austrian minister a draught for a protocol which comprised three heads: The position of Austria and Prussia should be that of absolute neutrality as far as Russia was concerned, but they should be armed and ready to defend themselves against the threats and pressure of the Western powers. In case these powers should attack Austrian or Prussian territory or any state of the Germanic confederation, Russia, Prussia, and Austria should combine to assist the territory imperilled. And, finally, if it happened that the events of the war changed the face of things in the East, the Tsar would agree not to come to any conclusion without a preliminary understanding with his allies. It was no simple convention, therefore, but a veritable treaty of defensive alliance which Russia intended to submit to Austria. Whatever it was, Count Buol, with courteous firmness, absolutely declined to sign it, and when Count Orlof called to remembrance the perfect accord which had existed for forty years between the three Northern powers in maintaining the general order of Europe, and finally reproached the Austrian government for deserting the obligations and forgetting the principles of the alliance, he received the plain answer that the spirit of conservatism influenced those who watched over the integrity of the Ottoman Empire, rather than the man who had already begun to attack it. On the third of February an order signed by the Emperor Francis Joseph raised to thirty thousand men the army of observation stationed in Transylvania. On the eighth the Vienna Conference held a session to receive Count Buol's report of his despatches to the Austrian envoy at Saint Petersburg; the able and resolute conduct of the Austrian minister was unanimously approved. The same day Count Orlof left Vienna.

At Berlin the negotiations were conducted with less formality, but rather, one might say in the true sense of the word, as a family affair. Since he was brother-in-law of King Frederic William the Fourth, Nicholas thought it unnecessary to send an envoy extraordinary. His accredited representative, Baron Budberg, was commissioned, in the first place, to put into the King's hands an autograph letter, and then to give the minister, Baron Manteuffel, the draught of the protocol supported by a letter from Count Nesselrode. Two rival influences were at work on the somewhat weak and fickle mind of King Frederic William: on one side was the royal house, followed by the whole aristocratic, or, as it was called, the feudal party, decidedly inclined toward Russia; on the other, the Prime Minister, hostile to that power and sustained in the Chambers and out of them by the opinion of the liberal and parliamentary middle classes. Instead of applying to Baron Manteuffel, it was without his knowledge, that Baron Budberg, passing by the King's minister, obtained an audience of Frederic William and gave him his brother-in-law's letter. This proceeding so like that of Prince Menshikof, aggrieved Baron Manteuffel, who immediately resigned; but as his resignation was not accepted, he retained his place with increased strength. Baron Budberg resented it, and he was dismissed more quickly and less courteously than Count Orlof had been. The despatch of the thirty-first of January, sent by Baron Manteuffel to the Prussian minister at Saint Petersburg, stated, in substance, that the protocol of the fifth of December and the negotiations arising from it had created between the four powers a mutual engagement from which Prussia was unable to withdraw, and, on the other hand that if it adopted the principle of an armed neutrality its action would be fettered in view of contingencies whose reach could not be foreseen. In a second despatch, after showing that, under a disguise, what Russia asked for was not only a defensive alliance but a genuine and effective concurrence, Baron Manteuffel did not hesitate to make an allusion to the Hungarian insurrection, which was equally disagreeable to the Court of Saint Petersburg and Vienna, in calling up the memory of services rendered by the one and ill acknowledged by the other, and he added proudly that if Russia had nothing to fear from the spirit of revolution, Prussia had shown its ability to crush it without foreign assistance.

LETTERS OF NAPOLEON THE THIRD AND THE EMPEROR NICHOLAS. — AUSTRIA AND PRUSSIA AGREE WITH FRANCE AND ENGLAND TO MAINTAIN THE TURKISH EMPIRE.

When official and regular diplomacy has reached the end of its resources, direct communications from sovereign to sovereign in the way of autograph letters are expedients of doubtful value. "We have left to us the shadow of a shadow of hope," said Earl Fitz-William in the House of Lords, referring to a letter written with the approbation of the English government by the Emperor Napoleon the Third to the Emperor Nicholas, on the twenty-ninth of January. After stating the part which had been taken by France and England, Napoleon made the following proposition: "Should your Majesty be as desirous as myself of a pacific conclusion, what would be more simple than to declare that an armistice shall now be signed, that things shall resume their diplomatic course, that all hostilities shall cease, and that the belligerent forces shall return from the places whither motives of war have led them? Thus the Russian troops would abandon the principalities, and our squadrons the Black Sea. If your Majesty preferred to treat directly with Turkey, you might appoint a plenipotentary who could negotiate with a plenipotentary of the Sultan a convention to be submitted to the four powers. Let your Majesty adopt this plan, upon which the Queen of England and myself are perfectly agreed, and tranquillity will be re-established and the world satisfied. There is nothing in this plan which is unworthy of your Majesty, nothing which can wound your honor; but if, from a motive difficult to understand, your Majesty refuses this proposal, then France as well as England will be obliged to leave to the fate of arms and the chances of war that which might now be decided by reason and justice."

The reply of the Emperor Nicholas, dated February eighth, reached Paris ten days later. It was negative, as might have been expected. The Tsar indulged in recriminations against England and France: "I have made for the maintenance of peace, all the concessions, both in form and substance, compatible with my honor, and in claiming for my co-religionists in Turkey a confirmation of the rights and privileges which they long ago acquired at the price of Russian blood, I demanded nothing which was not confirmed by treaties. If the Porte had been left to itself, the difference which holds Europe in suspense would long ere this have been settled. A fatal influence has intervened to throw everything into confusion. I learn that the two powers, while protecting the reinforcement of Turkish troops on their own territory, have resolved to prohibit to us the navigation of the Black Sea, that is to say, apparently to take from us the right to protect our own coasts. I leave it to your Majesty to consider if that is, as you say, the way to facilitate the conclusion of peace, and if, in the alternative which is laid before me, I am allowed to discuss or examine, even for a moment, your proposals for an armistice, the immediate evacuation of the Principalities, and for a negotiation with the Porte of a convention to be submitted to a conference of the four courts. Would you yourself, if you were in my place, accept such a proposition? Would your national feeling allow you to do so? I am bold to answer, no. Allow me then in my turn the right of thinking as you yourself would think. Whatever your Majesty may decide, threats will not induce me to recede. My trust is in God and in my right, and Russia, as I can pledge, will prove herself in eighteen hundred and fifty-four what she was in eighteen hundred and twelve." We shall find again, in the manifesto of February twenty-first, the invocation of that terrible year: "But Russia will not betray its holy mission, and if enemies invade its borders, we are ready to meet them with the firmness bequeathed to us by our forefathers. Are we not still the same Russian nation whose valor is attested by the memorable events of eighteen hundred and twelve? May the Almighty help to prove this by deeds."

On the twenty-seventh of February two despatches of similar import were sent from Paris and London to Saint Petersburg; they contained a summons to the Tsar to withdraw his troops from the Principalities before the thirtieth of April at the latest. A refusal to submit or to answer would be considered as tantamount to a declaration of war. It was the thirteenth of March when the courier reached Saint Petersburg; the next day, the French and English consuls placed the summons in Count Nesselrode's hands. On the eighteenth they were invited to call upon the Chancellor, and received this laconic communication: "The Emperor thinks it unbecoming to make any reply." Mr. Michele, the English consul, then asked what would be the consular arrangements between the belligerent powers when war was once declared. "That will depend entirely upon the course which the French and English governments adopt," said Count Nesselrode; "we shall not declare war."

On the seventh of March the French Minister of Finance brought in a bill to negotiate a loan of two hundred and fifty million francs, saying, " Important maritime armaments and expeditions to distant shores will soon be attended with sacrifices which are not provided for in the estimates or by the ordinary means of the treasury." The loan was authorized, and all the members of the Legislative body proceeded to the Tuileries to present the bill to Napoleon, who felt much pleased with this expression of their confidence and support. The English House of Commons had already granted the Queen's government an extraordinary subsidy of three million pounds sterling, for the necessary increase in the army and navy. On the twenty-seventh of March a message of the Emperor Napoleon and a message of Queen Victoria, read before the parliamentary assemblies of the two nations, informed the world that a state of war had succeeded the suspension of diplomatic relations between England and France on one side, and Russia on the other. A treaty signed at Constantinople assured the Porte of the armed assistance of the two powers, who were solemnly engaged to each other by a treaty of alliance signed at London on the tenth of April.

Of the two German powers, Austria was the most decided, because the presence of the Russians in the Principalities gave reason for more disquietude. Thus, at Saint Petersburg it had supported strenuously the summons made by France and England, while Prussia simply held aloof. Likewise, when France and England proposed to substitute for the rather theoretical protocols of the conference a regular treaty of quadruple alliance equally binding on all parties, Austria declared itself ready to subscribe, but the King of Prussia, from family scruples, refused his signature. Baron Manteuffel, however, before the Prussian parliament as well as in his diplomatic conversations, did not cease to declare that his government was in moral accord with the other three powers, and, in fact, Prussian representation at the Vienna conference did not hesitate to sign the protocol of the ninth of April, one of the most important acts of that diplomatic body. The territorial integrity of the Ottoman Empire, as an absolute condition for every transaction having peace in view, was proclaimed anew, and the evacuation of the Principalities was insisted upon. Moreover, the governments represented at the conference agreed not to make any engagement with Russia or any other power which did not adhere to this principle until first a common conference had been held.

"At this solemn moment," as it was expressly said in the protocol, in which France and England were about to pass from debate to battle, in which, consequently, the exclusively diplomatic campaign pursued for nearly a year came to an end, it was not a matter of indifference that the two other powers should recognize "the necessity of stating anew the union of the four governments on the ground of principles."

CHAPTER VII.

THE CRIMEAN WAR.

1853–1855.

Military Arrangements of France and England.—The Allied Armies at Gallipoli and Varna.—Siege of Silistria.—Bombardment of Odessa.—Expedition into the Dobrudsha: the Cholera.—The Crimea.—Battle of the Alma.—Sevastopol.

MILITARY ARRANGEMENTS OF FRANCE AND ENGLAND.—THE ALLIED ARMIES AT GALLIPOLI AND VARNA.—SIEGE OF SILISTRIA.—BOMBARDMENT OF ODESSA.

ON the eleventh of March Marshal Saint Arnaud was appointed commander-in-chief of the French expedition to the East. General Vaillant succeeded to the Ministry of War. Although at Marseilles there reigned the greatest confusion, and neither the naval nor the military arrangements were completed, General Canrobert, who commanded the first division, was ordered to depart on the nineteenth. At Malta he found fifteen thousand English soldiers who had left England in February. They were under the command of Lord Raglan, who, under the name of Lord Fitzroy Somerset, had fought in the Peninsular war with the Duke of Wellington. He was a man sixty-six years old, and had lost his right arm at the battle of Waterloo.

Napoleon was inclined to fortify the peninsula of Gallipoli. In his instructions to Marshal Saint Arnaud he said: "The peninsula of Gallipoli is selected as the principal site of disembarkation, because it should be, as a strategical point, the basis of our operations, — that is to say, the place for our stores, ambulances, and provisions, and from whence we may easily march forward or re-embark." Gallipoli was the largest city on the peninsula, and though it was not walled, and had for defence only an ancient ruined castle, the immediate vicinity of the isthmus of Bulaïr, an excellent anchorage, and a shore favorable for disembarkation determined its selection. The houses, for the most part of wood, were built in irregular rows on the side of a steep hill sloping to the water. The streets were narrow and filthy. The inhabitants, a wretched mixture of Turks, Greeks, and Armenians, amounted to fifteen or sixteen thousand souls.

The troops, immediately upon their arrival, began to form an intrenched camp, consisting of a series of field-works about thirteen kilometers in length, running from the Sea of Marmora to the Gulf of Saros. The town was divided into two portions, of which the western was given to the English. Two mosques were transformed into powder-magazines, and the *muezzin* were replaced by watchmen in the tapering minarets. Before these field-works were finished, however, the troops were removed to the Bosphorus; the British, ten thousand strong, making their camp at Scutari on the Asiatic shore, and the French, about double in point of numbers, occupying the vicinity of Constantinople.

The Russians meanwhile had crossed the Danube at Braïla, Galats, and Ismaïl, taken the small fortresses of Matchin, Isaktcha, and Tultcha, and were occupying the southern part of the region called Tartary Dobrudsha, bounded by the Danube, the Sea, and the Wall of Trajan.

Lord Raglan left England on the tenth of April, in company with the Duke of Cambridge, and on the twenty-ninth reached Constantinople, whither he was followed ten days later by Marshal Saint Arnaud. On the twenty-second of April the first hostilities on the part of the allied fleets were begun in the

Black Sea. Several weeks before, the English steam-frigate Furious approached Odessa with a flag of truce, for the purpose of removing the English residents. The Russians fired upon the frigate; Baron Osten-Sacken, the commandant, claiming that soundings had been made and that the flag of truce was used to cover hostile investigations. Odessa is situated on a line of cliffs which curve inward, forming a shallow bay. At the southeastern extremity a long fortified mole ran out for the protection of shipping. The town was otherwise defended by seven batteries, and there was a strong citadel on the west, mounting heavy cannon. On the day mentioned a fleet of five English and three French steam-frigates approached Odessa, and, after an incessant cannonading of ten hours, destroyed the batteries and the mole; many factories, warehouses, and shops were set on fire, and Count Vorontsof's magnificent palace was damaged. The city and the port were spared as far as practicable. The Emperor Nicholas, in a manifesto, held up to the detestation of his subjects the action of the allies in attacking Odessa "on a day in which the inhabitants were assembled in the Orthodox Temple to celebrate the death of the Son of God, crucified for the redemption of humanity, — a city of peace and commerce where all Europe in its days of scarcity and famine always found open granaries."

Marshal Paskićvitch, toward the end of April, came to take command of the army under Prince Gortchakof. He concentrated a large force in the vicinity of Bukarest and then crossed the Danube at Kalarash. Silistria was invested and underwent a regular siege, which lasted until the twenty-third of June, when the Russians dismantled their batteries, evacuated their positions, and retired to the left bank of the Danube. The siege had been a long and costly one: many furious engagements put to the test the bravery of the Turks and Russians. On the night of the second of June Musa Pasha was killed by a shell; on the thirteenth the Russians made a grand attempt to take the place by storm, but they were repulsed.

General Shilders was killed. General Lüders, Count Orlof, Prince Gortchakof, and Prince Paskiévitch were wounded. On the night of the eighteenth of June a final effort was made. This also failed. Lieutenant Nasmyth, an English volunteer in the Turkish service, wrote to the Times: "The Russians had sixty guns in position at Silistria, and threw upwards of fifty thousand shot and shell, besides an incalculable quantity of small-arm ammunition. They constructed more than three miles of approaches and sprung six mines; yet during forty days not one inch of ground was gained, and they abandoned the siege, leaving the petty field-work, against which their principal efforts had been directed, a shapeless mass from the effects of their mines and batteries, but still in possession of its original defenders." It was estimated that the Russians lost twelve thousand men by wounds and disease at the siege of Silistria.

They were also suffering severely in their occupation of the wilderness of Dobrudsha. The Dobrudsha is a region of which the soil is sandy, allowing water to sink away so that brooks and springs are almost unknown. It is "an immeasurable expanse covered with parched blades of grass. Nowhere, not even in the villages, is a tree or a shrub to be found." Malarial fevers are prevalent in this dreary region, especially during the hot summer months.

EXPEDITION INTO THE DOBRUDSHA: THE CHOLERA.

On the nineteenth of July Marshal Saint Arnaud decided to send an expedition against the Russians in the Dobrudsha. It was designed as an experiment to occupy the minds of the soldiers, and accustom them to enduring the toils of war and long marches. The marshal also desired to make trial of a new body of troops which he had just incorporated. Attached to the Bulgarian army were twenty or thirty thousand bashi-bazuks, who, at their own expense, fought, either on horse or on foot, under the Turkish government. It occurred to Marshal Saint Arnaud to form these irregulars into a body of cavalry, under French officers; they would then be able to do good service against the Cossacks. On the sixth of July the number of these Oriental Spahis, as they were called, amounted to almost twenty-five hundred men, well armed with muskets and lances. One division of the French army, consisting of upwards of ten thousand men, left their camp on the twenty-first of July, "impatient to see the Russians, glad, joyous, charmed, to cross woods, brooks, verdure-clad ravines; but at the heights of Baltchik the country suddenly changed. From that point to Kustendjé the ground sank away by an insensible decline. Trees failed; tall, dry grasses, undulating in the wind like the waves of the sea, took their places; no more running streams were to be seen, but, at intervals, brackish pools, neglected wells, often filled up, almost always fetid, and miserable, deserted villages. As the column approached, the inhabitants disappeared with their herds into the depths of the plain. On the twenty-fifth of July the division encamped near Mangolia; only four cases of cholera had occurred since they started, and those at the first stage. On the twenty-sixth the distance they marched was short, but on the two following days it was a long and painful journey under a burning sun. On the twenty-eighth the column, passing Kustendjé, stopped at the village of Pollas near a pond. Here the cholera broke out. Twenty-seven men were sick that day." The first regiment of Zouaves came by sea to Kustendjé, and three days after landing they had more than fifty cases. They had one or two encounters with the Russians, in which the bashi-bazuks acted without discipline, and committed such excesses that their commander, General Yusuf, was obliged to write a letter in the name of the French army, disavowing their atrocities. The order was given to retreat to Varna. The march lasted twenty days. All the means of conveyance were encumbered with the sick; there was no medicine, and nothing to drink except unhealthy water. Provisions gave out. It was a terrible journey.

Of the men who engaged in this unfortunate expedition, nearly twenty-five hundred perished, and another thousand had to be sent back to France. The cholera also attacked the English forces, and spread with alarming rapidity throughout all the troops at Varna. Marshal Saint Arnaud, in a private letter to the Secretary of War, complained bitterly of the misfortunes of the army: "The cholera is overwhelming and decimating us. Those whom it spares are left in a fearful state of feebleness and enervation. Up to this time I have lost two thousand, and nearly five thousand are sick. We must escape from this sepulchre of Varna, where fevers, already threatening, in a month will succeed the cholera."

It had been decided to strike Russia a mortal blow, not on the Danube, but in the Crimea. The long and weary delay at Varna had been caused partly by the entire lack of preparations by the French government, and partly by the uncertainty which Austria showed in regard to entering into the armed alliance. But a month after the Crimean expedition was fully determined upon, Lord Raglan and Marshal Saint Arnaud received word that Baron von Hess was expecting orders from Francis Joseph to attack the Russian right wing in Moldavia in September, and was desirous that the three allied armies should co-operate with him in driving the Russians from the Principalities by simultaneously attacking their left flank. But the two commanders felt obliged courteously and firmly to decline the invitation. The climate of the Danube valley was so deleterious to their soldiers that it seemed too great a responsibility to carry on a campaign in such a difficult country, and the indigenous cavalry, which might have done excellent service, was rendered useless by Turkish fanaticism and their unwillingness to serve under French "giaours." It was therefore decided to break up the camp at Varna and carry the war to the Crimea. On the twenty-fourth of August Marshal Saint Arnaud wrote to the Minister of War: "When you read this letter, the army will be at sea on its way to the Crimea. On the second of September these magnificent fleets, in company, will weigh anchor at Baltchik, the general rendezvous, and bear away to Sevastopol. All my plans are matured; I think nothing has been forgotten, nothing neglected which could assure success, and I am confident that we shall not fail. May Heaven only grant us fair weather and a smooth sea. Now it is necessary to think of the future. The undertaking is immense, and the object makes difficulties of small moment. Therefore I want to strike the blow; but I have no idea that the Russians will abandon this magnificent booty without a struggle. Menshikof is brave and headstrong. We shall have much to do. Gaps will be made in our ranks; we must devise means to fill them. I do not want to spend an eternity before Sevastopol, and allow the Russian armies to come by way of Perekop to dispute my conquest. I desire to take Sevastopol in all haste, to get the mastery of the Crimea, so as to choose a good field in which to await the Russians, if, indeed, I do not manage to blockade the port of Perekop. This word Sevastopol has had a magic effect. Every one has revived, the coldest have become enthusiastic; this spirit is gaining ground, and the cannon will do the rest."

The fleet destined to carry the French army to the Crimea amounted, in all, to one hundred and seventy-two ships; nine frigates bore the Turkish division; the English fleet was composed of ten ships of the line, fifteen steam-frigates, and one hundred and fifty magnificent transports. On the seventh of September, after several delays, the united squadron proceeded to the Crimea. Several days before they were encouraged by the news of the capture of the fortress of Bomarsund on the sixteenth of August. Bomarsund was the key to the Gulf of Bothnia, and was garrisoned by more than two thousand men. The Russians decided to evacuate the Principalities which were then occupied by the Austrians, according to an agreement with Europe and the Sultan. The war on the Danube was ended. The Crimean war had begun!

THE CRIMEA. — THE BATTLE OF THE ALMA.

The Crimea, known to the ancients as the Tauric Chersonese, is a quadrangular peninsula, bathed on the north by the Sea of Azof, and on the other three sides by the Black Sea. It is united to the mainland by the isthmus of Perekop, which the allies intended to occupy. The shallowness of the Bay of Perekop, however, and the entire absence of water on the isthmus, made this seem impracticable. Communication with the continent, moreover, is easily effected by the long, narrow tongue of Arabat, which separates the Sea of Azof from the Sivash or Putrid Sea, and reaches to within a hundred meters of the mainland, a distance easily crossed by boat. This is the usual route to Kertch or Theodosia. Farther to the west a bridge over the Putrid Sea connects the peninsula of Tchongar with the Crimea.

The southern portion of the Crimea is occupied by three parallel lines of mountains, of which the one farthest to the south is the loftiest. All the mountains form a precipitous wall on the southern side, but slope gently toward the north. The summits are level plateaux; the most important, Tchatir-Dagh, rises fifteen hundred and sixty meters above the level of the sea. This whole region is well provided with rivers and streams; the Salgir runs northeast into the Putrid Sea; the Tchernaia, or Black River, emptying into the harbor of Sevastopol; the Belbek, the Katcha, and the Alma run west. The southern Crimea is picturesque, well-wooded, and its valleys are perfect gardens. A level plain, or steppe, occupies the remaining two thirds of the peninsula. In spring and autumn it is verdant, in summer bare and burnt, in winter covered deep with snow. This region is inhabited by bands of Tartars, who keep their flocks and are peaceful and kind. Their number at the time of the Crimean war was about two hundred and fifty-seven thousand, out of a population of four hundred and thirty thousand, composed, for the rest, of Turks,

Bulgarians, Armenians, Jews, Germans, and Russians. In the interior of the Crimea are only three cities: Simferopol, the capital of the province, Baktchi-Sarai, and Karasubazar; on the sea-coast there are six: Eupatoria, on the Bay of Kalamita, Sevastopol, and Balaklava, Theodosia or Kaffa, Kertch, and Ienikalé. The only road really worthy of the name was the one constructed by Prince Vorontsof, which reached from Simferopol to Sevastopol, by way of Alushta, through one of the most beautiful countries in the world.

The Russian army in eighteen hundred and fifty-four had an available force of seven hundred thousand men distributed on a line of two thousand kilometers from the Gulf of Bothnia to the Caspian Sea. There were two hundred and seven thousand in Finland, around Saint Petersburg, and along the Baltic to the Prussian frontier; one hundred and forty thousand in Poland, one hundred and eighty thousand in Bessarabia and on the Danube, thirty-two thousand near Odessa and Nikolaief, thirty-nine thousand in the Crimea, forty-six thousand between the Don and the Caucasus, and fifty-five thousand on the frontier of Turkey in Asia. In September, eighteen hundred and fifty-four, there were really fifty-one thousand men in the Crimea, twelve thousand of whom were at Kertch and Ienikalé under the command of General Khomutof, who was charged with the defence of the eastern part of the peninsula. Prince Menshikof, with thirty-three thousand foot-soldiers, twenty-seven hundred cavalry, twelve hundred Cossacks, and seventeen hundred artillery men, defended Sevastopol. The majority of the infantry was encamped near Sevastopol; the sixteen battalions, with thirty-two field-pieces and six hundred Cossacks, were distributed between the Katcha and the Alma. The destruction of the fleet brought eighteen or nineteen thousand excellent sailors into the land service.

It was evident that the Russian government had no especial anxiety about the expedition to the Crimea, although the English press had intimated the probability of it. Odessa was considered far more likely to be the objective point of the attack. Prince Menshikof was surprised on the tenth of September to see four ships bearing the French and English flags approach Sevastopol. His surprise was changed to apprehension when, three days later, a thick cloud of black smoke, as it were, precipitated a countless host of hostile ships.

The allies decided to disembark at Eupatoria, and the landing was completed on the fourteenth of September, the anniversary of Napoleon Bonaparte's entrance into Moscow. On the nineteenth the armies began their march against Sevastopol. After a march of sixteen kilometers, through a dry and undulating country which showed some signs of cultivation, they reached the banks of the Bulgarak, where they encamped for the night after a slight skirmish with Cossack cavalry. On the morning of the twentieth the signal-gun fired from the fleet was answered by drums and trumpets in the allied armies, while from the heights of the Alma floated down the sound of Russian hymns, and the popes with their crosses were seen passing to and fro, sprinkling the kneeling hosts with holy water.

As soon as Prince Menshikof had known of the occupation of Eupatoria and the arrangements for landing the allied armies, he sent for aid from General Khomutof at Theodosia, and at the same time posted as strong a force as was possible upon the heights of the Alma. The river runs from east to west through a narrow cañon covered with trees and bushes. A timber bridge, on which the road from Eupatoria crossed the Alma, had been partially destroyed, but the stream was fordable, except at the latter part of its course. There were three villages, or groups of houses, on the right bank, buried in gardens and vineyards, — Tarkhanlar, Burliuk, Almatamak. The descent from the heights to the Alma was steep; it was almost impossible to reach the terrace above Almatamak.

The weakest point, Prince Menshikof's position, was an open gap opposite Burliuk, through which led the road from Eupatoria; and here he stationed his strongest batteries. The total of the army on the heights of the Alma was between thirty-five and forty thousand men, with ninety-six cannon. Prince Gortchakof commanded the right wing, composed of sixteen battalions. He had also charge of the centre, sustained by the four battalions of Borodino. General Kiriakof commanded the left wing, consisting of the regiments of Biélostok and Biest, with those of Tarutino and Moscow.

The attack had been ordered to begin early in the morning, but, owing to delay in the British camp, it was nearly one o'clock before General Bosquet could get his column in marching order. A detachment crossed the river by the shallow bar near its mouth, and, clambering up the almost perpendicular face of the cliff, surprised the Russian flank who retired toward the centre. The Russian generals could not at first believe the evidence of their eyes, but Menshikof, seeing that his left wing was in danger, sent the Moscow regiment and soon after half of the general reserve; but the main body of the French had now reached the plateau, and upon them depended the result of the day. If they succeeded in forcing back the Russians the game was theirs, but there was no retreat for them. The precipitate face of the plateau prevented any hope of escape if they were repulsed. But just at the critical moment Marshal Saint Arnaud, seeing the position of General Bosquet's Hussars, sent the first and third divisions to his assistance. They crossed the Alma by the new fords discovered by the sharpshooters, and in spite of the efforts of the Russian artillery to prevent them, succeeded in reaching the level plateau. The Russians were now drawn back in confusion; the regiments of Minsk and Moscow had lost more than fifteen hundred men, together with their colonels and the majority of their other officers. A final encounter took place near the telegraph station, but this was decided in favor of the French.

The Russian battalions retreated in good order toward Sevastopol. But while the contest was thus decided on the plateau, there was still some doubt of the sequel on the other side of the ravine. The English division, under command of the Duke of Cambridge, had renewed the attack upon the fortification built on the slope of the bank above Burliuk. Prince Gortchakof encouraged the Russians by his presence; his coat was riddled with bullets and his horse was killed under him as he led the battalions of Vladimir to the charge. The British line began to give way; the retreat in a moment would have been general, as the Russians with wild yells rushed forward, bayonets in hand, had not Marshal Saint Arnaud, hearing of the resistance offered by the Russians, sent several batteries to the assistance of his allies. The raking fire was too terrible to withstand. When the order came from Prince Menshikof for the regiment of Vladimir to give up their post behind the fortification, where they took refuge, only ten officers were left; all the rest were killed or wounded. It was four o'clock; the soldiers of the allied armies had not eaten since morning; they were too weary to follow the retreating Russians. The battle had lasted three hours, and the total loss on the Russian side had been more than fifty-seven hundred men, while the French lost thirteen hundred and the English two thousand. All three armies covered themselves with glory. Marshal Saint Arnaud gave his enemy credit for bravery and discipline, but he criticised their tactics as being, like those of the English, fifty years behind the times. "Just as Lord Raglan was the pupil of the Duke of Wellington, so Prince Menshikof followed the rules laid down by Suvorof for the use of Kutusof." On a Champ de Mars the manœuvres of the masses of infantry would have been marvellous for precision, but on the battlefield the slowness and precision proved their ruin. Quicker action would have prevented the French division of Canrobert from setting foot on the plateau.

Just before the allied armies reached the Crimea the Emperor Nicholas, convinced that a new system of tactics was desirable for his armies in order to give them greater mobility, issued the necessary regulations, but, as they were not fully understood, they caused confusion and disorder and led to the loss of the battle.

On the night after their defeat the Russians encamped on the Katcha; they blamed their carbines and their rifles; they were angry but not discouraged. The next day they continued their retreat, and pitched their tents south of Sevastopol.

The battle of the Alma was a thunderbolt to Russia. Since eighteen hundred and twelve no enemy had landed on its soil; the Crimea, protected by a formidable fleet, impregnable fortresses, and a numerous army, seemed secure from all attacks. Now the army was beaten, and the Black Sea fleet which had retreated to the harbor of Sevastopol served only to obstruct the channel.

SEVASTOPOL.

"The traveller who comes from the northern coasts along the western shore of the Crimea is obliged to make a long détour around a spur projecting to the southwest from the mountainous region of the peninsula. A light-house stands on the extreme point of this sharp Cape Chersonese. It occupies the apex of a triangle, which is washed on two sides by the Black Sea, and is cut off on the east by the abrupt crags to which the Russians have given the name of Mount Sapun. The territory included between these crags and the sea is called the Plateau of Chersonese, a soil henceforth historic and sacred, because it served as the intrenched camp for the armies of France and England, and thither came three of the greatest nations of the world to end their disputes, as it were, in lists; and there thousands of heroic soldiers, who fought for the possession of Sevastopol, sleep their last sleep.

"The geometric extent of the plateau is about one hundred

and twenty-five square kilometers; its greatest elevation is nearly three hundred meters, with a general slope from southeast to northwest. This is the direction also of the numerous ravines which furrow its surface, and whose outlets form a succession of creeks, some running up from the open sea, others from the deep inland gulf which serves as a harbor for the port of Sevastopol. The contrast between this hospitable northern shore and the inaccessible cliffs on the south is as striking as possible.

"It sometimes happens that several ravines unite in forming a single creek. The largest are in reality enormous clefts whose bare sides, like ruined walls, expose to view the limestone foundations a hundred meters thick, on which rests the thin layer of earth which barely covers the plateau. Such, for example, is the largest of the three ravines whose common mouth, called the South Bay, twenty-four hundred meters long and four hundred wide, deservedly became the principal military port of Russia on the Black Sea. On the left bank of this bay were laid the foundations of Sevastopol not a hundred years ago.

"The houses, constructed at first on the narrow ridge which preserves the name of City Mountain, have gradually crept westward down to the lower level of the valley into which opens Artillery Bay, and have even climbed up the opposite slope, so that the Artillery quarter has finally crowned the other side of the valley, now called the Central or City Ravine. The marine establishment, in order to give room for the growing demands of the fleet, have been transported to the other side of the port, and on the right bank has grown up the Karabelnaïa quarter around the bay having the same name. Barracks, hospitals, magazines, workshops of all sorts have rapidly covered this western part of Sevastopol; basins have been hollowed out, dry docks, large enough for the largest ships, have been constructed, immense earthworks undertaken, and enormous foundations prepared for the great palace destined to replace the ancient admiralty, which, built in the infancy of the city, was now unsuitable.

"Seen from the western side of the harbor, Sevastopol delighted the eye and the mind with a most attractive and varied spectacle, as it lay spread out on the slopes of the City Mountain, cut through by its two magnificent streets, lined with elegant houses built of handsome white stone, gay with gardens and green boulevards in the daytime, lighted in the evening by innumerable gleams of gas, while its arsenals, its quays, and its port were filled with life and animation.

"Numerous churches lifted their cupolas above the public and private edifices of the city. This soil, venerated by the Russians as holy ground, had been pressed under foot toward the end of the tenth century by the first Christians of their race. It was in the ancient city of Kherson, subjugated by his arms, that the Grand Prince Vladimir made his profession of Christianity in nine hundred and eighty-eight. At a distance of two kilometers west of Sevastopol, on the heights overlooking the Quarantine Bay, among the ruins left by the different generations who have occupied in succession this corner of the world, — from the Greeks to the Genoese, — a church dedicated to Saint Vladimir is built on the place where the Pagan conqueror, won over to the faith of his enemies, received baptism."

While Sevastopol was well protected on the water side by Fort Quarantine, by Fort Konstantin on the north, and Fort Alexander on the south, and by four other strong casemated fortresses, — so that a ship trying to enter the harbor would be exposed to the cross-fire of six hundred guns, — on the land side it was almost defenceless.

The Emperor Nicholas in eighteen hundred and thirty-seven had designed a plan for fortifying the city. A line of eight bastions, four to the west and four to the east, connected by a crenellated wall, the whole extending a distance of seven kilometers, was to be built. But now, more than sixteen years after the Emperor's visit, only one bastion was completed, and that the nearest to the harbor; a few slight attempts had been made to trace the connecting walls, but the vast design was scarcely more than begun.

When in the spring of eighteen hundred and fifty-four the European journal spoke of the probabilities of attacking Sevastopol, the Russians looked upon the idea as chimerical, but in order to be on the safe side, work was resumed on the bastions crowning the heights according to the original plan. On the hill of Bambor an earthwork like a redan was formed, capable of holding seven cannon. A thousand meters distant, on the summit of the Malakof hill, the engineers of the marine corps finished a sort of round tower, ten meters high and about forty-five in circumference. An earth embankment in the form of a semicircle surrounded this at some distance, and protected the masonry. Farther to the north there were two earthworks, and these four fortifications completed the defence of the Karabelnaïa. Out of one hundred and forty-five cannon distributed over the seven kilometers from the Quarantine to the Careening Bay only forty belonged to this part of the defence.

When the victory of the Alma opened to the allies the way to Sevastopol, and after the first moment's surprise had passed, the Russians set to work to repair years of carelessness and official peculation. "Sevastopol, by the character of its population, was particularly well fitted for resistance. It was less a city than a military colony; of its forty-two thousand inhabitants, thirty-five thousand belonged to the army and navy; the remainder, artisans and merchants, were dependent on the former for their labor or trade. There were few women, scarcely five thousand, and all were wonted to the robust and healthy activity of a seafaring people. Thus there were no lazy throngs nor unemployed classes, — the usual elements of disorder; there were no political divisions and no social antagonism; in a word, there was no internal enemy against which the defence had to take precautions or leave forces to protect the rear. On the contrary, the mental discipline was easy and sure, because two great principles, patriotism and religious faith, were brought into play. The military chiefs could call upon God and the guardian saints of the city without being blamed or ridiculed for weakness. They were respected because they were real models of patriotic devotion and moral excellence. It was not that the leading spirit, Prince Menshikof, was popular; his exalted rank, his icy dignity, his severity, repelled rather than attracted men. They had not yet had sufficient time to become accustomed to him and to understand him. It was the two vice-admirals, his principal lieutenants, Nakhimof, acting commander of the fleet, and especially Kornilof, the head of the marine staff, who won the sympathy and confidence of all; but neither of them had ever sought or bought popularity by any favoritism. Besides these two names, dear to the Russian sailor, we must add that of an officer of engineers, a new-comer, who quickly won the esteem and gratitude of the public. Sent from the army of the Danube to the Crimean army, and arriving only at Sevastopol on the twenty-second of August, Lieutenant-Colonel Todleben had just joined Prince Menshikof's staff when the event of the fourteenth of September and its consequences suddenly brought him into notice and gave him immediately a principal part to play in the defence."

Kornilof was anxious to take the whole squadron, and, if possible, surprise the enemies' fleet moored near Cape Lukul. He thought that thus he might disperse the armada and cut off the victors of the Alma from their source of supplies. At any rate, each one of the Russian captains might select one of the most formidable of the French or English ships and blow up his own ship and his adversary. But Prince Menshikof and the council of war vetoed this proceeding, and Kornilof was obliged to sink seven vessels at the mouth of the harbor. Seven months' provisions, three thousand cannon, and eighteen thousand men eager to avenge the ruin of the fleet were transferred to the land service. Since the fourteenth of September the Russians had not ceased to labor night and day at the defences. In a very short time, thanks to their marvellous activity, the stony soil of the Chersonesus was raised in redoubts and in ramparts crowned with fascines. The bastions of the Centre, of the Flagstaff, of the two Redans, and of the Malakof, all afterwards so celebrated, bristled with the guns taken from the navy. Admirals Kornilof, Istomin, and Nakhimof, all of whom were to die on the bastion of the Malakof, directed the defence.

On the twenty-fourth of September Prince Menshikof abandoned his position to the south of Sevastopol and encamped his army near Baktchi-saraï. He was afraid lest his communications with Simferopol and Southern Russia would be cut off.

He left to defend the city a total of thirty thousand men. Lieutenant-General Moller had charge of the city and the Karabelnaïa; Kornilof commanded the northern fortification and the western side of the harbor. He was expecting every moment the assault of the enemy, when, to his surprise, they deserted the Belbek, and made the plateau of the Chersonesus their objective point. Assisted by Todleben, he took charge of the defence; soldiers, sailors, merchants, women, and children lent a helping hand; six thousand men labored with all energy on the earthworks. At night they were relieved by a squad of three thousand distributed along the whole line. It is still thought by many officers that at this time a bold march of the allies on Sevastopol would have made them masters of the town. "During the night of the twenty-sixth an alarm was raised. A battalion of the regiment of Tarutino entering into the city was mistaken for a hostile band, and had it really been what it was supposed to be, the fortress of Sevastopol would have run some risk. The next morning the priests of the principal churches were asked by Kornilof to bless the inhabitants and the troops; they passed in solemn procession along the lines; behind them rode the admiral, haranguing marines and soldiers. "Children," said he, "we are to fight the enemy to the last extremity. Each one of us must die at his post. Kill the man who dares to speak of going back. If I order you to retreat, kill me."

On the twenty-sixth of September the English had taken possession of Balaklava, and the French were encamped on the Fediukhin heights, which rose above the right bank of the Tchernaïa, and looked down on the undulating plain of Balaklava. It was found that the port of Balaklava was not of sufficient size to accommodate both fleets, and by the advice of a captain acquainted with the region, the French fleet was transferred to the harbor of Kamiézh, which proved to be more convenient and suitable than that of Balaklava.

It had been agreed upon that, while the army of observation should protect the approaches of Balaklava and Mount Sapun with field-works, the rest of the troops should begin the attack of the military port, the English concentrating their action on the Great Redan, opposite the Karabelnaïa, the French against the Flagstaff Battery. Balaklava was naturally protected on the east and west; the English had, therefore, to defend only the north side. On the night of the ninth of October the first intrenchments were begun. At six o'clock in the morning the French had dug a line of trenches a thousand meters long, capable of sheltering a man erect. The English, during the same time, had formed their trench about twelve hundred meters distant from the Great Redan. Batteries also were constructed and fortified with cannon of heavy calibre. The seventeenth of October was set for the first bombardment.

The French army at this time amounted to forty-two thousand men, besides a division of five thousand Turks. The English had twenty-two thousand. On the other hand, Prince Menshikof, during the first days of October, added thirty battalions to the garrison of Sevastopol. The French batteries were armed with forty-nine cannon, the English on Mount Vorontsof and the Green Mountain had seventy-three. The Russians could answer the French with sixty-four pieces, the English with only fifty-four, although the ramparts were provided with more than treble that number.

On the morning of the seventeenth of October, at six and one half o'clock, the allies began the bombardment, which lasted for more than three hours without special result, when the explosion of a powder-magazine and the terrible cannonade of the Russians finally silenced the French batteries. The English, being more advantageously placed, were more successful, and the ruins of the Malakof tower and of the Great Redan proved the effect of the forty-seven hundred projectiles which the English guns had thrown. Taken as a whole the advantage of the day belonged to the Russians; the fleet which entered into a contest with the batteries on the shore had retired worsted; the French batteries were reduced to inactivity, and the damages inflicted by the English were repaired in twelve hours, under the enemy's fire. It was on this seventeenth of October that the brave Admiral Kornilof was killed by a cannon-ball. His last words were: "My God, bless Russia and the Emperor! Save Sevastopol and the fleet." For three days longer the bombardment continued without further result than the expenditure of vast quantities of ammunition, and the loss of many of the combatants on both sides. During all this time a force of two or three thousand men worked each night at the difficult and dangerous task of bringing the approaches nearer the Russian lines. On the twenty-fifth of October the French parallels were within three hundred and sixty meters of the Flagstaff Battery, while the English second parallel, barely traced as yet, brought them within nine hundred meters of the Great Redan.

The English army, badly sheltered, ill-provided with suitable clothes, exposed to all sorts of privations, was suffering a diminution of more than a hundred men a day; at the same time the Russian army, with which the beleaguered city was in perfectly free communication, was being largely augmented. The Tsar had gradually withdrawn from the Principalities the army of occupation, and the attitude of the Austrian and Turkish armies was so peaceful that the left bank of the Pruth was left almost undefended. Thus the Tsar could reinforce his army at Sevastopol.

The English at Balaklava occupied a camp threefold larger than was necessary, and, in order to defend the outposts, a guard of a thousand Turkish soldiers had been added to their own pickets. For some time Prince Menshikof had been meditating an attack upon Balaklava. He fixed upon the twenty-fifth of October for the execution of his plan, and placed General Liprandi at the head of eighteen thousand men, who formed at the village of Tchorgun on the Tchernaïa. At five o'clock in the morning Liprandi's corps marched three columns against the redoubts which protected the English camp. Prince Menshikof also gave orders to General Zhabokritski to bring about five thousand men from the heights of Makenzie to Mount Fediukhin as a reserve.

At daybreak the Russians attacked the redoubts occupied by the Turks, who after a slight resistance fled, without even spiking their cannon. The Russians then took possession of the redoubts and advanced against the English forces, who formed with great rapidity and repelled the cavalry attack of General Rizhof. Had not Lord Cardigan's Light Brigade been too far in the rear, the day might have been won for the English. After this check the Russians held aloof and tried to tempt the English to descend from their excellent positions. At noon Lord Raglan thought that he saw the Russians removing the field-pieces from the redoubts which they had captured, and he sent orders to have the cavalry advance rapidly and try to prevent them from accomplishing their object. This order was sent by Captain Nolan, who was obliged to make a long détour, and in the interval the state of affairs changed. The Russians kept their position on the side of the hills and Mount Fediukhin; the cavalry and flying artillery had re-formed, and in a solid rank were drawn up in the plain. Lord Raglan's order was considered peremptory, however, and the Earl of Cardigan placed himself at the head of the Light Brigade, whose terrible ride into the "jaws of death" has become so famous. The six hundred, in their impetuous charge, broke through a whole army, and then were obliged to return the same deadly way. Five hundred horses lay dead upon the field. Two hundred and fifty men were either killed or severely wounded. After this glorious but useless action the day passed with no further event. The advantage may be said to have remained with the Russians, who obtained a foothold in the valley of the Tchernaïa, and, as it were, blockaded the English in Balaklava.

While the French and English commanders had agreed to attempt storming the city on the seventh of November, Prince Menshikof had decided to make a general attack upon the allies. His objective point was the southern extremity of the plateau of Inkermann, the weakest part of the English defence, and he intrusted the principal operation to General Dannenberg. A division against the French left wing was to be conducted by General Timoféief. Prince Gortchakof, with twenty-three thousand men, had charge of the division against Balaklava.

Favored by the mist which succeeded a dark and rainy day and night, the Russians early on the morning of the fifth approached the English camp unsuspected. The alarm was given by some pickets, who escaped capture by the advanced guard of the Russians. After a few moments' confusion the English formed in line and faced the Russians, but were driven back to their tents. Here the Russians were unfortunate enough to lose General Soïmonof, who was shot down as he rushed to the front to encourage his men. They immediately fell back in disorder, and, though they were reinforced by the regiments of Uglitch and Butirsk, they remained for the rest of the day "abandoned, forgotten, and one might say ignored, by the general-in-chief."

On the left wing eight battalions belonging to the main division, and consisting of five thousand eight hundred and forty Russians, met a brigade of seventeen hundred and seventy English troops, who were driven back from a small sand-bag battery, afterwards called the Slaughter-House Battery, from the deadly nature of the struggles which took place in its vicinity. It was in a measure the key of the English position, and time after time it was taken and lost. Not long before nine o'clock General Dannenberg's division, which had been delayed, arrived, and it seemed as if the battery would be definitely gained by the Russians. The English were tired out with three hours of gallant fighting in defence of the defile, "this Thermopylæ of Inkermann." It was the arrival of the French which saved the day. A battalion of only sixteen hundred and fifty came to their assistance before the Russians had passed the battery of sand-bags. The Russians, thinking it was the whole French army, fell back a little. This was an extraordinary blunder on their part, for, had they immediately advanced only five or six hundred meters, they would have prevented the arrival of French reinforcements.

At eleven o'clock the battle was over. Thanks to the timely arrival of the French and the confusion in the Russian ranks, the attempt to overwhelm the English camp had failed. The Russian army on this day lost eleven thousand eight hundred men, killed, wounded, and missing; nearly a third of those engaged in an action "badly conceived, badly conducted." The English lost twenty-six hundred out of twelve thousand, and the French about eighteen hundred out of forty-two hundred.

The battle of Inkermann caused the indefinite postponement of the grand assault which had been planned for the seventh of November. On the fourteenth a tremendous hurricane inflicted great damage upon the fleets, especially the English ships in Balaklava Bay. The pecuniary loss was reckoned at nearly two million pounds sterling, and more than a thousand men were drowned.

The allies now encamped for the winter before Sevastopol; both besiegers and besieged could continually receive reinforcements and supplies. It was like two armies intrenched opposite each other and keeping all their communications. The winter was severe, and the French and English, especially the latter, suffered from great hardships, from cold and disease; but they succeeded in establishing themselves more and more firmly, braving, in a corner of the Crimea, all the forces of the empire of the Tsars.

Toward the last of January Omer Pasha decided to bring forty-five thousand of his Danubian army to the Crimea, and, on the tenth of February, twenty thousand Turks had already reached Eupatoria, from which point they could, with comparative ease, trouble Simferopol or Perekop. When advices of the landing of the Turks at Eupatoria reached the Emperor Nicholas, he commanded General Wrangel to invest the town. A portion of the army of the South under Prince Mikhail Gortchakof was added to his forces. Nicholas was not satisfied, however, with a mere blockade; he sent an imperative order to take the place by assault, in order to avenge upon the Turks of Omer Pasha the insult inflicted by this invasion of the sacred soil of Russia.

General Wrangel made a careful survey of the town, which had been strengthened and fortified under the direction of two French officers. He reported, on the eighth of February, that an attack upon Eupatoria would be unlikely to succeed. But General Khrulef, the commandant of the artillery, declared that he would guarantee a successful assault if the charge of it were conferred upon him. Prince Menshikof, who was as impatient as the Tsar, immediately gave General Khrulef the necessary authority. He divided his twenty thousand men into three columns, which, on the night of the sixteenth of February, formed about four kilometers from Eupatoria, while hundreds of laborers threw up hasty earthworks to protect the artillery. Early in the morning they opened a vigorous cannonade from sixty-six pieces, and at ten o'clock the first assault was given by the left wing. It failed completely. General Khrulef had not the audacity to order the other two columns to rush into certain destruction. His first onset caused a loss of nearly eight hundred men. The failure of this attempt to drive the Turks into the sea was so severe a blow to Prince Menshikof, who had promised again and again to lead the Russian armies to a glorious success, that he resigned his position, and was succeeded by Prince Mikhail Gortchakof, the brother of the general who held important commands at Alma and Inkermann. While the allies were digging trenches, boring mines, and multiplying the batteries in front of Sevastopol, the Russian engineers, under the direction of Todleben, strengthened the town fortifications and built new ones, — the Transbalkan, Selinghinsk, Volhynia, and Kamtchatka redoubts, — which sprang up almost like magic, and caused the allies wonder and admiration. The chances of taking the city by storm seemed less and less, when, suddenly, the news of the Emperor's death came to Sevastopol, and brought some hope that peace might be immediately re-established.

On the twenty-sixth of December, eighteen hundred and twenty-five, Nicholas had been consecrated, in the blood of conspirators, the armed apostle of the principle of authority, the exterminating angel of the counter-revolution. This position he had held for thirty years, not without glory. He had subdued the Polish, Hungarian, and Rumanian revolutions, and prevented Prussia from yielding to the seductions of the German revolution, and to the appeals of disaffection in Holstein. He had, if not humiliated, at least troubled the French revolution in all its legal phases, — July royalty, republic, and empire. He had saved the Austrian Empire, and hindered the creation of a democratic German empire. He stationed himself wherever the contrary principle made its appearance. People surnamed him the Don Quixote of autocracy: like Cervantes' hero, he possessed a chivalrous, generous, and disinterested spirit; but, like him too, he represented a superannuated principle in a new world. His part of chief of a chimerical Holy Alliance became more visibly an anachronism, day by day. Since eighteen hundred and forty-eight, particularly, the "aspirations" of the people were in direct contradiction to his theories of patriarchal despotism. This opposition was apparent throughout Europe. The Tsar's prestige began to suffer. In Russia he still contrived to sustain it: his successes in Turkey, Persia, the Caucasus, Poland, and Hungary, and the apparent deference of the European princes, permitted him to play his part of Agamemnon among kings. Russia thought its external greatness was sufficient compensation for its internal subjection. People forgot to exclaim at the interference of the police, at the fetters imposed on the press, at the intellectual isolation of Russia, and they renounced the control of government, diplomacy, war, and administration. The hard-working monarch, they thought, would foresee all, watch over all, and bring all to a happy conclusion. The men with liberal "aspirations," the discontented and critical spirits, were not listened to. In reply to the objections timidly expressed by a few was urged the monarch's success. It seemed to justify absolute confidence in the government, and relinquishment of themselves.

The disasters in the East caused a terrible awakening. The invincible fleets of Russia were forced to take refuge in the ports, or to retreat into the harbor of Sevastopol. The army was vanquished at the Alma by the allies, at Silistria by the much-despised Turks. Fifty thousand Westerns installed under Sevastopol were insulting the majesty of the empire. The immense superiority of the navy of the allies allowed them to attack Russia in all its seas; Odessa had been bombarded;

the Russian settlements on the coasts of the Caucasus, Redut-Kalé and Sukum-Kalé, had been burned by the Russians themselves. In the Baltic, Kronstadt was blockaded; Sveaborg was bombarded. In the White Sea the fortified monastery of Solovetski was attacked. In the Sea of Okhotsk the Siberian ports were blockaded; the arsenal of Petropavlovsk was destroyed, and their position on the Amur was threatened. The allies of old had failed. Prussia was allowing matters to take their own course; Austria was openly playing the traitor. The silence of the press had, during thirty years, favored the thefts of the government officials; the fortresses and the armies had been ruined beforehand by administrative corruption. The nation had expected everything of the government, and the Crimean war appeared as an immense bankruptcy of autocracy; the absolute and patriarchal monarchy stopped payment at the demands of the Anglo-French invasion. The greater men's hopes had been, — the more people expected the conquest of Constantinople, the upheaval of the East, the extension of the Slav Empire, the deliverance of Jerusalem, — the harder and more cruel was the awakening. Then a vast movement was felt in Russia. Tongues were unloosed, and in default of the press an immense manuscript literature was secretly distributed. The government was pelted with unexpected charges, accusing the Emperor, the ministers, the administration, the diplomatists, the generals, every one at once. "Arise, O Russia!" said one of these anonymous pamphlets. "Devoured by enemies, ruined by slavery, shamefully oppressed by the stupidity of *tchinovniki* and spies, awaken from thy long sleep of ignorance and apathy! We have been kept long enough in serfage by the successors of the Tartar khans. Arise, and stand erect and calm, before the throne of the despot; demand of him a reckoning for the national misfortunes. Tell him boldly that his throne is not the altar of God, and that God has not condemned us forever to be slaves. Russia, O Tsar, confided to thee the supreme power, and thou wert to her as a god upon earth. And what hast thou done? Blinded by passion and ignorance, thou hast sought nothing but power; thou hast forgotten Russia. Thou hast consumed thy life in reviewing troops, in altering uniforms, in signing the legislative projects of ignorant charlatans. Thou hast created a despicable race of censors of the press, that thou mightst sleep in peace, and never know the wants, never hear the murmurs, of thy people, never listen to the voice of truth. Truth! thou hast buried her; thou hast rolled a great stone before the door of her sepulchre, thou hast placed a strong guard round her tomb, and in the exultation of thine heart thou hast said, 'For her, no resurrection!' Now, on the third day, Truth has risen; she has come forth from among the dead. Advance, O Tsar! appear at the bar of God and of history! Thou hast mercilessly trodden Truth under thy feet, thou hast refused liberty, at the same time that thou wast enslaved by thine own passions. By thy pride and obstinacy thou hast exhausted Russia; thou hast armed the world against her. Humiliate thyself before thy brothers. Bow thy haughty forehead in the dust, implore pardon, ask counsel; throw thyself into the arms of thy people. There is no other way of salvation for thee." More than once toward the end of his life the Tsar was seized with doubts, but this advocate of absolute power could not make atonement. "My successor," he said, "may do what he will; I cannot change." He could not change, he could only disappear. He was a man of another age, an anachronism in the new Europe. When, from his villa of Peterhof, he could follow the manœuvres of the enemy's fleet, when he heard raised against him the voice of the hitherto silent nation, then this proud heart bled — the "iron Emperor" was broken. He longed to die. The failure of the attack upon Eupatoria was a mortal blow. On the twenty-seventh of February, eighteen hundred and fifty-five, having at the time a bad influenza, he went out without his great-coat to review his guard. It was a damp day, with the cold at twenty-three degrees Centigrade. His doctor,

Karrel, tried to restrain him. "You have fulfilled your duty," replied the Emperor, "let me do mine." Other imprudences aggravated his illness. He gave his last instructions to his heir, and himself dictated the despatch which he sent to all the great towns of Russia, — "The Emperor is dying." On the eighteenth of February, or, in accordance with the new style, the second of March, he died.

CHAPTER VIII.

THE CRIMEAN WAR.

1855–1856.

ACCESSION OF ALEXANDER.—END OF THE CRIMEAN WAR.—TREATY OF PARIS.

ACCESSION OF ALEXANDER.

ALEXANDER SECOND was born on the twenty-ninth of April, eighteen hundred and eighteen. His mother was Alexandra Feodorovna, the Princess Charlotte of Prussia, daughter of Friedrich Wilhelm the Second. The poet Zhukovski, his tutor, instructed him in the ancient languages; he was taught to speak French and German, and particular attention was paid to Russian. Zhukovski implanted in him a love for his country and liberal ideas. He interested him early in the subject of emancipation. His Empress mother cultivated the sympathetic side of his nature, while Nicholas, his father, who was kindly and tender in the family, subjected him to the stern discipline of a soldier. In his youth he was initiated into the science of government and taught practical armory.

At the age of sixteen Alexander reached his majority, and on the fourth of May, eighteen hundred and thirty-four, took the oath of succession in the chapel of the Winter Palace. He became the Emperor's first adjutant, Hetman of the Cossacks, commandant of the guard of lancers, and Chancellor of the University of Finland. His duty as adjutant obliged him to accompany his imperial father on journeys of review and inspection. At the age of twenty he travelled in Germany with Count Orlof, and was received with the honor befitting his rank. At the court of Hesse-Darmstadt he selected for his wife the accomplished Wilhelmine Maximiliane Marie, daughter of the Grand Duke Louis the Second. The wedding took place on April twenty-eighth, eighteen hundred and forty-one, the Princess assuming the Greek religion and the name of Maria Alexandrovna.

In eighteen hundred and fifty Alexander journeyed through the South of Russia, visiting the battle-field of Poltava, passing through New Russia and Bessarabia to Nikolaïef, to Sevastopol and the Caucasus. He was received in Tiflis with most imposing ceremonies. The population came out to meet him in gay apparel and bearing floral offerings. At night the city was illuminated, the fountains flowed with wine, the mountain Artebar, opposite, was adorned with a temple of flame on which glowed his name, streams of fire in many colors dashed down the mountain-side, and the river Kura was one blaze of light. He had at this time an opportunity to apply his military knowledge. He gained a victory over the Tcherkesui, and won the decoration of the George order.

When Alexander ascended the throne of Russia he was already thirty-seven years of age. His father, only a few hours before his death, said to him: " All my care, all my endeavors, have been directed for Russia's welfare. I was anxious to continue to labor so that I might leave you the empire steadfast and orderly, safe against dangers from without, thoroughly prosperous and at peace. But you see at what a time and under what circumstances I am dying. God has willed it so. You will find the burden hard to bear." It was Alexander's duty to preserve the honor and integrity of his empire. Almost all Europe was opposed to him. A burdensome war was bequeathed to him. His treasury was depleted. The people were anxious for peace, and the dying Nicholas had caught the murmurs of uneasiness and had heard the demand for sweeping reform. The new Emperor issued the following manifesto to the nation when he assumed the rule: "We, Alexander the Second, by the grace of God Emperor and Autocrat of all the Russians, King of Poland, etc., notify all our faithful subjects that it has pleased God in his unsearchable wisdom to overwhelm us all with an unexpected terrible blow. Our beloved father, the Emperor Nikolai Pavlovitch, has this day, February eighteenth, departed this life after a short but severe illness which towards the last developed with incredible rapidity. No words can express our grief, which is shared by all our faithful subjects. While we submit to the mysterious dispensations of Divine Providence, from the same source alone do we seek consolation and hope to be given the strength to bear the burdens which have been laid upon us. As our beloved father, of sorrowful memory, devoted all his efforts every hour of his life to caring for the welfare of his subjects, so also do we in this sad and solemnly important moment, as we assume our hereditary thrones of the Russian Empire, of the Kingdom of Poland inseparable from the same, and of the Grand Principality of Finland, take, in the presence of the invisible God who rules our destinies, the holy vow, constantly to hold before our eyes, as our sole aim, the welfare of our Fatherland. And may Providence, who has chosen us for this high calling, so guide and protect us that we may preserve Russia at the highest point of power and glory, and accomplish the designs and wishes of our illustrious ancestors, — Peter, Catherine, Alexander the Blest, and our father of imperishable memory. The tried zeal of our beloved subjects, their ardent prayers uniting with ours before the throne of the Almighty, will be our support."

This manifesto, which closed with a command to the Russian people to take the oath of allegiance to the Emperor and his heir-apparent, Nikolai Alexandrovitch, was sent to Moscow and also to the imperial ministers abroad, who were instructed by the chancellor Nesselrode in regard to Alexander's designs. He desired to protect Russian integrity and honor, and at the same time to bring the war to a close as speedily as possible. Freedom of worship and the welfare of the Christian population of the East were to be guaranteed. The Danubian principalities were to be secured in their privileges, free navigation of the Danube established, and an end was to be put to the rivalry of the great powers, so as to prevent a recurrence of the disturbances in the East.

In spite of Alexander's proclamation, in which he proposed to accomplish the designs and wishes of his illustrious ancestors, the funds arose on all the exchanges of Europe. It was well known that Russia was anxious for peace. The Emperor, however, addressed the diplomatic corps at his court in a way that showed that he would accept no dishonorable conditions: "I declare solemnly before you, gentlemen, that I shall remain true to all my father's convictions and persist in clinging to the political principles which served as a line of conduct for my uncle the Emperor Alexander and my father. These principles are those of the Holy Alliance; if this Alliance no longer exists it is assuredly not my father's fault. His designs were always open and straightforward, and if they were here and there misjudged, doubtless God and history will render him full justice. I am entirely willing to give my hand to an understanding under the conditions which he had adopted. I also am anxious for peace. I wish to put an end to the horrors of the war. But should the conference opened at Vienna have a result incompatible with our honor, I shall renew the conflict, together with my faithful Russia, and I will then rather go to destruction than yield." But the new sovereign knew better than any one how little the ambitious projects of Peter and Catherine were appropriate to the difficult circumstances in which he was placed. It was rumored that a serious quarrel estranged the Emperor from his brother Konstantin, who was supposed to be more inclined to war than the former; and when this found no confirmation, it was whispered that

Alexander was acting not from his own impulse, but under Konstantin's instigation. All such rumors were stopped by the action which Alexander took in appointing his brother High Admiral of the Russian navy, with unrestricted powers. He made him, also, Regent in case he should die before his son Nikolai attained his majority.

On the fifteenth of March, eighteen hundred and fifty-five, the representatives of England, France, Austria, Turkey, and Russia met in Vienna. The demands of the allies were based upon the four points which had already been under consideration. These were: That Russia abandon the control over Moldavia, Valakhia, and Serbia; give up its claim to control the mouths of the Danube; agree that all treaties allowing it a preponderance in the Black Sea should be abrogated; and, finally, renounce the exclusive protectorate of the Christians in the Ottoman dominions. Baron Bourqueney, the representative of France, wished so to limit the Tsar's power that Prince Alexander Gortchakof, who was at first inclined to be yielding, felt that the demands were exorbitant, and asked time to refer to the Tsar. But when the proposal to close the Black Sea was refused, the representatives of England, France, and Turkey declared that their instructions forbade them to go farther. Titof, the second Russian ambassador, tried to show it was not from the Russian side that the obstacles to a settlement arose. In this he was seconded by Gortchakof, who claimed that proof positive of Russia's singleness of intention was furnished by its willingness to agree either to the opening the Black Sea to all ships of war, or to the closing it to all ships of war. Nearly a month of inactivity ensued, during which notes were exchanged, and Count Nesselrode pointed out officially that the fruitlessness of the conference was entirely the fault of the western powers. The fourteenth and last session took place on the fourth of June, when it was proposed to consider certain new propositions of Count Buol-Schauenstein's, who was indefatigable in his zeal to bring about an agreement. France and England, however, declined to discuss them, considering that Russia's refusal to reduce its active forces was a practical answer to the proposal. The conference accordingly came to an end, and the only advantage it produced was in showing clearly the relationship in which the great powers were to each other. Austria, in December, eighteen hundred and fifty-four, had agreed to defend the Principalities against Russia, and Prussia had undertaken to assist Austria; but in this conference Prussia was disgusted by the quibbles and chicanery which had prevented any satisfactory result, and consequently had prevented Austria from vigorously espousing the cause of France and England. Moreover, the rejection of Buol-Schauenstein's propositions somewhat piqued Austria, and the Emperor Francis Joseph, alleging financial reasons, withdrew sixty thousand of his forces from Galicia, so that Russia felt justified in transferring its Galician army to the Crimea. It began to be suspected in England that Austria was in league with Russia, and although the Clarendon ministry succeeded in disproving this, there nevertheless remained a considerable party who believed that nothing but unfavorable circumstances prevented the declaration of war.

END OF THE CRIMEAN WAR.

On the sixteenth of April Napoleon and the Empress Eugénie paid a visit to Queen Victoria. Nothing was left undone to show honor to the distinguished visitors, and the good feeling which existed between the two nations was much enhanced. The visit was returned in the middle of August, and the alliance still more strongly cemented by the hospitalities which the French Emperor showed to Victoria and the Prince Consort.

Meanwhile the Crimean war continued. Victor Emmanuel, King of the Sardinian States, had become bound by a military treaty signed at Turin on the twenty-sixth of January, to furnish an army of fifteen thousand men in case the war against Russia should be prosecuted. The first division, numbering about seven thousand men, together with officers and stores, set sail for the Crimea in May. They were warmly welcomed by their allies, and were assigned a camping-ground to the west of the French.

During the months of March and April numerous encounters took place between the besiegers and the Russians, while each party tried to strengthen its defences. The Russians occupied many rifle-pits, by means of which they annoyed those who were constructing the zigzags and parallels. On the seventeenth of March the whole British force was put under arms, and a tremendous struggle ensued, in which the French bore the brunt of the attack, but did not succeed in driving the enemy back from their rifle-pits. Two days later Admiral Istomin, commander of the Karabelnaïa, was killed by a cannon-ball, and was laid in the Cathedral of St. Vladimir, beside Kornilof. On the night of the twenty-second, which was windy and dark, a body of fifteen thousand Russians made a double sortie from Sevastopol, one column being directed against the French to the northeast of the Mamelon, and the other against the left wing of the English. The assault was so vigorous and sudden that the French had to leave their trenches, but afterwards, being reinforced, they captured them again. This sortie was exceedingly bloody, and was called an Inkermann on a small scale. The Russians hoped by means of it to destroy the works directed against the Malakof, which was now the point of attack, being justly considered the key to Sevastopol. The Russian loss was about thirteen hundred; the French perhaps half as many.

The October bombardment had not been renewed. After an enormous number of projectiles were hurled upon the town, doing considerable damage to life and property, it was decided that Sevastopol could be taken only by siege. Consequently for nearly half a year nothing was done beyond the occasional repulse of sorties, and the regular investment of the town. On the ninth of April the second bombardment began. For many days in succession all the batteries of the allies poured a stream of red-hot shot, bombs, and cannon-balls against the walls and other defences of the town. On the first day twenty thousand projectiles were thrown by two hundred and fifty guns. The weather was unpropitious. Lord Raglan's despatch to the English ministry said : " Much rain had fallen in the course of the night, and it continued during the day, accompanied by a tempestuous wind and a heavy mist which obscured everything and rendered it impossible to ascertain with any degree of accuracy the effect of the fire." All day long the bombardment was carried on. Dr. William H. Russell thus describes the scene at the close of the day : —

"The sun descended into a rift in the dark gray pall which covered the sky, and cast a pale yellow slice of light, barred here and there by columns of rain and masses of curling vapor, across the line of batteries. The outlines of the town, faintly rendered through the mists of smoke and rain, seemed quivering inside the circling lines of fire around familiar outlines, — the green cupola and roofs, long streets and ruined suburbs, the dock-yard buildings, trenches, and batteries."

From the ninth to the twentieth the Russians had suffered a loss of six thousand one hundred and thirty men, the French fifteen hundred and eighty-five, the English two hundred and sixty-five. On the Tsar's birthday a Te Deum was sung in the Cathedral and a salvo of one hundred and one guns was fired against the enemy in honor of the occasion.

But the second bombardment, like the first, in spite of the enormous consumption of powder and shot, was on the whole a failure. It caused much loss of life, but the material damage done was easily repaired. On the first of May the French by a gallant attack captured all of the Russian rifle-pits near the Central Bastion on the southwest side of the city. The next day the Russians, several thousand strong, attempted to regain the important position which they had lost, but they were driven back. Their killed and wounded were about nine hundred, while the French lost nearly eight hundred.

On the fifth, ninth, and eleventh of May the Russians made desperate sorties, in which the British parallels were the points of attack; but nothing resulted from them except loss of life. On the twenty-second a tremendous conflict took place between the French and the Russians. The Russians, anxious to make good the position lost at the beginning of the month, set large numbers of men to construct lines of gabions between the Quarantine Battery and the Central Bastion, enclosing a considerable surface outside of the town defences, and threatening the French rear. It was seen by the French commander that these works must be stopped at all hazards, and at nine o'clock in the evening two strong bodies of men were sent out to make simultaneous attacks in different places. The Russians were in full force, as if awaiting an attack. During the whole night the battle raged, the ground being contested step by step. Time after time the ambuscades near the Quarantine changed hands. The attack made by the French right wing was a failure; they were completely overwhelmed by the superiority of the Russian fire. The French, however, were successful on the left, and the lines of gabions were transferred into defences against the Russians. On the night of the twenty-third the attempt was renewed, and this time with success. The French penetrated so far within the Russian lines that it was deemed safer to withdraw; which they did after destroying a strong battery behind a previously unknown fortification. The Russian loss was upwards of five thousand.

On the sixteenth of May Canrobert telegraphed to Napoleon; "My health and my mind, overwhelmed by a constant strain, do not allow me longer to bear the burden of a great responsibility. My duty towards my sovereign and my country compels me to ask you to transfer the chief command to General Pélissier, a skilful and experienced leader." Three days afterwards Canrobert was relieved by the Emperor's orders.

Aimable Jean Jacques Pélissier was of an Irish family long settled in France. He was a soldier from his childhood, and had served with distinction in Africa. He now succeeded to the chief command of the French forces, and announced that he would take Sevastopol. By reinforcement, his army now amounted to one hundred and twenty thousand men. The British had their full complement of thirty thousand; the Turks had about fifty thousand, and fifteen thousand Sardinians, under Alphonso de la Marmora, had just arrived, raising the total number of the allies to two hundred thousand, — a number too large for effective operations. The whole force of the Russians in the Crimea had been reduced to one half of that number. Pélissier had hardly assumed his command before a naval expedition was planned and carried out with success by the allies. About sixty men-of-war carrying a force of fourteen thousand eight hundred infantry, besides various corps of cavalry, artillery, marines, and engineers, set sail on the twenty-third of May for the Strait of Kertch. The Russians, seeing the approach of so strong a fleet, blew up Fort Pavel, between Kertch and Ienikale, and evacuated the town of Kertch, setting fire to many granaries and burning the steamers in the harbor. The allied troops under Sir George Brown and General d'Autemarre, having disembarked, advanced and took possession of the town, nowhere meeting the enemy, and simply destroying some military establishments. General Wrangel, on leaving Kertch, had burned many tons of corn and flour to prevent them from falling into the hands of the allies. Captain Lyons, on the twenty-fourth, anchored just beyond range from Ienikale, and saw the Russians blow up their magazine, containing more than thirty thousand kilos of powder. The next day, many of their batteries having also been dismantled, he was enabled to clear a passage into the Sea of Azof, where, in three days, he announced that he had destroyed more than a hundred vessels belonging to the Russian government. Much property was also annihilated along the shores. Lyons sent a despatch to the home government to the effect that he had captured seventeen thousand tons of coal and one hundred cannon, destroyed nearly two hundred and fifty vessels, and rendered unavailable at Berdiansk and Genitchesk six million rations of corn and flour. Early in June the fleet sailed against Taganrog, a town very difficult to approach owing to the shallowness of the bay. Lyons sent a demand to surrender, which was refused, whereupon the hostile fleet began the bombardment. The custom-house and various government buildings were set on fire, and much private property was destroyed. Mariopol, a corn-exporting place, was next attacked, and the same work of destruction accomplished. The Russians were cut off from every base of supplies with the exception of Perekop. They evacuated Anapa on the fifth of June, after exploding the powder-magazine, spiking the guns, and burning the stores of coal and grain. A Turkish garrison was stationed in the town, and by them the Circassians were urged to revolt.

While these destructive but not specially glorious operations were being conducted in the Sea of Azof, the siege of Sevastopol was vigorously prosecuted under the new and energetic general. The Russians still maintained themselves, daily increasing their defences and bringing into the city immense quantities of provisions and military stores. The previous bombardment had destroyed many hundred houses; the theatre was in ruins; there was not a building that had not suffered; the streets were ploughed up by cannon-balls and filled with barricades.

Early in June a council of war was held by the allies, and it was determined to open the third bombardment on the afternoon of the sixth, and when it should reach its maximum violence, to make a threefold attack on the defences of the Russians. The French were to undertake the capture of the White Works or the redoubts on Mount Sapun, and also the Mamelon or Green Hill, separated from the former by the so-called Careening ravine; the English were to attempt the Quarries facing the Redan, and separated from the Mamelon by the Karabelnaïa ravine. The cannonade continued until the afternoon of the seventh, when the assault was to be attempted. The troops were at their posts; twelve battalions of Turks were to serve as a reserve corps and protect the heights of Inkermann. Lord Raglan took his station on Cathcart's Hill; General Pélissier, from the Victoria redoubt, was to fire six rockets as the signal for the simultaneous attack to be made. At quarter of seven the rockets were sent up, and with cheers the three divisions dashed across the open spaces between their trenches and the works to be taken. The Quarries were found almost undefended, but fully half a dozen unsuccessful attempts to regain them were made by the Russians.

General Bosquet was intrusted with the French attack. At the signal the troops under fire from the Mamelon, the Malakof, and the Redan quickly advanced against the first, scrambled up the parapet, fought their way through the embrasures, and captured the redoubt, contesting it inch by inch with a Russian corps which had been concealed behind the Mamelon. Once, indeed, they were driven down the hill by a powerful body of Russians, and would have lost their advantage had not the reserves, under Brunet, supported them. The Mamelon remained in the hands of the French, and was immediately turned against its former possessors. Its name was changed to the Brancion Redoubt, after Colonel de Brancion, who was the first to plant the eagle on the redoubt, and who fell in the assault. The French attack on the White Works was quick, bloody, and successful. The Russians were obliged to abandon the Volhynian and Selinghinsk redoubts, thereby losing control of the Careening Bay and an important road connecting Inkermann with the city. During these three days the French suffered a loss of more than five thousand, the Russians of more than six thousand men, among whom was General Timoféïef, who had led the great sortie against the French left wing at the battle of Inkermann.

General Pélissier held another council of war on the fifteenth, and laid before Lord Raglan, Omer Pasha and General de la Marmora his plan for an assault on the eighteenth, the anniversary of the battle of Waterloo. It was agreed that the cannonade should open early on the morning of the seventeenth, and continue for several hours into the next day, at the end of which time the French were to attack the Malakof, and the English the Redan.

Thirty-six hours before the assault General Bosquet, who had offended Pélissier in some trifling matter, was ordered to transfer his command to General Regnaud de Saint-Jean d'Angély. It was a grave mistake. The new commander had too little time to study the ground, he was unacquainted with his troops, and they with him. Bosquet was sent to the valley of the Tchernaïa to take command of a body of twenty-five thousand men.

About four o'clock on the morning of the seventeenth the batteries opened fire along the whole line, from the Quarantine to the mouth of the Tchernaïa. The cannonade continued all day. At night the battery of the Barracks, the Great Redan, Malakof, and many other of the Russian works were badly beaten down; but in spite of the loss of life under the deadly fire, the garrison bravely kept at work repairing the damages. Sevastopol had a working force of forty-three thousand infantry, and eleven thousand attached to the artillery service. About half of these men were employed in the Karabelnaïa suburb under the supervision of General Khrulef. General Pavlof commanded the infantry.

The signal for the assault was to be given by a rocket from

the Victoria redoubt at three o'clock in the morning of the eighteenth. General Khrulef, suspecting that a decisive action was about to ensue, had his troops all stationed as early as two o'clock. But Pélissier, at midnight, had not left his headquarters to take his position on the Victoria redoubt. The Russian battalions were all at their posts, nine in the Malakof, as many more in the Grand Redan and its subordinate batteries, when, finally, Pélissier mounted his horse to accomplish the long ride before him. But he had not ridden far before suddenly the roar of cannon and the rattle of musketry were heard. General Mayran, whose duty it was to attack the works flanking the northeast of the Malakof, mistook the fuse of a shell for the rocket which Pélissier was to fire. The two brigades of his division dashed forward in the face of a raking fire which soon stopped them. General Mayran himself fell mortally wounded, and was succeeded by General de Failly.

When Pélissier arrived at the Victoria redoubt, he found Lord Raglan had been waiting for him an hour. The signal was now regularly given. Brunet's division, which also had been delayed, now boldly attacked the north side of the Malakof. At the first onset the general himself was killed, and though the men succeeded in crossing the three hundred meters which lay between them and the battery, they were so broken by the galling fire that they had to retreat. D'Autemarre, with two battalions, succeeded in gaining possession of the Gervais battery and a group of houses standing near the Malakof. But the Russians, having repulsed the attacks on the other side, now turned their whole attention to the left flank, and after a gallant resistance D'Autemarre was forced to withdraw. The English also suffered from the terrible fire of the Russians, and after two unsuccessful attempts were obliged to give up the capture of the Redan. Major General Eyre distinguished himself by gaining a portion of the very suburb of the city, where, in the shelter of several houses, he maintained himself the whole day.

On the nineteenth the allies, for the first time during the siege, asked for a truce. The loss of both sides had been enormous. The Russians counted five thousand four hundred and forty-six, of whom all but fifteen hundred were the result of the bombardment. General Todleben was wounded in the head. The English lost nearly two thousand, among whom were Sir John Campbell, who was killed; Sir George Brown, General Eyre, and Harry Jones, who were wounded. The French killed, wounded, and missing amounted to more than three thousand five hundred.

This unfortunate day nearly cost Pélissier the chief command. The Emperor ordered Marshal Vaillant to send a despatch to the Crimea putting General Niel in Pélissier's place. But the minister of war, being convinced that it would be ruinous to remove Pélissier, took it upon himself to send the despatch by mail rather than by telegraph. The next day the Emperor was persuaded that Vaillant was right, and the letter was countermanded when it had reached no farther than to Marseilles. Pélissier retained the chief command, and General Bosquet returned to the right wing.

After the defeat of the eighteenth of June much sickness broke out in the allied armies. Nearly a sixth of the French forces were in the hospitals. Lord Raglan, overwhelmed with fatigue and chagrin at his ill success, fell a victim to the cholera, and died on the twenty-eighth. He was succeeded by General James Simpson, who had been sent by Lord Palmerston on a mission of investigation. One of the last acts of the Emperor Nicholas had been to decree that every month of service in the Crimea should count as a year. It was only an act of justice to the brave army of defence, who, in spite of their success in June, saw that the toils of the enemy were approaching closer and closer. General Todleben lay with his leg badly injured by a cannon-ball, and from his couch still directed the work of defence. Nakhimof, on the eleventh of July, was observing the French works from the summit of the Malakof, when a bullet struck him in the head. He lived only two days. The Russian army suffered from lack of provisions. The destruction of the granaries on the Sea of Azof, and the occupation of Kertch and Ienikale, obliged them to bring grain from a distance of a thousand kilometers, over roads that were so nearly impassable that a large part of the provisions were often consumed before they reached their destination. All of these disasters and difficulties showed that a crisis was approaching. This was still more plainly proved on the sixth of August, when, under the direction of General Buchmeyer, a floating bridge across the harbor, nine hundred and eighteen meters long and five meters wide, was begun. This bridge, connecting Fort Nikolaï with Fort Mikhail, was completed in three weeks, and assured the garrison a retreat in case of need.

On the ninth of August Prince Gortchakof assembled a council of war by which the question was discussed, whether it would be best to continue the passive defence of Sevastopol with no distinct end in view, and only in order to gain time or to take a vigorous offensive against the enemy. General Khrulef wished to engage in the most radical system of offensive warfare, either by making a general sortie from the Karabelnaïa against the Victoria redoubt and the Green Mamelon, or by destroying the city and attacking the allied army with all the Russian forces. General Osten-Sacken was in favor of evacuating the city and taking some other place to defend. Todleben, who was at Belbek, laid up with his wounds, being asked his opinion, spoke strongly against any such measures, seeing that the enemy were far superior in numbers. But General Vrevski, who had been sent from Saint Petersburg especially to urge a decisive action, was so strenuous in his views, that finally Prince Gortchakof decided to attack the allies on the Tchernaïa River. He had, however, small hope of success. The day before he gave his orders he wrote to Prince Dolgoruki, Minister of War: "There is no doubt about it, I am attacking the enemy under wretched circumstances. His position is very strong: upon his right hand Mount Hasford, almost perpendicular, and well fortified; upon his left, the Fediukhin heights, at the foot of which runs a deep canal with steep banks and filled with water, which cannot be crossed except upon bridges which must be built under the direct fire of the enemy. If things go wrong it will not be my fault. I have done my best, but the task has been too difficult ever since I came to the Crimea."

On the evening of the fifteenth of August the Russian corps camped on the heights of Mackenzie were ordered to be ready to attack the enemy at daybreak. The French general, D'Allonville, who was constantly on the watch for any movement among the Russians, immediately notified Pélissier that an attack was imminent. General Herbillon, with seventeen thousand eight hundred and fifty-eight men and forty-eight cannon, was encamped on the left bank of the Tchernaïa, occupying the Fediukhin heights. The Sardinian army, amounting to about nine thousand men, was on Mount Hasford, with thirty-six field-pieces. Gortchakof's whole effective force was seventy thousand, and the march from the heights of Mackenzie to the bridge of Traktir, or the Tavern, occupied the entire night, although the distance was only six or eight kilometers. A thick fog made the darkness almost impenetrable. Gortchakof's plan was to divide his army into three portions, the cavalry and a part of the artillery remaining as a reserve, with two divisions of infantry, in the middle of the undulating plain, while General Read attacked the French, and General Liprandi the Sardinian position. The reserves could then be made effective to complete a partial victory on either hand. Under the cover of the fog the two divisions of Liprandi endeavored to surprise the outposts on the heights of Shuliu. They succeeded in gaining the heights of Tchorgun, where they posted a battery directed against Mount Hasford. Toward five o'clock in the morning the atmosphere cleared, and the grouping of the various forces became apparent. Gortchakof was about to make Mount Hasford his principal point of attack, when, without waiting for the order to begin the battle, General Read crossed the Tchernaïa and tried to storm the Fediukhin heights. The right wing drove the French from the Redan which faced the Traktir bridge, but were completely routed by Zouaves and Turcos of General Camou, and driven across the river again. Meanwhile the centre, passing the narrow but deep aqueduct by means of flying bridges, began to press heavily against the weakened division of General Faucheux, which was relieved, just in time, by three battalions sent by General Camou. The Russians were driven back across the canal and the river. The bridge remained in the hands of the French. Liprandi was now called down from the heights of Tchorgun, and the reserves were brought into action.

The French had eighteen field-pieces on the Fediukhin heights, which, instead of replying to Gortchakof's batteries, concentrated their fire upon the Russian infantry massed near the Traktir bridge. Nevertheless, the bridge was again gained, the canal crossed, and, for the third time, the Russian infantry dashed up the face of the slope. Again the French came down against them like an avalanche. For a few moments there was a fierce struggle, but it was in vain. The Russians began to give way, and soon their rout was complete. The aqueduct and the Tchernaïa were choked with wounded and dying. Many were drowned. Generals Wranken, Veimarn, and Tulubief were severely wounded. General Read was killed by a bursting bomb, and General Vrevski, as he was standing by Prince Gortchakof, had his head carried off by a cannon-ball. The battle of the Traktir had failed. About nine o'clock, while cannon-shots were still exchanged, the Russian army began its retreat. It was far into the afternoon before the last company had disappeared.

On the following day the French and English batteries

began in concert a heavy cannonading, which was directed against the defences of the Karabelnaïa. It crumbled the parapets, and dislodged the batteries; it killed the garrison at the rate of a thousand men every four-and-twenty hours. Meanwhile the sappers and miners worked steadily at their dangerous task of advancing the parallels nearer and nearer to the Malakof. About one o'clock, on the night of August twenty-ninth, seven thousand kilograms of powder and three hundred and fifty large bombshells accidentally exploded at once in the Brancion redoubt. Masses of stones, trunks of trees, and fragments of iron were scattered about in all directions, into the Karabelnaïa, beyond the docks and among the English trenches. Glass was broken in Forts Pavel and Nikolai, three kilometers distant. Thirty-one men were killed outright, and more than two hundred were bruised and wounded. The English also numbered several victims of the catastrophe. Nevertheless, amid all the confusion a couple of brave gunners calmly proceeded to fire all the uninjured cannon in the battery opposite the Malakof. In two days the last traces of the accident had disappeared; the immense hole, twenty meters wide, thirty long, and four deep, was filled up, and again converted into a redoubt. As the works of the allied armies approached nearer and nearer to the Russians, their losses became proportionally heavy. Their trenches were swept by the rifle-bullets and cannon-balls sent from the Malakof and the Redan. The Malakof was protected by a palisade of sharpened stakes, above which rose a parapet of earthworks more than six meters high and of great thickness. A ditch seven meters deep and eight meters wide separated this parapet from three tiers of batteries well provided with heavy cannon. Besides the sheltered places for riflemen, there was a large space enclosed for infantry.

The fifth of September was the day set for the final bombardment of Sevastopol. On the eighth the assault was to take place.

The French batteries mounted in all more than six hundred cannon. The English had about two hundred, while, on the other hand, the Russians, according to Rousset, had thirteen hundred and eighty. In accordance with the order, the bombardment began, — the bombardment which Gortchakof characterized as infernal. Rousset thus describes the final scenes: —

"At times the fire diminished, almost ceased, and when the enemy, deceived by these lulls, and, anxiously on the watch for the assault, issued from their covers to mount upon the ramparts, then the allied batteries, suddenly firing in volleys, overwhelmed them with shot and shell. This first day the besieged made desperate but useless efforts to sustain the struggle. The night caused no interruption to this storm of iron and of fire; it gave only a more terrific expression to its fury. The spectacle of this drama had an awful majesty. From the bosom of the Great Harbor, beneath a sky of brilliant red, a column of flame reflected its ruddy glow upon the mountains and the sea as far as the eye could reach. A great transport, the Berezan, hit by a red-hot shell, burned like an enormous beacon to light up the immense spectacle. The two days and nights which followed finished the ruin of what had been Sevastopol. When the Russians, after the peace, returned once more, there remained standing fourteen houses, scattered witnesses of its ancient splendor. From all sides arose the smoke of burning buildings; and on the night of the seventh the black silhouettes of another frigate, and then of a second ship, were seen amid the devouring flames. The frigate held two hundred tuns of alcohol; the fiery jets with which it burned cast a livid tint on the sides of the bastions which were being bombarded. The scene now was terrible, and, according to the Russians themselves, it produced a painful impression on the minds of the defenders of Sevastopol.

"The enclosure of the place was overturned. All that the besieged could do was to embank the powder-magazines, to strengthen the protections, to replace at least a few of the dismounted cannon, and to clear the embrasures; but at the price of what sacrifices! On the seventh it cost forty killed and wounded to maintain one single gun. In the evening, about eleven o'clock, just as two boats from the north shore, with great cargoes of powder, were coming alongside of the city wharf, a rocket fell hissing upon one of them. The explosion had terrific effects. Everything in the vicinity was destroyed. Heavy thirty-six-pounders, hurled into the air, fell again to the earth and killed many persons. The powder thus destroyed was meant for the chambers which had been dug under the cornice of the Malakof. From the seventeenth of August to the fourth of September the garrison of Sevastopol had lost twelve thousand seven hundred men. In the three days which preceded the assault it lost seven thousand five hundred and sixty. During these three weeks the French troops had three thousand eight hundred and fifteen men disabled."

After the battle of Traktir Prince Gortchakof thought seriously of evacuating Sevastopol. On the twenty-fourth of August he wrote to the minister of war that there was not to be found in all his army a single man who would not call it madness longer to continue the defence. A week later his mind underwent a complete change. "I am resolved," he wrote to the same minister on the first of September, — " I am resolved to continue to defend the south side with all our resources, and as long as possible, for it is the only measure left to us." On the eighth of September the garrison of Sevastopol was made up of ninety-six battalions belonging to forty regiments of infantry, of one battalion of sharpshooters, three battalions of sappers, three cohorts of militia, and four thousand gunners from the fleet, the only survivors of the eighteen thousand brave marines who began the defence. The actual number of these troops was about fifty thousand men.

Under the superior authority of Count Osten-Sacken, chief of the whole garrison, General Semiakin commanded in the city. Under him General Khrushtchof was in charge of the defence of the first section, including all between the sea and the Central Bastion. The second section, which comprised the Flagstaff Battery, was under command of General Schultz. General Khrulef commanded in the Karabelnaïa. The three sections of the suburb corresponding to the Great Redan, the Malakof, and the Little Redan were under the orders, respectively, of General Pavlof, General von Bussau, General Sabashinski. The special reserve of Malakof was commanded by General Lisenko.

Every morning since the fifth of September the Russians had been expecting the assault; but as time went by with no crisis, they imagined that the eighth day would pass as the preceding had done, and, when the lunch-hour drew nigh, they for the most part withdrew under the protection of their works.

At eleven o'clock General Pélissier took his position in the Brancion redoubt on the Green Hill. For some two hours the cannonading had been carried on with less violence, but just before twelve it began again with full vigor and lasted twenty minutes; then suddenly it stopped entirely. "The bugles sound, the drums beat, the men are on the double quick. The last parallels have brought them within twenty-five meters of the Malakof, and the Zouaves of the first regiment, with Colonel Collineau at their head, cross the space at a bound. They need neither flying bridges nor ladders; half choked up by the débris of the escarp, the ditch is no longer an obstacle. The slope is mounted; some leap over the parapet; others, under the masks, through the embrasures. The Russians are taken by surprise; the platform in front of the Tower has at first scarce any defenders, with the exception of the gunners, who, armed with ramrods and handspikes, sustain the struggle hand to hand, and are killed, bravely standing by their guns.

The soldiers of the regiment of Modlin have been kept behind their bomb-proofs by the bombardment; now, as they hear the noise of the assault, they hasten forth, but in confusion, in straggling groups, without any fixed purpose. Meanwhile the second battalion of the first Zouaves, then the seventh infantry, led by Colonel Decaen, come to reinforce their comrades. The Russians are driven back, and try to form again behind the first trenches of the fortification. General von Bussau, commander of the redoubt, the colonel of the regiment of Modlin, and most of his officers are killed."

The French flag floated from the parapet of the Malakof. At the Little Redan, after a temporary success, the French were driven out by the Russians. The English, also, attacked the Great Redan, and at first drove back the regiment of Vladimir, which defended it. But the regiments of Kamtchatka, Iakutsk, and Suzdal came to their assistance, and this work was regained by the Russians. Twice the English tried to win it back, and twice were they driven out with terrible slaughter. Everywhere, except at the Malakof, the Russians were successful; but with the loss of that important fortification all was lost. General Pélissier thus described its position: "The fortification of Malakof, which is a sort of citadel made of earth, three hundred and fifty meters long by one hundred and fifty wide, crowns a hill which commands the whole interior of the Karabelnaïa suburb, flanks the Redan attacked by the English, is only twelve hundred meters from the south port, and threatens the only anchorage left to the vessels as well as the only way of retreat open to the Russians, — the bridge of boats which they have thrown from one shore of the harbor to the other." And Malakof was fairly won. About five o'clock Prince Gortchakof gave the order to evacuate the south side of the city. At midnight the barricades were left deserted, and then began the fires and explosions which brought back the memory of Moscow. Throughout the night a steady stream of infantry poured across the bridge;

one after another the forts were blown up, — the Flagstaff and Garden batteries, the Quarantine, Forts Alexander and Nikolai; the fleet was scuttled and sunk, with the exception of the steamers, which were busy in towing across boats laden with stores. At quarter past seven the bridge was severed from the south side, and the Russian army was safe. Dr. William H. Russell expressed the general dissatisfaction with the result of the bombardment and assault, when he wrote as follows to the London Times : —

"This Redan cost us more lives than the capture of Badajoz, without including those who fell in its trenches and approaches; and although the enemy evacuated it, we could scarcely claim the credit of having caused them such loss that they retired owing to their dread of renewed assault. On the contrary, we must in fairness admit that the Russians maintained their hold of the place till the French were established in the Malakof, and the key of the position was torn from their grasp. They might, indeed, have remained in the place longer than they did, as the French were scarcely in a condition to molest them from the Malakof with artillery; but the Russian general possessed too much genius and experience as a soldier to lose men in defending an untenable position, and his retreat was effected with masterly skill and with perfect ease, in the face of a victorious enemy. Covering his rear by the flames of the burning city, and by tremendous explosions which spoke in tones of portentous warning to those who might have wished to cut off his retreat, he led his battalions in narrow files across a deep arm of the sea which ought to have been commanded by our guns, and in the face of a most powerful fleet. He actually paraded them in our sight as they crossed and carried off all his most useful stores and munitions of war. He left us few trophies and many bitter memories. He sank his ships and blew up his forts without molestation; nothing was done to harass him in his retreat, with the exception of some paltry efforts to break down the bridge by cannon-shot or to shell the troops as they marched over."

The Russian loss, on the eighth of September, amounted to nearly thirteen thousand men, while the allies had a total of more than ten thousand killed, wounded, and missing.

On the eleventh the French took possession of the city, while the English established themselves in the Karabelnaïa. A battery was immediately directed to shell the steamboats which had taken refuge in the creeks of the northern side, but before the first shot had been fired the Russians themselves either burnt or scuttled them all.

The allied forces now amounted to about two hundred and twenty-nine thousand men; and Prince Gortchakof, having just received his last reinforcements, was able to oppose to them an army of one hundred and fifty thousand, of which one hundred and fifteen thousand were concentrated in the vicinity of Sevastopol, Baktchi-saraï, and Simferopol. In October, by orders sent from Paris and London, a powerful fleet, under Admirals Bruat and Lyons, was sent along the coast for the purpose of capturing several important fortresses. Kinburn was situated on the bay of the Dnieper, where two large rivers, the Dnieper and the Bug, united their waters. About eleven kilometers from the mouth of the latter is the admiralty town of Nikolaeïf. Kherson, the capital of the government of the Taurid, is situated on the Dnieper. The entrance to the bay is narrow; it was then defended by two forts, — Otchakof on the north, on the south the fortress of Kinburn, situated on a narrow tongue of sand. The fortress, which mounted eighty-eight cannon and held a garrison of fifteen hundred men, was under the command of General Kohanovitch. The fleet came within sight of Odessa, but this city was spared the horrors of a bombardment. On the fourteenth of September they anchored off Kinburn, and preparations were made to storm the fort. The firing began three days later and lasted several hours, when the artillery of the Russians, being completely disabled, ceased to reply. A flag was sent to the commander, and he was allowed to surrender as a prisoner of war. The next day the Russians themselves blew up Fort Otchakof, but they retained the towns of Arabat and Genitchi, and the allied fleet, after leaving a strong garrison at Kinburn, sailed back to the Crimea without having accomplished much of decided importance beyond the destruction of immense quantities of provisions and ship-timber. Napoleon, to be sure, wished to make Kinburn a base of operations, and take possession of the left bank of the Dnieper. The lateness of the season, however, and the knowledge that the Russians would simply withdraw into the depths of the steppes, decided Pélissier against this plan. The English were bent upon driving the Russians entirely from the Crimea, and proposed to make a descent upon Kaffa, and, if possible, capture the Russian stores at Karazubazar; but this also was not listened to by the French. About this time General Simpson was succeeded by General Coddington. The campaign of eighteen hundred and fifty-five dragged along with no actions of importance. The French and English laborers dug some eighty kilometers of trenches. The cannonading after the twenty-sixth of October was suspended by Marshal Pélissier, but was kept up irregularly by the Russians.

On the fifteenth of November a powder-magazine containing fifty thousand kilos of powder, six hundred thousand cartridges, four thousand bombs, and an enormous quantity of rockets and explosives, blew up. Dr. Russell says: " I was riding from headquarters, reading my letters, and had just reached the hill or elevated part of the plateau at the time, and happened to be looking in the very direction of the park when the explosion took place. The phenomena were so startling as to take away one's breath. Neither pen nor pencil could describe them. The earth shook. The strongest houses rocked to and fro. Men felt as if the very ground upon which they stood was convulsed by an earthquake. The impression of these few moments can never be eradicated. One's confidence in the stability of the very earth was staggered. *Suppositos incedimus ignes.* What part of the camp was safe after such a catastrophe? The rush of fire, smoke, and iron, in one great pillar, attained a height I dare not estimate, and then seemed to shoot out like a tree which overshadowed half the camp on the right and rained down missiles upon it. The color of the pillar was dark gray, flushed with red, but it was pitted all over with white puffs of smoke which marked the explosions of the shells. It retained the shape of a fir-tree for nearly a minute, and then the sides began to swell out, and the overhanging canopy to expand and twist about in prodigious wreaths of smoke, which flew out to the right and left, and let drop, as it were, from solution in its embrace, a precipitate of shells, carcasses, and iron projectiles. The noise was terrible, and when the shells began to explode the din was like the opening crash of one of the great cannonades or bombardments of the siege."

The cause of the explosion was not absolutely known. It caused the French a loss of thirty-eight dead and more than a hundred wounded; the English, twenty-one dead and one hundred and sixteen wounded.

The French would willingly have preserved the docks and forts which had been built at enormous expense, and seemed as if intended to outlive time itself. Some of them were hewn out of solid rock. Many of the soldiers were lodged in large buildings, which the Russians had not had time to destroy before they left the city. But toward the middle of January, eighteen hundred and fifty-six, orders came to blow up Fort Nikolai and the great barracks. It was no small work to destroy them. Fort Nikolai required fifty thousand kilos of powder. Colonel Langlois thus described its destruction: "This gigantic mass, which seemed indestructible, we saw uprooted, rise heavily into the air, then its walls, a moment before so beautiful, were thrown down in horrible chaos. All its parts, broken up, crushed, piled together, were shot through by jets of murky fire, accompanied by thunder. The whole thing seemed to come toward us, driven by the wind, through clouds of smoke and dust, the most frightful, the most impenetrable that could be imagined. The attentive ear could hear the crash of the avalanche which followed. In one instant all was over, and of this immense Fort Nikolai there remained only a vast shapeless mound where not a stone nor a fragment could be used as the meanest abode."

After the evacuation of Sevastopol Russia seemed still unwilling to submit. Gortchakof announced to the army assembled on the north side of the harbor that he would "not voluntarily abandon that country where St. Vladimir had received baptism." Alexander, after promising the Muscovite nobles to continue the war for the sake of glory, journeyed to the south, and was at Nikolaïef when Kinburn was taken. He had left behind him an encouraging manifesto to the people. "I take the present and past occurrences," he said, "to be the unsearchable will of Providence, who has brought upon Russia this heavy hour of trial. But Russia has been often tried, and even more severely, and God, the Lord, has always sent his all-holy and invisible aid. So now also will we put our trust in him; he will be a protection and guard to Russia, to orthodox Russia, which has taken up arms for the sake of the right, for the cause of Christianity. Comforting to me are the continual proofs that each and all are ready to sacrifice property, family, and the last drops of lifeblood, in order to sustain the integrity of the empire and the honor of the fatherland. In these feelings and acts of the people I find consolation and strength, and, bound inseparably heart and hand with my faithful and noble people, with trust in the help and grace of God, I repeat the words of the Emperor Alexander the First, — 'Where right is, there is God.' "

Alexander visited the Crimea and Sevastopol, and mourned over the ruins of the fair city. The Bee newspaper officially announced to Europe, that the war was now becoming serious, and that since Sevastopol was destroyed a stronger fortress would be built. Gortchakof was recalled, and General Lüders was put in command of the army. But the fact could no longer be disguised, that the country wished for peace. This war had cost two hundred and fifty thousand men. An irredeemable paper currency had completely driven out the precious metals; the banks paid only in paper, and that of the government was refused by the public. England, however, manifested the most warlike disposition. Under Lord Palmerston and Lord Panmure its army was newly organized and abundantly equipped. From a lack of men and equipment it had passed almost to the other extreme. The war party were anxious to retrieve England's reputation, and show the world that its prowess, under more favorable circumstances, could equal that of France. They felt, too, that Russia had not been sufficiently humiliated. But Austria, now that the allies had proved themselves successful, again came to the front with proposals of peace. Russia was more inclined to treat, for the reason that since June its army operating in Turkish Armenia and Georgia had been victorious. General Muravief, after a long siege of Kars, which was gallantly defended by Colonel William, an Englishman in the service of Turkey, obliged the garrison to capitulate on the twenty-fifth of November. The news of this success partially consoled Russia's military vanity. Napoleon, also, was anxious to come to an understanding. He wished to be the one to restore peace to Europe. He took pains to communicate his pacific desires to the Court of Saint Petersburg. Count Esterhazy left Vienna in the middle of December, carrying to the Russian Emperor a note in the threatening form of an ultimatum, which contained the original four guarantees, revised and changed to suit the changed circumstances. The Russian cabinet was particularly displeased with the proposal to rectify the borders of Bessarabia, which was practically a plan to cause Russia to give up part of its territory. Since the capture of Kars, it had been confidently hoped that that stronghold might be exchanged for Sevastopol, Eupatoria, Kinburn, and Kertch. But no modification would be admitted in the ultimatum. After a long struggle, during which Count Esterhazy nearly broke off the negotiations, Alexander was brought to sign the preliminaries of peace on the basis proposed. On the sixteenth of January the Tsar yielded. On February first a protocol, signed at Vienna, officially ratified the adhesion of France and England to the Austrian propositions, and named Paris as the place where the congress should meet to regulate the treaty.

TREATY OF PARIS.

England was represented by Lord Clarendon and Lord Cowley, France by Count Walewski and Baron de Bourqueney; the Grand-Vizier Ali-Pasha and Diémil-Bey were sent by Turkey, Cavour and the Marquis de Villamarina by Sardinia; Austria sent Buol-Schauenstein and Baron von Hübner; Russia was represented by Baron Brunof and Alexéï Orlof. They met at the office of Foreign Affairs. The hall was magnificently decorated; a table covered with green cloth was arranged with twelve seats. All reporters were excluded, with the exception of Benedetti, who was made secretary. Count Walewski was unanimously chosen president. An armistice, to last till March thirty-first, was immediately agreed upon and telegraphed to the Crimea. The allied armies received the news with exultation; the Russians, in sullen silence.

It was proposed to discuss first of all the third point, and the question arose whether the arsenal at Nikolaïef should be destroyed. Lord Clarendon recognized that Nikolaïef was not on the Black Sea, but he claimed that ship-yards were contradictory to the principle established in the preliminaries. But finally, when it was formally promised in the name of the Tsar that the ship-yards on the Bug should not be employed for any considerable works, the plenipotentiaries declared that they were satisfied. This was considered an auspicious beginning.

The second point, which included the question of territory to be taken from Russia in exchange for Sevastopol and the other towns occupied by the allies, caused some difficulty. The restitution of Kars was not considered sufficient, a strip of land must be taken from Bessarabia and added to Moldavia. This included the important towns of Ismaïl and Reni. It was the Austrian representatives who were strongest in favor of keeping Russia entirely from the Danube. The discussion lasted through two sittings. The "duel" finally was ended by the success of Austria. Count Orlof bent over to his neighbor Cavour, and said, "The Austrian plenipotentiary does not know what this rectification of border will cost his country in tears and blood." Brunof, too, had expressed his dissatisfaction with the Austrian arrogance by this muttered criticism: "Count Buol speaks as if Austria had taken Sevastopol." The sittings were interrupted in the middle of March by the birth of a son to Napoleon. When they were resumed, on the eighteenth, Baron von Manteuffel, Prussian Prime Minister, and Count von Hatzfeld were admitted to the congress. The only point left to decide was the relation which Turkey should bear toward Europe, and the difficult question as to the treatment of the Christian population under the Ottoman control. The question was thus settled: "The Emperor of the French, the Emperor of Austria, the Queen of Great Britain, the King of Prussia, the Emperor of Russia, and the King of Sardinia declare that the Sublime Porte is admitted to share the advantages of international law and European concert. Their majesties agree, each separately, to respect the territorial independence and integrity of the Ottoman Empire, and in common to guarantee the strict observance of this engagement, and will consider, consequently, every act tending to attack it as a question of general interest. . . . His majesty, the Sultan, in his constant solicitude for the well-being of his subjects, having granted a firman, which, by ameliorating their lot without distinction of religion or race, consecrates his generous intentions towards the Christian populations of his empire, and, wishing to give a new proof of his sentiments in this respect, has resolved to communicate to the contracting powers the said firman, which is the spontaneous utterance of his sovereign will. The contracting powers declare the great value of this communication. It is perfectly understood that in no case does it give the said powers the right to interfere either collectively or separately with the relations of his majesty the Sultan and his subjects, nor with the interior administration of his empire."

Peace was signed on the thirtieth of March, on the following basis: Russia renounced its exclusive right of protection over the Danubian principalities, and all interference with their internal affairs. The free navigation of the Danube was to be effectually secured by the establishment of a commission in which the contracting parties should be represented. Each of them should have the right to station two sloops of war at the mouth of the river. Russia consented to a rectification of frontiers which should leave Turkey and the Rumanian principalities all the Danubian delta. The Black Sea was made neutral ground; its waters, open to merchant-ships of all nations, were forbidden to men-of-war, whether of powers owning the coasts or of any others. No military or maritime arsenals were to be created there. Turkey and Russia could maintain each six steamboats of eight hundred tons, and four of two hundred to guard the coast. The *hatti sherif*, by which the Sultan Abdul-Medjid renewed the privileges of his non-Mussulman subjects, was inserted.

Thus ended the Crimean war. When the news came to Sevastopol, the armies which had been opposed to each other in so many deadly battles began to fraternize. Social gatherings and complimentary reviews took the place of sorties and hand-to-hand conflicts. The past was forgotten. The garrisons were recalled from Kinburn, Eupatoria, and Kertch. Preparations were made to leave the place where so much suffering had been undergone, where so many glorious deeds had been done. By the beginning of July the last French soldier had gone. Pélissier was received with rapturous enthusiasm. Napoleon gave him the title of "Duc de Malakof." But the results of the war were to be long felt in all the countries of Europe. France counted more than eighty thousand men who were killed or died of disease and exposure, besides thousands who came home only to die. England lost twenty-two thousand, the Piedmontese army a tenth of that number; the Turks upwards of thirty thousand. It cost England in money alone fifty million pounds sterling.

Russia lost by the treaty of Paris both the control of the Black Sea and the protectorate of the Eastern Christians, thus annihilating the fruits of the policy of Peter the Great, Anna, Catherine the Second, and Alexander the First. Thus they were compelled to ruin the fleets and naval arsenals created by Potemkin, the Duc de Richelieu, the Marquis de Traversay, and Admiral Lazeref. Thus the fortresses of Sevastopol, Kinburn, and Ienikale were deserted. The treaties of Kaïnardji, Bukarest, and Adrianople were made of no avail, and the hopes of conquest and dominion to which they had given rise were all destroyed. The imprudent policy of Nicholas had cancelled the work which two centuries of successful progress had accomplished.

CHAPTER IX.

ALEXANDER THE SECOND AND THE REFORMS.

1856 – 1877.

IMPERIAL MANIFESTOES AND DECREES. — THE ACT OF THE NINETEENTH OF FEBRUARY, EIGHTEEN HUNDRED AND SIXTY-ONE: JUDICIAL REFORMS; LOCAL SELF-GOVERNMENT. — THE POLISH INSURRECTION. — INTELLECTUAL MOVEMENT: MATERIAL PROGRESS: EDUCATION.

IMPERIAL MANIFESTOES AND DECREES.

ON the thirty-first of March the Emperor announced the conclusion of peace in the following manifesto: "The bloody and obstinate war which for nearly three years has been disquieting Russia is now ended. It was not instigated by Russia, and even before it began our Father of imperishable memory, who now rests in God, solemnly declared to all his faithful subjects, as well as to all foreign powers, that the sole aim of his endeavors and wishes was to assure the rights of our co-religionists in the East, and to protect them from every form of oppression. A stranger to selfish designs, he had no thought that his righteous demands would lead to the horrors of war. These horrors he looked upon with deep pain as a Christian and the sympathetic father of the people that God had intrusted to his care, and he did not cease to reiterate his desire for peace. But no result followed the negotiations, which shortly before his death were opened, touching the conditions of this peace alike necessary to all nations. The powers which had formed an alliance hostile to us continued to expend their strength in warlike preparations.

The war took its course, and we have continued it with absolute confidence in the grace of the Almighty, with firm trust in the invincible zeal of our beloved subjects.

"They have justified our expectations. In this time of heavy trials our faithful brave armies, as well as all classes of the Russian people, have shown themselves worthy of their high calling. In our whole Empire, from the shores of the Pacific even to the Black and Baltic Seas, has prevailed the single thought, the single resolution, to fulfil duty, to protect the fatherland at any cost of property or life. Husbandmen, who had never left the plough and the fields which they cultivated, hastened to take up arms for the holy struggle, and were not inferior to our experienced warriors in bravery and self-renunciation. New and brilliant heroic deeds have glorified even these latter days of our contest with mighty opponents. The enemy was driven back from the coasts of Siberia and the White Sea, as well as from the walls of Sveaborg, and the courageous defence of the southern ports of Sevastopol for eleven months, in the face and under the fire of the besiegers, will live in the memory of the latest posterity. In Asia, after the famous victories of the two preceding campaigns, Kars, together with its numerous garrison, which comprised almost the whole male population of Anatolia, was obliged to surrender to us, and the best Turkish troops coming to its assistance were compelled to retreat."

This manifesto then went on to commend the result of the peace in the establishment of the rights of the Christians, and declared that the concessions made were inconsiderable. It ended with the expression of a wish for righteousness and mildness, so that all might enjoy the fruit of peaceful labor under the protection of the laws.

During the year which followed the signing of the Paris treaty, Alexander issued decrees allowing foreign ships to enter Russian ports, and establishing the northwestern provinces on a peace footing. The law of eighteen hundred and forty-nine, which limited the number of students in the universities to only three hundred, was repealed, the excessive fee for passports was abolished, new journals and newspapers were allowed to be published, and the disgraceful schools, to which soldiers were obliged to send their sons, were restricted. Alexander, meeting the joyous and expectant minds of his people with these concessions, became popular. De Mazade tells of a witty Russian who said, if Nicholas had forbidden his subjects to appear in the streets, and if Alexander had only revoked this prohibition, he would have been immediately regarded by the Russians as one of the most free-minded monarchs of his day.

Alexander's programme for the future was hinted at in an address which he made to the deputies sent to him by the national aristocracy at the time when he went to Moscow to celebrate the declaration of peace: "Gentlemen, the war is at an end, for before I left Saint Petersburg I hastened to ratify the treaty of peace which had been signed in Paris by the assembled plenipotentiaries. I am glad to be able officially to communicate these tidings to you, and to repeat in presence of the nobility of Moscow the words which I addressed to my people in my last manifesto. Russia had the ability to defend itself with energy for years, and I am convinced that whatever forces should be raised against it, it would be invincible in its own territory. Yet for the best interests of the land I was obliged to listen to such propositions as were consistent with our national honor. War is an exceptional state of affairs, and the greatest results gained from it scarcely balance the evils which it brings in its train. It had interrupted the trade of the kingdom with the majority of the nations of Europe. But undoubtedly I should have continued the struggle, had not the voice of the neighboring nations spoken out against the policy of previous years. My father, of imperishable memory, had his reasons for proceeding as he did. I knew his plans, and they had my heartiest sympathy. But the end that he had in view will be reached by the Treaty of Paris, and this way I prefer to war. There are many among you, I know well, who regret that I assented so quickly to the propositions laid before me. It was my duty, as a man and the head of a great empire, without delay either to reject or accept them. This duty I have fulfilled faithfully and conscientiously. I am convinced that, under the difficulties of the situation, it will be to my advantage, and that, erelong, every devoted friend of Russia will acknowledge the wisdom of my purposes and plans for the future of the land. Even on the supposition that fortune had remained as steadfastly on our side as it did in Asia, still the empire would have exhausted its resources by maintaining considerable armies at different places, and at the same time the greater part of the soldiers would have been withdrawn from agriculture and manufacture. Even in the government of Moscow, mills, machine-shops, and factories had closed their doors. I prefer the actual prosperity of the arts of peace to the idle glory of battles. Accordingly I have opened the Russian ports to trade, the boundaries to the free exchange of foreign commodities. I desire that in the future the barter of the products of all lands and the raw goods or manufactures to which our soil gives rise may be as free as possible in our markets. Hereafter many projects will be submitted to your judgment which will aim to promote internal industry, and I desire that every noble man should manifest his interest."

Alexander the Second was crowned on the seventh of September, eighteen hundred and fifty-six. Previous to the coronation he went to Warsaw, where he promised the Polish nobles that they should be treated with the consideration due to the members of the family of which he was the head. He ended his address to their marshals with the warning that they should cease to indulge in chimerical notions. Forgetfulness of the past was the key-note of the Emperor's promise, but their future happiness would depend upon their wisdom and their renunciation of visionary projects. Contrary to precedent, the Emperor continued his journey to Berlin, where he was received in great honor by the Prussian princes. Austria was not visited. Alexander returned by the way of the Baltic provinces, and in his addresses held out to them the promise of important reforms.

On the very day of his coronation appeared the long-expected manifesto, which was written in that mystic religious tone peculiar to the Russian Tsars. It dealt first with the orders and decorations to be granted to those who had served faithfully in the Crimean war, — soldiers of all ranks, surgeons, civilians, chaplains, noblemen. Certain provinces had suffered peculiarly from the effects of the war; the Taurid, Bessarabia, the governments of Kherson, Iekaterinoslaf, and the coasts of the Baltic had been laid desolate; the manifesto promised peculiar indulgences and assistance to these, in order that the last traces of the ruin might disappear as soon as possible. The Emperor then, in a series of thirty-eight articles, made provision for freeing the country from certain burdens which, in its impoverished condition, were unendurable. The most important of these were the conscriptions and the taxes. A new census was promised, by which the rates of taxation might be equalized. No conscription should take place for four years, unless it were made absolutely necessary by some unforeseen complication. Both of these ordinances were of great importance, because the pecuniary ability of the noblesse depended upon the laborers, and the army had drained away from agriculture so many, that the proprietors were threatened with ruin, and some were unable to pay even the capitation taxes. Debts of private persons in arrears to the state were remitted, aggregating twenty-four million rubles. The position of the Jews was somewhat improved, and it was decreed that the children of soldiers and sailors, who formerly had belonged to the state, should be restored to their parents, and allowed to choose their own profession. The manifesto finally took up the subject of pardons for political crimes. Some of these prisoners were allowed greater liberties in the places of their banishment; others were granted permission to choose a residence in the interior provinces of Russia; and still others were allowed to live anywhere in the whole empire, including Poland, with the exception of the two capitals, Saint Petersburg and Moscow. Among those pardoned were the survivors of the revolution of eighteen hundred and twenty-five, the participators in the troubles caused by the secret societies in eighteen hundred and twenty-seven, and the Polish conspirators of eighteen hundred and thirty-one. The patent of hereditary nobility was restored to many who still survived, or was given to their legitimate children. This measure was of great consequence, because more than a hundred of the principal boyar families had been implicated in the revolution with which Nicholas's reign began, and there was scarcely a family in Poland which had not sent a member to the mines or wastes of Siberia.

The Emperor signed also, on the seventh of September, a number of different decrees, the execution of which occupied the administration during the rest of the year. They were mainly to carry out the provisions of the manifesto.

ACT OF THE NINETEENTH OF FEBRUARY, EIGHTEEN HUNDRED AND SIXTY-ONE: JUDICIAL REFORMS; LOCAL SELF-GOVERNMENT.

In the manifesto which announced to his people the termination of the Eastern war, Alexander expressed his conviction that "by the combined efforts of the government and the people" the public administration would be improved, and that justice and mercy would reign in the courts of law. He understood that the disasters of the Danube and the Crimea must in a great measure be imputed to the administration, protected as it was by the silence of public opinion, the slavery of the press, and the rigor of the police and of the censorship. The events of eighteen hundred and fifty-five taught the important lesson that a people in which the majority of the agricultural classes was subjected to serfage could not rival the European nations in intellectual, scientific, or industrial progress, and it is clear that, in modern warfare, success is the resultant of all the moral and material forces of a state. The system of governing Russia without giving the people a voice in the management of their own affairs, of conducting all public business in the routine and silence of the bureaux, was condemned. The officials, so haughty under Nicholas, bowed their heads under the public execration. The term *tchinovnik*, which once had so formidable a meaning, became a term of derision and contempt; public opinion naturally associated it with everything superannuated, ridiculous, or odious. The servants of the autocracy, who had formerly flaunted their official rank on all occasions, now overwhelmed by the weight of a crushing responsibility, showed that they felt half ashamed by taking pains to hide their pompous titles and the decorations which no longer commanded respect. It seemed as if the conservative Russia of Nicholas the First had sunk into the earth; every one called himself a Liberal. A breath of audacious hope, of courageous enterprise, passed through the country. "All thirsted for reforming activity. The men in authority were inundated with projects of reform, — some of them anonymous, and others from obscure individuals; some of them practical, and very many wildly fantastic. Even the grammarians showed their sympathy with the spirit of the time by proposing to expel summarily all redundant letters from the Russian alphabet! The fact that very few people had clear, precise ideas as to what was to be done did not prevent, but rather tended to increase, the reform enthusiasm. All had at least one common feeling, — dislike to what had previously existed. It was only when it became necessary to forsake pure negation, and to create something, that the conceptions became clearer, and a variety of opinions appeared. At the first moment there was merely unanimity in negation, and an impulsive enthusiasm for beneficent reforms in general."

The movement, which in eighteen hundred and one affected only those in the immediate vicinity of Alexander, now spread throughout Russia. A thousand voices were raised in the papers, in the reviews, and in the books, all suddenly emancipated; in the drawing-rooms and in the streets, where the bewildered police forgot to spy. What had been whispered timidly in the manuscript literature of the last months of Nicholas was now printed freely. "The heart trembles with joy," said one of the leading organs of the press, "in expectation of the great social reforms which are on the point of being carried out, — reforms which are thoroughly in accordance with the spirit, wishes, and hopes of the public. The ancient harmony and community of sentiment which, in all but short and exceptional periods, have always existed between the government and the people, are completely re-established. The absence of all sentiment of caste, the feeling of common origin and brotherhood, which binds all classes of the Russian people into a homogeneous whole, will permit the easy and peaceful fulfilment, not only of those great reforms which cost Europe centuries of struggle and bloodshed, but also many reforms that the nations of the West, enchained by their feudal traditions and their caste prejudices, are even now in no state to accomplish." And again: "We have to fight in the name of the highest truth against egotism and the petty interests of the moment. We must prepare our children from their tenderest years to take part in the struggle that awaits every honest man. We have to thank the war for opening our eyes to the dark sides of our political and social organization, and it is now our duty to profit by the lesson. But it must not be supposed that the government can, single-handed, cure us of our faults. The destinies of Russia are like a stranded ship, which the captain and the crew alone cannot move, and which nothing but the rising tide of the national life can raise and float." As

Mr. Mackenzie Wallace says: "Hearts beat quicker at the sound of these calls to action. Many heard this new teaching, if we may believe a contemporary authority, 'with tears in their eyes;' then 'raising boldly their heads, they made a solemn vow that they would act honorably, perseveringly, fearlessly.' Some of those who had formerly yielded to the force of circumstances now confessed their misdemeanors with bitterness of heart. 'Tears of repentance,' said a popular poet, 'give relief, and call us to new exploits.' Russia was compared to a strong giant who awakes from sleep, stretches his brawny limbs, collects his thoughts, and prepares to atone for his long inactivity by feats of untold prowess. All believed, or at least assumed, that the recognition of defects would necessarily entail their removal. When an actor in one of the Saint Petersburg theatres shouted from the stage, 'Let us proclaim throughout all Russia that the time has come for tearing up evil by the roots!' the audience gave way to the most frantic enthusiasm. 'Altogether a joyful time,' says one who took part in the excitement, 'as when, after the long winter, the genial breath of spring glides over the cold, petrified earth, and nature awakens from her death-like sleep. Speech, that was long restrained by police and censorial regulations, now flows smoothly, harmoniously, majestically, like a mighty river that has just been freed from ice.'

"Under these influences a multitude of newspapers and periodicals were founded, and the current literature entirely changed its character. The purely literary and historical questions which had hitherto engaged the attention of the reading public were thrown aside and forgotten, unless they could be made to illustrate some principle of political or social science. Criticisms on style and diction, explanations of æsthetic principles, metaphysical discussions,—all this seemed miserable trifling to men who wished to devote themselves to gigantic practical interests. 'Science,' it was said, 'has now descended from the heights of philosophic abstraction into the arena of real life.' The periodicals were accordingly filled with articles on railways, banks, free-trade, education, agriculture, communal institutions, local self-government, joint-stock companies, and with crushing philippics against personal and national vanity, inordinate luxury, administrative tyranny, and the habitual peculation of the officials. This last-named subject received special attention. During the preceding reign any attempt to criticise publicly the character or acts of an official was regarded as a very heinous offence; now there was a deluge of sketches, tales, comedies, and monologues, describing the corruption of the administration, and explaining the ingenious devices by which the *Tchinovniks* increased their scanty salaries. The public would read nothing that had not a direct or indirect bearing on the questions of the day, and whatever had such a bearing was read with interest. It did not seem at all strange that a drama should be written in defence of free-trade, or a poem in defence of some peculiar mode of taxation; that an author should expound his political ideas in a tale, and his antagonist reply by a comedy. A few men of the old school protested feebly against this 'prostitution of art,' but they received little attention, and the doctrine that art should be cultivated for its own sake was scouted as an invention of aristocratic indolence. Here is an *ipsa pinxit* of the literature of the time: 'Literature has come to look at Russia with her own eyes, and sees that the idyllic romantic personages which the poets formerly loved to describe have no objective existence. Having taken off her French glove, she offers her hand to the rude, hard-working laborer, and observing lovingly Russian village life, she feels herself in her native land. The writers of the present have analyzed the past, and, having separated themselves from aristocratic *littérateurs* and aristocratic society, have demolished their former idols.'"

The delicate questions that the Russian press feared to bring forward, and the great personages that it did not dare to attack, were left to the exiled Herzen in London, with his terrible *Kolokol*, or *Bell*, the dread of dishonest officials. The proscribed numbers of the *Kolokol* made their way by thousands into Russia, were laid on the table of the Emperor, and revealed to him the most secret iniquities. Wallace quotes the following anecdote, which shows how thoroughly Herzen was acquainted with what was done in the ministries, and how mercilessly he exposed all abuses. One number of the *Kolokol* contained a violent attack on an important personage of the court, and the accused, or some one of his friends, considered it advisable to have a copy specially printed for the Emperor without the objectionable article. The Emperor did not at first discover the trick, but shortly afterwards he received from London a polite note containing the article which had been omitted, and informing him how he had been deceived.

In their eagerness for reform the people wished everything to be undertaken at once, but it was soon seen that all questions remained in abeyance till that of the emancipation of the peasants was settled. Whether it was a question of self-government, of education, of industrial liberty, of military service, or legal equality, it was sure to come back to social reform, which therefore must be made the starting-point.

The unfree population of Russia amounted, at the time of the emancipation, to forty-five million eight hundred and sixty-three thousand and eighty-six individuals, divided into twenty-three million three hundred thousand Crown peasants, nine hundred and thirty-six thousand four hundred and seventy-seven peasants of appanages, — institutions such as churches, schools, hospitals, mines, and factories, — twenty million one hundred and fifty-eight thousand two hundred and thirty-one attached to the soil and belonging to proprietors, and one million four hundred and sixty-seven thousand three hundred and seventy-eight *dvorovuié*, or domestic servants. The peasants of the Crown and of the appanages might be considered as freemen, subject to the payment of a rent, or of other well-defined dues, settled by the state, which was represented either by the administration of the domain or by the department of the appanages. The Crown peasants even enjoyed a sort of local self-government. They regulated their affairs in the commune, or *mir*, through an elder and an elected council. Their differences were judged by elected tribunals, — the tribunal of the village and the tribunal of the *volost*, or district, which tried cases according to the peasant customs. Nothing more was needed than to give the name of freemen to men substantially free. This was done when their personal liberty was proclaimed, and when certain restrictions on their right to come and go, to acquire new lands, or to dispose of their goods, were abolished. This was accomplished by a series of edicts, the first dating July, eighteen hundred and fifty-eight.

The case of peasants belonging to private owners and the position of the *dvorovuié* was different. The emancipation of twenty-two million five hundred thousand men was to bring about the most prodigious social change which has taken place in Europe since the French Revolution. The liberation of the peasants, properly so called, which would make them owners of part of the soil which they cultivated, was an enterprise surrounded with difficulties on all sides. On the question of personal liberty, all were in accord, but there were disagreements regarding the question of proprietorship. To solve this difficulty it was necessary to go back to the historic origin of Russian property, to choose between the systems and theories formulated by different schools of historians. The most authoritative of these proved that serfage was not introduced into Russia by the conquest of one race by another, for it was in those very provinces conquered by the Russians — in the Finnish or Tatar countries — that serfage did not exist, while its greatest development was to be found in the midst of the conquering people. Serfage had been sanctioned by a series of acts emanating from the throne; and the nearer a province was to the Muscovite centre, the more ancient and the more firmly established was serfage found to be. The northern regions were exempt from it; in the governments of Arkhangel and Vologda at the time of the emancipation there were only six serfs, and they belonged to nobles who had no estates. It seemed, therefore, to be a Muscovite institution, a creation of the Tsarian power. It took its rise in the period when, under the pressure of the Mongol yoke, Russian society formed itself into a rigorous hierarchy, in which the sovereign of Moscow arrogated to himself absolute authority over the nobles, as the nobles did over the peasants, — their subjects. The institution sprang from the new wants of the infant state. The grant of lands to the military class, to the nobles, was the recompense for the service exacted from them; the revenues of the soil constituted their pay, and were to defray the expenses of their outfit and equipment. They were, besides, delegated to govern and administer the lands of their domain, and to pay to the prince the amount of the poll-tax which they were charged to collect. But the land had no value without the hands that cultivated it, the revenues of an estate diminished as the number of peasants diminished; the noble who was deserted by his peasants was ruined, and in no condition to serve the prince. In order that military service might be secured, and that the produce of the tax might suffer no diminution, it was necessary to hinder the emigration of the peasants. The interest of the noble, as well as the interest of the state, demanded that the liberty of coming and going should be restrained, that the noble should be armed with a formidable authority over the peasant, and that the laborer should be fixed to the soil. Almost everywhere, without any intervention on the part of the legislature, the husbandman gradually became a serf. Legally free, the peasant had become a slave; in the eyes of the law, a simple tenant for life, the noble had become in fact the proprietor of the land, the owner of the peasants. The state of things created by arbitrary power was afterwards legalized by a series of legislative acts, which, one after the other, curtailed the liberty of the muzhik and increased the authority of the lord. Such were the decrees of Feodor Ivanovitch in fifteen hundred and ninety-two and fifteen hundred and ninety-seven, of Boris Godunof in sixteen hundred and one, of Vasili Shuïski in sixteen hundred and seven, of Peter the Great in seventeen hundred and twenty-three, and of Catherine the Second for Little Russia in seventeen hundred and eighty-three.

The peasant, while resigning himself to this condition of affairs, had not entirely lost all sense of his rights. His ancient right to the ownership of the land he expressed to his master, after his own fashion, in the proverb, "Mui vashi no zemlia nasha," that is to say, "We are yours, but the land is ours." He forgot less easily than the government the fact that the peasant's obligation to serve the lord was on the same plane with the lord's obligation to serve the Tsar. When Peter the Third in his short reign freed the nobles from the obligation of serving the state, the peasant expected that the corollary of this first ukas would be a second edict, setting free the peasant from his bondage to the soil and from paying dues to the lord. Hence the troubles of seventeen hundred and sixty-two, the insurrection of seventeen hundred and seventy-three, when a false Peter the Third appeared, with the intention, as it was supposed, of finishing the work of the deceased Emperor. During the campaign of eighteen hundred and twelve the peasants for a moment believed that Napoleon was bringing them liberty, and the agitation was revived during the Crimean war. Serfage was decidedly the weak point of Russia. An invader might always have the possibility of supplementing his own offensive operations with a servile war.

We have seen the efforts at emancipation under Alexander the First, and the ukas of Nicholas in eighteen hundred and forty-two. The latter, by the decrees of eighteen hundred and forty-five, eighteen hundred and forty-seven, and eighteen hundred and forty-eight, recognized the right of individuals and communes to acquire landed property. Prince Dolgoruki, one of Nicholas's enemies, has not been able to refuse him this testimony: "However hostile he may have been to the doctrine of liberty, we must do him the justice to say that he never ceased through the whole of his life to cherish the idea of emancipating the serfs." In eighteen hundred and thirty-eight he established a committee under the direction of Count Bludof, with instructions to investigate the emancipation question. The proceedings of this assembly were interrupted in consequence of the bad harvests of the following year, and in eighteen hundred and forty were entirely suspended. He was obliged to bequeath this task to his son.

A few days after the Treaty of Paris was signed, in March, eighteen hundred and fifty-six, Alexander the Second, in an address to the marshals of the Moscow nobility, while guarding himself against the notion that he aimed at the instant emancipation of the serfs, invited "his faithful nobles" to seek the proper means to prepare for the execution of this measure. These were his words: "For the removal of certain unfounded reports, I consider it necessary to declare to you that I have not at present the intention of annihilating serfage; but certainly, as you yourselves know, the existing manner of possessing serfs cannot remain unchanged. It is better to abolish serfage from above than to await the time when it will begin to abolish itself from below. I request you, gentlemen, to consider how this can be put into execution, and to submit my words to the noblesse for their consideration." The Muscovite proprietors showed, however, but little enthusiasm, and the Emperor was disappointed, for he had hoped that his ancient capital would be the first to begin the great work. He now saw clearly that such a measure could be carried out only by an energetic exercise of the imperial power, and he appointed, on the fourteenth of January, eighteen hundred and fifty-seven, a secret committee composed of high states-officials. This "chief committee for peasant affairs," or "chief committee for the amelioration of the condition of the serfs," as it was afterwards called, spent half a year in studying the history of the question. This same year the nobles of the governments of Kief, Volhynia, and Podolia, dissatisfied by the result of the measures taken by Nicholas the First in the institution of the "inventories," which regulated the mutual obligations of masters and serfs, "took," says Schnitzler, "a desperate resolution. They declared themselves ready to emancipate the peasants, either because they thought that the bare idea of so radical a measure would alarm the government, or because they hoped that the emancipation would necessarily be based on the idea of a proportionate pecuniary indemnity." Whether their expressed desire for a revision of the inventories warranted such a violent assumption or not, it furnished the Emperor with the occasion he sought to give the question a decisive impulse. By an imperial rescript he authorized the nobility of the three Lithuanian governments to proceed with the work of emancipation, although the word itself was carefully avoided. In the supplementary considerations, however, it was stated that "the abolition of serfage must be effected not suddenly, but gradually." He sent this edict — known as the Rescript of Nazimof — and the ministerial instructions which formed its commentary, to all the governors and all the marshals of the nobility throughout the provinces of the Empire, "for their information," and also, adds the circular, "for your direction, in case that the nobles of the government, confided to your care, should express the same intention as the three Lithuanian governments." The nobles of St. Petersburg, Nijni-Novgorod, and Orel made a reply which encouraged the Emperor: they begged permission to call a committee for deliberation. During the year eighteen hundred and fifty-eight thirty-three districts declared their wish to discuss the matter, but only nineteen established their committees.

Another encouragement came to him from the press, almost

the whole of which hailed with enthusiasm a measure "which was to open a new and glorious epoch in the national history." "All sections of the literary world," says Mr. Mackenzie Wallace, "had arguments to offer in support of the foregone conclusion. The moralists declared that all prevailing vices were the product of serfage, and that moral progress was impossible in an atmosphere of slavery; the lawyers asserted that the arbitrary authority of the proprietors over the peasants had no firm legal basis; the economists explained that free labor was an indispensable condition of industrial and commercial prosperity; the philosophical historians showed that the normal historical development of the country demanded the abolition of barbarism; and the writers of the sentimental, gushing type poured forth endless effusions about brotherly love to the weak and oppressed."

Already the question was not one of giving the peasant his liberty alone. In order to prevent the peasant, now free, but detached from the soil, from falling into the hands of his ancient master, and into a state of dependence more insupportable than that of the past; to hinder the formation of an immense proletariat, more hungry and more dangerous than that which, it was said, threatened the kingdoms of the West, — it was necessary to give the newly liberated classes some property, to reconstitute and strengthen the Russian commune, whose strong unity and indestructible life formed the best rampart against pauperism. Many proprietors associated themselves with this movement; they trusted that the abolition of the serfage of the peasants would have as its consequence the limitation of the autocratic authority of the Tsars, and that by enfranchising their serfs they would themselves gain political liberty. More than once it was proposed to re-establish the ancient council called *duma*, or *sobor*, as a kind of national parliament which under more modern forms would allow the country to become associated in the exercise of the supreme authority.

The government, supported by the addresses of many bodies

of the noblesse, ordered the creation of committees of landowners, charged to examine the question. Forty-six of these committees, composed of thirteen hundred and thirty-six landowners, assembled to discuss the rights of twenty-three millions of serfs and of one hundred and fourteen thousand six hundred and ninety-seven proprietors. The forty-six committees unanimously pronounced for the abolition of serfage without any recompense, but opinions were divided as to the distribution of lands and the conditions of indemnity. The Emperor had again to interfere. In eighteen hundred and fifty-nine he called a chief committee, composed of twelve persons, over which he presided during its first sessions. He afterwards resigned the presidency to Prince Alexis Orlof. This committee, in conjunction with some of the provincial committees, more than once opposed passive resistance to the beneficent schemes of the sovereign. The Emperor went through the provinces, appealing to the conciliatory spirit and devotion of his nobility, reprimanding those who hung back, and reminding them that "reforms came better from above than from below." To subdue the resistance of the superior committee he created another, to which the old one was subordinated, and which he packed with men devoted to the new idea.

The new "imperial commission" did not content itself with elaborating the materials furnished by the provincial committees. Directly inspired by the Emperor, who sent them his paper on "the progress and issue of the peasant question," they took into their own hands all the points of legislation, by which course they ran the risk of throwing into opposition many proprietors who were well disposed, but who complained that they had never been consulted, and that the commission seemed desirous of depriving them of the merit of their sacrifices. The commission gradually gave to the reform a more and more radical character. It admitted the principle that the emancipation should not take place gradually, but that the law should insure the immediate abolition of serfdom; that the most effectual measures should be taken to prevent the reestablishment of the seigniorial authority under other forms, by a liberal organization of the rural communes; and that the peasant should become a proprietor on the payment of an indemnity. From these deliberations resulted the new law, announced by the manifesto of the nineteenth of February, or third of March, eighteen hundred and sixty-one, according to the New Style.

The fundamental principles of the new legislation may be summed up thus: The peasants hitherto attached to the soil were to be invested with all the rights of free cultivators. The peasants, in consideration of certain quit-rents fixed by law, should obtain the full enjoyment of their enclosure or *dvor*, and also a certain quantity of arable land, sufficient to make certain the accomplishment of their obligations towards the state. It was provided that this "permanent enjoyment," or usufruct, might be exchanged for an "absolute ownership" of the enclosure and the lands, on the payment of purchase-money. The lords were to grant the peasants or the rural communes the land actually occupied by the latter; in each district, however, a maximum and a minimum were to be fixed. On the whole, there was an average of three *desiatins* and a half, or more than nine English acres, for each male peasant; but it varied from one *desiatin* to twelve; that is to say, the peasants in general received less in the Black Land, and more in the less productive zones. The government was to organize a system of loans, which would permit the peasants immediately to liberate themselves from their lords, though they would remain debtors to the state. The *dvoro-vuić*, who were neither attached to the soil, nor members of the commune, were to receive only their personal liberty, after they had served their masters for two years. To bring the great work of partition into seigniorial and peasant lands to a happy conclusion, to regulate the amount of the dues, the conditions of repurchase, and all the questions which might arise from the execution of the law, the temporary magistracy of the *mirovuié posredniki*, or mediators of peace, was instituted, who showed themselves for the most part honest, patient, impartial, equitable, and who deserve a great part of the honor of this pacific settlement.

The peasants, freed from the authority of their former masters, were organized into communes; or, rather, the commune, the *mir*, which is the primordial and antique element of Slavo-Russian society, acquired a new force. It inherited the right of police and of surveillance, held by the lord over his subjects; it administered and judged with more liberty the suits of the peasants. In accordance with the ancient Slav law, the land bought from the lord remained the common property of all the members of the *mir*: each peasant held as his private property only his enclosure and the land thereto pertaining. Arable lands are subject, at more or less frequent intervals, to partition among the heads of families, and are possessed by them only by way of usufruct. The law, which does not permit a final partition of the common land, except when two thirds of those interested consent, will long maintain against the destructive action of new manners and new wants this old European institution, which in Western countries has disappeared for centuries, in France especially, and has left no trace, other than in so-called communal properties. The communes, freed from the control of the lords, were grouped, as in the case of the imperial domains, into *volosti*, or districts having from three hundred to two thousand male members; a *volost* tribunal received the appeal from the communal justices, and a *volost* municipality was charged to watch over the common interests of all the villages under its jurisdiction. The mayor of the commune was called *stárosta*; the head of the *volost* was called *starshiná*, and was made responsible for the peace and order of the community. The Russian peasants were thus given a complete system of local self-government, of an absolutely rural character, for the former lord was strenuously kept apart from it. Since his ancient domain had been divided into seigniorial and peasant lands, he ceased legally to be an inhabitant of the village. His interests being perfectly distinct from those of the peasants, he was forbidden to meddle either with them, their elections, their administration, or their justice.

The great emancipation measure was, in fact, a dissolution of partnership between masters and peasants. It imposed sacrifices on both the interested parties. If the proprietors were forced to renounce their seigniorial rights, the *obrok*, or money-dues, the statute-labor, and part of their lands in exchange for an indemnity, the peasant found it hard to be obliged to buy the very ground whereon his cottage stood; the soil which his ancestors had cultivated in the sweat of their faces, even the land reserved for the lord, they regarded in many places as their own property, because it had been cultivated by them from time immemorial. The division imposed by the law seemed to them a system of spoliation. The discontent often showed itself in an obstinate resistance to the advice of the "mediators of peace," by their refusal to acquit themselves of legal obligations, and to enter into negotiation with the lord for the purchase of the land. They persuaded themselves that the nobles and officials had falsified the edict of the Tsar, or that a fresh act of emancipation, the true one, was to be proclaimed. A strange ferment arose in many provinces; it was necessary to call out the soldiery, and three times the troops had to fire on the people. In the government of Kazan ten thousand men rose at the call of the peasant, Anton Pétrof, who announced to them that the Emancipation Law was a forgery, and proclaimed the true liberty. General Apraxin was sent out against him, and was obliged to have recourse to powder and ball. A hundred perished, and the chief himself was taken and shot. The emancipation was none the less a beneficent and essential reform, of which the present generation will have to pay the price, while its good results will develop in future generations. The Russian peasants owe their liberty above all to the firm will of the Emperor; to the generous efforts of the Grand Duke Konstantin, and of a German princess, the widow of the Grand Duke Mikhail Pavlovitch, the Grand Duchess Helena, who in eighteen hundred and fifty-nine gave an example by emancipating her own peasants; to the enlightened patriotism of General Rostovtsof, who died before the law was promulgated, of Panin, Minister of Justice, of Nikolaï Miliutin, of Prince Tcherkasski, of Iuri Samarin, all members of the Imperial Commission, of Koshelef, Solovief, Zhukovski, Domotuvitch, and others; and to a large number of the proprietors, many of whom granted their peasants more than the maximum of land fixed by law.

As a reward for their sacrifices, the upper classes in Russia demanded reforms and more political liberty. In the two principal cities, Moscow and Saint Petersburg, strenuous efforts were made to obtain this influence and position. Some of the more radical newspapers demanded the abolition of the nobility, but this extremism found little general support. The discontented nobles, headed by Nikolaï Besobrasof, felt that the sacrifices which they had been compelled to undergo deserved a recompense in the extension of their political rights. A constitutional assembly with representation of all classes, and a house of nobles, were desired by both aristocrats and liberals. Prince Shtcherbatof in Moscow proposed to send an address to the government asking for a general commission of inquiry into the needs and wishes of the country, and the meeting passed the motion by a large majority. The discussions, however, became so angry and excited that the police were obliged to interfere. In Smolensk, Prince Gurko made a motion to abolish all the rights of the nobles and to demand a constitution. Here again the police interfered in the most summary manner. In Tula and Tver similar radical measures were discussed. At the latter town thirteen justices of the peace refused to abide by the decree of emancipation, and announced their intention of acting according to their own judgment. The government felt obliged to interfere: the decrees of the assembly were declared to be of no effect, and the rebellious justices were put in prison and released, after a fortnight's detention, only because the Emperor felt that extreme measures were dangerous. The address of the Moscow nobles was answered with a reprimand; that of the Tula nobles was unnoticed. But if the nobles were refused the re-establishment of the *duma*, that is to say, constitutional government, at least great reforms were accomplished in legal matters and in provincial administration.

In judicial affairs, the edicts from eighteen hundred and sixty-two to eighteen hundred and sixty-five introduced innovations sanctioned by the experience of Western states in former times. "Explicit, minute rules were laid down for investigating facts and weighing evidence; every scrap of evidence and every legal ground on which the decision was based was committed to writing; every act in the complicated process of coming to a decision was made the subject of a formal document, and duly entered in various registers; every document and register had to be signed and countersigned by various officials who were supposed to control each other; every decision might be carried to a higher court and made to pass a second time through the bureaucratic machine." Public accusation and defence now succeeded to this written and inquisitorial procedure. The trial of crimes and misdemeanors was placed in the hands of a jury. "In studying the history of criminal procedure in foreign countries, those who were intrusted with the task of preparing projects of reform found that nearly every country of Europe had experienced the evils from which Russia was suffering, and that one country after another had come to the conviction that the most efficient means of removing these evils was to replace the inquisitorial by litigious procedure, to give a fair field and no favor to the prosecutor and the accused, and allow them to fight out their battle with whatever legal weapons they might think fit. Further it was discovered that, according to the most competent foreign authorities, it was well in this modern form of judicial combat to leave the decision to a jury of respectable citizens. The steps which Russia had to take were thus clearly marked out by the experience of other nations, and it was decided that they should be taken at once. The organs for the prosecution of supposed criminals were carefully separated from the judges on the one hand, and from the police on the other; oral discussions between the public prosecutor and the prisoner's counsel, together with oral examination and cross-questioning of witnesses, were introduced into the procedure; and the jury was made an essential factor in criminal trials." In eighteen hundred and sixty the duty of making criminal inquiries was taken from the police and given to special magistrates, called *sudébnuié sledovateli*, or *juges d'instruction*, who were nearly independent of the public prosecutor; and district courts were established, having jurisdiction over a group of several districts. Appeals were carried up to *sudebnuia palatui*, or "palaces of justice," similar to the French courts of appeal, but which reversed the sentences of the first judges only in cases where the law was misinterpreted or misapplied. "When a case, whether civil or criminal, has been decided in the justice of peace courts or in the regular tribunals, there is no possibility of appeal in the strict sense of the term, but an application may be made for a revision of the case on the ground of technical informality. To use the French terms, there cannot be *appel*, but there may be *cassation*. If the law has evidently been misinterpreted or misapplied, if there has been any omission or transgression of essential legal formalities, or if the court has overstepped the bounds of its legal authority, the injured party may make an application to have the case revised and tried again. This is not, according to French juridical conceptions, an appeal.

The court of revision (*Cour de Cassation*) does not enter into the material facts of the case, but merely decides the question as to whether the essential formalities have been duly observed, and as to whether the law has been properly interpreted and applied; and if it be found on examination that there is some ground for invalidating the decision, it does not decide the case, but merely hands it over to be tried anew. According to the new Russian system, the senate is the sole court of revision, alike for the justice of peace courts and for the regular tribunals." The senate thus crowns all this organization, in which we find certain wholly French ideas.

The justices of the peace constitute a separate hierarchy: the *mirovoi sudiá*, or judge, elected by the landed proprietors of the district, forms the head of a tribunal of arbitration and of ordinary police; the jurisdiction of the justice of peace courts is much more extensive than in France, and includes the civil cases not exceeding five hundred rubles, or about three hundred dollars, and criminal cases where the penalty does not exceed three hundred rubles, or more than a year's imprisonment. "When any one has a complaint to make, he may go to the justice of the peace, and explain the affair orally, or in writing, without observing any formalities; and if the complaint seems well founded, the justice at once fixes a day for hearing the case, and gives the other party notice to appear at the appointed time. When the time appointed arrives, the affair is discussed publicly and orally, either by the parties themselves, or by any representatives whom they may appoint. If it is a civil suit, the justice begins by proposing to the parties to terminate it at once by a compromise, and indicates what he considers a fair arrangement. Many affairs are terminated in this simple way. If, however, either of the parties refuses to consent to a compromise, the matter is fully discussed, and the justice gives a formal written decision, containing the grounds on which it is based. In criminal cases the amount of punishment is always determined by reference to a special criminal code." The sentence can be appealed from only when the sum involved exceeds thirty rubles in civil, and fifteen rubles or three days' imprisonment in criminal cases. In this case the appeal is taken, not as in France before the district tribunal, but before the *mirovoi siezd*, or assembly of justices of the peace for the district, whose verdict can be annulled only by the senate.

The Russian provinces, or *gubernii*, are divided into *uïezdui*, or districts. In each district the law of eighteen hundred and sixty-four institutes a district council, the *uïezdnoé zemstvo*, formed by deputies elected every three years, in certain fixed proportions, by the three orders of the state, — the landed proprietors, or gentlemen, the rural communes, and the towns. The council assembles at least once a year, and is replaced in the interval between its sessions by a permanent executive committee. The functions of the district council, which occupies in the administrative hierarchy the rank immediately superior to the municipal councils of the towns and to the councils of the rural *volosti*, consist in the care and repair of the roads and bridges, the watching over education and sanitary affairs, the inspection of the state of the harvest, and the power to take measures for the prevention of famine. Above the district council was instituted the general council, the *gubernskoé zemstvo*, elected, not by the primary electors, but by the district councils of the province; in these there was to be found, as a general thing, a larger proportion of noble deputies than in the other assembly, in consequence of the tendency of the peasants to avoid all public charges. The general council occupies itself with affairs concerning several districts, and votes the provincial budget. Such is a summary of the system of self-government with which the present reign has endowed Russia.

Corporal punishments, that blot on ancient Russia, were abolished in the army and the imperial tribunals. They remain in vigor only in the tribunals of the peasants, who, from their attachment to the ancient patriarchal customs, still apply some blows with a whip to delinquents. The censorship was mitigated; the newspapers of both capitals received the right to choose between submitting to the examination of the censors and the liberty of appearing at their own risk and peril. In this case an arrangement borrowed from the second French empire is applied,—after three warnings, the paper may be suspended or suppressed. The periodical press of Saint Petersburg and Moscow has developed in a surprising manner in an atmosphere of comparative liberty; on the other hand, the provincial press, even in the largest towns, such as Kief and Kazan, scarcely exists. That of Warsaw is in an exceptional situation; that of the Baltic provinces enjoys a greater freedom.

Since eighteen hundred and fifty-nine the table of receipts and that of the state expenses have been given a kind of publicity. The estimates of revenue are divided into three heads: ordinary receipts, including direct and indirect taxes; *recettes d'ordre*, or receipts from the sale of law reports published at government expense, the produce of the state mines, and the like; and extraordinary receipts, such as sums borrowed in the European money markets. The expenditures are subdivided into four heads: ordinary expenses, anticipated deficits, *dépenses d'ordre*, and temporary disbursements for the aid of railroads, and other enterprises. The Trans-Caucasus, Finland, and Turkestan are usually sources of far greater expenditure than income. If there is ever a surplus, it comes from Central or Southern Russia. In eighteen hundred and seventy-eight the receipts were six hundred million three hundred and ninety-eight thousand four hundred and twenty-five rubles, of which nearly forty millions were borrowed. The following year the ordinary revenue was five hundred and ninety-five million four hundred and sixty-one thousand seven hundred and twenty-four rubles, and the ordinary expenditure five hundred and ninety-three million seventy-nine thousand seven hundred and seventy-three rubles.

Nine million three hundred and sixty-seven thousand seven hundred and sixty-six rubles were borrowed for the purpose of continuing the railroad system. On the first of September, eighteen hundred and seventy-eight, the interest on the public debt was one hundred and thirty-three million six hundred and seventy-six thousand seven hundred and nineteen rubles, which had increased in the following year to one hundred and fifty-six million five hundred and seventy-seven thousand five hundred and twenty-six rubles. The total debt in eighteen hundred and seventy-eight was two thousand four hundred and fifty million rubles, not including the paper currency, which in eighteen hundred and seventy-nine was eleven hundred and thirty-four millions of rubles. In eighteen hundred and sixty foreigners acquired all the civil rights accorded to natives, and which are held by Russians in foreign countries. The barriers raised by Nicholas between his empire and Europe have been partially overthrown. The Jews — at least those exercising a trade — were authorized to remove from Poland and the western governments into the interior of the empire. The universities have been freed from the shackles imposed by Nicholas, the limitation of the number of students abolished, the charges of study lowered, and numerous scholarships created.

THE POLISH INSURRECTION.

Great hopes awakened in Poland at the accession of the new sovereign; they went as far as the re-establishment of the constitution, and even to the reunion of the Lithuanian provinces with the kingdom. The awakening of Italy had made that of Poland appear possible; the concessions of the Emperor of Austria to Hungary led men to expect the same from Alexander the Second. On the death of Prince Paskiévitch, in eighteen hundred and fifty-six, General Mikhail Gortchakof was appointed vice-regent of Poland, and the system of administration was changed for a simpler and milder form. The in terview of the three Northern sovereigns at Warsaw, in October, eighteen hundred and sixty, caused a certain irritation among the people. It is necessary also to take into consideration the intrigues set on foot by the Polish committees abroad. If many Poles counted on the support of Alexander the Second to help them to raise their country, others wished for complete emancipation from Russia. There existed, therefore, two parties in Warsaw and in the foreign committees; the one wished to take Italy as an example, the other would be content with the new lot of Hungary. The emancipation of the peasants was in Poland, as in Russia, the question of the day; but the conditions of the problem were different in Warsaw from what they were in Moscow. The personal liberty of the rustics had been decreed by Napoleon the First, at the time that the Grand Duchy was created; but as they had received no property, they continued to farm the lands of the nobles, and paid their rent either in money or by statute labor. The substitution of a quitrent in money instead of labor was the first step in the path of reform, which might be carried further by allowing the husbandman to become a proprietor, by paying annually a fixed sum towards the purchase of the land, and putting means of credit at his disposal. The Agricultural Society, consisting of more than five thousand members, and presided over by Count Andréï Zamoïski, found that it was for the interest of the Polish nation to anticipate the Russian government, and to secure to the native nobility the honor of emancipation; the government, on the contrary, represented by Mr. Mukhanof, Director of the Interior, decided that it was to its advantage to fetter the activity of the society, to forbid the discussion of the question of purchase, and to confine its functions to the mutation of statute labor into fixed dues.

This disagreement between the Agricultural Society and the government increased the agitation which already existed at Warsaw. On the twenty-ninth of November, eighteen hundred and sixty, on the occasion of the thirtieth anniversary of the revolution of eighteen hundred and thirty, demonstrations, at once national and religious, took place in the streets of the capital; portraits of Kosciuszko and Kilinski were distributed, and a patriotic hymn was sung expressing the prayer for the freedom of the fatherland. On the twenty-fifth of February, eighteen hundred and sixty-one, the anniversary day of the battle of Grokhov, the Agricultural Society held a meeting to deliberate on an address, in which the Emperor should be asked for a constitution. Tumultuous crowds gathered in the streets, singing national songs; the Polish flag, the white eagle on a red ground, was unfurled and received in the market-place with the wildest enthusiasm. The gens-d'armes made use of their sabres to quell the tumult, and several Poles were wounded. On the twenty-seventh, on the occasion of a funeral service for the victims of the preceding insurrections, there was a new demonstration, which had to be suppressed, with the loss of five killed and ten wounded. Prince Gortchakof, Viceroy of Poland, touched by these strange manifestations, in which the disarmed people confined themselves stoically to facing the musketry without interrupting their songs, labored with Count Zamoïski for the restoration of order. He promised a strict investigation of the murder of several priests by the Cossacks; granted permission to form a committee of safety, consisting of several of the most prominent citizens; and expressed his willingness to receive an address to the Emperor. The address, asking the Emperor for a restoration of the national government, and appealing to his generosity and justice, circulated in Warsaw, and was filled with sixty thousand signatures; one hundred thousand persons in perfect order joined the procession at the funeral of the victims of the twenty-seventh of February.

The Emperor received the address; but while he was unwilling to grant a constitution, he made, however, many important concessions. By the ukas of March twenty-six, he decreed a council of state for the kingdom, a department of public education and of worship, elective councils in each government and each district, and municipal councils at Warsaw and in the principal cities of the kingdom. The Marquis Vićlopolski, a Pole belonging to the party which hoped for the reestablishment of Poland by Russia, was named director of public worship and education.

These concessions were calculated to reconcile at least the constitutional party. Unhappily their effect was destroyed by the sudden dissolution, on April the sixth, of the committee of safety, the citizens' police, and the Agricultural Society, in which the mass of the people had placed their hopes. The demonstrations continued, the city was illuminated, and the Roman Catholic priests especially did their best to sow discontent. On the seventh of April a crowd assembled in the square of the *Zamok* before the castle of the viceroy, and demanded that the edict of dissolution should be withdrawn; but in consequence of the hostile attitude of the troops sent out by the viceroy, it dispersed without any result. On the eighth of April the multitude reappeared, more numerous and more violent than before, shouting that they wanted a country; a postilion, who was driving a postchaise, played on his cornet the favorite air of Dombrovski's legions, "No, Poland shall not perish." The crowd, composed in great part of women and children, and headed by priests with crucifixes, presented a passive resistance and an invincible inertia, on which the charges of cavalry had no effect. The troops, at last losing patience, irritated by shouts and even missiles, had recourse to their arms, and fifteen rounds of shot laid two hundred dead and a large number of wounded at the feet of the statue of the Virgin. On the following days the people appeared only in mourning, in spite of the prohibition of the police. This uneasy state of things was prolonged for many months. The government made yet one more attempt at conciliation when, on the death of Prince Gortchakof, the Emperor appointed Count Lambert as viceroy, with orders to apply the reforms decreed in March, eighteen hundred and sixty-one; but the effect of his nomination was weakened by the presence at his side of men devoted to the policy of repression. On the tenth of October a procession of Poles and Lithuanians celebrated at Hodlevo, on the Polo-Lithuanian frontier, the four hundredth anniversary of the union of the two countries. The humanity of the Russian commandant allowed the fête to be held without the shedding of blood, though the procession was not permitted to enter the city of Lublin.

The anti-Russian party had not given up the struggle. On the fifteenth of October, on the anniversary of Kosciuszko's death, the people flocked to the churches of Warsaw; the military authorities caused the churches to be surrounded by detachments, without seeing that the inoffensive inhabitants, alarmed at this display, would refuse to leave the churches, and that it would be necessary to drag them out by force. In fact, after a useless blockade that lasted all day and until four of the next morning, the soldiers had to break their way violently into the cathedral, and carry two thousand people to the fortress. This was declared to be a desecration of the churches, and they were closed by the administrator of the Archbishop. The Protestant and Jewish ministers followed his example, and thus the disorder spread. Count Lambert loudly complained to General Gerstenszweig, the military governor. After a fierce altercation the latter blew out his brains, and Lambert was recalled.

He was succeeded, on the fifth of November, by Count Lüders, who began a period of thorough reaction, and caused a considerable number of influential Warsovians to be transported. But the demonstrations only increased in violence. The newly appointed Archbishop Fiélinski reopened the churches in February, eighteen hundred and sixty-two. On the twenty-ninth of April, the Emperor's birthday, an amnesty was promulgated, but caused little change. The Grand Duke Konstantin, made viceroy on the eighth of June, eighteen hundred and sixty-two, again tried the policy of reconciliation. Viélopolski, one of the promoters of the address to the Emperor, was appointed chief of the civil power and vice-president of the Polish State Council; at the same time Polish gentlemen were nominated governors of the provinces, and directed to carry out the reforms decreed in the ukas of March, eighteen hundred and sixty-one. The Jews were emancipated, the condition of the peasants was ameliorated, the Catholic clergy were promised redress for their grievances, and the University of Warsaw was granted native-born instructors. But the fanaticism of the Poles was rampant. Enthusiasts attempted the lives of the government officials. On the twenty-seventh of June General Lüders was severely wounded by an assassin; on June second three attempts were made upon the Grand Duke himself; and in August Viélopolski was twice the object of assassination. Violent men profited by all the errors of the government to push things to extremity, and to turn its good intentions to its disadvantage. The Poles of Warsaw committed the error of disquieting Russia about the provinces which it regarded as Russian, and an integral part of the empire; the proprietors did not content themselves with demanding, in an address to Viélopolski, that the government of Poland should be Polish, which was reasonable and just, but insisted that the Lithuanian palatinates should be reunited to the kingdom. The upper classes of Podolia in October expressed the same wish with regard to that province, to Volhynia and the Ukraina. These imprudences caused the exile of Zamoïski, and the arrest of the Podolian agitators.

All understanding became now impossible; an exercise of arbitrary authority precipitated the explosion. Since the peace of Paris the usual military conscription had been suspended in Poland, in order to give the country chance of recuperation; but in September, eighteen hundred and sixty-two, the order came for a renewal of the offensive measure. Viélopolski, who was aware of the dangerous state of public opinion, conceived the desperate expedient of ordering the military to seize all the instigators of disturbances throughout Poland, and place them in Russian regiments. He thus hoped to render them harmless.

During the night of the fifteenth of January, eighteen hundred and sixty-three, between the hours of one and eight, the recruits, thus arbitrarily chosen, were taken from their houses, from their very beds, and hastily carried away to the army. Students, usually exempted from serving in the ranks, were this time not spared: the conscription was especially enforced upon men upwards of fifteen years of age who had no settled profession, and hence were at leisure to attend to political agitation. Before the conscription had taken place, many escaped into the woods, where their friends brought them provisions, clothing, guns, and ammunition. The official journal of Warsaw published an account of the seizure of the recruits, and added that there had been no resistance; that, on the contrary, the young men marched to the barracks contentedly and even gayly. This was a last insult. In all circles the anger and indignation of those whose friends had been so summarily taken from them knew no bounds.

The conscripts who escaped from the police formed the nucleus of the rebel bands which appeared at Blonié and at Siérotsk. Before the first of February encounters took place between Poles and Russians at Radom, Plotsk, Lublin, and other places. The fighting soon became universal. A secret central committee, which received implicit obedience though its members were not known, addressed a proclamation to the people with a summons to arms, and on the twenty-second of January was established as a provisional government. Decrees were issued granting those peasants who fought in the national army liberty and free possession of property. The peasants, however, generally showed reluctance in coming forward: it was from the city population, the clergy, and many of the nobility that the revolutionists received encouragement. But the aristocratic party, or the "Whites," held with Vićlopolski at least during the early months of the insurrection. When the Western powers expressed sympathy and offered diplomatic intervention, then the heads of the Agricultural Society began to participate in the revolution, because they feared, if they longer held aloof, that Russia would declare the revolt to be merely that of a mob, and because they feared also that they were losing moral influence and giving Poland into the hands of demagogues.

Mićroslavski was chosen dictator, but was soon defeated and driven over the border. Langiévitch, appointed dictator on the twelfth of March, was also obliged to take refuge in Galicia, where he was arrested by the Austrian authorities. Archbishop Fićlinski addressed a letter to the Emperor, begging him "to put an end to this war of extermination," and showing that the only way to do so was to give the Poles an autonomous administration. Alexander, on the thirteenth of April, offered amnesty to all who would lay down their arms within a month; but the central committee, which acted as dictator, repudiated the amnesty, and its influence was so great that no one attempted to take advantage of the Emperor's mercy. It also passed a decree declaring every act which was calculated to hinder its authority or weaken the revolutionary impulse to be high treason, punishable by death, and the decree was executed rigorously. The war, however, could by no means assume the great character of those of seventeen hundred and ninety-four and of eighteen hundred and thirty-one; there was now no Polish army to struggle seriously with that of Russia: it was a petty war of guerillas and sharpshooters, who could nowhere hold their own against the Russians, but who plunged into the thick forests of Poland, and concealed themselves there, or who fled only to appear farther on and harass the columns. There were no battles, only skirmishes, the most serious of which was that of Vengrov, on the sixth of February, eighteen hundred and sixty-three. A few chiefs made themselves names: among these were Leof Frankovski, Sigismond Padlevski, Kasimir Bogdanovitch, Miélentski, the energetic Bossak-Hauke, who afterwards fell under the French flag in the fields of Burgundy, the French Rochebrune and Blankenheim, Miss Pustovoïzhov, Siérakovski, an ex-colonel in the Russian army, who was hanged after his check in Lithuania, the priest-soldier Matskiévitch, Narbutt, a son of the historian, and Lélével, a Warsaw workman who adopted this pseudonym.

The Russian liberals, since the accession of Alexander, had felt strong sympathy for Poland. Their wishes for the new régime, their hatred of old institutions, had common ground. Polish freedom was discussed in the same breath with Russian freedom. Herzen and Bakunin, the leaders of radicalism, were the champions of free constitutions and perfect liberty for both countries. The London exiles embraced the defence of Polish independence with passionate enthusiasm; the *Kolokol* summoned the officers of Polish regiments to refuse to fight against the cause of freedom. Liberal Russia was undecided what course to take, which side to choose.

It was at this critical period that Mikhaïl Katkof, the editor of the Moscow Gazette, spoke the word which was to decide the momentous question. He declared that Russia had no right to amuse itself with liberal ideas in face of the danger that was threatening on the side of Poland; that every Russian patriot had only one duty, and that was to crush all rebels who endangered the unity of the state. He declared that Russia had long enough shown forbearance, and allowed the rebels to do as they pleased; had long enough restrained the arm of vengeance for the sake of Utopian liberalism. The point in question, according to him, was not that of concession to Poles, but whether Russia was to be obliged to give up the border lands which for more than fifty years had been its undisputed territory. He showed how the Russian state must be maintained in its entirety if the liberal plans for the future were to be carried out. Only foolish sentimentality could see in the Poles aught else than foes to Russia. "He who has a spark of patriotic honor within his breast must forever break with these traitors, nor sheathe his sword until the last rebellious Pole lies prone upon the ground." This utterance of Pan-slavism had a tremendous effect. When the revolution had spread all over Lithuania, then Katkof demanded " the restoration of the Russian character of the Lithuanian land and the old national freedom which had once prevailed there." The democrats were easily persuaded that a contest with the Poles and against their claims on Lithuania was a liberal work; the orthodox Philo-slavs were assured that they ought to resist the Polish Catholic party, and restore the Greek church to Lithuania; and the Pan-slavists were taught that the Poles were suborned to Roman Catholicism and Western ideas, and must be brought back to orthodoxy and nationality. The Moscow Gazette also harped on the danger of Western intervention and a foreign war. Thus all parties united against Poland and in favor of Russianizing the Lithuanian lands. Katkof also succeeded in getting General Muravief, who had hitherto been hated by every liberal as a military despot of the deepest dye, appointed to crush the revolt with his brutal power. His cruelty was looked upon as the highest virtue. He was to restore the Russian character to the northwest provinces. "Muravief interpreted this phrase with the most frightful reality. In a land whose cultured classes for centuries had consisted of nothing but Poles and Catholics, in which the ideas of culture and Polish rule had always been synonymous, the national governor-general treated the Poles as foreigners, forbade the use of the Polish language and the employment of Polish letters, ordered hundreds of Catholic churches to be closed under the pretext that they had been Russian four centuries before, and executed all this with the approval of the Russian press and the Russian public. As incapable as they had been at Moscow and Saint Petersburg, in the years from eighteen hundred and fifty-nine to eighteen hundred and sixty-one, to distinguish between anarchy and freedom, equally incapable were they now of distinguishing the right of self-preservation from the rudest barbarism and the trampling underfoot of all human rights. Patriotic phrases were spoken without thought, and there was no horror that was not invested with some show of patriotism, and thus pronounced salutary. There was no banquet and no public demonstration which did not end with telegrams sent to the Russian leader at Vilna and to the Moscow journalist."

The exasperated Russians treated the towns and villages concerned in the insurrection with great cruelty. The village of Ibiany was destroyed; all the Polish chiefs taken with arms in their hands were shot or hanged. General Muravief in Lithuania declared that it was "useless to make prisoners." Count Berg, who in July was appointed Vićlopolski's successor as vice-president of the council, and, on the departure of the Grand Duke Konstantin for Saint Petersburg, on the twenty-fifth of August, eighteen hundred and sixty-three, was made viceroy, took the severest measures of repression. All the higher and lower offices of state were filled with Russians. All sorts of punishments were inflicted upon the unhappy Poles. So, too, Dlotovskoï, in Livonia, and Annenkof, in the Ukraina, were the agents of a rigorous system of cruelty and repression. Fićlinski, Archbishop of Warsaw, was transported into the interior of Russia, as a punishment for having written his letter to the Emperor.

The sympathy of Europe became aroused. On the fifth of January, eighteen hundred and sixty-three, the French minister Billault, in the tribune of the Corps Législatif, blamed the "baseless hopes excited in the minds of patriots, whose powerless efforts could only bring about new evils"; he recommended the insurgents to the clemency of Alexander. Then France, England, and Austria decided to have recourse to diplomatic intervention, and invited the other powers who had signed the Treaty of Vienna to join in their efforts. They laid before the

Russian government the notes of April, eighteen hundred and sixty-three, which invited it to put an end to the periodical agitations of Poland by a policy of conciliation. On June seventeenth the three powers proposed a programme with the following conditions: An amnesty; the establishment of a national representation; the nomination of Poles to public offices; the abolition of restrictions placed on Catholic worship; the exclusive use of the Polish language, as the official language of the administration, of justice, and of education; a regular and legal system of recruiting. This intervention of the Western powers, which was supported by no military demonstration, was rejected by the famous note of Prince Gortchakof, Chancellor of the empire, and the idea of a European conference was likewise rejected. Europe found itself powerless, and Napoleon the Third was forced to content himself, in his speech from the throne, with the declaration that the treaties of eighteen hundred and fifteen were "trampled underfoot at Warsaw." The conduct of Prussia was quite different. It concluded with Russia the convention of the eighth of February, eighteen hundred and sixty-three, for the suppression of the Polish manifestations, and thus laid the foundation of that Prusso-Russian alliance which was to prove so useful to its interests.

This insurrection cost Poland dear. The last remains of its autonomy were extinguished. To-day the "kingdom" is nothing but a name; in eighteen hundred and sixty-six the country was divided into ten provinces. The Russian language has replaced the Polish in all public acts; the University of Warsaw is a Russian university; the primary, secondary, and superior education all lend their aid to the work of denationalization. Poland lost its institutions without obtaining the benefit of those of Russia, — the *zemstva*, the jury, and the new tribunals. As the government held the nobles responsible for the insurrection, it therefore decidedly favored the peasants, authorizing them to "enter into full and entire possession of the lands which they held." The price of redemption which was to have been paid into the hands of the noble to indemnify him for his loss was extremely small, but even this was now transferred to the state, and only those nobles who took no part in the revolt were allowed to receive the advantage of it. This measure, which robbed the landed proprietors of Lithuania of three fourths of their wealth, was fully approved of by the Russian liberals. An ukas of the tenth of December, eighteen hundred and sixty-five, commanded all persons compromised in the revolt to sell their estates within a short time allotted; another law forbade persons of Polish descent and professing the Catholic faith to buy them in; Russians alone might be purchasers.

Katkof declared that the Germans in the Baltic provinces and the Swedes in Finland were as dangerous as the Poles, and that they ought to be Russianized; but the government replied that it was convinced of the loyalty of these provinces, and would leave them untouched. Finland, therefore, had all its privileges confirmed. In eighteen hundred and sixty-three, Alexander convoked the diet of the grand duchy, the second that had been held since the annexation to the empire. The German nobility of the Baltic provinces, more docile and more politic than that of Poland, were not disturbed. The University of Dorpat remained a German university; the government took measures simply to protect the language and religion of the empire against the propagation of the German tongue and of the Protestant religion. The bold demands of the Slavophil Iuri Samarin, in his "Russian Frontiers," a phenomenal pamphlet published in eighteen hundred and sixty-seven, and the lively polemic sustained against him by the Baltic writers, Schirren, Wilhelm von Bock, Julius Eckart, and Sternberg, did not lead to any important changes in the three governments of Livonia, Kurland, and Esthonia.

INTELLECTUAL MOVEMENT; MATERIAL PROGRESS; EDUCATION.

The Russian agitation began simultaneously with the troubles in Poland. At the beginning it seemed associated with the Polish movement. The students of Saint Petersburg made open manifestations of sympathy at the time of the Warsaw anniversaries; and the students of Kazan attended the funeral of Petrof, the insurgent peasant. Kovalevski, the minister of education, had prepared a project for allowing the utmost freedom in instruction and for the abolition of the old military system which treated the students like cadets. This project, borrowed from principles which had been tested in Germany, was submitted for examination to a committee composed of Count Viktor Panin, Minister of Justice, Prince Dolgoruki, the head of the secret police, Count Stroganof, and others who, thoroughly imbued with reactionary sentiments, passed an adverse judgment upon Kovalevski's project. He was obliged to retire, and was succeeded by Count Putiatin, a thoroughly incapable and narrow man. During the following winter Putiatin prepared a new law which took away from the students much of the freedom which they had before enjoyed; the entrance fee was raised; the students were forbidden to hold meetings, to continue their fund for the assistance of poor young men, and their libraries and conferences were closed.

This new law was scarcely noticed in consequence of the nearness of the vacation, but in the autumn it was received with a storm of indignation at Saint Petersburg, Moscow, Kharkof, and Kief. The students in a body refused to sign their acceptance of the distasteful requirements, and several hundred sent in a petition to Sresnevski, the acting vice-vector, in which they protested against the increase in the admission fee, the abolition of their fund, and the prohibition of their journal. The curator Philippson replied to this statement of their grievances by closing the lectures, the library, and the chemical department. On the twenty-fourth of September some nine hundred students, accompanied by a throng of people, proceeded to the curator's house to demand explanations. General Patkul, the head of the city police, and the Grand Duke Konstantin vainly attempted to disperse the excited youths. A deputation was sent to treat with the curator, and while the negotiations were going on, Count Shuvalof, General Patkul, and General Ignatief, with a body of soldiers, surrounded the students on all sides. The deputation could come to no terms with Philippson, who demanded as a preliminary the signature of the declaration; to this the students absolutely refused to submit. Finally, on the promise of the students no longer to disturb the peace of the city, Philippson, seconded by Ignatief, the governor-general, agreed to open the lectures again on the second of October, and the libraries and laboratories on the following morning, and that no one should be put under arrest.

On the twenty-fifth of September the news spread that the student deputies and spokesmen had been surprised during the night and thrown into prison. It was discovered, however, that the minister was the one in fault, and not Philippson, who had done his best to promote the interests of the students. The students therefore resolved to present an address to Count Putiatin, and while the paper was in circulation soldiers appeared with bayonets to take the university building, the gates of which were in possession of the students. But the demonstrations of the public in favor of the students were so pronounced that the troops were withdrawn. A deputation of five young men went to the minister, but were unable to get any satisfaction. They were allowed to depart in peace, but on the following night they and several other ringleaders were taken from their houses and incarcerated in the fortress, and the university building was guarded by a detachment of infantry. The young men were severely punished, the university lectures were closed for several months; but when the Emperor returned from the Crimea, the minister who had acted with such perfidy and severity was obliged to resign, and was replaced by Golovnin, the Secretary of State.

The student revolts in Moscow were even more serious. Collisions occurred between the discontented young men and the police, and several of the former were wounded. Professor Pavlof, who almost challenged insurrection, was forbidden longer to lecture, and was sent to Siberia without trial; the imprisoned students were treated with pitiless severity. But public opinion declared itself so strongly that a new statute was prepared which met the requirements of the time. General Ignatief, in consequence of his compliance with Putiatin's projects, was compelled to resign his post as governor-general of Saint Petersburg. He was followed by Prince Suvarof, "a man generally beloved for his humane disposition." His appointment was received with universal joy and gratitude.

Next in importance came addresses from the assemblies of nobles: that of Tver, in eighteen hundred and sixty-two, requested the abolition of privileges, and the convocation of a national assembly; in that of Tula a meeting of the States-general was discussed. Events in Poland soon gave the current of ideas a new direction. The Moscow Gazette, under Mr. Katkof, one of the most brilliant and original journalists of modern times, seized the leadership of opinion. It awakened the national Russian sentiment against the demands of the Poles, and declared to them that nothing now remained for Poland "but to unite its aspirations with those of Russia, and thoroughly to accept the principles which have been developed and are still in process of development in the political growth of the Russian people." It provoked demonstrations in honor of Muravief, glorified what it called his energetic and pacific measures in Lithuania, and audaciously ascribed the numerous fires which occurred in eighteen hundred and sixty-two to Polish emissaries. By making itself the advocate of Russian nationality, the press gained unexpected freedom, and Mr.

Katkof took advantage of it to impose upon even the ministers. He was the man of the new state of things, as Herzen had been that of the liberal movement at the beginning of the reign. On the fourth of April, eighteen hundred and sixty-six, Vladimir Karakozof, who had formerly studied at Moscow, fired his pistol at the Emperor as he was walking in the Summer Garden. It was found that the young man was not a Pole, but a Russian democratic socialist, belonging to a revolutionary society established in the two capitals. This attempt and that of Berezovski, at Paris, in eighteen hundred and sixty-seven, in the name of the Polish revolution, show how deeply men's minds were troubled. It would be idle to give a detailed account of the changes of ministers — sometimes progressive, sometimes reactionary — who reflected the impressions produced by events on the mind of the Emperor. Under a government which on the whole was liberal, Russia still continued to undergo transformation. It will be sufficient to enumerate a few of the results.

The preceding government bequeathed to Russia only three hundred and fifty kilometers of railway. In eighteen hundred and seventy-four there were less than sixteen thousand versts; in eighteen hundred and seventy-nine there were more than twenty thousand versts in active operation, and about seven hundred and thirty-six versts in process of construction. The net receipts of the fifty-three different lines had increased from about thirty million rubles in eighteen hundred and sixty-nine, to seventy-eight million seven hundred and eighty-five thousand four hundred and ninety-seven rubles in eighteen hundred and seventy-eight. The railways unite nearly all the large towns of Russia in Europe; in the north they end at Helsingfors and at Vologda; in the east at Nijni-Novgorod, Saratof, Samara, with a line projected as far as Orenburg; in the south at Kishenef, Odessa, Kherson, Sevastopol, and Taganrog, with a line projected as far as Vladikavkas. Russia is placed in communication with the west by means of the lines of Saint Petersburg and Berlin, Warsaw and Berlin, Warsaw and Vienna, and Kishenef and Iassy. The Caucasian line already unites Poti on the Black Sea to Tiflis; it will be prolonged as far as Baku on the Caspian, which will be connected by steam navigation with Krasnovodsk. The Siberian railway is at present under consideration. The four seas, the great lakes, the rivers and canals of Russia, are furrowed by numerous steamboats. The river Volga is navigated by the steamboats of four great companies which run from Tver to Astrakhan. Others go from Kama to Perm. They are remarkable for the comfort which they offer travellers. On the Caspian Sea there is postal service between Astrakhan, Derbent, Baku, Enzeli, and Ali-Alad. Steam navigation has tended to destroy the occupation of the *burlaki* who were accustomed to tow rafts and vessels from Astrakhan to Ruibinsk, a distance of more than three thousand five hundred kilometers. The telegraph and the postal service, of which the cost has been lowered, put the empire in rapid and regular communication with the whole world. In January, eighteen hundred and seventy-nine, there were eighty-eight thousand five hundred and eighteen versts of telegraph, with about double that length of wire. Of the two thousand one hundred and sixty-six offices, nine hundred and thirty-five belong to the state. During the preceding year five million three hundred and sixty-nine thousand nine hundred and thirty-five messages were sent, four fifths of which were on inland service. The financial statement showed a surplus. There were three thousand six hundred and seventy-eight post-offices in eighteen hundred and seventy-eight, conveying ninety-three million six hundred and ninety-two thousand five hundred and sixty-one letters and post-cards and sixty-three million three hundred and fifty thousand and sixty-four newspapers. The postal department is not, as yet, self-supporting.

Trade has also greatly developed. "The people are beginning to move," writes Mr. Herbert Barry, "and many manufactories are in course of construction. The Russians are clever at all handicrafts. An Englishman, the director of a paper factory which I was astonished to find in the middle of the Ural Mountains, told me that in England many years of apprenticeship were needed to make a good paper-worker, but that a Russian learned as much in three months as an Englishman in three years." The branches of commerce which have prospered the most are the manufactures of cotton and silk, the establishments in the interest of metallurgy, and steel foundries. In eighteen hundred and sixty-four there were estimated to be in European Russia fourteen million seven hundred and nineteen thousand horses, forty-three million sheep, and twenty-one million cattle, the annual income of which amounted to between three and four hundred million of rubles. In eighteen hundred and sixty-three more than one hundred and eighty million kilograms of iron-ore was produced, and two hundred and seventy-eight million four hundred and sixty thousand kilos of coal. In eighteen hundred and twenty-eight only a little more than five thousand kilos of gold were produced in Russia. In eighteen hundred and forty-seven the product was one hundred and eighty-five thousand two hundred and seven kilos. In eighteen hundred and sixty-five new mines were discovered in the Trans-Caucasus and the following year in Turkestan. Numerous banks have been started, even in some of the most remote towns of the empire.

Primary education in Russia leaves more to be desired than in any other country in Europe. Russia, with its nine or ten per cent of people who can read, is below even Austria, which reckons only twenty-nine per cent. In France the average is seventy-seven per cent. Owing to the efforts of the minister of public instruction, and the minister of war in his regimental schools, the average is slowly but surely rising. In eighteen hundred and sixty, out of one hundred recruits only two could read and write; ten years later eleven per cent was the average. The proportion in the German Baltic provinces was far greater, being one to eighteen; in Finland, one to twenty-one; in Poland, one to thirty-four. The population of Russia, in eighteen hundred and seventy-seven, was eighty-six million seven hundred and twenty-eight thousand. Primary education is more advanced in Poland because of the efforts of the government; in the Baltic provinces and in Finland, because of the Protestant culture; in Central Russia, because of the industrial influences. In eighteen hundred and seventy-one the minister, Tolstoï, in his report to the Emperor, enumerates twenty-four thousand schools attended by eight hundred and seventy-five thousand scholars, and four hundred and twenty-four superior primary schools, attended by twenty-seven thousand eight hundred and thirty scholars.

On the first of January, eighteen hundred and seventy-two, there existed one hundred and twenty-six *gymnasia* and thirty-two *progymnasia*, with forty-two thousand seven hundred and ninety-one pupils. At this same date Mr. Tolstoï had issued an order to introduce or confirm the study of Greek and Latin in these establishments. On the other hand, the regulation of the twelfth of May, eighteen hundred and seventy-three, instituted practical schools for the teaching of professions.

In eighteen hundred and seventy-six, the universities of Saint Petersburg, founded in eighteen hundred and nineteen; Moscow, founded in seventeen hundred and fifty-five; Kharkof, Kazan, Kief, Dorpat, founded in sixteen hundred and thirty, but reorganized in eighteen hundred and two; New Russia, or Odessa, founded in eighteen hundred and sixty-four, and Warsaw, founded in eighteen hundred and sixty-nine, — reckoned five thousand four hundred and sixty-six students and four hundred and fifty-seven free pupils. Among the students, thirteen hundred and twenty-five were the recipients of scholarships.

To the educational institutions for the daughters of the nobility, established by Catherine the Second and developed by Maria Feodorovna, wife of Paul, were added seminaries of a kind more appropriate to the new needs, and where young girls of all classes are received. These are the female gymnasia and progymnasia, — lyceums for girls, though not boarding-schools. The earliest of these schools were founded under the auspices of the late Empress, from the funds belonging to the fourth section of the imperial chancery. They are twenty-six in number, — six at Saint Petersburg, five at Moscow, fifteen in the provinces. The state of female education is thus well described by Julius Eckardt, the author of "Europe Before and After the War": "The miserable condition of female education was so notorious, so indisputable, and had been already, in the days of the Crimean war, a fact so universally lamented, that Norof, the Minister of Instruction at that time, was forced to confess it, in his report of eighteen hundred and fifty-six, to the Emperor, and to ask for an entirely new organization. The scheme prepared for this purpose was ready in May, eighteen hundred and fifty-eight, but could not be properly carried into effect, as the ministry of finance declared themselves unable to assign the necessary funds. The state, therefore, turned to the communes, the provincial estates, and private persons, who, in accordance with a statute ratified by the Emperor (and altered again on the tenth of May, eighteen hundred and sixty), were authorized to establish higher and lower 'female gymnasia,' after the pattern of similar schools in Germany, each of which, when established, should enjoy the patronage of the Empress. The matter, however progressed, very slowly, the government giving a very lukewarm support, and the communes and provincial diets being already burdened with too many other obligations to be able to raise larger sums. Newspapers and periodicals did all they could, and more, by discussing 'the woman's question' and the problem 'How to educate our girls,' and advancing the newest and most daring theories on this subject and its 'connection with our general development.' But, in spite of all this, the number of newly established schools remained small. At the end of eighteen hundred and seventy-two there were in Russia and Poland fifty-five female gymnasia and one hundred and thirty-one lower gymnasia, with a total of about twenty-five thousand female pupils. Since then no statistics have been published; but the regulations and directions have become all the more prolix and detailed. They extend to the smallest minutiæ of management: Who is to act as curator, and who as honorary curator, of each school; who is to nominate and appoint the heads and teachers of the different classes; what functions are to be performed by the conference of curators, composed of representatives of the state institutes, and what by the 'Pedagogic Conference,' conducted either by the director of schools in the province, or the inspector of the 'circle.'" Nowhere in Europe has such a vast development been given to the scientific education of young girls, and nowhere have they been given such easy access to liberal careers, and to government employments, such as in the telegraph and postal service. "In eighteen hundred and sixty-four the first Russian ladies were inscribed in the medical faculty of the University of Zürich. In eighteen hundred and sixty-eight, for the first time, a woman, who had completed her studies in midwifery, obtained permission to attend the lectures of the Medico-Chirurgical Faculty at Saint Petersburg. The incident created so much sensation, and was received so favorably by the leaders of public opinion, that other ladies soon followed suit, and seven years later the female medical students at Zürich could be counted by dozens, and at Saint Petersburg by hundreds. In eighteen hundred and seventy-two, special courses for married and unmarried women were opened at the Medico-Chirurgical Academy at Saint Petersburg, and more than five hundred females attended them. In eighteen hundred and seventy-three there were no less than seventy-seven Russian ladies studying medicine at Zürich. Although the right of practising has not yet been conceded to female physicians, there are now at Saint Petersburg several hundreds of female students; and the example thus set by the capital has been copied at the universities of Moscow, Kief, Kharkof, and Odessa." In eighteen hundred and seventy-nine, sixteen million two hundred and thirty thousand one hundred and sixteen rubles were devoted by the government to public instruction.

CHAPTER X.

LITERATURE AND ART DURING THE REIGN OF ALEXANDER THE SECOND.

1856–1880.

The Natural and Realistic Schools. — Influence of the French Novelists. — The Historical Drama and Novel. — History. — Periodicals. — The Artistic and Scientific Movement.

THE NATURAL AND REALISTIC SCHOOLS.

THE period which followed the Crimean war was remarkable for its literary activity. Under the stimulus of comparative freedom the press developed with unexampled rapidity. An earthquake had shaken the social edifice to the ground; it seemed as though all old things had passed away, and it was the duty of the hour to build anew with fresh materials upon untried foundations. A host of writers filled the periodicals of the day with crude and extravagant theories, hastily gathered from French, English, and German philosophy. Vast systems of improvement, which worked well on paper, were devised; lofty ideals, which could never be realized, were held up for emulation.

The natural school, of which Turgenief is the chief, found a wide field in delineating this chaotic state, in painting the figures which became typical of the men of the generation of eighteen hundred and forty, the enthusiastic theorizers who excelled in planning and talking, but left the real work to be done by others. Turgenief's "Rudin" is the prototype of this class of "useless men." He speaks fluently and eloquently, but the sound of his voice is of more consequence than the clearness of the ideas which are so abundant. He easily deceives himself and others, that he is full of the fire which purifies and the life which transforms. He proves how noble and honorable a thing it is to work for others and to be unselfish ; but at heart he is selfish, a profound egotist, unable to do more than project great enterprises. When the test comes he is found to be entirely wanting. His theories of self-sacrifice and loftiness of soul are seen to be mere words. He finally perishes without accomplishing anything by his life. "He is the sad product of a sad social state." Lavretski, in "A Nest of Noblemen," is another type of the same species. In this novel Turgenief describes also the quarrel between the two old parties, the Slavophils and the Occidentalists, revived by the question of reforms. Lavretski is a mild type of the Slavophil ; he has a wide acquaintance with his country and its needs ; he sees the absurdity of Panshin's application of Western notions, gathered in his study, to a people whose history and peculiarities are unique.

In eighteen hundred and fifty-nine appeared "On the Eve," which seems to have been a sort of prophecy that the country was approaching a crisis. The "useless men," the men of words, are supplanted by men of action. Rudin gives place to Insarof, more practical, a quiet worker, with less brilliancy and depth, but with greater moral earnestness than the former. "Father and Sons," published two years later, shows, as its name implies, the contrasts in society at this time of transition. Another type is given to us in Gontcharof's great novel, "Oblómof." Oblómof's education has been superficial, his character is weak and devoid of energy, consequently his normal state is that of an invalid ; he rarely leaves his chamber, he delights in his luxurious laziness, in his apathetic weariness. His friends try to stir him from his indolence, but their efforts are vain. At last he is aroused by a young girl. "Olga is the most beautiful ideal which an artist could gather from contemporary life in Russia. The elevation and breadth of her mind, the admirable harmony between her will and her heart, are so striking that the reader is disposed to doubt the poetic truth of the picture, and to deny that such a young girl could exist. But as you study her character throughout the book you find that she is always consistent; she is not a mere conception of the author's imagination, but rather a real person whom we have not yet been fortunate enough to meet. It is she rather than Stolz who is the ideal of the new Russian life; from her we expect the revivifying word which is to awaken and inspire Oblómof." Oblómof allows her influence to control him, and for a time emerges from his apathy, but when the question arises of marriage with Olga, and he considers all the duties, the cares and responsibilities which will devolve upon him, he sinks back into his former state. Olga marries his friend Stolz, who is his complete opposite, a man of energy, iron will, and fully developed life.

Rudinism and Oblomovism were two of the chief maladies of the time, and the difference between their two types is the difference between Turgenief and Gontcharof. "Turgenief is above all the painter of the mind, Gontcharof of the heart. Turgenief's characters are full of life; they develop every instant by their contact with the world. Gontcharof simply makes pictures; his portraits are marvellous for their finish and delicacy of design, but they are too abstract, too far removed from real life; they lack animation and movement."

While Pisemski is inferior to Turgenief in skill of psychologic analysis, and to Gontcharof in the artistic development of details, he holds a high place in the literary history of Russia. His characteristics are brilliancy and strength, a power in devising dramatic situations, a poetic appreciation of the life of the time, absolute freedom from artificiality, and faithfulness to his ideal of truth. In the best of his romances, the "Thousand Souls," published in eighteen hundred and fifty-eight, Pisemski struck a fuller chord than in his earlier novels, which were barely freed from the influence of Gogol. He brings out vividly the lack of individuality, the mental paralysis, the many sides of incapacity which were a result of the cankerous disease of slavery. Kalinovitch, the hero, has all the vices of the age. He is winning in his manners, but at heart egotistic, selfish, ambitious, venal. He is resolved to have honors and wealth at any price, and to attain his end he ruthlessly sacrifices the love of Nastasia, who has left everything to nurse him through illness; and by marrying the immoral and deformed daughter of a wealthy old general's widow, the owner of a thousand serfs, he gratifies his ambition. He constantly advances in political position, until finally he becomes governor of the province where he had begun his career as director of the gymnasium. With all the energy of his character he now declares a pitiless war upon the officials whom he finds guilty of peculation or of accepting bribes. He tries to forget his moral suffering, his own faithlessness to a higher ideal, in his absolute justice, his unwavering severity to all offenders. His official acts bring upon him the hatred of the community; his wife turns against him; he is removed from office, when he is abandoned by all. Nastasia again comes to his aid, and upon the suicide of his wife marries him, "because she was the only thing left to him in this world, and because it was her duty to sustain and cherish the life of this great mind, — a wreck, but still precious."

Pisemski, in a "Thousand Souls," gives an accurate picture of the new type of officials who made their appearance at the time of the reforms. Kalinovitch has the faults of the age which is going by, but he has also the characteristics of the new era about to be inaugurated. The vices and qualities natural to a period of transition are thus seen in the same person. The contrasts and contradictions of his life are well sustained by the author.

Besides the writers whom we have mentioned, and Dostoïevski, the painter and historian, *par excellence*, of the victims of fate and social oppression, and who published his novel, "The Downtrodden and Oppressed," in eighteen hundred and sixty-one, we may mention, among the writers of the natural school, Kokaref, whose sketches and tales are interesting as autobiography; Madame Zhadovska, author of "Far from the Great World"; and a lady who, under the pseudonyme of Marko Vovtchok, published a series of Little Russian tales which Turgenief translated. Her specialty is the life of the Russian peasants and serfs, and the manners and customs of the small proprietors. "Marko Vovtchok seems to listen to the still distant murmur of the future life of the people; her writings breathe, as it were, a perfume of Russia, by offering images familiar and precious to every Russian, expressed in a style thoroughly national and popular." "Masha," "Igrushetchka," and "Iekaterina" are among the best known of her works.

The first few years of Alexander's reign, and the changes which they introduced, stimulated the satiric spirit; its principal exponents were Andréi Petcherski and the formidable Shtchedrin. Petcherski's light tales, "The Bear's Lair" and "Bygone Years," enjoyed great popularity. Saltuikof was a provincial governor and privy councillor, who, under the pseudonyme, Shtchedrin, in his "Provincial Sketches" and his "Prose Satires" makes an especial study of the officials and their surroundings, of their tendency to exaggerate trifles and to insist on routine. He uses a whip of serpents in his attacks on the foibles of society. Sometimes his wit and satire are inartistic and incomplete, but his characters are generally careful and exact types belonging to an interesting and peculiar age.

The dramatic literature of this period counts three principal names,—Ostrovski, Potićkhin, and Pisemski. Ostrovski wrote, in eighteen hundred and fifty-eight, "The Lucrative Place," treating nearly the same subject as Pisemski in his "Thousand Souls"; in "The Storm" he gives a vivid picture of family despotism among the merchant class. "Ostrovski's talent lies in his deep knowledge of the soul, and his skill in opening and exposing the human side of every individual apart from the social position which he occupies." Potićkhin is far inferior to Ostrovski. Pustozerof, the artificial and thoroughly disagreeable hero of "Tinsel," is an official of almost superhuman disinterestedness, who scorns any one devoid of this virtue, though he may possess all the others. Potićkhin's unfamiliarity with the stage makes his characters too much like puppets, although the separate scenes are managed with some skill. Pisemski wrote, besides his novels, a powerful drama, "The Bitter Destiny," which gives also a vivid picture of the unhappy relations existing between the proprietors and their serfs. The success of these dramatic and romantic pictures of contemporary society stimulated a host of imitators, among whom may be mentioned Slavutinski, Diakonof, the author of "The Prosecutors," Count Sollohub, and others.

The Emancipation divides the literary history of Alexander's reign into two distinct epochs. The first, as we have seen, was a period of transition and of sudden awakening. The natural school took upon itself to show the insufficiency of the old generation to grasp the new order of things. But now the great act which liberated twenty-three million serfs was accomplished, and a hundred questions of reform were elevated into the region of reality. Such a complete overturn necessarily had a tremendous effect upon the minds of those in whose midst it occurred. The nation may be said to have grouped itself into hostile camps: there were the retrogrades and conservatives, who were startled by the changes taking place, and saw before them only danger and disaster; who remembered the revolutions which had deluged France with blood, and who predicted the same fate for Russia; who saw in the agitators opposed to them only Nihilists disposed to reject all authority in religion, in morals, in politics, in the arts and sciences. The Liberals, on the other hand, felt that what had been done was incomplete and faulty. They wished the new laws to be applied in their integrity, without being warped to suit old exigencies. When the reaction came, many of them joined the Nihilists, who demanded that the serfs should not only be freed, but put on a basis of equality with the more favored of the land, that all class distinctions should be abolished, and that the most liberal institutions should be given them. Herzen defined Nihilism as the most perfect freedom from all settled concepts, from all inherited restraints and the historical impediments which hamper the progress of the Western intellect. Tchernishevski, whose romance "What is to be Done?" was forbidden by the censor, was the first to make Nihilism popular. It was not strange that the younger generation, the students in the universities and the hot-headed enthusiasts of the intellectual centres, should sometimes carry this doctrine to extremes. Nor was it strange that the leaders of the natural school, seeing the confusion and turmoil, should show themselves hesitating, sometimes even hostile, because they comprehended only the exaggerated side of the new tendencies.

Turgenief, in his novel, "Smoke," published in eighteen hundred and sixty-seven, paints the monstrous evils of this spirit of negation. He shows how all the "reforms, the discussions, the theories, the opinions, the progress of the Russian people, the Russian life itself, is only smoke." The author was vigorously assailed by the critics; he was charged with attacking his country and with caricaturing the younger generation, which he was unable to understand and appreciate.

"If Turgenief is superior to Pisemski in the variety and perfection of his types, in the analysis of the human heart and in beauty of design, Pisemski, on the other hand, excels in the power of vigorously presenting nature and life, which sometimes causes his creations to be as repulsive as the reality itself." In eighteen hundred and sixty-three he published his "Troubled Sea," in which he makes a study of the disgusting and comic side of Nihilism, showing the grossness and sensuality, the low materialism of the men who scorn morality and religion, and believe that marriage is only a social contract to be made and broken at pleasure. Pisemski may have felt that he went too far, for in his next novel, "The Men of Eighteen Hundred and Forty," he gives a picture of a bygone age; but when this failed to be appreciated as it deserved, he came back to the subject of Nihilism, and wrote, in eighteen hundred and seventy-two, a new romance, "In the Vortex," and in the following year two comedies, "The Mines" and "Baal."

Besides Dostoïevski, who wrote the remarkable psychological studies, "Crime and Punishment" and "Mauvais Esprit," and Gontcharof, who likewise painted the social effects of Nihilism in the blackest colors in "The Abyss," we find other followers of the natural school taking the same desperate view. "Marévo," by Kliutchnikof; "No Issue," by Stebnitski, who gives the history of a young Nihilist, Liza Bukharef, and a Socialist, Raïner; and the many romances of Madame Khvotchinski, better known by her pseudonyme of Krestovski,—all take the different phases of the modern spirit, and treat it either with open ridicule or with an overdrawn fidelity which approaches caricature.

The natural reaction against a one-sided treatment of a subject brought to the front a new school of writers, who especially devoted themselves to faithful realistic descriptions of the lower orders of society. By their very wish to fill the void left by the natural school they have gone to the other extreme, and have often indulged in disagreeable exaggerations. The leading exponent of this "literature of the muzhik" is Reshetnikof, whose great novel, "Podlipovtsui," gives a striking picture of the *burlaki*, or rough sailors of the Volga. His favorite themes are poverty, wretchedness, and the brutality of ignorance. The other writers of this realistic school are Uspienski, who wrote "The Ruin" and other stories, and delights in the more jovial side of the peasant life; Pomialovski, whose "Molotof," "Brother and Sister," and "Mikhaïlof," partly autobiographical, and written in a rough, desultory style, show the influence of Dostoievski; Sleptsof, author of "Hard Times"; Avdićef, who wrote "Between Two Fires," and others. Had Reshetnikof not died at the early age of twenty-nine, and had he fulfilled the promise of his youth, it might have been that he would have settled definitely the laws of the new school of realism. Unhappily it "has neither authorities nor principles, nor a definite path. Between the field preferred by the natural writers and that chosen by the realistic writers, there is an immense void which no one has as yet attempted to fill. Turgenief seems to have come near it in his 'Panin and Baburin.' But is the union of the two schools possible? That is a question to be answered by the writers of the future."

INFLUENCE OF THE FRENCH NOVELISTS. — THE HISTORIC DRAMA AND NOVEL.

While George Eliot, Dickens, and Thackeray have had great influence upon the literature of Russia, it is a curious fact that Victor Hugo, Eugéne Sue, and Dumas have found imitators only among an inferior order of writers. Another Krestovski, an officer of the army, in his "Mysteries of Saint Petersburg," had a considerable success; but when he persisted in disregarding the advice of his critics, and published "The Troops of Panurges," it was found that he had reproduced the faults and not the excellences of the former. His last novel, "The Outlaw," published in eighteen hundred and seventy-three, is the greatest failure of all, and "marks the complete decadence of his powers." Boborikin, in "On the Road," "Dr. Tsuibulka," and other stories, shows much wit and imagination, but is lacking in seriousness and depth. Averkief, Avsienko, and Markiévitch have written several romances for the *Russki Viéstnik*, but they deserve only faint praise.

Although the society novel has thus far been preferred by Russian authors, yet the department of the historical romance and drama has by no means been neglected. Count Alexéi Tolstoï wrote "Prince Screbrianui" and the celebrated drama, "The Death of Ivan the Terrible," both of which give vivid pictures of the time of Ivan the Fourth. His other dramatic works, "The Tsar Feodor Ivanovitch" and "The Tsar Boris," form, with the latter, a sort of historical trilogy. The first is, by all odds, the greatest. Count Leof Tolstoï added to the literature of the Napoleonic war of eighteen hundred and twelve his immense romance, in five volumes, entitled "War and Peace," which is considered one of the masterpieces of Russian literature. The work is divided into two distinct parts; and although a multitude of characters appear upon the scene, there is no confusion or lack of clearness. Count Sahlias, in his "Partisans of Pugatchef," imitates the methods of Alexéi Tolstoï, but is far inferior to his model.

Russian history is remarkably rich in dramatic episodes, and many of these have been seized upon by the Slavophil authors and made the subjects of historical plays. Yet, as Courrière justly observes, "Russia has not yet found its Corneille, its Shakspere, or its Schiller. The dramatic writers, borrowing Pushkin's Shaksperian methods, endeavor to bring out the leading figure in the most vivid light. The character of the hero is shown even in its slightest psychological details, hence the other *dramatis personæ* are sacrificed and obliged to keep in the shade like modest satellites around a brilliant sun. The action suffers, the plot is of no account, scenic effects are wholly wanting, the issue of the drama is foreseen and excites no interest, — there is no illusion. Speeches, monologues, and conversations, smacking of bombast and rhetoric, take the place of all this." Meï wrote "The Bride of the

Tsar" and "The Lady of Pskof," but his own productions are not equal to his translations of the ancient Folk Songs, such as the "Tale of the Troops of Igor," which are noticeable for their grace and artistic beauty. "Kozma Minin," "The Voïevod," "Tushmo," and "The False Dmitri and Vasili Shuïski" are Ostrovski's principal historical plays. The last mentioned is the best. "The subject of the play is full of grandeur. The scenes are truly dramatic. The characters of the False Dmitri and of Shuïski are well portrayed. But Ostrovski confines himself too closely to the domain of facts." His plays are apt to be long and monotonous. Ostrovski and Tolstoï found an imitator in Averkief, who in eighteen hundred and seventy-two wrote "Bygone Days at Kashira," representing society in the latter half of the seventeenth century. The success of this drama at Moscow was immediate and complete; at Saint Petersburg it was not so well received. "Vasili the Blind and Prince Shemiaka," by the same author, did not enhance his reputation.

The Crimean war and the abolition of serfage did not seem to inspire the Russian muse to very lofty heights. Between eighteen hundred and fifty and eighteen hundred and sixty the public read with interest the satiric verses of Shtchedrin, Nekrasof, Pisemski, and Minaüf. Maïkof wrote the "Council of Clermont," which relates the sufferings of the Eastern Christians. But his poems are chiefly lyrical. Fet is one of the chief representatives of what may be called "the school of Heine." He delights in picturing the soul weary of life and pleasure-seeking, and he varies his theme with celebrating the azure of the sky, the voice of the waves, and the dreamy eyes of the young maiden. Pleshtchéef, Polonski, and Madame Zhadovska belong to the same lyric school. Polonski is devoted to dreamy sadness. "Under a sombre and fantastic coloring, his verse, which is timid and sometimes even rough and inharmonious, nevertheless reveals an exquisite appreciation of the life of nature."

Benediktof, who is considered to be a follower of Derzhavin, is a poet who delights in singing of justice, disinterestedness, and patriotism. His poems, however, have been scarcely more popular than those of Madame Zhadovska, which have a certain merit of simplicity and naturalness. "Her favorite themes are a dreamy contemplation of nature, solitude, and the memories of a brilliant and happy past forever gone from sight." Rosenheim, Shevtchenko, the patriotic poet of Little Russia, and Nikitin, the postilion lyrist, the poet-laureate of poverty, are names which have a certain reputation.

HISTORY.

In the field of history proper, great activity has been shown, partly owing to Karamsin and partly to the struggle between the Slavophils and the Occidentalists. In eighteen hundred and thirty-four the government founded the Archæological Commission, which was charged to examine and publish ancient chronicles and documents. A short time after, the Historical and Antiquarian Society of Moscow began to publish historical collections. The Academy of Sciences instituted the Archæografic Commission. These societies were emulated by similar ones in Vilna, Kief, Odessa, and other cities. The subject has been still further stimulated by reviews devoted to the publication of historical documents: *Russki Arkhiv*, edited by Barténief, the *Russkïa Stariná*, "Ancient Russia," and the "Collections of the Imperial Society of Russian History," started in eighteen hundred and sixty-seven. The three great names in this department are Pogodin, Kostomorof, and Solovief. Pogodin, a pupil of Karamsin, makes history a true science. His "Critico-historical Sketches" are devoted to the Russia of the Middle Ages. His last work, "Russia up to the Invasion of the Tatars," shows a deep study of the ancient chronicles, and contains many curious and interesting facts about the life of the Slavs at the time of the Grand Princes. Pogodin took an active part in the controversy about the authenticity of "The Chronicle of Nestor," which was attacked by Katchenovski, the editor of the *Viestnik Evropui*, Kostomarof, and Ilovaiski, who tried to prove that the Variagi were not Scandinavians. Kostomarof has published many historical works, among which may be mentioned his "Historical Monographs and Researches," "History of the Fall of Poland," "History of Russia in Biographies." His "Bogdan Khmielnitski," his account of the "Revolt of Stenka Razin," and his "Studies of the Nationalities of Northern Russia" prove him to be a careful and conscientious historian. Solovief, called the Augustin Thierry of Russia, has left behind him a prodigious monument to his painstaking researches in his "History of Russia from the Earliest Times," which at the time of his death had reached as far as the reign of Catherine the Second, in twenty-six volumes. Ustrialof, besides a "History of the False Dmitri" and the "Tales of Prince Kurbski," published a "Life of Peter the Great," in the preparation of which he was allowed to study the secret archives of the European capitals. He wrote also a History of Russia in two volumes, bringing it down to the Crimean war. Zabiélin in his "Private Life of the Tsars, Tsaritsas, and the Russian People in the Sixteenth and Seventeenth Centuries," Bogdanovitch in his "Campaigns of Suvarof," his "History of Alexander the First," and his "History of the War in the East," and Miliutin in his "Campaign of Seventeen Hundred and Ninety-nine" (which was also written by Mikhailovski-Danilev), have made themselves authorities by their accuracy and fairness. We may mention, further, Pekarski's "Science and Literature under Peter the Great," which gives the nomenclature of five hundred and ninety-one works, and Puipin's "Progress of Ideas under Alexander the First." Shtchebalski has published a monograph upon the Princess Sophia, and Semevski upon the Mons family, which was intimately connected with Peter the Great. The epoch of Alexander the First was further illustrated by Baron Korf's "Biography of Count Speranski,"

Kovalevski's "Bludof and his Time," and by the works of Popof. Bantuish-Kamenski, whose "Dictionary of Celebrated Russians" was well known, added another remarkable series in his "Biographies of the Russian Generals and Field Marshals."

The Russian professors have paid especial attention to the antiquities and mythology of the Eastern Slavs. Sreznievski made a study of the heathen forms of worship; Kotlarevski became famous by his book on the "Funeral Rites among the Pagan Slavs"; Afanasief left a thorough monograph on the poetic ideas of the Slavs regarding nature. Tales, legends, superstitions, and popular songs have been collected by Terestchenko, Iakushkin, Sakharof, Kirićevski, Ruibnikof, Shein, Bezsonof, Miller, and others. Fréhn, Savélief, Kunik, and Schubert have made studies of numismatics. Annitchkof and Todleben have described the siege of Sevastopol, while General Fadéief and Colonel Obrutchef have published valuable statistical works on the military resources of the country. Prince Galitsuin has published several parts of a "Universal Military History," which have received much praise.

Historical studies have not been confined to Russian topics. Kudriavtsef, who died in eighteen hundred and fifty-eight, left a remarkable study of the "History of Italy until the Time of Charlemagne"; Leontief and Babst wrote upon ancient Greece, Eshevski upon the Middle Ages, Vuizinski upon the Papacy and English history. Nor has the history of Russian literature and language been neglected. Sukhomlikhof, Lavrovski, Bishop Makari, and Archbishop Philaret have written on the chronicles and sacred literature of Russia. Dobroliubof made his début as a critic in eighteen hundred and fifty-six, and wrote continuously for five years. He is remarkable for the clearness and simplicity of his views, and his keen logic. Buslaïef's "Historical Grammar of the Russian Language" deserves to be mentioned for its knowledge of the dialects of Russia and the ancient monuments of its literature. Hilferding wrote "Letters on the History of the Serbs and Slavs of the Baltic." Galakhof, Kuraulof, and Vodovozof have also published works of merit on Russian literature.

PERIODICALS.

The development of the daily press in Russia began with the reign of Alexander. Herzen, the illegitimate son of a Muscovite noble, Ivan Zhakovlef, who left him at his death a fortune of half a million rubles, had established at London a free press and an organ of liberalism, the *Kolokol*, which published an address to the new Emperor, demanding from the son of Nicholas atonement for the misery which his father had brought on an entire people, a complete breach with the ruthless system of universal servitude and recklessness, accordance with the liberal ideas of the time, and above all the immediate abolition of serfdom as an earnest of future agreement between people and ruler. Herzen expressed the ideas which had been vaguely in the minds of thousands. His utterances struck the chords of popularity, and he immediately became as absolute a ruler in Russia as the autocratic Tsar. The *Kolokol*, though prohibited, found its way across the boundaries, and was read in the palace and in the izba of the peasant. In eighteen hundred and fifty-nine, at the great Iarmarka of Nijni-Novgorod, the police seized one hundred thousand copies which were introduced by the way of Asia. The *Kolokol* published correspondence from all parts of Russia. State secrets were divulged; the names of political prisoners confined in the dungeons of Schlüsselburg and the mines of Siberia were printed, with the numbers by which they were known to their keepers alone. The misdeeds of the pettiest officials, as well as those of higher rank, were made public; nothing escaped the vigilance of the agents of this enterprising refugee. The government organs were notorious for their dulness and insipidity. In self-defence the censorship was relaxed, and private enterprise was allowed to establish new journals. In eighteen hundred and thirty there were only seventy-three periodicals of any kind; in eighteen hundred and fifty there were, perhaps, double this number; but between eighteen hundred and fifty-eight and eighteen hundred and sixty, fifty large journals sprang into existence in Saint Petersburg alone, seventeen in Moscow, and ten in the provinces. Liberality became the popular notion. Everybody rushed into print. The periodicals were filled with translations from all the foreign political and economical works which had appeared in the last half-century. Hobbes, Darwin, Jeremy Bentham, Buckle, John Stuart Mill, Vogt and Ruge, and Louis Blanc became household names. There are at present to be counted in Russia about five hundred journals, of which four hundred are in the Russian language. The two chief representatives of the daily press are the *Golos*, or the "Voice," and the Moscow Gazette. The *Golos*, under the management of Kraïevski, has the largest circulation. It favored the withdrawal of the five hundred million of paper rubles issued during the Crimean war, and a return to a solid specie basis. The Moscow Gazette has taken opposite views. In eighteen hundred and sixty-three it ceased to belong to the university, and passed into the hands of the valiant Slavophil, Mikhaïl Katkof, and became the organ of the landed proprietors of the interior. It has had a great influence over government councils, and counted among its contributors many officials, — Miliutin, Muravief, and others. The Russian World, at one time edited by Kostomarof, has published General Fadeïef's plans for reforming the organization of the Russian army, and his criticisms upon the division of the country into great military commands. The *Invalide*, the official organ of the war minister, replied with some acerbity. Other dailies published in Saint Petersburg are the Saint Petersburg Gazette, devoted to the Slav interests, the Banking Gazette, which expressed its sympathy for France in the war of eighteen hundred and seventy and eighteen hundred and seventy-one, and the *Novoe Vremia*, conducted somewhat upon the principles of the Paris *Figaro*, and having the same circulation as the *Golos*.

The most important of the reviews which have a general interest is the *Viestnik Evropai*, or "European Messenger," with a circulation of nearly seven thousand copies. It is edited by Stasiulévitch, who succeeded Katchenovski, and professes a moderate liberalism. Its specialties are history and criticism. Katkof, whose influence superseded that of Herzen, besides editing the Moscow Gazette, has charge of the *Russki Viestnik*, which is the constant upholder of Panslavism and Slavophilism. It is modestly followed in this course by the *Grazhdanín*, or "Citizen," founded in eighteen hundred and seventy-two by Gradovski, and edited by Prince Metcherski and Dostoïevskí. The *Sovreménik*, or "Contemporary," edited by Panaïef and Nekrasof, which had at one time eight thousand subscribers and ten times as many readers, was suppressed, soon after the publication of Tchernishevski's novel, "What is to be done?" and gave room to the *Otetchestvennui Zapiski*, or "Annals of the Country," which is now under the direction of Kraïevski. We must also mention the *Diélo*, or "Deed," an advanced liberal sheet, and the *Slovo*, or "Word," the organ of the Socialists. In consequence of the disturbances of the Nihilists and the alarming attempts upon the Emperor's life, an ukas was enacted on the fifth of April, eighteen hundred and seventy-nine, by which the governor-generals were granted the right, without warning, to suspend or suppress any periodical or journal whose tendencies were considered injurious. In consequence of this the Courier, of Moscow, was obliged to close its doors. Already the *Grazhdanín* had been suspended, the *Golos* interdicted for five months, and the *Sovreménik* suppressed. The enlightened and liberal action of Prince Melikof is, however, making an entire change in the disposition of the press. Among comic papers may be mentioned the *Svistok*, or "Whistle," in which Dobroliubof, under the pseudonyme of Konrad Lilienschwager, wrote articles of reckless satire. In eighteen hundred and fifty-seven Plushard began to publish the *Veseltchák*, or "Merry Andrew," assisted by Benidiktof, Pogoski, Count Sollohub, Lenkovski, better known as Baron de Brambéous, whose name made the paper a success. At the death of the latter, Lvof took charge of the *Veseltchák*, but his talents were not equal to his opportunities, and the paper soon perished. The same fate attended the *Gudók* and the *Zanoza*. In eighteen hundred and fifty-nine Kurotchkin founded the *Iskra*, or "Spark," which was very successful, and for four years was the only comic paper in Russia. It amused the public by the boldness with which it published all sorts of scandals and allusions, which were not difficult to refer to prominent individuals. Afterwards a part of its editors separated from its management and started a new paper called the *Budilnik*, or "Alarm Clock." These two are the only humorous papers worthy of mention.

THE ARTISTIC AND SCIENTIFIC MOVEMENT.

The Russians are a thoroughly musical people. Their folk-songs, of a plaintive and minor character, bear an impress which is all their own. The Ukraïna and Podolia is especially the home of an indigenous and beautiful music. At one time improvisers from this land of song were to be found in all the great houses of Russia. Perhaps the greatest composer now living is a Russian. Anton Rubinstein was born in eighteen hundred and twenty-nine. His reputation as a pianist is also unequalled. He has composed several operas on Russian subjects, such as "Dmitri Donskoï," "The Hunter of Siberia," "Vengeance," and others. Other Russian composers of note are Tchaïkovski, Leshetitski, Siérof, Lvof, Dragomirof, and Dorgomuizhski.

Orthodoxy, by proscribing statues in the churches, is largely responsible for the small number of great sculptors which

Russia has produced; there are a few names, however, which are worthy of mention. Martos sculptured the monument to Minin and Pozharski at Moscow. Halberg erected a statue of Catherine at the Academy of the Fine Arts. Mikiéshin was the sculptor of the monument at Novgorod, which was unveiled in September, eighteen hundred and sixty-two, on the occasion of the thousand years' anniversary of the Russian Empire. The same artist, in eighteen hundred and seventy-four, at Saint Petersburg, erected a statue to Catherine the Second, surrounded by the great men of her time. Orlovski sculptured statues of Kutuzof-Smolenski and Barclay de Tolley at Kazan. The majority of sculptors who have won a European reputation are in reality Poles. Antokolski, Kruinski, Riger, Kamenski, Godebski, and Pimenef have exhibited excellent work. Runeberg, who has illustrated the legend of Cupid and Psyche in marble, is a Finn. At the Paris exposition of eighteen hundred and seventy-eight, Tchizhof was the only purely Russian sculptor who attracted attention.

Russia has produced many distinguished painters. One of the best at the present time is Vereshtchagin, whose pictures of East Indian landscapes are famous for the brilliancy of their coloring. Ivan Aïvazovski, the painter of marine landscapes, is of Armenian origin. He was born in eighteen hundred and sixteen, and lives at Theodosia in the Crimea, which has inspired some of his finest pictures. Alexéi Bogoliubof, a pupil of Vorobief, Isabey, and Achenbach, is his chief rival in this class of landscapes. One of his finest efforts is his "View of Nijni-Novgorod." Feodor Brunni is the rector of the Academy of Fine Arts; his specialty is religious subjects. Nikolai Svertchkof excels in his pictures of horses and snow-scenes. The latter are also favorite subjects with Klever. Other landscape painters of note are Meshtcherski, Priashnikof, and Shishkin, the painter of forest scenes. Among portrait painters are Makarof, Pavel Pleshanof, Vasili Tropinin, Zarenko, and Alexander Kharlamof, who exhibited excellent portraits of Monsieur and Madame Viardot and their friend, Ivan Turgénief.

The Russian painters have rivalled the Russian authors in their choice of historical subjects. Iakobi painted the marriage of a jester and a dwarf in the famous ice-palace on the Neva. Pelevin has shown a picture representing a boyar reading to Sophia the ukas of her brother, Peter the Great, commanding her seclusion in a convent. Two of his pictures relate to Ivan the Terrible, one of them a portrait. Litovtchenko has painted the same Tsar exhibiting his treasures to the English ambassador. Others who have made choice of historical subjects are Konstantin Flavetski, Kotsebue, Gay, and Semigradski. The three Makhovski brothers have illustrated Oriental manners and customs, especially those of Cairo.

Among the painters of *genre* subjects and of Russian peculiarities are Gustaf Brudkovski, Baron Klodt, Pavel Fetodof the Russian Hogarth, Koshilef, Vasili Perof, and Popof. Sterenberg, Vereshtchagin, and Repin have painted the wild scenes of army life, camps, and battles. Bronikof executed the frescos in the Russian church at Paris. At Moscow the magnificent Church of the Saviour, projected by Alexander the First, is in process of completion after the plans of Mr. Tonn.

The lines of railway which intersect Russia have necessitated the building of extensive bridges. At Kief a bridge, five hundred and seven sazhens in length, was built in eighteen hundred and seventy. In eighteen hundred and seventy-two the bridge across the Dnieper at Krementchug was completed. It is four hundred and fifty-seven sazhens in length. The bridge on the Orenburg railroad, crossing the Volga seventeen versts from Suizran, the longest in the world, was opened in eighteen hundred and eighty. It has thirteen iron arches, each weighing one million three hundred and forty-three thousand one hundred and sixty kilograms. The total length is six hundred and ninety-six sazhens, the height above the river is eighteen and one third sazhens, and the cost was four million six hundred and thirty thousand rubles. The design was due to Professor Biéleliubski, and it was erected under the care of Chief Engineer Berezin.

The Russians have always shown a great passion for geographical investigation. The discoveries made by Alexander von Humboldt in the interior of Asia were at the command of the Russian Emperor, Nicholas. In eighteen hundred and thirty-four Vasili Feodorof, the astronomer, reached Lake Balkash, and determined the mouth of the river Lepsa, which flows into it. Eight years later Messrs. Karelin and von Schrenk explored the country of the Dzungarian Kirghiz between Lake Balkash and the river Ili. Baer and Hilmersen edited passages from von Schrenk's travels. In eighteen hundred and forty-five the Imperial Russian Geographical Society was founded at Saint Petersburg. With an annual income of twenty-five thousand dollars, it has been enabled to render immense services to human knowledge in its explorations and investigations of the most distant and difficult provinces of Siberia and Central Asia. Branch societies, each with a limited circle of work, have been established at Tiflis, Irkutsk, Vilna, and Orenburg. The geography and topography of Russia proper has been made the object of most thorough investigation. In eighteen hundred and fifty-one Colonel Kovalevski penetrated to the very borders of Chinese Dzungaria, established trading posts at Kulja and Tchugutchak, and determined the boundaries between the two nations. In eighteen hundred and fifty-seven the astronomer, Professor Semenof, ascended to the summit of Tian-Shan, or Celestial Mountains. The southeastern provinces of Orenburg have been subjected to a geometrical survey by Captain Miélitski, the well-known explorer of Lake Baikal, and Captain Antipof, who published an account of their investigations, with maps. About the same time Borshtchof, the botanist, accompanied by Mr. Siévertsof, made a geological survey of the parts of the same province lying between the Ural Mountains, the sea of Aral, and the Caspian. In eighteen hundred and fifty-eight the Geographical Society sent an expedition to explore the Persian province of Khorâsan, under the command of Nikolai Khanuikof, the explorer of Bukhara and the steppes of Central Asia. Other members of this expedition were von Lenz, the astronomer, and Dr. von Bungl, the botanist. A detailed account of this expedition, by Khanuikof, was published in Paris in eighteen hundred and sixty-one. In eighteen hundred and sixty-three Captain Butakof took soundings of the Sir Daria, and determined its navigable channels as far as Bailduir-Tugai. Western Siberia has been thoroughly surveyed and mapped. Lieutenant Tatarinof found gold and coal on the southern shores of the Kara-Tau Mountains, only ninety kilometers from Turkestan and Tchemkend. Makshéief the statistician, the archæologist Favitski, and Radlof the philologist, connected with Captain Holmstrom's expedition west from Lake Balkash through the Golodnaia, or Hungry Steppe, made full and interesting reports. The mountain regions of Tarbagatai were explored by Struve and Potanin, who so completed the topographical survey of the region that a "map of the province of the governor-generalship of Turkestan" was published in eighteen hundred and sixty-eight. Siévertsof, by his explorations of the Upper Sir Daria and the regions beyond the Tian-Shan Mountains, has convinced himself that the inland seas of Central Asia were originally united with the Arctic Ocean, and that probably the Caspian was separated earlier from the Black Sea than the Black Sea was from the Mediterranean. Przhevalski travelled through southern and southeastern Mongolia, from Lake Dalai Nor to the northern boundaries of the Havos province, and sent home a diary of his journey. He afterwards received a permit from the Chinese government to extend his travels to Lake Kuku Nor and Thibet. In company of Puiltsof and two Cossacks the indefatigable explorer had succeeded, at last accounts, in completely traversing the difficult regions of Thibet. Another traveller, Matuzovski, published in the Turkestan Times of Tashkent an account of his adventures in Bokhara and the vast wilderness of Mongolia. A Russian exploring expedition under Stebnitski and Radde, in the interests of trade, extended their researches from the east shore of the Caspian to Khiva, and established posts on the Oxus in Bokhara. Still another expedition went from Krasnovodsk to Khiva, and a botanical section attempted scientific investigations of the Sea of Azof. Maksimof has thoroughly explored the coasts of the Black Sea, and the same service has been performed on the Aral by Butakof and Siévertsof. Von Middendorff has made extensive journeys through Siberia, bringing to light its immense resources. Central China has been investigated by Timovski and Kovalevski. Golovnin has devoted himself to Japan. Kashgar has been visited by Valishurof. Krashianikof's description of Kamtchatka is a standard work, and has been translated into most European languages. Lütke has also travelled in Russian America, and Soritchef and Vrangel have explored the icy seas of the far North. While Nikolai Muravief, Piotr Tchihatchof, Sosnovski, Kostienkof, and Fedtchenko have made explorations of Central Asia, and Norof, Muravief, and Umanes in the far East, Zhakovlef has made investigations in Italy, Botkin has described Spain, and Platon Tchihatchef has visited South America. The energy and enterprise of the Russian explorers easily put them in the front rank.

Ethnography and philology can count some illustrious names: Castren, Sjœgren, Schiefner, Bethlinjk, Dorn, Kunik, Lerch, Wiedmann, Kanikof, Brosset, Storch, and Kœppen. In the natural sciences Brandt, Ovsiannikof, and Gappert have made names for themselves. Koksharof is an authority in mineralogy; Kuppfer has especially studied meteorology; Iakobi has written monographs on galvanism and the treatment of platinum; Engelhardt, Fritzsche, and Shishkof are names well known to the students of chemistry; Iabloshkof is the inventor of the electric light called by his name. In astronomy Struve may be mentioned, and Savitch has prepared a valuable work on the calculus. Simonof, who died in eighteen hundred and fifty-five, Lobatchevski, who died the following year, Buniakovski, Tchebuitchef, Forsch, and Maievski are famous mathematicians. In the same field Ostrogradski, who died in eighteen hundred and sixty-one, has published works on algebra, Somof on geometry.

Vernadski was the first Russian advocate of free trade. The surgeon Pirogof has won a European reputation. In the early part of the year eighteen hundred and sixty-three the ministry of the interior, composed of representatives of the different departments, organized a council with the special purpose of improving and unifying the methods of collecting statistics. This statistical council was afterwards established on a firmer basis, and it was owing to the efforts of its members and the co-operation of the imperial family, that during the next ten years both capitals witnessed numerous statistical congresses and meetings for the purpose of exhibiting the products and resources of the country. Russia has thus been enabled to invite the learned men of Europe to its international gatherings, — to the Ethnographical Congress of eighteen hundred and sixty-seven at Moscow, the Exhibition of Manufactures and Industries at Saint Petersburg in eighteen hundred and seventy, the Polytechnic Exhibition of Moscow in June, eighteen hundred and seventy-two, and the Statistical Congress of Saint Petersburg, held during the same year, — as well as to the series of archæological meetings of Saint Petersburg, Moscow, Kief, and Kazan from eighteen hundred and sixty-nine to eighteen hundred and seventy-seven, and the Congress of Orientalists at Saint Petersburg in eighteen hundred and seventy-six. The International Polytechnic Exhibition of eighteen hundred and seventy-two opened on the eleventh of June with a grand celebration of the two hundredth birthday of Peter the Great, was attended by the representatives of Germany, Austria, England, France, Belgium, and Sweden, and numerous deputations came from Bohemia, Galicia, Hungary, Montenegro, and other Slavic lands. The exhibition was opened by the Grand Duke Konstantin, the Emperor's brother; the celebration took place on the square in front of the Troitska bridge. A cantata, written by Polonski and set to music by Tchaikovski, was sung under the direction of Davuidof, a professor in the Moscow Conservatory. Russia also took part in the Vienna Weltausstellung in eighteen hundred and seventy-three, and the expositions of Philadelphia in eighteen hundred and seventy-six and Paris in eighteen hundred and seventy-eight.

CHAPTER XI.

ALEXANDER THE SECOND.

1856 – 1880.

THE ADVANCE OF RUSSIAN POWER BEYOND THE CAUCASUS. — GORTCHAKOF'S CIRCULAR NOTE. — SHAMIL AND THE CIRCASSIANS. — CENTRAL ASIA. — THE KHANATES. — THE KHIVAN EXPEDITIONS. — RELATIONS WITH CHINA, JAPAN, AND THE UNITED STATES.

GORTCHAKOF'S CIRCULAR NOTE. — SHAMIL AND THE CIRCASSIANS.

THE Russian policy of territorial aggrandizement was explained by Prince Gortchakof, the Chancellor of the Empire, in a circular note dated November twenty-first, eighteen hundred and sixty-four, and sent to the courts of Europe. He showed that the position of Russia in Central Asia is similar to that of all civilized states brought into contact with semi-savage nomad tribes, lacking a fixed, social organization. Commercial relations and the security of the frontiers can be protected only by reducing these turbulent neighbors to a state of subordination. But when this result has been obtained, and the tribes on the frontier have become peaceful, they are in turn exposed to the attacks of more distant tribes, and the state is bound to defend them and punish those who commit the depredations. The only way to have any moral influence over these Asiatic tribes is to establish fortified posts among them, and by a greater or less display of force to bring them to submission. "But beyond this second line other tribes still more distant soon come to threaten, in their turn, the same dangers, and require the same measures of repression. The state thus finds itself obliged either to abandon this ceaseless labor and give over its frontiers to perpetual disorder, which renders all prosperity, all security, all civilization, an impossibility, or to accept the alternative of plunging deeper and deeper into barbarous countries where, at every onward step, the difficulties and expenses are increased. Such has been the lot of every country placed in similar conditions. The United States in America, France in Algeria, Holland in its colonies, England in India, all have been irresistibly forced, less by ambition than by imperious necessity, to follow this line of progress, in which the principal difficulty is to know where it will end." The circular then goes on to state the principle upon which Russia has undertaken to establish its rule in Central Asia. The civilization of the continent is accepted as the special mission of Russia. "No agent has been found more efficacious for the spread of civilization than commercial relations. Their development everywhere demands order and stability, but in Asia there must be a complete change in the customs of the people. The first thing that the Asiatic tribes must learn is, that more is to be gained by favoring and protecting the caravan trade than by robbery. These elementary ideas can be made a part of the public conscience only where there is a public, that is, a social organization, and a government to direct and represent it."

Russia's occupation of the Caucasus dates from the year seventeen hundred and twenty-two, when Dagestán was invaded by Peter the Great, who established Russian garrisons at Tarki and Bakú. In eighteen hundred and six, and again in eighteen hundred and thirteen, many provinces were given by formal treaty into the protection of Alexander the First. Before eighteen hundred and twenty-four nearly the whole of Dagestán was under control of the Russians. About this time the fanatic Kazi-Mollá began to advocate the doctrine of

Muridism, which was rather a political than a religious movement. A Murid signifies a person who walks in the ways of truth, who follows the second part of the Korán, the "Tarikat," or book of moral laws. Kazi-Mollá was born in seventeen hundred and eighty-five, and after studying the Arabic language and the Korán with his grandfather, the learned Ismaïl, and with Saïd-Effemdi, the liberal friend of Iermolof, he began to acquire influence with the mountain tribes. He is reported to have been married twice, but to have separated from his brides on the first day because they were unable to preserve silence. The first ideas of Muridism were brought to the Caucasus by Mollá-Mahmúd. After Kazi-Mollá had joined this sect in eighteen hundred and twenty-five, the doctrine spread with remarkable rapidity. Kazi-Mollá began by endeavoring to exterminate the vice of drunkenness, which he punished by inflicting forty blows with a rod. One of his immediate followers was the celebrated Ben Mahomet Shamil, "the Prince of Believers," who was born at Imri in seventeen hundred and ninety-seven. After studying philosophy, and living as a recluse monk till he was twenty-seven years of age, he entered with his whole heart into the revolution of the Caucasus. Most of the tribes of Dagestán were roused by the religious and political preaching of Kazi-Mollá, who advocated a holy war against "the unfaithful." Iermolof entered Dagestán in eighteen hundred and thirty-one, and stormed the Aul, or fortified village of Imri. Kazi-Mollá was killed, and Shamil was severely wounded. His escape was considered miraculous, and that circumstance, added to the position in which the Mollá was found, — with one hand grasping his beard and the other pointing to heaven, — caused the fanaticism of the Murids to blaze forth more violently than ever. Hassam-Bey succeeded Kazi-Mollá, but was assassinated in eighteen hundred and thirty-four. Shamil seized the treasure of the Mollá, and was immediately recognized as the Iman, or chief. He continued the struggle with the Russians with indifferent success. In eighteen hundred and thirty-nine he was surrounded in the fortress of Akhulgo, situated on an inaccessible rock. His escape from General Grabbe's army, who took the fortress, was again considered miraculous. He reappeared at Dargo, in the Andi Mountains, and in eighteen hundred and forty-two he ruled over the souls and bodies of more than three quarters of a million of men. He formed this population into a military organization, in which every man from the age of sixteen to sixty was obliged to serve. By means of his marvellous escapes, his sudden appearances, his fasting and prayers, he succeeded in making his people look upon him as divine. The success which he enjoyed against the Russians in eighteen hundred and forty-two was not continued after Prince Vorontsof was appointed to the command. In eighteen hundred and forty-five Dargo was captured after a protracted siege. The following year he went into the Kabarda and seized Zhergebil, a fort built by the Russians. There he withstood a fortnight's siege in eighteen hundred and forty-seven, and finding his position growing untenable, he escaped to the mountains. He had lost so many men during his campaign on the Terek and Kubán, that during the Crimean war he was enabled to gain little advantage by the withdrawal of Russian troops. In eighteen hundred and fifty-eight Prince Bariatinski, the energetic governor of the Caucasus, seized the pass of Argun, won the battle near the village of Ismaïl, and after a long siege captured Veden, the fortified residence of Shamil, on the eleventh of August, eighteen hundred and fifty-eight. The Lesgi abandoned him, and at last he was captured, after a heroic defence, in his castle of Gunib in eighteen hundred and fifty-nine. Prince Bariatinski sent the old hero to Saint Petersburg, where he was received with due honor by Alexander. He was allowed a residence at Kaluga, where he finished his days. After the capture of Shamil the Tcherkesui, or Circassians, in spite of Mahomet-Emin, were obliged to submit to the Russians

Mahomet himself went to Saint Petersburg to confirm his allegiance to the Tsar. The emigration of the mountaineers, encouraged by England from hostile feelings toward Russia, rendered the latter government, on the other hand, the service of relieving the country of its most turbulent elements, and of making room for colonization. The Murshids, or teachers of truth, urged the Mahometans to abandon the homes of their ancestors. Many of them died on the route. Very few ever reached the Turkish shores, and of those some returned afterwards without waiting for permission. The Russian conquest was secured by numerous fortresses called Kreposti and strategic routes, as, for instance, that from Vladikavkas to Tiflis, the capital of Georgia. The Russian element, attracted by this beautiful and imposing country, has rapidly increased north of the Caucasus. Churches and schools have been established, and the wonderful wealth of these regions is being surely developed.

CENTRAL ASIA.

Mr. Eugene Schuyler, in the Conclusion to his interesting and valuable work on Turkestan, indulges in the following reflections: "Central Asia has no stores of wealth and no economical resources. Neither by its agricultural nor by its mineral wealth, nor by its commerce, nor by the revenue to be derived from it, can it ever repay the Russians for what it has already cost, and for the rapidly increasing expenditure bestowed upon it. Had Russia known fifteen years ago as much about the countries of Central Asia as she does now, there can be hardly a doubt that there would have been no movement in that direction. . . . Despite the drain upon the Imperial exchequer, it is practically impossible for Russia to withdraw from her position in Central Asia. . . . On the contrary, as far as one can foresee, Russia will be compelled in the future to advance still further. It seems now to be impossible for her to remain where she is. Kashgar, Bukhara, and the Turkoman country must be either annexed or they must be reduced to a position of real and not nominal vassalage."

Mr. Schuyler then goes on to show what will be the ethnical and political boundaries of Russia in Asia: "She will have under rule in Central Asia all the Mahometan peoples of Turkish race. On the east her neighbor will be China, and as the Russians are not disposed to get into difficulties with that empire, we may expect few boundary disputes. On the south the frontier will be the Oxus, separating the Russian domains from Afghanistan, as agreed upon by arrangement with England. Although the rulers are Afghans, and of different stock, yet the inhabitants of Balkh and the province south, as far as the Hindu Kush, are of Turkish origin. This range would therefore form the true ethnical frontier of Russia on the south, and it must be remembered that mountains are always better barriers and boundaries than rivers. On the west the Russian frontier will join that of Persia, which is inhabited by men of a different race, and although Mussulmans, yet of a sect violently hated by the inhabitants of Central Asia. If any difficulty with England ever arise, it will probably be in Persia, where at present Russian influence is paramount, and not elsewhere."

The gradual growth of Russian influence in Asia is well condensed, in an historical sketch of Russian policy in Asia, by Professor Grigorief, forming an appendix to Mr. Schuyler's Turkestan. Turkestan is a sandy region traversed by the Syr Daria and the Amu Daria rivers. The river Syr, known to the ancients as the Iaxartes, rises from a glacier in the Djittim-Tau range of the Tian-Shan Mountains, to the south of Lake Issik-Kul, at an elevation of about thirty-six hundred meters above the sea. After receiving several tributaries, the Naryn, as it is called for its first five hundred kilometers, is joined by the Kara-Kuldja, which rises in the Alai Mountains. From the junction the river, now called the Syr Daria, flows by Khodjent, and, after forming the vast marshes of Bakali-Kapa, falls into the Sea of Aral to the west of Kazalinsk. The shallows in the lower course of the river are the great obstacle to its navigation, and all attempts to better it have been unavailing. Schuyler tells of an old legend that the whole valley of the Syr Daria was at one time so thickly settled that the bulbul could fly from branch to branch of the fruit trees, and a cat could walk from wall to wall, from house-top to housetop, all the distance from Kashgar to the sea. Many large and flourishing cities existed along the banks, and the mounds which enclose their ruins disclose pottery, household utensils, and other evidences of early civilization. The desert, which has usurped this cultivation, is rapidly growing under the influence of the strong winds which blow the sands continually toward the south and southwest.

The Amu Daria, which the ancients called the Oxus, rises in Lake Sari Kul, on the northern slope of the Hindu Kush Mountains, in the territory of Pamir, called by the Hindus the roof of the world. The Oxus, which now empties by many mouths into the Sea of Aral, in all probability once flowed into the Caspian. Major Wood, who accompanied Colonel Sobolef's Amu Daria exploring expedition in eighteen hundred and seventy-four, believes that the course of the river may have been changed by means of the irrigation canals near Khiva, which took off so much water during the summer floods that the silt deposited in the river-bed gradually accumulated beyond the power of the water to wash it away. It has been proposed to turn the waters of the Amu Daria once more into their old channel. A well-defined bed exists, through which it was believed that if the dams on the Laudan were removed the river would once more fall into the Caspian near Krasnovodsk; but an insuperable difficulty exists in the comparatively small supply of water, owing to the destruction of the forests in Central Asia. Mr. Schuyler says: "In order to have sufficient water for navigation, it would seem to be necessary to destroy the irrigation systems, and this, by diminishing, if not putting an end to the productive power of the countries of Central Asia, and thus destroying the commerce, would remove the only reason for which navigation is considered necessary."

The government of the Syr Daria is the most extensive of the four provinces which form Russian Turkestan; it is subdivided into eight districts, and inhabited by five different peoples besides Russians, Tatars, Jews, Hindus, Chinese, and Persians. The most numerous are the Kirgiz, who belong to six tribes, and make up nearly sixty per cent of the population. The principal towns are situated on or near the upper course of the Iaxartes. Tashkent, the principal city of the Kurama district, and the residence of the governor general of Turkestan, has more than one hundred thousand inhabitants, and a Russian population of six thousand. The Russian town is well built and possesses a theatre and a public library, where can be found Russian, English, French, and German books. The projected railway uniting Orenburg, Samarkand, and Siberia will undoubtedly be of great advantage to the city. The walls of the city are more than twenty-five kilometers in length, three or four meters in height, and built of solid blocks of clay. The town is entirely hidden in beautiful gardens and orchards.

Khodjent, the key of the Fergana, is situated on the Syr Daria, and its population is variously estimated to be from eighteen thousand to fifty thousand. It lies on the direct route between Kokan and Bukhara, and was, therefore, a cause of contention between these two countries. It was captured by the Russians on the fifth of June, eighteen hundred and sixty-six. Khodjent is usually considered the site of Alexandria Eskhaté, or the Last Alexandria, founded by the great conqueror whose exploits are still matters of legend throughout the whole region.

Tchimkent, Aulié-Ata, and Turkestan are the other chief

cities. At Turkestan is the "incomparable mosque" of Hazret Iasavi, the Mussulman Apostle of Central Asia. Hazret Hodja Akhmet Iasavi was the founder of the sect Iahria, and died about eleven hundred and twenty. The mosque over his tomb was begun by Timur, or Tamerlan, in thirteen hundred and ninety-seven. Bektchusin gives the following description of it: "It is built on a space outside the fortifications of the city, surrounded by a lofty wall of clay flanked at the corners with bastions provided with artillery. . . . Two minarets joined together by a stone coping form the front of the mosque. Its top and its two cupolas have no roof. It is divided in the interior into three portions. The first, situated under the dome, forms a vast hall sixteen sazhen in height; on the right and left are four chambers filled with tombs. On the left front a door leads into the principal mosque, forming the second division, in which the religious exercises are performed, but only on Fridays. In the centre is a good-sized chamber in which are to be seen the tombs of Hazret and his family. Toward the right is a long corridor with a small opening at the extremity, and likewise filled with tombs. From this corridor you enter a vast chamber where you see the sacred well. Near the mosque is a small round edifice adorned with a cupola and covered with mosaics. The mosque of Hazret is constructed of square-pressed tiles; the walls are strengthened by great wooden girders. All the beams are of wood. The ceiling of the great hall surmounted by the cupola has a moulding of alabaster. The mosque and the cupolas are covered on the outside with a beautiful mosaic tiling. On the whole length of the upper cornice, which is made of blue tiles, there is an Arabic inscription taken from the Koran. Unfortunately it is almost illegible, from the effects of time." All that is left of this inscription are the words: "The work of Hodja Hussein, a native of the city Shiraz." The Hazret mosque is considered the most sacred in all Central Asia, and its clergy are supported by pious gifts, by taxes from the caravansaries and shops of the city, and by the products of certain fields cultivated by the Mollás. It was somewhat damaged by the Russians during the siege of the city, and was saved from complete destruction only by the bravery of Sheikh-el-Islam, who, at the peril of his life, flung out the white flag from the minaret.

On the upper course of the Syr Daria and the Naryn is the khanate of Kokan, with its capital of the same name. The khanate is an almond-shaped valley two hundred and fifty-seven kilometers in length and about one hundred and five in width, surrounded on all sides by lofty mountains, those to the south rising to a height of from fifty-seven hundred to seventy-six hundred meters. The Southern Kokan or Alai Mountains were explored by Fedtchenko in eighteen hundred and seventy-one. The whole valley is remarkably fertile, and is watered by the small streams which descend from the mountains and by numerous canals filled by the Syr Daria. Mr. Schuyler speaks of the unusual fertility of this ancient valley of Fergana, and the Hungarian traveller, Mr. Ujfalvy, describes the capital as the most interesting city of Central Asia. Before its annexation the khanate contained about a million inhabitants, governed arbitrarily by the khan, who imposed the most grinding taxes and was a "frightful tyrant."

On the Upper Oxus is the province of Balkh, the cradle of our race, "of the thousand gates," whose capital city stands on the ruins of the ancient Baktra, and was during the Middle Ages a centre of civilization. It was then called Um-el-Bilâd, or Mother of Cities. Balkh was formerly an independent khanate, but since eighteen hundred and forty it has formed a province of Afghanistan.

Between the Syr and the Amu there is a considerable valley through which flows the Zerafshan, which rises in a large glacier, twenty-five hundred and ninety-two meters above the level of the sea. The glacier, which is fifty-six kilometers in length, has been explored by Baron Aminof. The Zerafshan descends with a rapid current from the mountains, and not far from Samarkand divides into many branches, most of which, being employed for irrigation, are expended before they reach the Amu Daria. The district of the Zarafshan is divided into three cantons, the most important of which is near the centre of the valley, and has nearly one hundred and twenty-five thousand inhabitants. Its capital is Samarkand, which was known as Marakanda in the time of Alexander the Great, and was a flourishing city, whose walls, according to Quintus Curtius, were seventy stadia in circumference. It was at Samarkand that Alexander killed his old friend and adviser, Klytos. The great Asiatic conqueror, Timur, made the city his capital, and both he and his successors spared no pains in making it worthy of its beautiful situation; and in Baber's time it was "a wonderfully elegant city." The mosque in honor of Kazim Ibn Abbas, called Shah Indeh, or the Living King, was erected by Timur in thirteen hundred and twenty-three, and its ruins are even now among the most beautiful of Central Asia. Madame Ujfalvy-Bourdon thus describes this mosque: "The decoration is so magnificent that the mind is overwhelmed. The walls are covered with superb enamelled bricks; large surfaces are decorated with rich mosaics; there are round or rectangular panels with designs in relief of remarkable workmanship. There are admirable columns, pediments, groined vaults with corbel recesses of extraordinary beauty. The delicate and slender pillars are full of grace, and the groined ceiling is incomparable for its elegance, its boldness, and at the same time its purity of lines." There are other remarkable mosques, colleges, and public buildings; but, according to Mr. Schuyler, the most interesting monument of Samarkand is the Gur-Amir, or Tomb of Tamerlan, an octagonal building surmounted by a melon-shaped dome, and having two minarets in ruins. The tombstone of the great conqueror is a superb slab of greenish-black jade, which has around its edge a complicated inscription giving his name and titles and those of his ancestors. Timur died in fourteen hundred and five. Since the occupation of the city by the Russians everything about the mosque has been put in repair, and a guardian appointed. Samarkand has about thirty-five thousand inhabitants, and is the residence of the governor general of the district and other Russian authorities.

Bukhara and the districts north of it are watered by the Shahri-rud and other canals, which take their water from the Zarafshan. The city of Bukhara is called, officially, Al Sherif, or The Noble; it is the centre of trade for this part of Asia, and its bazaar, according to Mr. Petrofski, in eighteen hundred and seventy-two, was five times larger than that of Tashkent. He estimated the yearly transactions of the Bukharian market at forty million rubles.

On the Lower Oxus is situated the khanate of Khiva, in the midst of a fertile oasis, surrounded by the sandy desert of Kara-Kum, nine hundred and sixty-five kilometers from Tashkent, eight hundred and five from Krasnovodsk on the Caspian, and nearly fifteen hundred from Orenburg.

On the other side of the Tian-Shan Mountains is situated the khanate of Kashgar, the powerful state of Eastern Turkestan, founded in eighteen hundred and sixty-four by the bold and able Iakub Khan. Iakub's father, according to Mr. Kurupatkin, was Ismet-Ulla, a native of Khodjent, who made a livelihood by reciting prayers at the bedside of the sick. He removed to Pskent, a small village lying about fifty kilometers from Tashkent, and married. When Iakub was a lad, Ismet separated from his wife, who then married a butcher, in whose house Iakub was brought up. On the death of his parents he became a *batcha*, or public dancer, and was taken to Kokan by a wealthy man of that place. Iakub finally came into the service of the governor of Tashkent, who married his foster-sister, the daughter of the butcher of Pskent. Iakub began to receive political advancement. He helped defend the fortress of Ak-Mesjed against the Russians in eighteen hundred and fifty-three, and in eighteen hundred and sixty-four fought them near Tchemkent; but in both cases, in spite of his bravery, he was defeated. The same year a revolution broke out in Kashgar, and Khodja-Buzurk Khan was besought to come back to the throne of his fathers. Iakub took a handful of adventurers, and after ridding himself of the weak and pleasure-loving Khodja, and poisoning his cousin, Katta-Tura, he succeeded in uniting under his own sceptre the provinces of Kashgar, Ianyssar, Iarkand, and Khotan, and extended his power far to the east. He took in succession the titles Bek and Atalik-Ghazi, and was finally recognized as Amír-el-Muminein, or Commander of the Faithful, by the Sultan, who sent him valuable gifts. Mahmud Iakub is said to have united in his character all the virtues and vices of his race. He was brave, energetic, persevering, but, at the same time, cruel, wily, and treacherous. By his remarkable genius he succeeded in making himself the most powerful monarch in Central Asia.

The principal cities of Eastern Turkestan are Kashgar, Iarkand, Khotan, Aksu, Ush-Turfan, and Ianyssar. Iarkand is the largest of all these cities, and has thirty-two thousand houses and from two to four hundred thousand inhabitants. Kashgar was formerly the most western city of the Chinese Empire. It has from fifty to one hundred thousand inhabitants, and is surrounded by a clay wall. Many famous mosques and colleges are situated in Kashgar, and it is distinguished by the tomb of Apak-Khodja, surmounted by a lofty dome covered with blue enamelled tiles. The other cities have from four to twelve thousand houses. All of these states, whose fertility depends on the Amu, Syr, Iarkand, and Kashgar rivers, lie on the commercial route to India and China, and the English have always looked with uneasiness upon the progress of the Russians in these regions.

In the reign of the Empress Anna many hordes of Kirgiz sent in their submission to Russia; but for more than a century, as Professor Grigorief asserts, in order to defend themselves from their new subjects, the Russians were obliged to shut themselves in by a line of fortresses requiring large garrisons, and the efforts made to bring them to obedience were entirely without avail. They still continued to plunder the caravans which set out for Central Asia, and to render all commercial relations with Kokan and the other cities impracticable. Even the armed caravans, which were instituted in eighteen hundred and twenty-four at a cost of two hundred and thirty thousand rubles, were robbed, and proved an unprofitable investment. It was during the reign of the Emperor Nicholas that the Kirgiz were brought under perfect control. Colonies of Russians were planted on the northeastern shores of the Caspian and in the Trans-Irtuish steppes. The Siberian Kirgiz rebelled under their khan, Kenisar Kasimof, and were assisted by the Kirgiz of Orenburg. For six years Kasimof defied the Russians, but was finally defeated and killed in eighteen hundred and forty-four. During the following three years other tribes became tributary to Russia, and it proved to be necessary to protect them from the Kokandians and Khivans by erecting the fortifications of Raim, Kopal, and Viernoć. The Khivans were not especially troublesome, but the Kokandians, who had established themselves in the valley of the Syr and on the slopes of the mountains, regularly took tribute from all the Kirgiz, and occasionally invaded the Trans-Ural and Tchu steppes, treating the natives with the greatest barbarity. Russia was obliged in eighteen hundred and fifty-three to enter into a war with Kokan. The principal fort belonging to Kokan on the Syr Daria was Ak-Mesjed, or White Mosque, situated about four hundred and eighty kilometers from Aralsk. The first movement which the Russians made against it was in July, eighteen hundred and fifty-two, when they sent a detachment of four or five hundred men with two field-pieces under Colonel Blaremberg; but, being unprovided with the proper equipment, they succeeded only in destroying the outer works. On their way down the river they captured three auxiliary fortifications. The following year the fort was attacked by General Perovski, and after a three weeks' siege was taken by storm on the twenty-seventh of July. During the progress of these operations a small detachment proceeded a hundred versts farther up the river and captured Djulek, which was the extreme of Russian advance until the campaign of eighteen hundred and sixty-three. After the heroic defence of Ak-Mesjed the Kokandians made repeated but unsuccessful attempts to recapture it. The Russians henceforth held it and named it Fort Perovski.

In eighteen hundred and sixty the Kokandian general, Khanaiat Shah, with an army of thirty thousand men, started to drive out the Russians from the province of Semirietch, or the Seven Rivers, and to sack Viernoé, which had only a small garrison. Colonel Kolpakovski concentrated his troops at the small fort Kastek, at the foot of the pass where the attack was expected. But Khanaiat Shah crossed the mountains by another route and attacked Uzun-Agatch, intending after he had captured it to blockade Kastek, and thus without opposition to make himself master of Viernoé. As soon as Colonel Kolpakovski was informed by a messenger, who succeeded in escaping through the lines, of the true state of affairs, he marched out with eight hundred men and six guns, and by a flank movement succeeded in defeating an army of more than fifteen thousand Kokandians and Kirgiz, thus completely establishing the power of the Russians north of the Alai-Tau Mountains.

In eighteen hundred and fifty-four it was planned to siege Tchimkent and the city of Turkestan, thus forming a fortified line connecting Orenburg and Siberia, and serving as a complete protection to the Kirgiz. But this plan was not carried out until eighteen hundred and sixty-four, when Colonel Tchernaïef, with twenty-five hundred men from Siberia, and Colonel Verevkin, with twelve hundred men from Orenburg, were detailed to accomplish the conquest. General Tchernaïef took Aulić-Ata, or Avliata, by assault on the sixteenth of June. Turkestan was taken about the same time. In the following October the two columns united and carried Tchimkent by storm. They thus gained command of one of the richest districts of Kokan, "the granary of all the country between the Tchu and the Syr Daria." It was at this time that Prince Gortchakof despatched the celebrated circular note to the foreign courts. The fears of the English were somewhat calmed by its frankness and candor. But hardly was it in the hands of its readers before the Russians were again involved with the Kokandians, who were irritated at the encroachment of their conquerors. In December, eighteen hundred and sixty-four, Alim Kul, with a large force, endeavored to recapture Turkestan the Holy, but without success. The Amir of Bukhara, troubled at the approach of the Russians, had already invaded Kokan and taken possession of Khodjent and several other places. General Tchernaïef resolved to act on the offensive. Having failed, in October, eighteen hundred and sixty-four, to take Tashkent by assault, he now attacked and took the small fortress of Niazbek, about twenty-five kilometers northeast of Tashkent, commanding the water supply of the city. Meanwhile the Alim Kul, the Regent of Kokan, with six thousand men and forty guns, entered Tashkent, and on the twenty-first of May attacked the Russian camp, which had been brought down to within ten kilometers of the city. After a severe fight the Kokandian army was driven back and Alim Kul was killed. An embassy was then sent to the Amir of Bukhara offering the submission of the city, but the Amir demanded as a hostage the young khan, Seid Sultan. Seid Sultan was not disposed to put himself into the hands of Mozaffer, and fled on the night of the twenty-first of June. A small party of Bukharians, led by Ishan Bek, then entered the city. General Tchernaïef was now in a difficult position. He had only two thousand men and a dozen guns; the walls of the city were twenty-five kilometers in circumference, and could not be subjected to a regular siege. He could not withdraw and allow the Amir of Bukhara to take the city, nor could he meet him in a pitched battle. He therefore resolved upon a bold stroke; and on the morning of the twenty-seventh of June Captain Abramof surprised the watch and opened the Kamelan gate, which led to the highest part of the town. By the evening of the following day the whole city was brought to terms. The Russian loss was only twenty-five killed and one hundred and seventeen wounded, while that of the defenders was about thirty thousand. The loss of Tashkent, the commercial emporium of the province, a city of between fifty thousand and three hundred thousand inhabitants, was a death-blow to the independence of Kokan. Khudaïar, who had the prudence to send his congratulations to the Russians upon their capture of Khodjent in eighteen hundred and sixty-six, was unmolested for ten years. He succeeded in putting down a series of revolts by his subjects, who were exasperated by his tyranny. These revolts broke out in eighteen hundred and seventy-one, and became more serious every year until eighteen hundred and seventy-five, when, being abandoned even by his two sons, who joined the insurgents, Khudaïar quitted his capital with his harem, and with a treasure estimated at five million dollars escaped to Tashkent, and was allowed to live at Orenburg. His eldest son, Nasr-Eddin, was then made khan by the Russians, but proved to be weak and incapable. Having been drawn into a war with the Russians, he lost his throne and was sent to Vladimir. On the anniversary of the emperor's accession to the throne Kokan was annexed under the historic name of Fergana. In process of time it bids fair to prove Russia's most valuable possession in Central Asia. The population is variously estimated to be from six hundred thousand to a million.

The caravan trade between Bukhara and Russia was carried on without interruption until the capture of Tashkent. At that time the Amir Mozaffar Eddin, again intervening in the civil wars of Kokand, came into collision with the Russians. Having seized Khodjent, he sent a message to the Russians ordering them to become Mahometans and to evacuate the conquered territory. General Tchernaïef sent Struve, Tatarinof, and Glukhovski to the khan, who imprisoned them, but was obliged to liberate them after the battle of Irdjar on the twentieth of May, eighteen hundred and sixty-six, which brought about also the conquest of Samarkand and the annexation of the district of the Zarafshan. On the eighteenth of October the fortress of Djisakh, the last important stronghold belonging to the khan in the valley of the Syr, was taken by storm by the Russians after a week's siege. Mozaffar was now somewhat disposed for peace, but the priesthood made use of the indignation of the people at the increase of taxes and stoppage of trade, to demand a vigorous prosecution of the war. In spite of the frantic attempts of the Mollás to raise the holy war, Mozaffar was defeated at Zera-Bulak, which led to the treaty of the fifth of July, eighteen hundred and sixty-eight. By this treaty the Amir promised to give as a war indemnity one hundred and twenty-five thousand gold tillas, or about four hundred thousand dollars, the last instalment of which was paid in eighteen hundred and seventy. Bukhara itself would have been annexed, had not the Russian generals feared to weaken their conquests by extending them. The annexation of the province, moreover, is of comparatively small consequence; and as long as trade can be conducted on an equitable basis, it is better for Russia to treat Bukhara as a vassal state. The agriculture of the country is not in as flourishing a condition as that of Kokan.

In July, eighteen hundred and sixty-seven, by an imperial ukas, the organization of the territories bordering on China and the Central Asian khanates was changed, and the government of Turkestan was created. Alexander placed at the head of it a governor general, or *iarim padishah*, who imitates the pomp and magnificence of the Eastern monarchs by whom he is surrounded. Besides the viceroy, there were appointed military governors for the two provinces into which the new government was divided. Prefects or commandants administer the departments or districts of the provinces, while the nomad population, divided into auls and volosti, is governed by elders chosen by the people. The cost of acquiring nearly all the territory occupied by the Russians in Central Asia is given by Mr. Schuyler as nine hundred thousand rubles, of which five hundred thousand were paid by Bukhara. The deficit in the budget for the five years following eighteen hundred and sixty-eight was nearly nineteen millions of rubles.

THE KHIVA EXPEDITION.

The relations of Russia with Khiva began early in the seventeenth century. The first three expeditions were made by the Cossacks of the Iaïk, and resulted in their complete discomfiture. In June, seventeen hundred and seventeen, Prince Bekovitch-Tcherkasski was sent to Khiva by Peter the Great, who in seventeen hundred had been besought by the khan Shaniaz to take his nation under Russian protection. Prince Bekovitch and his whole army were treacherously massacred, and the successive khans, protected by the deserts which girdle the fertile oasis, have been able to defy the power of the Russians, whom they have captured and enslaved with impunity. The Perovski expedition, in eighteen hundred and thirty-nine, was a complete failure, and the treaty which Danilevski induced the khan to sign in eighteen hundred and forty-two remained a dead letter, for the very next year Khiva offered aid to Kenisar, and soon after sent forces to destroy the new forts which the Russians had established in the steppe. At last the patience of the government was exhausted. Mohammed Rakhim sent insolent replies to General Kaufmann's letters, and he was accused, though in all probability unjustly, of furnishing aid to the Kirgiz. In eighteen hundred and seventy-two Colonel Markozof conducted a reconnoitring expedition into the steppe, starting from Krasnovodsk with the intention of getting as near as possible to Khiva. Thirst and privations, together with the constant attacks of the Turkomans, decimated his forces, and he was obliged to retreat. The following year it was resolved to bring the khan to terms. Three columns advanced against Khiva from three different sides. Markozof, with twenty-two hundred men, succeeded in reaching the wells of Igdy after a terrible march of twenty-nine days. Bad provisions, the intense heat, and the imprudent management of the commander, who was anxious to win the honor of taking Khiva, caused the failure of the expedition. It returned to Krasnovodsk after nearly two months of struggles in the desert with wandering tribes of Turkomans. The second column, under command of General Verevkin, started from Orenburg, and, after a comparatively easy march, reached Khiva, which might have been taken, had it not been arranged beforehand for General Kaufmann to be given the glory of the conquest. Kaufmann set out from Tashkent, and after a severe march through the Kizil-Kum desert, where nearly nine tenths of his ten thousand camels perished, and where the whole expedition was very nearly lost, he arrived at Khiva, and on the tenth of June he received the peaceful submission of the city. According to all accounts, however, the glory of the conquest belonged to General Verevkin's detachment. The vanquished khan acknowledged himself the "obedient servant" of the White Tsar, and renounced the right of entertaining direct relations with neighboring sovereigns and khans. The portion of his states on the right bank of the Amu Daria and the delta of the river as far as the Taldik branch was annexed. The free navigation of the Amu was reserved exclusively to Russians, who were to be permitted also to construct harbors and piers on the left bank, under the protection of the khan. Extensive mercantile and agricultural privileges were secured; all the towns and villages were opened to Russian trade, for the safety of which the Khivan government held itself answerable. Complaints and claims against Khivan subjects were to be immediately settled by the Khivan authorities. Quarrels with Russian subjects living in the khanate were to be decided by the nearest Russian authorities. A fine of two million two hundred thousand rubles was imposed upon the Khivan government as a partial offset to the war, which cost the Russians probably three times as much; but in consideration of the condition of the country the payment was extended over a period of twenty years, the balance each year bearing five per cent interest. The Turkomans were declared Russian subjects in eighteen hundred and seventy-five, and the khan, deprived of the tribute which he had collected from them, and despised by his subjects for his submissiveness, found his difficulties constantly increasing. In eighteen hundred and seventy-six he entreated to be allowed to exchange his domains for a pension. The reply was not given immediately, but annexation is only a question of time. In eighteen hundred and seventy-three only the fear of a conflict with England, a consequence which was averted by Count Shuvalof's mission to London, prevented the reduction of Khiva to the condition of a Russian province.

The Kirgiz and Turkomans being subdued, Kokan and Samarkand annexed, Khiva and Bukhara tributary states, only one of the princes of Central Asia still defied the Russians. This was Iakub, Khan of Kashgar, who, with his army of forty thousand men, disciplined by Polish or Anglo-Indian officers, with his arsenals and his foundries, made headway against the "Infidels" and defended the passes of the mountains. In eighteen hundred and seventy General Kolpakovski anticipated Iakub Khan by occupying the Chinese province of Kuldja, from which the rebellious Mussulmans had expelled the troops of the Celestial Empire after the most frightful massacres, and which the khan coveted. The Russian government was not pleased at this accession of territory, and immediately informed the Chinese Emperor of the occupation of the province and of its willingness to restore it to China as soon as a sufficient force was brought to preserve order. China, however, did not care about it, and meanwhile it has been administered by the Russians.

In June, eighteen hundred and seventy-two, a commercial treaty was signed with Iakub, who for the first time was recognized by Russia as an independent sovereign. Nevertheless, the caravans which were sent to Kashgar were molested and robbed. The Russians made further advances by occupying the valley of the Naryn and building Fort Narynsk. Their support of the Chinese caused Iakub unexpected difficulty. Iakub the Badaulet, or Fortunate, was assassinated in eighteen hundred and seventy-seven. After his death the Chinese entered Eastern Turkestan. In December, eighteen hundred and seventy-seven, they captured Yarkand, Kashgar, and Khotan. Kuli Bek, the oldest son and the successor of Iakub, took refuge in Russian territory, and Eastern Turkestan was again in the hands of the Celestials.

The character of Russian colonization is thus described by M. Cucheval-Clarigny: "All these enterprises will profit civilization at the same time that they consolidate the Russian power; but the chief strength of the latter lies in the qualities which make of the Russian soldier the most admirable instrument of conquest and colonization. Docile as well as brave, easily contented, supporting without complaint all fatigues and privations, and ready for everything, the Russian soldier constructs roads, clears canals, and re-establishes the ancient aqueducts. He makes the bricks with which he builds the forts and the barracks which he inhabits; he fabricates his own cartridges and projectiles; he is a mason, a metal-founder, or a carpenter, according to the need of the hour, and the day after he is dismissed he contentedly follows the plough. With such instruments at its disposal, the Russian power will never give way: a few years will suffice to render final the conquest of any land on which it has set foot."

In these countries, for centuries devastated and dishonored by Mussulman fanaticism, by wars between the khans, by brigandage, and by traffic in slaves, the Russians appear as the soldiers of civilization, and as a general thing bring with them a more humane and equitable rule. Following on the banks of the Oxus and Iaxartes the traces of Alexander the Great, they complete the revenge of the Iranian race against the Turanian peoples, who, under the lead of Tchingis Khan, invaded semi-Greek Baktria and ruined the ancient Macedonian colonies.

RELATIONS WITH CHINA, JAPAN, AND THE UNITED STATES.

In the middle of the seventeenth century the Siberian Cossacks, by their ambition for conquest, disquieted the Chinese government. The first embassy for the purpose of establishing commercial relations was sent by the Tsar Alexis in sixteen hundred and fifty-four, but neither this nor the succeeding attempts met with success. By the treaty signed in Fort Niptchu at Nertchinsk, on the twenty-seventh of August, sixteen hundred and eighty-nine, the Chinese shut off the Russians from the Pacific for one hundred and fifty years, and kept control of the left bank of the Amur in spite of the attempts of the governors of East Siberia to regain it. The Russian government confined trade with China to the trans-Baïkal boundary town of Kiakhta, and the caravan trade, confirmed by the treaty of Burinsk in seventeen hundred and twenty-seven, was given up. In eighteen hundred and forty the English declared war upon China, and the Celestial authorities went to the Russian legation at Pekin for counsel and assistance. The Russian government did not take advantage of this state of affairs, but contented itself with the treaty of

Kuldja, by which trade with Western China was legalized. The operations of Count Nikolaï Muravief upon the Amur resulted, in eighteen hundred and fifty-three, in the foundation of several forts, which did not attract much attention in China in consequence of internal disturbances and English complications. In eighteen hundred and fifty-six the lands along the Lower Amur were incorporated into the province of Kamtchatka under the title of East Siberia, the capital of which was Nikolaïevsk. Admiral Putiatin went to Tien-tsin in August, eighteen hundred and fifty-seven, for the purpose of reaching a diplomatic understanding. The treaty of Tien-tsin gave the Western Powers the right of establishing representatives at Pekin.

The following year, on the twenty-eighth of May, Muravief concluded the treaty of Aigun, which secured to Russia all the left bank of the river Amur, a territory of two million square kilometers, which has since been divided into the province of the Amur and the Maritime Province. By the same treaty the right of navigating the tributary rivers, Zungari and Usuri, was granted to Russian traders. The treaty of Aigun was confirmed by that of Tien-tsin, signed by Putiatin on the thirteenth of June, eighteen hundred and fifty-eight, and Russia was also assured all the advantages which France and England had gained. General Ignatief, in March of the following year, went by way of Kiakhta to his post as ambassador in Pekin, where his indefatigable endeavors for still pleasanter relations met with gratifying success. The steamboats of the Amur Company plough the waters of the river for twenty-four hundred kilometers, from Nertchinsk to the sea, and place Russia in direct communication with San Francisco and the islands of the Pacific. In eighteen hundred and sixty maritime Mantchuria was annexed, and the plan was broached of transferring the capital from Nikolaïevsk to Vladivostok, which is connected with Saint Petersburg by a telegraph wholly on Russian soil. In eighteen hundred and seventy-eight Kuldja had become the most prosperous of the imperial provinces of Central Asia. Tso Tsung Tang preferred a formal demand of the province, and toward the close of the year Chung How was sent to Saint Petersburg to negotiate a treaty. Six months were spent in fruitless endeavors to come to terms. At last Chung How was induced to sign a convention by which China should take possession of a portion of Kuldja, pay Russia an indemnity of five million rubles, and grant Russian subjects the right of trade. Chung How was degraded on his return, the treaty was abrogated, and great preparations were made for war. The forts on the Peïho were furnished with Krupp cannon, the fleet was strengthened by iron-clads with twenty-five ton guns, and a well-disciplined army of one hundred thousand men was ready to appeal to arms. The peace party, however, prevailed, and hostilities, if not averted forever, were at least postponed.

Russian dealings with the insular empire of Japan began in the eighteenth century. In seventeen hundred and eighty some Japanese were shipwrecked on the coast of Siberia, and were obliged to teach the Japanese language at Irkutsk. This was the first of the Eastern languages to be officially taught. In eighteen hundred and three the circumnavigation of the world was accomplished by Russian ships for the first time. The commander made a stop at Japan, but his actions were injurious to Russian interests. A half-century later Admiral Putiatin explored the Chinese waters, and on the seventh of February, eighteen hundred and fifty-five, signed the treaty of Simoda, which opened to Russian trade the ports of Simoda, Hakodade, and Nagasaki. Two years before this the Russian American Company took possession of the northern portion of the island of Sagalin, known to the Japanese as Karafuto, in relation to which Japanese envoys were sent to Saint Petersburg. Finally, in eighteen hundred and sixty-seven a convention was signed by Stremulkof on the part of Russia, and by Koidé no Kami and Ishikawa Kawachi no Kami on the part of

Japan, in accordance with which the island was to be jointly occupied by the two nations. In eighteen hundred and seventy-five Russia ceded to Japan the Kurile Islands, and in return occupied the whole of Sagalin. The coal-fields of Dui promise to prove very valuable.

The relations of Russia with the United States have always been very friendly. The first treaty, concluded in eighteen hundred and twenty-four, declared the navigation and fisheries of the Pacific free to both nations, and regulated the suppression of illicit trade. In eighteen hundred and thirty-two a second convention was signed by James Buchanan and Count Nesselrode, guaranteeing the citizens of the United States the right to enter the ports, places, and rivers of the Alaskan territory under the full protection of the government. On the thirtieth of March, eighteen hundred and sixty-seven, Russia sold to the United States, for a sum of seven million two hundred thousand dollars in gold, its possessions in the north of the continent, amounting to one million four hundred and eighty thousand square kilometers, with a population estimated at seventy-five thousand, mostly Indians. Although Russian America was discovered by Russian traders as early as the first half of the seventeenth century, it was not until the death of Peter the Great that Captain Behring, a native of Jutland, in the Russian service, was sent to make investigations. After a two years' voyage in which, by his timidity and indolence, he failed to carry out any of his instructions, he returned to Saint Petersburg. Throughout the century various trading expeditions were organized. In seventeen hundred and seventy-nine Catherine made a decree that the Aleuts should pay tribute and have dealings only with Russian companies. In seventeen hundred and ninety-nine the Emperor Paul gave a charter to the Russian American Company, which henceforth controlled all the coasts of America north of fifty-five degrees north latitude. In consequence of an unfavorable report upon the management of the company by Pavel Golovin, the charter was not renewed. The average annual income of the company for the twenty-one years preceding its dissolution was upwards of nine hundred and sixty-six thousand silver rubles. The original capital of the company was ninety-eight thousand silver rubles. The average annual tax paid to the Russian crown is stated by Mr. William H. Dall to have been two hundred thousand rubles. On the eighteenth of October, eighteen hundred and sixty-seven, the Russian Commission formally transferred the "territory, dominion, property, dependencies, and appurtenances" of Russian America to General Rousseau. The transfer was made under mutual salutes of artillery, and since that time the United States has controlled this province, whose value has been the subject of much dispute.

CHAPTER XII.

ALEXANDER THE SECOND.

European Relations from 1856 until 1877.

AUSTRIA AND ITALY.—PRUSSIA AND DENMARK.—IMPERIAL INTERVIEWS; THE FRANCO-PRUSSIAN WAR.—THE PRUSSIAN ALLIANCE.—GORTCHAKOF'S CIRCULAR NOTE OF 1871.—REORGANIZATION OF THE ARMY.

AUSTRIA AND ITALY.

IN eighteen hundred and fifty-six Prince Alexander Gortchakof succeeded Count Nesselrode as Chancellor of the Empire. The necessity under which the country was placed, of recovering from the consequences of the Eastern war, was expressed in one of his earliest circulars: "Russia is not sulking, it is convalescing." Peace with the great powers was absolutely essential in order to carry out the reforms of which the Empire stood in need.

Russia, however, was able to repay Austria for the part it took in the Crimean war. Austria's plans for getting a preponderating influence in the Danube states were upset by the counter-game which Russia played in the Paris conferences. By the convention of eighteen hundred and fifty-eight, the Principalities of Valakhia and Moldavia were allowed to become one state, which bore the historic name of Rumania. In spite of the protests of the Porte and the convention of the nineteenth of August, Russia, supported by France, which had already grown cold to its old ally, Austria, caused Prince Alexander Kuza to be raised to the throne. In Serbia the revolution of eighteen hundred and fifty-eight resulted in the deposition of Prince Alexander Karaiurévitch and the re-establishment of the old prince, Milosh Obrenovitch, a faithful friend and vassal of Russia. At the conferences of Paris there was a visible growth of good feeling between Russia and France. France favored the demands of the Rumanians, Serbians, and Montenegrins against Turkey, and was graciously pleased to respond to Prince Gortchakof's observations on "the wretched and precarious situation" of the Christians of Bosnia, the Herzegovina, and Bulgaria. Russia was disposed to keep neutral in regard to the complications in Italy. It proposed a conference to settle the difficulties without recurring to a European war. The programme, which was supported by France, included peace between Austria and Sardinia, evacuation of the Papal States by the French and Austrians, a confederation of the small Italian States, and a deliberation touching the reforms to be effected in Rome, Naples, and the rest of Italy. The other great powers willingly acceded to this proposal; but Austria, feeling that it was derogatory to be put on an equal footing with the small state of Sardinia, added such conditions that the Congress was abandoned. The Austrian troops then crossed the Tessin. Russia's firmness prevented a general European war. The Italian revolution was allowed to take its course. Peace was declared on the seventeenth of October between France and Austria. In March, eighteen hundred and sixty-one, Victor Emanuel took the title of King of Italy, and in August of the following year Alexander formally granted him recognition, and soon after signed a commercial treaty with him. But while Russia acceded to the Emancipation of Italy, it was not so ready to favor that of the Christians in the East. It applauded the French occupation of Syria in eighteen hundred and sixty, at the time when the Druses massacred the Christians of Palestine, and would have even wished it to be more important and more prolonged.

But the diplomatic demonstration of France in eighteen hundred and sixty-three, arising from Polish affairs, destroyed the growing intimacy of the two states, and threw Russia into the Prussian alliance. To maintain this the Russian Chancellor made irreparable sacrifices to Bismarck, "the man of blood and iron."

PRUSSIA AND DENMARK.—IMPERIAL INTERVIEWS; THE FRANCO-PRUSSIAN WAR.

When it seemed likely that the royal line of Denmark would be extinguished by the death of Frederic the Seventh, Duke Christian of Augustenburg, the heir apparent, was forced to accept an indemnity of two million thalers and renounce his right in favor of the collateral line of Holstein-Sonderburg-Glücksburg. This settlement was considered at the time of doubtful legality, and when Christian the Fourth, of Glücksburg, mounted the throne, Duke Frederic of Augustenburg protested that his father's abdication was not binding on his posterity. The German Confederation took up the cause of Frederic, and declared war against Christian the Fourth in eighteen hundred and sixty-four. Russia allowed Denmark to be crushed. It was obliged to give up Schleswig-Holstein and pay an indemnity. Russia's former relations with Denmark were renewed, however, in eighteen hundred and sixty-six, when the Tsesarévitch, Alexander, was married to the Princess Dagmar, the daughter of King Christian the Fourth. She had been betrothed to Alexander's oldest brother, who died at Nice in April, eighteen hundred and sixty-five.

After the Danish war was ended, Austria and Prussia had a dispute as to the possession of Holstein. The question at issue was in reality of deeper moment, and involved the supremacy over Germany. War was only postponed by the convention of Gastein on the fourteenth of August, eighteen hundred and sixty-five, by which Prussia assumed temporary sovereignty of Schleswig, Austria of Holstein; and Lauenburg, on the payment of two and a half million Danish dollars, went to the Prussian Emperor. Although Gortchakof made no formal alliance with Bismarck in eighteen hundred and sixty-six, Russia allowed Prussia not only to expel Austria from the Germanic Confederation, but to dethrone the reigning houses of Hanover, Nassau, and Cassel, all of them more or less nearly related to the imperial house of Russia. Those of Darmstadt, Baden, and Würtemberg, which had given emperors to Russia, were subordinated so as to constitute Germany, formerly inoffensive, into a mighty military power, holding on the Baltic, the Vistula, and the Danube interests diametrically opposed to those of Russia.

The Emperor of the French had long been desirous of territorial extension toward the east, and the peculiarly loose relationship which Luxemburg bore to Germany after the Austro-Prussian war and the dissolution of the German Bund offered the requisite opportunity. Prussia was requested to withdraw its troops from the Grand Duchy; when this was not done the war feeling in France rose to a fever heat. Pacific measures were proposed by Prince Gortchakof. A conference was opened in London on the seventh of May, eighteen hundred and sixty-seven, in which the five great powers, together with Belgium, Holland, and Italy, decided that the Grand Duchy of Luxemburg should be erected into a neutral sovereign state under the house of Nassau and Orange. The King of Prussia then agreed to withdraw his troops from the castle. Only the great Paris Exposition prevented the French from expressing their disapproval of this treaty by a declaration of war.

In June, eighteen hundred and seventy, the sovereigns of Prussia and Russia had an interview at Ems; on the ninth of July Prince Gortchakof told the English ambassador that Russia did not feel at all alarmed at the power of Prussia; but this confidence was to be put to a new proof. Four weeks after the interview at Ems the Franco-German war broke out.

The official journal of Russia said: "The imperial government has made every endeavor to avert the war. Unfortunately, the rapidity with which hostile resolutions were taken rendered nugatory our efforts for the maintenance of peace. The Emperor is resolved to observe neutrality so long as Russian interests are not disturbed by the results of the campaign. The Russian government assures its support to all endeavors calculated to limit the operations and to shorten the duration of the war."

This threat of protecting Russian interests was extremely disagreeable to Austria. Count Andrassy made public declaration that although Hungary had nothing to win by participating in the war, and much to lose, yet, rather than allow a Russo-Prussian alliance, it would be justified in taking such a step. "The instant Russia enters the war," said the Hungarian minister, "it will find us also on the battle-field; and Russia's ally, whoever he may be, will be our enemy. We have declared this publicly many times during the last twelve months, and yet once more we repeat it: Hungary, and Austria as well, has only one natural opponent in Europe, and that is Russia. To this opponent we will give battle wheresoever and with whomsoever we find him, and welcome is any ally who comes to our aid against Russia."

Russia, on the other hand, declared that the moment Austria attempted to assist the French, the Prussian frontiers would be protected by Russian troops. Prussia was thus enabled to withdraw its troops from Silesia and Poznania and bring them into active service. The menacing attitude of Russia toward Austria carried with it Italian neutrality, and in the same way Denmark was kept from entering the conflict, although Danish sympathies were strongly pronounced in favor of the French, and the Marseillaise Hymn was sung with fervor at the reception of the French fleet.

After the battle of Metz, when England tried to prevent Prussia from taking Alsace and Lorraine, Russia again came to the assistance of William the First, and protested that after the immense expenditure of blood and treasure it was right that the Prussians should receive a proper compensation. France found itself isolated in Europe. Russia had not only prevented the formation of the "league of neutrals," but by diplomatic means had discouraged the collective intervention of Europe.

On the third of September the Emperor, hearing of his uncle's victory at Sedan and the surrender of Napoleon, drank his health, and broke the glass to give his toast greater solemnity. On the twenty-seventh of February, eighteen hundred and seventy-one, the Prussian monarch sent this telegram, announcing the capture of Paris: "We have thus reached the end of this glorious and bloody war, which was forced upon us by the frivolity of the French. Prussia will never forget that she owes it to you that the war did not enter upon extreme dimensions." Alexander immediately replied, offering his sincere congratulations and sympathy as a "devoted friend." The understanding between William and Alexander was not broken by the nephew's advice to use moderation; in the words of M. Soul: "This intimate and sympathetic exchange of private letters did not for a moment alter the friendship of the two sovereigns. The King of Prussia received the observations of his nephew without impatience; and the Tsar, although his entreaties always remained fruitless, was never affronted by the refusals of his uncle."

The mission of M. Thiers at Saint Petersburg in September, eighteen hundred and seventy, had no results. He had audiences with Prince Gortchakof, with Alexander Alexandrovitch, with the Emperor himself. But he received only soft words; among others, that "the former enemy of France would do more for it than its former ally, England." The Emperor said: "I cannot express to you how grieved I am to see your country in so desperate a situation. I can only advise moderation, as I have always done; and I assure you that King

William will be as magnanimous in peace as he was great and victorious in war." Thiers's check in Russia caused his efforts in Austria, Italy, and England to remain fruitless. He had counted on other influences in Russia. He knew well that there was a certain party which looked askance upon the gigantic strides Prussia was taking in Europe, and the nation did not contemplate the fall of France and the overthrow of the equilibrium of Europe in favor of Prussia with the same eyes as did the government. Subscriptions were everywhere opened for the benefit of the wounded French, and the news of the smallest successes of France excited public joy. Mr. Eugene Schuyler, the *chargé d'affaires* of the United States, wrote to his government under date of the seventeenth of August, eighteen hundred and seventy: " Great exertions are being made here to induce the government to abandon its neutrality and to declare itself on one side or the other. It seems to be the general opinion that if the country were prepared for war it would declare it and try to draw from it certain political advantages, such as a revision of the treaty of Paris and territorial extensions on the Black or Baltic Sea. The feeling in favor of France is perhaps stronger since the recent successes of Prussia, and the leading journals have every day articles showing how unfortunate for Europe and for free government would be the increase and consolidation of a great military power like North Germany. . . . The officers of the army are said to be nearly unanimous in favor of France and of a war with Prussia, and I know of several occasions when toasts have been drunk to the ruin of the Germans and of 'Fritz.' It is difficult to see how Russia would gain any advantage by taking part in a war of this kind even if Austria were engaged. Meanwhile the government is using every effort to prepare for eventualities. It is impossible not to notice that the vicinities of all the barracks show a great stir. Hospital wagons and camp equipage are being repaired and put in order. The cartridge factories are running constantly day and night, turning out about half a million metallic shells daily. These are now being filled and sent to the frontier in large quantities. . . . The late successes of the German army have directed attention to the vulnerable points of Russia in case of the complete victory of Prussia. There are two, Poland and the Baltic provinces. . . . In the Baltic provinces all the political power is possessed by some two hundred thousand German nobles and merchants, who still keep the privileges granted them by Peter the Great on the conquest of the country, to the exclusion of the two millions of natives and Russians who do not speak German. Any attempt of the Imperial Government to introduce the Russian language instead of the German as the official language, or to make liberal reforms in the judicial proceedings or in the city government, is vigorously resisted by the Germans, who immediately cry out that they are oppressed and persecuted. Their leaders have more than once pointed to Prussia as their natural defender and protector, and there is a party in Prussia which has espoused their cause, and threatens difficulties with the Russian government. These questions indeed in the North German Reichstag have always been evaded and opposed by the Prussian government; but people here think that should Prussia be successful and Germany become united, a strong effort will be made to make the Baltic question an international one, to claim the Baltic provinces as part of Germany and to detach them from Russia."

THE PRUSSIAN ALLIANCE.

It will be remembered that Bestuzhef-Riumin, the chancellor of Elisabeth, finding the Prussia of Frederick the Second too powerful, and the annexation of Silesia disquieting for Russia, fought the seven years' war to "diminish the forces" of his ambitious neighbor. Alexander the First dared all the power of Napoleon for the sake of Oldenburg and the Hanse Towns, and it was not strange that the Russians, who were well aware of what Prussia had gained by this ten years' alliance, should feel somewhat jealous. Prussia had acquired provinces and kingdoms, fortified harbors, and a formidable army, and was mistress of the situation. Charles of Hohenzollern-Sigmaringen, a prince related to the royal family of Germany, was firmly established on the throne of Rumania, and thus secured Prussia's influence in the East. Russia had recognized the formation of the German Empire on the twenty-fourth of January, eighteen hundred and seventy-one; the Tsar gave the military order of Saint George to the Crown Prince of Saxony; the princes Frederick William and Frederick Charles bore the title of Russian field-marshals.

Although the demands of the Baltic writers found an echo in public meetings and in the press of Berlin, and although it was a significant fact that Herr Kattner dedicated to the German army his book on the "Mission of Prussia in the East," yet, on the other hand, the danger was scouted by many of the Russian newspapers and statesmen. It was said, the stronger Germany proves to be, so much the greater protection against attacks from the West will Russia find it. A writer in the Northern Press declared that he could understand England's jealousy of the newly constituted Germany, or the bitter feelings of the house of Hapsburg-Lorraine, or the ambition for recognition as a first-class power by Italy, or the anxieties and antipathies of the Scandinavian states, but he could not see why Russia should take umbrage at the growth of Germany, or for a moment believe that there was any danger of its harboring designs upon the Baltic provinces.

The *Golos* newspaper, on the other hand, in a series of articles showed that Russia was the only power which could not afford to acquiesce in the aggrandizement and conquests of Prussia. The last article ended as follows: "Russia ought to keep its neutrality so long as its interests are untouched. But they may be touched if at a coming congress or at the conclusion of peace the treaty of Paris remains unchanged. Russia has not hindered the forcible unification of Germany, and in its turn does not think of a forcible unification of the Slavonians. But it has a right to demand that its position on the Black Sea and on the banks of the Danube be lightened. We may hope that these lawful demands will be respected in the General European Congress which will probably follow the present war."

In reality the Russian policy, while serving Prussia and cajoling France, was directed to one single end, the revision of the treaty of eighteen hundred and fifty-six. It was a question, however, whether Prussia would give its support to Russia in its Eastern policy; as it was expressed by Count Benedetti, the French minister, in Berlin, "Any conflict in the East subordinates the German Chancellor to Russia, and he will try to avert it." This was proved in the Greco-Turkish difference of eighteen hundred and sixty-nine. Russia is a card in his game for events that may take place on the Rhine, and he considers it necessary that the rôles should not be inverted, that he should not himself become a card in the game of Saint Petersburg.

GORTCHAKOF'S CIRCULAR NOTE OF EIGHTEEN HUNDRED AND SEVENTY-ONE.

On the thirty-first of October Prince Gortchakof addressed a circular to the six powers. He therein stated that the experience of fifteen years proved that the principle on which the signatory power relied for preventing a conflict between the powers bordering on the Black Sea, or between either of them and the maritime powers, was nothing more than a theory; that Russia had disarmed so thoroughly as to be liable to fall an easy prey even to a secondary state possessed of a navy; that the treaty had been violated with impunity by the other powers, and the imperial cabinet was therefore placed "under the necessity of examining the consequences which might follow for the political position of Russia."

Confiding in the equitable sentiments of the powers which signed the treaty of eighteen hundred and fifty-six, the Emperor declared that he held himself no longer bound by those stipulations, and felt that he was entitled and obliged to announce to the Sultan that he should henceforth use his own discretion in regard to the number and size of the men-of-war afloat in the Black Sea.

The English government received this circular with "deep regret," because it was felt that the assumption of a right to renounce any one of the terms of a treaty involved the assumption of a right to renounce the whole. After an exchange of courteous despatches between the two governments, it was agreed that Russia's demand for a revision of Article Two, which placed a limitation on its maritime forces in the Black Sea, should be laid before the conference which Prussia had convened in London.

On the thirteenth of March, eighteen hundred and seventy-one, the powers formally abrogated the neutralization of the Black Sea. Turkey, which at first protested that it would make every sacrifice rather than allow the act to pass, found itself so harassed by its relations with Syria, with Montenegro, with Persia, with Bulgaria, that it was obliged to give a reluctant consent. Russia, which had already begun to prepare for contingencies, in eighteen hundred and seventy-two resolved to reorganize the port and harbor of Sevastopol and build the dock-yards of Nikolaïef.

After the fall of France the Emperors of Russia and Germany, carrying with them the Emperor of Austria, undertook to constitute what was called the Alliance of the Three Emperors for the regulation of the affairs in the east and west. On the twenty-seventh of August, eighteen hundred and seventy-two, Alexander, who was at Novotcherkask, solemnly addressed the hetman of the Cossacks. "God grant," said he, advancing to the centre of the church, "that it may not be necessary to shed again your precious blood; and at the present moment I see no danger threatening us. In order still more to consolidate peace, I have decided to undertake a journey abroad, and I hope that it will not be without results for us. But in case of necessity, I am persuaded that the troops of the Don will reply to my appeal with the ardor they have always shown for the defence of our fatherland." This speech of the Emperor awoke grave apprehensions. The conference of the three emperors in September was attended with great magnificence. There were present Count Andrassy and two of the ablest Russians of the day, Baron Jomini and Mr. Hamburger; Alexander was accompanied by two of the Grand Dukes, by his brother, Count Berg, the Polish viceroy, and by a brilliant staff. This Congress of Berlin, the journey of the Emperor William to Saint Petersburg in eighteen hundred and seventy-three, and frequent interviews between the heads of the state, made the good understanding between them obvious to the eyes of Europe.

REORGANIZATION OF THE ARMY.

The novel situation in which Europe has been placed by the developments of the Prussian military power obliged the empire of the Tsars to reorganize its military system also, and bring its army to a development of which Peter the Great never dreamed. At the time of the Crimean war, and even after the emancipation, the main body of the army had consisted almost entirely of peasants, each landed proprietor being obliged to furnish a contingent from his serfs; the crown peasants were selected by magistrates. Thus the composition of the army was of the poorest material, and the extreme length of service, varying from twenty to thirty years, practically used up the best part of a man's life. In eighteen hundred and seventy the Minister of War was ordered to prepare an improved plan of recruitment by which the obligation of military service should be extended to all classes of the population. A special commission, composed of members of different branches of the administration and of military specialists, was appointed, and the regulation drawn up by this commission was approved by the Emperor on the first of January, eighteen hundred and seventy-four. In the imperial proclamation which accompanied this ukas it was declared as a fundamental principle that the defence of the throne and of the country was the sacred duty of every Russian subject, and the entire male population was called upon to share in the military service without exemption by purchase or by providing substitutes. Theological students and members of the priesthood, doctors of medicine and surgeons, chemists, artists who have been sent abroad to complete their education, schoolmasters and the officers of state or of corporate bodies, together with all who are incapacitated by disease or bodily defects, are exempt from service. The only son of a widowed mother, or of parents who have attained the age of fifty-five, is also freed from the obligation of entering the army.

The active army is recruited by means of a levy made throughout the empire upon that class of young men who have reached the age of twenty years by the first of January of that year. The number of men annually reaching the age of twenty years is about seven hundred thousand, of which only a fourth are required to join the active army. The remainder enter the reserve. The ordinary term of service in the land forces is fixed at fifteen years, six of which are spent in service and nine in the reserve; in the naval forces the ordinary term is ten years, seven of which are spent in active service and three in the reserve. In time of war, however, the soldiers under arms must remain with the colors as long as their services are needed by the state.

Educated conscripts can obtain a reduction of their six

years' term of service in four different ways. Those who have completed a course of study at the universities, or other first-class educational establishments, serve only six months; those who have finished the course of six classes in the gymnasia, or have received the secondary course of instruction at other schools, serve eighteen months. If they have passed through the primary superior schools, they serve three years; if through the primary schools, four years. This law, therefore, has the character of a law guaranteeing social equality, and, moreover, offers a premium on education. Young men over seventeen years of age may still further abridge their time of service by voluntarily forestalling the conscription. After a service of three months, six months, or two years, according to their attainments in education, they are allowed either to enter the reserve or remain in active service with the rank of officers.

The Russian land-forces are divided into the regular army, the reserve, and the irregular troops. These forces comprise a field army numbering five hundred and sixty thousand men, which can easily be expanded to nine hundred thousand in time of war; a force of local troops for garrison duty and frontier service, varying from one hundred and fifty thousand to three hundred and twenty-five thousand men; Cossacks or irregular horsemen, numbering from forty-two thousand to one hundred and forty-three thousand men, who are used as auxiliaries to the field army; and a reserve of trained soldiers consisting of upwards of a million men on furlough in peace but liable to service in time of war. The militia thus includes all the male population of the empire between twenty and forty years of age, except the regular army.

In October, eighteen hundred and seventy-four, the first drawing was made in accordance with the new law. The imperial ukas called for one hundred and fifty thousand men. More than six hundred and ninety thousand were liable for service, of whom between twelve and thirteen thousand were exempted by law, nearly fifty thousand were discharged on account of physical incapacity, eighteen thousand were allowed to postpone their service until they had completed their education. About one hundred and forty-five thousand were incorporated into the army, while the rest were inscribed on the rolls of the militia.

The commander-in-chief of the army is the Emperor. All military affairs are controlled through the Minister of War, a general of high rank, to whom all officers and soldiers throughout the empire are subject. The empire itself is divided into fourteen circumscriptions, in each of which a ministry of war, on a small scale, directs the administration. Each circumscription is under the control of a chief, appointed by the Emperor. The chief has the command over every military person in the district, and is the president of a council, the majority of whose votes decides all questions relating to property and supply.

The enormous strides taken by the science of naval warfare induced the Russian government to place its marine upon a footing worthy of a first-class power. At the end of the year eighteen hundred and seventy-nine Russia possessed a total of two hundred and twenty-three men-of-war, carrying five hundred and sixty-one guns. Some of these new iron-clads are among the most powerful in the world. The Piotr Veliki, or Peter the Great, is a floating fortification of over ninety-five hundred tons measurement, and carries four thirty-five-ton guns. The Novgorod and the Admiral Popof are circular monitors, called Popovkas from the name of their inventor. The Russian fleet is also provided with a large number of torpedo-boats, the use of which has almost revolutionized the service.

In March, eighteen hundred and seventy-eight, the Russian navy was commanded by seventeen admirals, thirty-two vice-admirals, thirty-one rear-admirals, and more than a thousand captains and lieutenants. The crews are obtained by recruitment, except in the case of Finland, where they voluntarily enlist. The fleet has four divisions, assigned respectively to the Baltic, the Black Sea, the Caspian and Aral, and the Pacific Ocean.

Russia, together with the other states of Europe, has made endeavors to mitigate the necessary horrors of war. In eighteen hundred and sixty-seven it adhered to the Convention of Geneva for the relief of the wounded. In the following year the Explosive Bullet Treaty was signed at Saint Petersburg by representatives of all the European powers.

The new military system of Russia was scarcely inaugurated before events in the East put it to the severest test.

CHAPTER XIII.

THE EASTERN QUESTION.

1875-1877.

The Herzegovinian and Bosnian Insurrection. — Count Andrassy's Note. — The Turkish Massacres. — Diplomatic Measures. — The Berlin Memorandum. — Events at Constantinople. — The Serbian War.

THE HERZEGOVINIAN AND BOSNIAN INSURRECTION.

ON the first of July, eighteen hundred and seventy-five, an insurrection broke out in the Herzegovina, a Turkish province situated on the east side of the Adriatic Sea, and bounded by Kroatia, Bosnia, Serbia, and Montenegro.

This was not the first time, even since the Crimean war, that the Christian subjects of the Porte had raised the standard of revolt. In eighteen hundred and fifty-eight the Montenegrins and the Turks had several quarrels, which finally were settled by a European commission. Two years later the Herzegovinians, aided by the Montenegrins, rose against their tax-collectors, and continued the revolt until the autumn of eighteen hundred and sixty-two. In eighteen hundred and seventy-four the harvests failed; the tribute nevertheless was collected with relentless cruelty and unfairness, and the percentage was even increased. Christians were forced to labor on the public highways; their horses were taken for the army; the law-courts were corrupt; it was an impossibility to secure justice; honor and life itself were at the mercy of the Begs.

Driven to desperation, the raiahs sent their wives and children for safety into the Austrian province of Dalmatia, and took up arms against their Turkish masters. The bravery which they displayed in battle under the command of Lazaro Socica and their other leaders, the sympathy and encouragement given them by their neighbors in Serbia and Montenegro, and the fact that it was a mountainous country where they fought enabled them to hold the Turks, who were not strong in numbers or in leadership, at bay throughout the year.

The Christians of Bosnia, having like grievances with those of the Herzegovina, followed their example; on the fifteenth of August the revolt began in the neighborhood of Gradishka with the murder of a tax-gatherer at the hands of a Christian. The revolt spread rapidly in spite of the efforts of Dervish Pasha, the Governor of Bosnia, to check it. Montenegro would gladly have participated, but the Russian Emperor firmly forbade it; Prince Milan of Serbia with difficulty prevented his ministry from involving the country in the dispute. Toward the middle of August the European powers through their representatives offered their mediation, which the Porte at first refused but afterward accepted. It was proposed that a commissioner should be sent to the disturbed districts to investigate the alleged grievances, while the foreign consuls at Ragusa and Seraïevo should have interviews with the leaders of the revolt, show them that they must not expect assistance or intervention from the great powers, and advise them to lay down their arms, and trust to the Turkish commissioner. Server Pasha was appointed commissioner by the Porte, and in September went to the Herzegovina; but such was the popular distrust of the Turkish government that nothing came of this step. The insurgent leaders on the twelfth of September presented the consuls with a document which embodied a statement of their complaints, and which closed with these words: "Under the Turkish scourge we cannot and we will not live. We are human beings and not cattle. If you are not willing to help us, at least you cannot oblige us to enter into slavery again. We no longer put any faith in Turkish promises, and as to the mediation which you offer us we are thoroughly convinced that it will not have a feather's weight of influence with the Turks. We want freedom, real and absolute freedom. We will never fall alive into the hands of the Turks." What the insurgents desired chiefly was a guarantee from the great powers that the Porte would faithfully execute the reforms which it was so ready to promise. The Turkish commissioner was forbidden to enter into negotiation with the consuls, but to accept their reports singly.

The Christians seemed to be put upon an enviable footing, however, by the iradé which the Sultan granted on the second of October, and the ferman which followed on the twelfth of December, decrees which far outstripped the modest demands of subjects or allies. Equality was established, on paper, between Christian and Mohammedan, and all grievances were to be redressed. The courts of justice were to be reorganized so that the judges should be chosen from among men of acknowledged worth and probity, and hold their office during good behavior. The subjects of the Porte without distinction of religion should elect the members of all the other judicial and administrative bodies, and civil tribunals should settle disputes between all Mussulman and other subjects. The Sultan further decreed that taxes should be made lighter and fairer; that the tithe should be diminished and henceforth collected by tax-gatherers chosen by the people without distinction of creed; and that enforced labor should be abolished. Ecclesiastical affairs were also put upon a satisfactory basis, and all ranks and offices were accessible to non-Mussulman subjects of the Porte, and they were allowed to acquire real property and devise their estates by will.

Although nothing whatsoever was done toward carrying out these admirable reforms, the Porte took special pains to bring them to the knowledge of the powers, and it might possibly long have continued to deceive them, had not the financial condition of the empire come to a crisis which made people suspect the approaching end of the Ottoman power. In eighteen hundred and seventy-four the Turkish debt amounted to about nine hundred million dollars, and the deficit for eighteen hundred and seventy-five was nearly twenty-three millions. The Turkish ministers, finding that they were unable to borrow further from the European markets, saw themselves under the necessity of partial repudiation. By a decree issued on the sixth of October it was announced to the world that the interest on the national debt would be paid for the following five years half in gold and half in new five per cent bonds, and that the revenue derived from the customs, from salt and from tobacco, and the tribute paid by Egypt would be mortgaged as security.

This partial repudiation naturally alarmed the bondholders, a large proportion of whom were English, and a deputation waited on Lord Derby, the foreign secretary, urging him to devise some measure to enforce full payment of interest on the loans. Lord Derby denied that the government was under any obligation to interfere. In Parliament it was distinctly asserted that the Treaty of Paris forbade England meddling with the internal administration of the empire. The English government, in order somewhat to calm apprehensions, purchased in November, for twenty million dollars, nine tenths of the shares of the Suez Canal, owned by the Khedive of Egypt, and announced to the world that free passage through Egypt must be maintained at all events.

COUNT ANDRASSY'S NOTE.

One of the results of the Turkish financial crisis was the revival of hope among the Christians. The insurrection in the northern provinces was still in progress. Both Austria and Russia felt that if it continued it might lead to serious complications. They therefore determined upon a new attempt to oblige the Porte to carry out its promised reforms, so that the Christians might be willing to return to their allegiance. Russia, Germany, and Austria came to an understanding, and Count Andrassy was given the difficult task of preparing a note which, bearing the signatures of the six powers, should make the Sultan's government see that they were in earnest. On the thirtieth of September, eighteen hundred and seventy-five, Russia and Austria came to an agreement about the wording of the note; and as Prince Bismarck made no objection, on the same day it was forwarded to France, Italy, and England for approval.

In his note Count Andrassy advised the Sultan to confirm the reforms which had been promised in the ferman of the twelfth of December, and in order that they might be carried out he proposed a special commission, composed of equal numbers of Mussulmans and Christians, who should take charge of the execution of the necessary measures. He thought the state should sell to the peasantry portions of waste land on easy terms, and the people might trust the promises of the Sultan so that he should solemnly confirm them and publicly accept the demands presented by the signatory powers.

The courts of Paris and Rome found no difficulty in adopting the Andrassy Note. In London there was considerable delay, and some doubt as to whether it were not a form of intervention. It was only when the Porte itself requested the English government to hesitate no longer, that the English cabinet gave a general assent.

The note was communicated to the Ottoman government in an informal way. Count Zichy, the Austro-Hungarian ambassador, called upon Rashid Pasha, the minister of foreign affairs, on the thirty-first of January, eighteen hundred and seventy-six, and read to him the note as a despatch directed to the Austrian ambassadors in Paris, London, and Rome. When he went away he left a copy. His example was followed by the Russian, French, Italian, and English ambassadors, who announced that the document met with their approval and they saw nothing in it to reflect on the spontaneity of the Porte or to conflict with the provisions of the Treaty of Paris.

The Grand Vizier laid the Andrassy Note before a ministerial council, and it was voted to accept four of the five demands without change. The fifth, which related to the expenditure of money raised by taxes in Bosnia and the Herzegovina for the best interest of these provinces, was to be changed in form but not in purport. Rashid Pasha's formal acceptance of the Andrassy Note was communicated in writing to Count Zichy on the thirteenth of February.

The rebels in the Herzegovina were not disposed to give up the struggle, and they refused the amnesty offered them in March by Ali Pasha. The Porte sent commissioners, who promised them all that they wanted on condition that they would lay down their arms. The Austrian government, finding that the Christians who fled to Dalmatia were spreading discontent throughout the southern boundaries, sent Baron Rodich as a mediator, and an armistice of ten days was arranged in March; but nothing came of this. Baron Rodich conferred with the insurrectionary leaders, with the refugees, with the Prince of Montenegro on the one hand, with the Turkish authorities on the other. The rebels declared that they were willing to lay down their arms, provided that in addition to certain financial concessions the Turkish government should withdraw the regular troops from all except six places, where small garrisons might be left under the eyes of Russian and Austrian agents, and disarm the native Mohammedan population. They also demanded a guarantee from the six powers that these reforms should be effected.

Russia also sent Mr. Veselitski to confer with the insurgents and with the Prince of Montenegro. This agent was presented with a memorandum stating their grievances and their expectations.

The Porte would not listen to the demands of the insurgents as presented through Baron Rodich, refused absolutely to disarm the native Mussulmans, or to concentrate its forces in a few small places, or to have a Russo-Austrian commission of supervisors, but confined itself to its promises, unguaranteed and untrustworthy as they were. Rodich threatened that Austria would set a guard on its boundaries, and no longer offered protection to refugees; the Turkish commissioners threatened that those who did not submit should be excluded from the benefit of the reforms. All these threats failed to bring back the refugees or make the rebels lay down their arms.

As the spring advanced, the revolution took more serious proportions. In the Herzegovina, on the fourteenth of April and the days following, the insurgents fought a pitched battle with Mukhtar Pasha, as he was marching from Gako to Niksikh, and drove him back with great loss. Mukhtar Pasha telegraphed to Constantinople that seven thousand Montenegrin subjects fought on the side of the insurgents. The intelligence was received by the Porte with indignation. War against Montenegro was threatened, a camp was established at Skutari, and preparations were made for immediate action. Only the desperate state of the finances and the exertions of the foreign ministers, who promised to renew their efforts at mediation, prevented the crisis.

THE TURKISH MASSACRES.

Difficult as was the position of the Turkish Empire, with a debt the interest on which amounted to seventy million dollars a year, with a serious insurrection unquelled in two of its provinces, and with signs of discontent among all its Christian subjects, it was made still more difficult by the outrage at Salonika, and by the Bulgarian atrocities which took place early in May, eighteen hundred and seventy-six.

On the sixth of May a fanatical throng of Mussulmans

cruelly murdered the consuls of France and Germany, living at Salonika, a town of Macedonia. On the preceding day a Bulgarian girl, supposed to be an unwilling convert to Islamism, arrived at the town to be confirmed in her new faith. A band of Greek Christians overpowered her escort and rescued her. The Mussulmans demanded the restoration of the girl, and their violence was so great that it was with some difficulty the mob was dispersed. The girl was believed to be concealed in the house of the German consul, and when the representatives of Germany and France imprudently ventured into the mosque where the excited throng had gathered, an altercation ensued and the two men were killed. French and German fleets were immediately sent to Salonika, and the murdered consuls were buried with great circumstance under the protection of troops landed in large numbers. Only the prompt action of the Turkish government in punishing the offenders and in making reparation to the families of the victims prevented a serious rupture.

But even this outburst of fanaticism had neither the elements of horror which made the massacres in Bulgaria so heartrending, nor the same wide-reaching influence upon subsequent events.

The Bulgarians, anxious to throw off the Turkish yoke, determined to take advantage of the perplexity caused by the Bosnian and Herzegovinian insurrection. They were instigated to this course by emissaries sent out by the revolutionary committee established at Bukarest, which without doubt was in communication with the Pan-slavic Society of Moscow. The chiefs of the insurrection had their plans nearly matured when the treachery of one of their number caused a premature explosion. On the first of May Nedjib Aga, a magistrate commissioned by the Governor of Bulgaria to make investigations, arrested and put in jail a couple of the conspirators. This was a signal for instant action. The imprisoned men were rescued, and the insurrection immediately spread through the villages of Klissura, Koprishtitsa, Panagurishta, Novoselo, and Bellova, and caused great alarm at Tatar-Bazardjik and Philippopolis. Telegrams were sent to Constantinople for regular troops, and as these were refused the beys of Philippopolis and Adrianople were obliged to meet the insurgents with an improvised militia composed of the Mussulman inhabitants of the region. These irregular troops, or Bashi-Bazuks, then proceeded to attack the villages of the Christians, who made almost no resistance and generally surrendered at the first demand. The Bashi-Bazuks burned and pillaged between sixty and seventy villages, destroyed eight thousand one hundred and forty houses, forty churches, and forty-three schools. Mr. Eugene Schuyler, who was sent by the American government to investigate these massacres, estimated the number of Bulgarians who were killed at fifteen thousand, a large proportion women and children. Others set the number at forty thousand. Bulgarian maidens were said to have been exposed for sale at Philippopolis at a price of only three or four *lire*. This massacre was entirely unjustifiable; it was said to be an insignificant rebellion at best, and the panic which might have served as an excuse was quickly over. Nor did the Bulgarians themselves give cause for such extreme measures. Mr. Schuyler says: "No Turkish women or children were killed in cold blood; no Mussulmans were tortured; no purely Turkish village was attacked or burned; no Mussulman house was pillaged; no mosque was desecrated or destroyed."

When the news of the Bulgarian atrocities reached Western Europe on the twenty-third of June, and was confirmed by later and more accurate statements, public opinion became greatly excited. The letters from Mr. McGahan to the Daily News, the report of Mr. Schuyler, Consul-General in Turkey, to Mr. Maynard, the official statements of Mr. Walter Baring, gave such terrible pictures of the scenes in Batak and other Bulgarian villages, that for once Englishmen forgot self-interest.

Four hundred public meetings were held in England, in which protests against Turkish misgovernment and barbarism were expressed, and criticism on English selfishness and partisanship was freely offered. Disraeli and several of the other ministers were blamed for their incredulity and flippancy. Lord Stratford de Redcliffe, Earl Russell, Gladstone, Granville, John Bright, Thomas Carlyle, Freeman, and other distinguished men published pamphlets and newspaper articles showing that England, which had been Turkey's chief supporter, was Turkey's accomplice in the crime.

The plea that the Turkish government was not accessory to these atrocities, and did not know of them till some time afterwards, was rendered idle by the fact that rewards and decorations were granted to the chief perpetrators. Akhmet Aga, who was responsible for the slaughter at Batak, and Nedjib Aga, who destroyed the village of Ienikeni after the inhabitants had thrown down their arms, were decorated with the order of the Medjidié. Shefket Pasha, whose soldiers pillaged Iamboli, was given a high position at Constantinople. Mr. Baring acknowledged in his report that the Turkish government gave a powerful handle to its enemies and detractors by the way it treated the agents engaged in the suppression of the insurrection. Those who committed atrocities were rewarded, while those who endeavored to protect the Christians from the fury of the Bashi-Bazuks were passed over with contempt.

A year later, in eighteen hundred and seventy-seven, the Porte was brought, by the protestations of the powers, to punish several of the guiltiest of the offenders, and on the eighth of June Akhmet Aga was sent with two others to Constantinople. But the promises to make good the injuries done to the Bulgarian towns were not kept; the suffering inhabitants were subjected to enforced labor, and attempts were made to collect the taxes.

DIPLOMATIC MEASURES.—THE BERLIN MEMORANDUM.

Immediately after the outrage at Salonika, and the despatch of the British fleet to Besika Bay, Prince Gortchakof and Count Andrassy met at Berlin, in order to confer with Prince Bismarck. The new Turkish ambassador had just reached his post in Berlin, and was endeavoring to put the most favorable construction on the acts of his government. The Russian agent Veselitski, and Petrovitch, the president of the Montenegrin Senate, who was charged with the representation of the Herzegovinian interests, also met with the three imperial chancellors. On the fourteenth of May the three ministers agreed upon a plan for the settlement of the Eastern Question. The object of the Memorandum, the preparation of which devolved upon Prince Gortchakof, was to this purpose: that the Porte should establish certain guarantees for the fulfilment of the reforms, and conclude a two months' armistice, during which negotiations with the disaffected Christians were to be opened. The bases for these negotiations were almost identical with the demands of the Christians themselves: that materials to rebuild the churches and houses destroyed should be furnished the returning refugees, together with food until they could support themselves; that this assistance should be distributed through a mixed commission composed of Christians and Mohammedans, while a committee of foreign consuls or representatives should oversee the application of the reforms; that the Christians should be allowed to carry arms, as well as the Mohammedans. The Memorandum concluded with these words: "If, with the friendly and hearty support of the great powers, and by means of an armistice, an arrangement could be concluded on these bases, and put into immediate operation by the return of the refugees, and the election of the mixed commission, a long step would be taken toward pacification. If, on the other hand, the armistice should expire without the objects of the powers being attained, the three imperial courts would be under the necessity of supplementing their diplomatic action by a common agreement to take more efficacious measures, according as such might be demanded by the interests of the general peace, to check the mischief, and prevent its further development."

The French and Italian governments immediately telegraphed their adherence to the terms of the Berlin Memorandum; England, after waiting six days, declined to adopt the proposals of the three Northern chancellors. The reason for the refusal was based partly on the disinclination of the British government to concur in so important a measure, in the preparation of which it had had no hand. Lord Derby declared that Turkey had not had sufficient time to carry out the reforms, and that the Berlin Memorandum, with its concluding threat of active interference, was a breach of international courtesy. The five other powers all expressed their regrets that England should break up the European Concert; the foreign minister of Italy said that he considered united action between all the powers to be the surest means of securing the maintenance of peace; in thus co-operating in the policy of the three imperial cabinets, the western powers would be in a better position to exert an influence over subsequent proceedings, in case the measures now proposed failed to bring about the pacification.

Prince Bismarck, while admitting that the articles of the Memorandum were open to discussion and amendment, regretted that England had felt obliged to withdraw from the cordial understanding established by the other powers, and hoped that her Majesty's government would do nothing to encourage the resistance of the Sultan. The Duc Decazes declared that if England stood aloof at this momentous crisis it would be a public calamity, and Count Andrassy offered to delay the presentation of the Berlin Memorandum at Constantinople, in the hope that the English government might still give its co-operation. But before the five powers could present the Memorandum, rapid changes on the Bosphorus rendered it an idle form.

EVENTS AT CONSTANTINOPLE.

The Russian ambassador at Constantinople was General Ignatief, who was supposed to exercise a great influence over Sultan Abdul-Aziz, and his Grand Vizier, Mahmud Neddin Pasha. He was sometimes called the Sultan's Mephistopheles. The more bigoted of the Mohammedans began to feel that Russian influence was too powerful a factor in the Turkish cabinet. The lack of success in putting down a small rebellion touched the Moslem pride; the financial difficulties which prevented a naturally rich country from paying its creditors abroad and its officers at home, worked great discontent among the more patriotic of the Turks. The idea became prevalent that General Ignatief and Mahmud Pasha were conspiring together to persuade the weak-minded Sultan to allow Russia to send him assistance. It was to be another Unkiar-Skelessi.

The Softas, or students of Constantinople, were fully persuaded of this, and on the eleventh of May they broke into open revolt, crying "Turkey for the Turks." Mahmud was deposed, and his place was filled by Mehemed Rushdi Pasha. Hairulah Effendi was made the Sheikh-ul-Islam, while the Hussein Avni Pasha, a member of the fanatical party of Old Turks, was named war minister and commander-in-chief. The leader of the reform party, Midhat Pasha, became an influential member of the cabinet, and prepared a scheme of financial and political reforms, which were laid before Abdul-Aziz. When the Sultan haughtily refused to consent to such a project, a cabinet council was held on the twenty-ninth of May, and the leaders of the opposing parties, laying aside their differences, agreed that the first thing to be done was to depose Abdul-Aziz. The Sheikh-ul-Islam, or chief of the Ulemas, declared that according to the Sacred Law the Sultan could be legally dethroned, and on the thirtieth of May Abdul-Aziz was forced to retire to Sheragan, and his nephew, Mehemet Murad Effendi, was proclaimed Sultan, with the title Murad the Fifth. He was a man weak in body and mind, and chiefly qualified for his high position by his good-will toward his ministers, whom he left in full control of affairs. The work of reform was immediately begun. The Imperial Hatt, announcing Murad's accession, was read with great solemnity before a large throng, and the ministers were charged to change the administration of justice, to pacify the provinces by granting concessions, to bring the army into a better condition, and to give assurances to the foreign powers. The treasures left by Abdul-Aziz were to be devoted to state purposes. The new Sultan offered to strike off a million and a half of dollars from the civil list, and to turn the income of the crown mines into the coffers of the state.

The new Sultan had scarcely been invested with his office when Abdul-Aziz was found lying dead in a pool of blood. A jury of nineteen physicians declared that his death was effected by his own hands with a pair of scissors, but whether it was a case of suicide or a political murder, the power of Murad the Fifth seemed to be established.

Before Hussein Avni had an opportunity to show his energy in bringing the provinces to peace, his career was suddenly ended. On the fifteenth of June, as the Turkish cabinet was in session in Midhat Pasha's palace, a Circassian officer named Hassan, who had been disgraced, rushed into the room and shot Hussein Avni. Rashid Pasha, the minister of foreign affairs, was too terror-stricken to move. Ahmed Kaïsserli, the minister of the marine, endeavored to pinion the assassin, was stabbed in several places during the struggle, and took refuge in flight. The other members of the cabinet escaped into an inner room. Hassan made sure of the death of Hussein and Rashid, and then, waiting till Ahmed Aga and Shukri Bey ventured back into the room, shot them also. Before he was secured he killed a police-officer, and wounded six of the men who had hastened from the nearest post. He was immediately tried and sentenced to be hung. The execution took place on the seventeenth.

Midhat Pasha became now the leading spirit. He was the hope of the younger men; he believed that the empire must be saved from ruin by a system of radical reforms which should benefit Christians as well as Mussulmans. He was the legitimate successor of Fuad Pasha, who died in eighteen hundred and sixty-nine leaving a scheme on paper for firmly establishing the Turkish Empire by means of uniting all elements into a mighty nation. Midhat Pasha was an enlightened man, educated in the school of French political ideas. He was supported by Abdul Kerim, who became war minister, and Savfet Pasha, who took the portfolio of foreign affairs.

After a reign of only three months Murad the Fifth, who had been reduced to a state of idiocy by drunkenness and dissipation, was deposed with his own consent, and was succeeded on the thirty-first of August by his brother Prince Abdul Hamid, a man in the prime of life, who was hailed by the Turkish press as a man of liberal ideas and favorably disposed to the Christians.

THE SERBIAN WAR.

The difficulties under which the Turkish government was laboring seemed to offer the Prince of Serbia a favorable opportunity to throw off his allegiance, which grew every day more and more intolerable. Although the Turkish garrisons were withdrawn in eighteen hundred and sixty-seven, the Porte had not kept its promise to return a certain fortress on the right bank of the Drina; complications about railway junctions had arisen which caused further bitterness of feeling. Recollections of ancient times, when Serbia was an independent Tsarate, governing Bulgaria, Macedonia, Albania, and

Thessaly, roused the flame of patriotism among the people, and it had been with difficulty that Prince Milan, in eighteen hundred and seventy-five, restrained them from making common cause with the Herzegovinians.

Early in June, eighteen hundred and seventy-six, Serbia began to make preparations for war. A national loan of twelve million francs was proposed for the purpose of freeing all men of Serbian race from foreign control, and restoring the ancient empire of United Serbians. The Porte demanded an explanation of the military movements which were being set on foot, and Prince Milan replied that Serbia was reorganizing its service on the principle of universal military obligation, and that the idea of waging war upon Turkey was preposterous. He justified the massing of troops upon the frontier on the ground that Serbian territory had been violated, but promised to send a peace commissioner to Constantinople to settle such difficulties as had arisen. The Porte, on the tenth of June, demanded the immediate payment of the arrears of the Serbian tribute, the withdrawal of the troops from the frontier, and the formal acknowledgment of Sultan Murad the Fifth ; but instead of acceding to these requirements, Prince Milan despatched an ultimatum to Constantinople, in which he called upon the Porte to withdraw its army from the Serbian frontier, and to recognize him as Viceroy of Bosnia under Turkish sovereignty.

The Bosnian insurgents, without waiting for the Sultan's reply, proclaimed Milan their prince on the twenty-eighth of June. On the following day Prince Milan left Bielgrad for the headquarters of the army at Deligrad, and on the second of July issued a manifesto to the people explaining the necessity of the warlike measures he had taken. The movement was declared to be purely national, and intended only to establish security and order in place of Turkish misrule and anarchy. Prince Milan promised to march at the head of his excellent troops, confiding in their patriotism and valor. " With us," he said, " are our brave Montenegrin allies, led by their noble chief, my brother Prince Nikita; with us are those valiant heroes the Herzegovinians, and those martyrs the Bosnians. Our brave brothers the Bulgarians await our coming, and we hope that the glorious Hellenes, the descendants of Themistokles and Bozzaris, will not long stay away from the battle-field. Forward then, noble heroes! Let us march in the name of Almighty God, protector of nations; let us march in the name of justice, liberty, and civilization."

General Tchernaïef, a retired Russian officer who had won some distinction in the capture of Tashkend in eighteen hundred and sixty-four, took the command of the Serbian army, which amounted to eighty thousand men, the larger part of whom were raw recruits. Three or four thousand Russians came to enlist under the Serbian flag. General Tchernaïef's headquarters were in Southern Serbia, at Alexinats, opposite Nissa, on the river Morava. Smaller divisions of the army were stationed in the east opposite the Turkish fortress Viddin on the river Timok, in the southwest and northwest on the rivers Ibar and Drina for the purpose of making common cause with the Bosnian insurgents and of keeping in communication with Montenegro, which declared war the day following the promulgation of Prince Milan's manifesto. Tchernaïef began the campaign by advancing boldly across the Morava into the territory of the enemy. He was defeated in engagements at Zaitchar and Iavor, and finally on the thirty-first of July was driven back by Abdul Kerim Pasha, who in turn crossed the boundary river and after some hard fighting captured Kniazevats. Tchernaïef then directed his march to the southwest, intrenched himself at Alexinats, and waited the attack of the Turks. The situation was alarming. On the twenty-fourth of August, after an indecisive battle had been fought for five days, Prince Milan declared to the foreign consuls his willingness to accept mediation; but the Turkish government offered peace on such humiliating conditions that not even England could advise Prince Milan to accept them.

After a short armistice hostilities were resumed toward the close of September, and although the Serbians, supported by many Russian volunteers, fought with greater steadiness than before, they were defeated at Alexinats, and on the twenty-third of October were driven back from Djunis. In the mean time the Montenegrins under Prince Nikita, having completely defeated Mukhtar Pasha and expelled the Turkish army, were demanding a rectification of frontier as the price of peace. In Serbia matters continued to go from bad to worse. The Turks occupied Deligrad on the first of November, and the Bashi-Bazuks were in full march to Bielgrad. Serbia lay at the feet of the Sultan. It was from the Tsar that help must come, and it came.

On the thirtieth of October Ignatief was directed by the Tsar to repair to Savfet Pasha, the Turkish minister of foreign affairs, and threaten to leave Constantinople with his suite, unless within four-and-twenty hours an armistice of six weeks or two months should be granted the Serbians. Sultan Abdul Hamid hastened to accept this ultimatum, and Serbia was saved.

On the second of November Alexander, who was then at Livadia in the Crimea, during a conversation with Lord Loftus, "pledged his sacred word and honor, in the most earnest and solemn manner, that he had no intention of acquiring Constantinople, and that, if he were forced by necessity to occupy a part of Bulgaria, it would be only provisionally, until the peace and security of the Christian population were secured."

In September the Tsar had proposed to the governments of England and Austria to take coercive measures to put an end to Turkish misrule. The programme was as follows: if the Porte refused the terms of peace offered by the powers, Bosnia should be occupied by an Austrian force, Russia should take control of Bulgaria, and the united fleets should enter the Bosphorus. Although Russia expressed its willingness to let the naval demonstration accomplish the purpose in view if it sufficed, this proposal did not meet the approval of the powers. England was in favor of a conference to be held at Constantinople. On the tenth of November the Tsar, in a speech delivered before the representatives of the nobles and the Communal Council of Moscow, after expressing his hope that the negotiations of the representatives of the great powers would bring about a peaceable and satisfactory settlement of all difficulties, used such threatening and warlike language that there could be little doubt of his real intention. "Should this general agreement," said Alexander, "not be brought about, and should I see that we cannot obtain such guarantees as we need to carry out what we have a right to demand of the Porte, I am firmly resolved to act independently, and I am convinced that in this case all Russia will respond to my summons should I consider it necessary, and should the honor of our empire require it."

On the day before, Lord Beaconsfield, at the Lord Mayor's Banquet at Guildhall, declared that England was ready for war, "and in a righteous cause would commence a fight that would not end until right was done." He had already received the Tsar's pacific assurances, made to Lord Loftus; but they were not published until the twenty-first of November, and in the mean time intelligence had come of the mobilization of Russian troops, and the floating of a new loan of a hundred million rubles.

The conference suggested by England met at Constantinople in December, eighteen hundred and seventy-six. In a series of preliminary meetings, from which the Turkish representatives were excluded, the propositions to be submitted to the government of the Porte were discussed, and on the twenty-third of the month occurred the first assembly of the Plenary Conference, as it was called. It soon became apparent that the Turkish plenipotentiaries were instructed not to come to any agreement involving concessions; when guarantees were demanded, they replied that the new and admirable constitution granted by the Sultan to his people was a sufficient surety that all necessary reforms would be carried out. At the eighth meeting of the conference, on the fifteenth of January, eighteen hundred and seventy-seven, Lord Salisbury read a modified ultimatum which the Sultan submitted to an Extraordinary General Council, composed of two hundred and fifteen members, including representatives of every class and creed. Lord Salisbury said, as the representative of the British government, that he was instructed "to declare formally that Great Britain was resolved not to give its sanction either to maladministration or to oppression, and that if the Porte, from obstinacy or indifference, offered resistance to the efforts made to place the Ottoman Empire on a surer basis, the responsibility of the consequences would rest solely on the Sultan and his advisers. The résumé which he now presented he declared to be the final communication from the plenipotentiaries, and if the principles of the proposals were not accepted at the time of the next meeting, the representatives of the six powers would consider the conference at an end, and would leave Constantinople."

Midhat Pasha opened the deliberation of the General Council with an address stating the condition of affairs, and plainly declaring that, in case of refusal to accept the proposals of the conference, Turkey would be left to its fate. France and England, he said, would not declare war against the Porte, but they had nothing to hope for from those powers. On the other side of the balance lay Turkish independence. The Grand Council was unanimous in favor of rejecting the proposals, and Savfet Pasha communicated the decision to the plenipotentiaries at the last meeting of the conference, held on the twentieth of January.

By the twenty-seventh of January the plenipotentiaries had all left Constantinople. Prince Gortchakof thus announced the failure of the conference: "At the proposal of the English government the cabinets agreed upon the bases and the guarantees of peace which should be discussed at a conference to meet at Constantinople. This conference, in its preliminary deliberations, arrived at a complete understanding, both respecting the conditions of peace and the reforms to be introduced. It communicated the result to the Porte as the firm and unanimous wish of Europe, but met with an obstinate refusal from the Turkish government. Thus, after more than a year of diplomatic efforts, showing the importance which the great powers attach to the pacification of the East, the right which they possess of insuring it in view of the general interests involved, and their firm desire to obtain it by means of a European understanding, the cabinets again find themselves in the same position as at the beginning of the crisis, which is, however, still further aggravated by the blood which has been shed, the passions which have been stirred up, the ruins accumulated, and the prospect of an indefinite prolongation of the deplorable state of things which weighs upon Europe, and justly preoccupies public opinion and the attention of the governments. The Porte pays no heed to its former engagements, to its duties as a member of the European Concert, or to the unanimous wishes of the great powers. Far from having progressed toward a satisfactory solution, the state of the East has grown worse, and remains a permanent menace to the peace of Europe, the sentiments of humanity, and the conscience of Christian nations." The Russian Emperor now wished to know what course would be taken by the powers under the circumstances, but it was not until the thirty-first of March that the signature of what was called the London Protocol took place. This memorandum stated the interest which the six powers took in the improvement of the condition of the Christian populations of Turkey, and the reforms to be introduced into the management of the provinces; it stated that the arrangement about to be concluded between the Porte and Serbia and Montenegro was a step taken toward pacification; it invited the Porte to put its armies on a peace footing, and to apply as soon as possible the measures promised for the relief of the Christians. It also stated the intention of the powers to watch carefully over the manner in which the Ottoman government fulfilled its promises, and it ended with a vague threat of interference in case their hopes were disappointed.

But while the representatives of the powers signed this document, they each added a separate qualification which destroyed its effect. Lord Derby declared that the protocol would be null and void unless it resulted in immediate demobilization of the Turkish and Russian forces. Count Shuvalof said: "If peace is concluded with Montenegro, and if the Porte, accepting the advice of Europe, shows itself ready to put its forces again on a peace footing, and seriously to undertake the reforms mentioned in the protocol, let it send to Saint Petersburg a special envoy to treat of disarmament to which his Majesty the Emperor would also consent. If massacres like those which have stained Bulgaria with blood should take place, it would necessarily put a stop to the measures of demobilization." The Turkish government on the tenth of April issued a circular declaring the London Protocol to be "destitute of all equity and of all obligatory character."

The Turkish ambassador in London, Musurus Pasha, delivered a copy of this circular to Lord Derby, who said he did not see what further steps the British government could take to avert the war which seemed inevitable.

CHAPTER XIV.

THE TURKO-RUSSIAN WAR

1877.

RUSSIA'S DECLARATION OF WAR.—THE PASSAGE OF THE DANUBE.—THE ADVANCE ACROSS THE BALKANS; SHIPKA PASS.—CAPTURE OF NIKOPOLIS.—REPULSE AT PLEVNA.—BATTLE OF SHIPKA PASS.—OPERATIONS ON THE LOM.—THIRD BATTLE OF PLEVNA.

RUSSIA'S DECLARATION OF WAR.

ON the thirteenth of April, soon after the publication of Turkey's refusal to accept the London Protocol, a council of war was held at Saint Petersburg, and it was determined to mobilize the entire Russian army, to establish reserves in the north as well as in the south, so as to be prepared for any crisis.

The Emperor, in company with his eldest son, left Saint Petersburg on the twentieth of April, and three days later reached Kishenef, the headquarters of the Army of the South. There he promulgated his manifesto, which ran as follows:—

"Our faithful subjects know the lively interest which we have always felt in the destinies of the oppressed population of Turkey. Our desire to improve and render their lot secure is shared by the whole Russian people, which now shows itself ready to offer fresh sacrifices in order to alleviate the position of the Christians of the Balkan peninsula. The life and property of our faithful subjects have always been dear to us, and our whole reign attests our constant solicitude to preserve to Russia the benefits of peace. This solicitude has never ceased to actuate us since the beginning of the deplorable events which took place in Bosnia, Bulgaria, and the Herzegovina. Our object has been, above all, to effect an improvement in the position of the Christians of the East by means of pacific negotiations in concert with the great European powers, our allies and friends. For two years we have made unceasing efforts to induce the Porte to grant such reforms as would assure the Christians of the Provinces against the arbitrary use of authority by the local magistrates, but the Porte has remained unshaken in its categorical refusal of any guarantee for the safety of the Christians. Having thus exhausted all pacific endeavors, we are compelled by the haughty obstinacy of the Porte to proceed to more decisive action. The sentiment of justice, the sense of our own dignity, imperatively demands it. By its refusal the Porte places us under the necessity of having recourse to arms. Profoundly convinced of the righteousness of our cause, and humbly trusting ourselves to the grace and help of God, we hereby make known to our faithful subjects that the moment foreseen when we pronounced these words, to which all Russia responded with such unanimity, is at last come. We expressed the intention to act independently whenever we should deem it necessary, and Russia's honor demanded it. We now invoke the blessing of God on our valiant armies, and give the order to cross the Turkish frontier."

On the same day Prince Gortchakof sent a circular to the powers, announcing the determination of his exalted master to "fulfil the duty imposed upon him by the interests of Russia, whose peaceable development was impeded by the constant troubles in the East."

The Turkish government, in reply to these manifestoes, did not hesitate to charge Russia with ambitious designs. The foreign minister in his despatch to the powers said: "The imperial government deems itself bound to declare that the Christian populations of the Herzegovina, of Bosnia, and the vilayets inhabited by the Bulgarians rose in insurrection solely at the instigation of Pan-slavic committees organized and paid by Russia; that Serbia and Montenegro took up arms against the sovereign power only through the direct intervention of Russia; that they could never have sustained the struggle without aid from Russia; and that, in fact, all the ills which for the past two years have scourged their portion of the empire are due to the action, open or secret but always present, of Russia." And again in the Sultan's address to his armies it was declared that Russia's only object in view was the complete annihilation of Turkish rights and independence.

Lord Derby replied to Gortchakof's circular with a despatch in which he expressed the deep regret of the English government at the action of Russia, and pointed out that it was a contravention of the Treaty of Paris, by which each and all the signatory powers had engaged to respect the independence and the territorial integrity of the Ottoman Empire. He ended by declaring that the Tsar had separated himself from the European concord, hitherto maintained; that the consequences of this step could not be foreseen, and that the British government felt bound to state that they could not concur or approve the Tsar's decision. Nevertheless England promised to observe neutrality so long as its own interests were not threatened on the side of the Suez Canal and India.

On the sixteenth of April a convention was agreed upon between Russia and Rumania, by which the former was allowed to use the railways, the rivers, the roads, ports, and telegraph lines in that country. All facilities for transportation were promised. This convention was approved by the Rumanian senate by a large majority, and as soon as it was brought to the notice of the Porte it resulted in a declaration of war. The proclamation of Rumanian independence followed on the twenty-second of May, and the army, amounting to thirty-eight thousand foot soldiers and eight thousand two hundred cavalry, with one hundred and twenty cannon, took the field, under command of Prince Charles.

THE PASSAGE OF THE DANUBE.

The force which Russia had collected in the south for the invasion of Turkey amounted to about two hundred thousand men, under the command of the Grand Duke Nikolaï, the brother of the Tsar. On the third week of April the Emperor reviewed the six army corps which had been assembling at Kishenef since the beginning of the month. On the very day of the declaration of war the troops began to cross the frontier in four columns at Ungeni, and a little south, at Besmatak, eighty kilometres southwest of Kishenef, and at Kubeï.

Owing to the lateness of the season, the impassability of the highways, and the insufficient accommodations afforded by the one railroad crossing Rumania, a month elapsed before the Russian army was concentrated opposite that portion of the Danube at which it was determined to effect the crossing. The headquarters were successively removed from Kishenef to Iassy, and from Iassy to Ploïesti, when the Emperor arrived on the sixth of June, with Prince Gortchakof and other distinguished officials. It was found impossible to cross the Danube upon the day set. The river was at this time about five metres above its normal level, and the Rumanian shore was in many places inundated. The railroad, which had insufficient terminal facilities, and a different gauge from the Russian track, was delayed in transporting siege guns, ammunition, the four pontoon trains attached to the army, the wooden pontoon built at Galatz, the two dozen torpedo-boats, and all the materials necessary for the operations. The army therefore remained in inactivity until the twenty-fourth of June.

Meantime the first shot had been exchanged between the belligerents at Ibraïla, on the third of May. A week later the Russian batteries threw a shell into the powder-magazine of the Turkish three-masted turret-ship Lufti-Djelil, and caused it to explode. Out of a crew of two hundred and seventeen men only two were saved. On the twenty-sixth of the same month, four Russian torpedo-boats, under the direction of Lieutenant Dubassof, managed to sink the Turkish monitor Seifé just below Matchin. The activity of the Russians thus prevented the Turks from making use of their fleet. At the beginning of the war they had eight large ironclads in the Danube below Braïla, and seven iron-plated gunboats and eighteen wooden ships between Hirsova and Viddin.

As early as May the Russians had restricted the Lower Danube fleet to the Sulina mouth of the river by laying a line of torpedoes across from Reni, while the barricade of torpedoes near Braïla, placed a few days later, protected the mouths of the Pruth and Sereth, and the town of Galatz. After the destruction of the Seifé, the Turks made only three attempts to use their ironclads. On the twentieth of June, while Commander Novikof, with ten steam launches brought overland, was placing a line of torpedoes across the river at Parapan for the purpose of isolating the Turkish monitors at Rustchuk, he was attacked by the Turks, but succeeded in accomplishing his object. On the twenty-third and twenty-fourth of June monitors put out from Nikopolis, but were driven back. Lieutenant Greene thus criticises the action of the Turkish navy, which was under control of Admiral Hobart Pasha, an ex-officer of the English service, and son of the Earl of Buckinghamshire: "After this date no Turkish gunboats ever left the shelter of their fortresses, and the history of the Turkish fleet on the Danube may be summarized as from first to last a complete failure. Two of their river ironclads were sunk, two more were captured subsequently at the surrender of Nikopolis, and the other three remained at Rustchuk till the close of the war. Of the large ironclads on the lower river, one was sunk by a stationary torpedo near Sulina in the month of October; the others remained idle in the port of Sulina. The only damage the whole fleet ever did was in wounding five or six men in one boat at Parapan, and in inflicting some slight injuries on three of the launches, which were subsequently repaired. It was not that opportunities were lacking for the flotilla to act. On the breaking out of the war they could have made an effort to prevent the capture of the bridge over the Sereth, and, failing in this, they might at least have destroyed it and thereby greatly delayed the Russian operations. Later on, if they had been vigilant and skilful, they might have destroyed a portion at least of the Russian flotilla of small launches; they might have protected their own ships with nettings, and used their small boats to drag for torpedoes, if they could not prevent them from being placed. But they did none of these things; and at the end of two months they found themselves isolated in sections by means of the torpedo barricades, and so alarmed by the loss of two of their ships, that the idea of a torpedo became a bugbear to them, and a few launches moving over the water with the motions of planting torpedoes were enough to make them retire under the guns of their forts." The strength of the Turkish navy in eighteen hundred and seventy-six was estimated at one hundred and thirty-two ships, and somewhat more than eighteen thousand men.

The Russian plan was to cross the Danube at two points. The crossing of the lower river was accomplished on the twenty-second of June. General Zimmermann, by means of boats, rafts, and steam-tugs, passed over at Galatz with two regiments, which after a short struggle, and a loss of five officers and one hundred and thirty-seven men, gained possession of the height of Budjak. The same night the town of Matchin was abandoned, and the whole of the Turkish force was immediately after withdrawn from the Dobrudsha. As soon as the flood in the Danube had sufficiently subsided, General Zimmermann was able to use the bridge which he had constructed near Braïla, and to transfer the main part of his force to the other side.

The crossing of the Middle Danube was a much more serious undertaking. The concentration of troops in the vicinity of Bukarest had made the Turks believe that the passage of the river would be attempted at Nikopolis, Giurgevo, or Oltenitsa. They strengthened also their works at Rustchuk, Turtukaï, and Silistria, and posted batteries along the river-bank. The first intention of the Grand Duke Nikolaï was to cross at Zimnitsa-Sistova, but a report that the height of the river would render this impracticable, for a moment threw his plans into confusion. While waiting for pontoons in order to cross at Nikopolis, he made a personal inspection of the river from Turnu to Zimnitsa, and finding that the passage at Turnu, opposite the strong works of Nikopolis, was rather too difficult, and that the water had fallen, he decided suddenly to force the river at a point just below Sistova where the island Vardim divides the Danube into two unequal streams, the widest of which could be crossed by a pontoon bridge, and the southern branch, measuring about six hundred meters, by boats. On the evening of the twenty-sixth of June the troops, numbering fifteen thousand men, under command of General Dragomirof, collected at Zimnitsa and launched the pontoon boat. The first division, led by Major General Ioltchin, landed on the Bulgarian shore and engaged in a close contest with the Turks, who were driven back. About five o'clock in the morning, three hours after the landing of the first division, General Dragomirof reached the southern bank with the third division, and took command of the attack. The Turks fought with great determination, but about two o'clock in the afternoon the Russians captured the heights behind Sistova, and soon afterwards entered the town itself. On the evening of that day the Turks had entirely abandoned their positions, and twenty-five thousand Russians were established in good defences on the southern heights. The passage of the river had cost only twenty hours of labor and a loss of eight hundred and twenty-one men. The construction of a bridge was begun on the twenty-eighth of June, but it was soon partially destroyed by a storm, and was completed only on the second of July. About this time the

Emperor and Grand Duke Nikolaï transferred their headquarters to the southern bank of the Danube, and Alexander immediately issued a proclamation to the Bulgarians in which he explained his action in defending the cause of the Eastern Christians, and promised that the life, liberty, honor, and property of all classes should be guaranteed. He also called upon them to form auxiliary forces, and to obey the Russian authorities so as to confirm their deliverance from Mussulman tyranny.

With the Russian occupation of the Danube line of defences, which was most strangely neglected by the Ottomans, closes the first period of the war.

ADVANCE ACROSS THE BALKANS; SHIPKA PASS.

On the fifth of July the Russians took possession of the bridge over the Iantra, near Biéla, and a detachment of cavalry captured the city itself. Two days later, Gurko, with fourteen hundred cavalry and six guns, put to flight the three thousand Turks who were stationed at Tirnova, the ancient capital of the Bulgarians. Thus the Russians had control of the two roads leading westward to the Balkans. On the twelfth of the month the Grand Duke Nikolaï changed his headquarters from Sistova to Tirnova. The Bulgarians brought bread and salt as a sign of hospitality, the women and children scattered flowers, and the priests came to meet him with songs.

General Gurko was detailed to cross the Balkans with his whole detachment. He knew that the Shipka Pass was guarded by a force of three thousand Turkish infantry, a few guns, and several bands of Bashi-bazuks; but certain Bulgarians offered to lead the Russians over a blind trail about half-way between the Elena and Travna passes. If he should succeed in issuing from the mountains on the south by the seventeenth of July, he was to attack the Shipka

Pass on that side, while one division of Cossacks should make a demonstration on the northern side. General Gurko sent his pioneers in advance to make this blind trail passable for his lighter artillery. On the twelfth of July he left Tirnova, and after a march of about sixty-seven kilometers surprised and captured the little village of Hainkioï, at the southern foot of the pass. The transportation of the artillery over this steep and difficult pass, which at the summit has an elevation of more than eleven hundred meters, was a remarkable feat of engineering. On the afternoon of July fourteenth the Russians were attacked by a force of about two thousand of the enemy, but won an easy victory. On the sixteenth of July Gurko began his march to Shipka, leaving at Hainkioï a detachment of three thousand five hundred men with fourteen guns, to keep possession of that pass. He turned southwest, and after marching about a dozen kilometers he met a body of Turks posted behind the Tundja brook, which flows out of the mountains at Uflani. The battle with the enemy occupied so much time that he was able on that day to get only half-way to Kazarlyk. By the next noon that town was in possession of the Russians, but they were too much exhausted by the heat and the labor of the day to advance against the Shipka Pass. The detachment, under charge of Prince Mirski, according to agreement, was to make an attack upon the Turks intrenched in the highway leading through the pass. This attack was to be supplemented by General Gurko. But General Gurko was a day too late. The attack made from the north by Prince Mirski's forces caused a loss of six officers and two hundred and five men, and, being unsupported, was a failure. The next day Gurko also made an isolated attack from the south, and gained some of the outer trenches; but when they found that they were not to be supplemented by Prince Mirski, they retired to Shipka. On the nineteenth it was intended to renew the attack, but during the night the Turks evacuated their position, and leaving their tents pitched, and abandoning their artillery and large supplies of provisions, as well as their wounded, they managed to escape in detached bodies to Philippopolis. Three passes over the Balkans were now in the hands of the Russians.

CAPTURE OF NIKOPOLIS.—REPULSE AT PLEVNA.

If the Russians wished to keep control of the defensive line of the Iantra, it was necessary for them to take the strongholds between the Vid and the Lom; their first offensive operation, therefore, was directed against Nikopolis, a town of eight or ten thousand inhabitants, which was a special menace to Sistova and the right wing. Nikopolis was defended by the citadel, an old half-mined fortress called Tuna-Kalé, and a few earthworks. The hills in the rear commanded the citadel. The Turkish garrison consisted of about twelve thousand men, for the most part distributed in the redoubts thrown up to the south and west of the city.

On the fifteenth of July, after a struggle which lasted all day, the troops under General Krüdener captured two of the chief positions of the Turks and drove them into the citadel. Fires were burning in many places; the Turks destroyed their stores and the principal buildings situated near the river; during the night a portion of the garrison tried to break through the Russian lines, but were repulsed. On the morning of the next day preparations were made for an early assault; but when Hassan Pasha saw that there was no chance of defending himself, he displayed a white flag, and submitted to an unconditional surrender. Seven thousand men became prisoners of war; the Russians took also six flags, one hundred and ten guns, more than ten thousand small arms, and two monitors which were scarcely injured. Their loss was about thirteen hundred men. A few days later the Russians occupied Lovtcha, and in accordance with instructions received by telegraph from the Grand Duke at Tirnova, proceeded to take Plevna, an important town situated about thirty-two kilometers from Nikopolis, and which was supposed to be almost undefended by the Turks. General Schilder-Schuldner, to whose care the capture of the city was intrusted, arrived at Plevna on the afternoon of the nineteenth of July. His little army of six thousand five hundred men, with forty-six guns, was distributed over a distance of twenty-seven kilometers, from Bukova to Tutchenitsa. He was surprised to find the city and the heights of Grivitsa occupied by a strong Turkish force. While General Krüdener had been engaged in the operations about Nikopolis, Osman Pasha was advancing from Viddin with forty thousand of the best troops of the Turkish army, intended to reinforce the garrison of the beleaguered city. Having come too late, he turned aside to Plevna. Although his march from Viddin to the Vid took many days, and a report of his movements had been brought to the Grand Duke, and although Turkish prisoners, even before the capture of the city, had announced the expected arrival of reinforcements from the west, no attempts were made to find out the facts. Thus the Turkish general was enabled to arrive upon the Russian flank without a single officer being cognizant of it. When the news of this criminal carelessness came to Saint Petersburg, the *Golos* demanded bitterly what the Cossacks, called the eye and ear of the Russian army, were doing.

General Schilder-Schuldner ordered a general attack on all sides on the morning of the twentieth. At half past five the Russians assaulted the Grivitsa heights. Four companies of infantry carried the western extremity, and pressed in to the very outskirts of the town, holding their position until ordered to retreat at twenty minutes past eleven. At nine in the morning the Russian right and left flanks had succeeded in reaching Plevna, but they were not in easy communication with each other, and the centre had completely failed to carry the main Grivitsa position. The Turks then, by the aid of reinforcements which arrived without the knowledge of the Russians, formed within the town, and came out in overwhelming numbers, driving them back with great slaughter to their lines of trenches. Seventy-four officers and two thousand seven hundred and seventy-one men were killed and wounded. Mr. Archibald Forbes telegraphed to the Daily News in regard to this the only serious reverse the Russians had as yet encountered: "It occurred through neglect of common military precautions. When the commander of the ninth corps proceeded against Nikopolis, he made the omission of protecting his flank, by not sending cavalry to occupy Plevna, then only weakly held. Afterwards an easy chance did not offer. The Turkish column from Viddin, marching too late to succor Nikopolis, turned aside and occupied Plevna. With intent to repair the blunder, General Krüdener sent three regiments of infantry against Plevna, and without a previous reconnoissance. These, after hard fighting, actually occupied the town. They had laid aside their cloaks and packs in the streets, and had quitted the fighting column formation, believing all was over, and were singing as they straggled along. No patrols had been pushed into the recesses of the town. No cavalry had been sent forward beyond. The whole business was slovenly to a degree. The penalty was paid. Suddenly from a hundred windows and balconies a vehement fire was poured into the troops straggling along the streets. They were beset on all sides, and had to retreat."

Osman Pasha was constantly receiving reinforcements, and working diligently to protect Plevna with earthworks and fortifications. He strengthened the Grivitsa redoubt and the lines connecting the numerous small villages in the vicinity of the town.

General Krüdener, though he was reinforced by a detachment of troops under command of Lieutenant-General Shakhovskoï, hesitated to make the assault, because he now knew the strength of the enemy's position and his own numerical inferiority. He applied for instructions to the Grand Duke, who on the twenty-eighth telegraphed from Tirnova, one hundred and twenty-eight kilometers distant, a peremptory order to attack. Accordingly General Krüdener made his preparations for an assault to be made on the thirtieth. He had a total of thirty thousand men, and the distance between the two wings was twenty-one kilometers. The attack was to be upon a strongly intrenched position; and the two columns, besides being insufficient in numbers, were entirely independent of each other. General Krüdener was ordered to attack the Turkish centre at the Grivitsa redoubt, which was the key of the position; General Shakhovskoï, with the left wing, was to assault the Turkish forces between Radishevo and Grivitsa, and General Skobelef was detailed to repulse any offensive operations, and prevent the arrival of reinforcements from Lovtcha. General Krüdener opened the attack upon the Grivitsa redoubt with his artillery. The cannonade lasted from half past eight until half past two, at which time the infantry began to advance. Their progress was hindered by the terrible and well-directed fire of the Turks. Again and again they neared the redoubt, but were driven back. At sunset Krüdener gave an order for a final assault from all sides. The brave Russians advanced to a distance less than a hundred meters from the Turkish works, but it was all in vain. The attack of the right wing was a complete failure, and it was with some difficulty that the Russians during the night managed to regain their old position.

On the left wing General Shakhovskoï by five o'clock had gained possession of two of the "middle group" of redoubts. It was impossible, however, for Shakhovskoï to hold the ground he had gained. It was now nightfall. He had no reserves, and he was surrounded by Turkish troops on three sides. Accordingly after dark his men were withdrawn in good order to the Radishevo ridge, and the next morning they reached Poradim. The dilatoriness of General Krüdener and the undue rashness of Prince Shakhovskoï had lost the day. It was only the consummate generalship of the younger Skobelef which prevented Shakhovskoï's forces from being entirely cut to pieces. Skobelef's little force was hotly engaged from morning until night, but he succeeded in keeping the Turks from occupying the second knoll of the "Green Hills." Shakhovskoï's retreat was thus assured.

The Russian loss in the second battle of Plevna was one hundred and sixty-nine officers and seven thousand one hundred and thirty-six men, or a quarter of all the men on the field. When the news of the repulse reached Tirnova, the Grand Duke hastily removed his headquarters, and panic seized upon the inhabitants of the whole region, who expected soon to see the Turks destroying the bridge, and the Bashi-bazuks murdering and mutilating in all their villages. The Turks, however, did not pursue their advantage, but safe in their intrenchments waited for further assaults.

At this time the Turkish strength was principally concentrated at three places. There was an army of fifty thousand men, under Osman Pasha at Plevna. Suleiman Pasha, with forty thousand men, had driven General Gurko back to Ieni-Zagra, and had taken a strong position there; while Mehemet Ali, who had been recalled from Montenegro to take the chief command in place of Abdul Kerim, was at Rasgrad with sixty-five thousand men. Other detachments at Lovtcha, Osman Bazar, and elsewhere, brought the total force to about one hundred and ninety-five thousand men. The Russians, on the other hand, had a strength of one hundred and twenty thousand infantry and twelve thousand cavalry, besides Zimmermann's detachment in the Dobrudzha. It was freely recognized that a terrible blunder had been made in beginning the campaign with insufficient forces. It was now impossible to carry out the original plan, and consequently the month of August was spent in inaction. On the third of the month the Emperor signed the order for the mobilization of the guard, the grenadiers, and two divisions of the line, bringing to the front a fresh army of one hundred and twenty thousand men and four hundred and sixty guns. He had already issued a decree calling out one hundred and eighty-eight thousand men of the militia to replace the actual and prospective losses by battle and disease. He also successfully appealed to Prince Charles of Rumania to bring his army to his assistance. The Russians were thus reinforced by thirty-two thousand infantry, five thousand cavalry, and eighty-four guns.

BATTLE OF SHIPKA PASS. — OPERATIONS ON THE LOM. — THIRD BATTLE OF PLEVNA.

It was Suleiman Pasha, on whose movements now depended the success of the Turkish arms. Mehemet Ali was anxious to unite the two armies, and make a combined attack upon the Russian left wing. In this case the Russians would have been obliged to give up the control of the Shipka Pass, and if the one hundred and twenty-five thousand men thus collected should gain the victory, the Sistova bridge was in their hands. Suleiman, however, sustained by the War Council, which directed the operations by telegraph from Constantinople, was determined to attack Shipka directly in front. He began his attack on the twenty-first of August; and, as Colonel Greene says, "Without gaining the least material advantage in so doing, he sacrificed the best part of the fine army he brought with him from Montenegro." General Gurko, whose scouts had penetrated to within one hundred and twenty-eight kilometers of Adrianople, after being obliged to retreat was summoned to Saint Petersburg to superintend the transportation of the troops which he was to command. General Darozhinski was left with about five thousand men at Shipka Pass, for the defence of which almost nothing had been done.

On the nineteenth of August Suleiman advanced against the Pass. The Turks secured the command of the Russian position on every side, but "for three days — August twenty-first, twenty-second, and twenty-third — less than eight thousand Russians and Bulgarians held in check the army of Suleiman twenty-five thousand to thirty thousand strong. During this time their only food was the biscuit — about one day's ration — which they had in their pockets when the affair began; the heat was intense, but the nearest water was at a spring between three and four miles back on the road toward Gabrova, and all that the men had to drink was the little which was brought back in their canteens by the men who carried the wounded to the rear. Whenever the firing ceased for a while, they lay down on the ground they were defending, and caught an hour's sleep; for it was the period of full moon, and night brought no cessation to the firing." Lieutenant Greene continues his comments: "For impetuous assaults and tenacious, dogged defence, for long-continued fighting and physical endurance, this five days' battle in the mountain is extremely remarkable; but there were no skilful manœuvres of the troops on either side. Although Suleiman took possession of heights flanking and nearly surrounding the Russians, yet he persisted in dividing his forces and making his strongest attacks upon their strongest position, Mount Saint Nicholas, thereby enabling them, though far inferior in numbers, to hold their ground at all points for three days, until the arrival of reinforcements."

Suleiman Pasha telegraphed to Constantinople for reinforcements, and the Shipka Pass remained in the hands of the Russians.

On the fifteenth of August the army under the Tsesarévitch, numbering forty-five thousand men with two hundred guns, was scattered over a distance of eighty kilometers, between Pirgos on the Danube and Eski-Djuma. Mehemet Ali, who commanded the Ottoman troops in the neighborhood of the four Bulgarian fortresses, determined to take advantage of the scattered condition of the Russians, and, if possible, to drive him back across the Lom. A decisive victory over the Tsesarévitch might give the Turks control of the line of the Iantra, and cut off all retreat by the bridge at Sistova. He had an excellent army, variously estimated to be from fifty thousand to eighty-five thousand strong. His first attempts met with some success; by the tenth of September he had forced the Russians beyond the Banitchka Lom, and was preparing to make a further advance when his plans were disarranged by the defeat of his troops at Tserkovna on the twenty-first. At the beginning of October the Russians had regained their old position on the Lom. Mehemet Ali's offensive movement had completely failed.

Meanwhile, to the Russians in the vicinity of Plevna nothing occurred of great importance. On the thirty-first of August Osman Pasha made an extensive sortie which was repulsed after some severe fighting. On the third of September Prince Imeretinski, assisted by General Skobelef and General Dobrovolski, took the important strategic village of Lovtcha. The Russians, having a superiority of numbers, succeeded by noon in capturing all the redoubts except one, the strongest, which protected the road to Plevna. This was carried about seven o'clock in the afternoon, after a desperate struggle in which all its defenders perished. The Russians were masters of Lovtcha, and were free to begin the third great assault upon Plevna, which, if it proved successful, "would probably lead to the complete defeat of the Turks throughout the whole theatre of war."

The military importance of the little town was explained by the fact that it was the meeting-point of roads leading to Viddin, Sofia, Shipka, Biéla, Zimnitsa, and Nikopolis. Since the two previous attacks upon the place by the Russians, Osman Pasha had worked strenuously to build fortifications upon the hills north and east of the town. In a month's time he had completed eighteen redoubts and several lines of trenches. His army on the first of September was roughly calculated to number fifty-six thousand men; the Russians, at the same time, were bringing against him more than ninety thousand men.

On the night of the sixth of September the troops began their advance, and, undiscovered by the Turks, succeeded in building two batteries, where they established twenty siege-guns opposite the Grivitsa redoubt, the key of the position on the north. For the next four days the cannonade continued without abatement while the troops were being disposed for the great assault which was fixed upon for the eleventh. The artillery fire from two hundred and fifty guns was to be continued at intervals all day until three in the afternoon, when the infantry should attack at three distinct points: the Grivitsa redoubt, redoubt number ten, situated a couple of thousand kilometers southeast of Plevna, and the two redoubts commanding the road to Lovtcha and belonging to the Krishin group. The fog, however, which hung over the whole region disarranged "this elaborate artillery programme." The Russians and Rumanians who attacked the Grivitsa redoubt, after a terrific struggle, which lasted from three until half past seven in the evening, were finally successful. A Rumanian soldier killed the Turkish standard-bearer and secured the flag; five guns also fell into the hands of the allies. The loss of the Rumanians was nearly twenty-six hundred men; their killed outnumbered the wounded; the Russian brigade lost about half as many.

At redoubt number ten the Russian attack failed completely, and resulted in tremendous losses. The dead and wounded were left on the field, and the Turks, in disregard of the convention of Geneva, sallied forth and barbarously mutilated their helpless opponents. All through this war, in fact, the Turks, especially the Bashi-bazuks, were distinguished for their wanton cruelty. Ambulances and surgeons were not spared, and those who carried the wounded from the field were shot down in cold blood.

General Skobelef, who had charge of the third column, took one of the redoubts in the bend of the Lovtcha road, after an hour's severe fighting, in which he lost three thousand men. On the next day, however, as he was not reinforced, after repulsing five attacks of the enemy he was obliged to give up his extremely critical position and withdraw. Though most of his officers were shot down, and though he exposed himself recklessly at the very front, he escaped without a scratch. MacGahan thus described his appearance at the close of the battle: "His uniform was covered with mud and filth, his sword broken, his cross of Saint George twisted round on his shoulder, his face black with powder and smoke, his eyes haggard and bloodshot, and his voice quite gone. He said: 'I have done my best; I could do no more. My detachment is half destroyed; my regiments do not exist; I have no officers left; they sent me no reinforcements, and I have lost three guns. I blame no one. It was the will of God.'" The third great repulse at Plevna had cost the Russians eighteen thousand men out of sixty thousand brought into action. The Grand Duke acknowledged that the Russians were defeated, not because the position at Plevna was impregnable, nor because they did not have sufficient forces, but because they were ignorant of the enemy's position, and failed to confine their assaults to the Grivitsa and Krishin redoubts, concentrating their efforts there. As it was, Skobelef was sent forward almost as into a funnel, leaving commanding positions on both sides of him, and attacking a position which led to nothing, and was untenable after it was gained.

It was now determined to make a regular investment of Plevna, and General Todleben was summoned from Saint Petersburg to superintend the operation. The days which followed the great assault were marked with no actions of importance. The Rumanians, on the eighteenth of September, and again on the nineteenth of October, made vain attempts to capture the second Grivitsa redoubt. The Turks worked almost unhindered at their fortifications, and General Kruilof failed entirely to keep Shevket Pasha from sending provision trains into Plevna from Orkhanie. It was estimated that owing to Kruilof's incompetence Osman received sixty days' full rations for an army of sixty thousand men. Shevket came with five thousand men and a large train, and had an interview with Osman, in which it was agreed upon that the former should fortify the strong points defending the road to Orkhanie. This was done, and Osman Pasha was in full communication with his point of supplies.

General Todleben's plans of investment comprised the capture of these fortified places. General Gurko was put in command of an army of thirty-five thousand infantry and ten thousand cavalry, and after a determined battle, which nearly resulted disastrously, he succeeded in storming Gorni Dubnik on the twenty-fourth of October. The Russians captured one Pasha, fifty-three officers, more than two thousand men, besides guns and ammunition. On the twenty-eighth Ismail Hakki, the commander of Telis, capitulated, with one hundred officers, three thousand men, and an immense amount of ammunition destined for the defence of Plevna. When this news reached Shevket Pasha he evacuated Rodomirtsa, which was immediately seized by the Russians. On the second of November the investment of Plevna was complete. General Todleben, secure in the knowledge that sooner or later Osman must be reduced by famine to capitulation, resolutely refused to compromise his chances by another assault. Although he was now completely blockaded by an army of one hundred and sixty thousand men, Osman Pasha replied to a flag of truce sent on the thirteenth of November, that he and his brave army were resolved to shed the last drop of blood for the honor of their country.

In the second week of December he made an attempt to break through the Russian lines with about forty thousand men. In this he was defeated and obliged to surrender at discretion. Lieutenant Greene says: "Certainly that must be called a brilliant defence which arrested the Russian advance and completely paralyzed their whole plan of campaign and all their movements for five months; which caused them to call forth vast reinforcements from Russia, and pending their arrival to supplicate the aid of a petty principality; which killed and wounded and spread disease among nearly forty thousand of his enemies, and caused the affairs of a mighty empire to be directed during half a year from miserable huts in obscure villages of a foreign land."

While the investment of Plevna was leading to the destruction of Osman Pasha and his fine army, Suleiman Pasha, who had again vainly attempted to dislodge the Russians from Shipka Pass, and had then been transferred to the Army of the Quadrilateral in place of Mehemet Ali, tried to break through the detachment of the Tsesarévitch, but, handling his forces unskilfully, he was driven back across the Lom. After the fall of Plevna, he placed portions of his troops in Shumla and Rustchuk, and took the remainder south of the Balkans. In the Dobrudzha, General Zimmermann was confined to a purely defensive rôle. He covered the Russian line of communication against any attacks from that direction.

General Gurko, in the first week of November, took a detachment of thirty-six thousand men and went along the Sofia road toward the Balkans, in order to engage with Mehemet Ali Pasha, who was now trying to come to the aid of Plevna. The Turks were in possession of all the roads across the Balkans. Gurko succeeded, in a week's time, in dislodging the enemy from Pravets, Etropol, and all their strongholds at the foot of the Balkans, and in driving him back to the crest of the range. He also captured immense quantities of ammunition and supplies of every kind. The Roumanian reserve, crossing the Danube above Nikopolis, had captured Rahova on the nineteenth of November, and bombarded Lompalanka for six days, causing the Turks to retire. The country between the Danube and the Balkans for a distance of two hundred and fifty-six kilometers was absolutely in the hands of the Russians. After the capitulation of Plevna, they could in safety cross the Balkans and advance toward Constantinople.

CHAPTER XV.

THE TURKO-RUSSIAN WAR.

1877.

The Campaign in Asia. — Reverses. — Battle of Aladja-Dagh. — Storming of Kars. — Passage of the Balkans. — Advance upon Constantinople. — End of the War.

THE CAMPAIGN IN ASIA. — REVERSES.

PASKIÉVITCH in eighteen hundred and twenty-eight, and General Muravief in eighteen hundred and fifty-five, conducted successful operations in Armenia, which resulted in practical gains for the Russians. At the outbreak of the war in eighteen hundred and seventy-six the Russian Cabinet resolved, if possible, to renew the traditions of those glorious exploits. The troops which were mobilized for this Caucasian campaign were under the general control of the Grand Duke Mikhaïl, the Emperor's eldest brother; and, exclusive of a detachment to guard the Black Sea coast and capture Batum, amounted to fifty-five thousand infantry and ten thousand cavalry, with two hundred and ten guns. Opposed to them were fifty thousand Turks, under Mukhtar Pasha, distributed at Ardahan, Kars, Erzerum, and other points. At Batum there were twenty thousand men. The Rion detachment advanced on the twenty-fourth of April against Batum; but, falling in with a Turkish force under Dervish Pasha, was defeated and driven back across the border, and for the rest of the campaign was occupied in preventing the Turks from landing reinforcements and in putting down insurrections stirred up by the Tcherkesui.

Simultaneously with the advance of the Rion detachment the other three columns of the Russians crossed the border. In order to penetrate to Erzerum they were obliged to capture Kars, the strongest fortress in Armenia, and to cross the Soganli Mountains. The plan of the campaign was to advance against the capital of Armenia after capturing Ardahan and Baïazid and investing Kars. General Loris-Melikof, after a four days' march from Alexandropol, established himself sixteen kilometers from Kars and cut off communication between that city and Ardahan; then, learning that the garrison of Ardahan was very weak, he sent a portion of his troops to co-operate with General Devel in the capture of that fortress. On the morning of the sixteenth of May the bombardment began; at night the Russians captured a fort which commanded the city. The next day, after a short but destructive bombardment, General Melikof gave the order to assault. It was then six o'clock in the afternoon; the Turks did not wait to defend their works, but fled precipitately, leaving the town in the hands of the Russians, who lost less than five hundred and fifty men. In the mean time General Tergukasof captured Baïazid, and left a small garrison there, which was almost immediately surrounded by a force of ten thousand infantry and a horde of many thousand Kurds. This little band of sixteen hundred Russians sustained a siege of twenty-three days, during which they were brought to the extremity of living on their dead horses. After the capture of Ardahan, Loris-Melikof returned to the neighborhood of Kars, and establishing sixty guns and mortars on three sides of the city, began the bombardment, which continued until the twenty-fifth of June, when, on account of the Russians having been completely repulsed at Zevin, he was obliged to raise the siege and retire to the border. The fruit of the summer campaign was simply the capture of Ardahan: but they had ten thousand men less than at the beginning of the war. The skirmishes and battles which took place in August and September were of not much importance, but resulted generally in the discomfiture of the Russians. On the twenty-fifth of August, Mukhtar Pasha, with ten thousand men, attacked the Russians at a little hill called Kizil Tepe. The battle lasted all day, but the Turks gained the position. Mukhtar Pasha, however, failed to follow up his advantage; with energy he might either have cut off the Russians from Alexandropol or compelled them to retreat.

BATTLE OF ALADJA-DAGH.—STORMING OF KARS.

Toward the end of September the long-expected reinforcements arrived, and the Grand Duke Mikhaïl, with fifty-five thousand infantry and eight thousand cavalry, was prepared to grapple with his opponents, who numbered about thirty-six thousand men and occupied the hills studding the plain of Kars. The Russians assaulted the Turkish left flank on the second of October; but, though they in places gained the advantage, on the whole the battle was a failure; they were obliged to retreat and leave the Turks in possession of the hills.

Mukhtar Pasha, however, believing either that the approach of winter would prevent the Russians from making any further attacks, or that his line of defence would be strengthened by being shortened, evacuated the hills on the night of October the ninth, and concentrated his troops on the heights of Vizinkioi, Avliar, and Aladja-Dagh, southeast of Kars. The Russians immediately assumed the positions left by the Turks, and prepared to dislodge them from the heights. General Lazaref, making forced marches by night and unrolling behind him a line of telegraph, established himself in the rear of the left flank of the Turks, in instant communication with the Grand

Duke's headquarters. On the fifteenth the assault upon the mountain took place, and, owing to the terrible execution of the Russian guns, which were loaded with shrapnel, was entirely successful. The right wing of the Turks, under command of Omar Pasha, was surrounded and obliged to surrender. Half of Mukhtar Pasha's army was destroyed, and the rest fled panic-stricken to Kars. In the hands of the Russians remained seven thousand prisoners, thirty-five guns, and immense stores of ammunition and provisions. Mukhtar Pasha himself, leaving the defence of Kars to Hussein Pasha, and abandoning Zevin and Ienikioi, retreated to Erzerum, where, with seventeen thousand or eighteen thousand men, he began to intrench himself. General Heimann pursued him, and on the fourth of November, in a battle which lasted all day, finally carried the line of fortification, captured the Turkish camp with forty-three guns and much ammunition, and forced Mukhtar Pasha to retire into the line of forts surrounding Erzerum. After several abortive attempts to storm the place, he settled down to wait for reinforcements, and was overtaken by winter.

The rest of the Russian troops were sent to the investment of Kars. Kars, a city of thirty thousand inhabitants, is situated in the plain and on the river of the same name. "Behind it on the west and southwest," says Lieutenant Greene, "are volcanic spurs jutting out from the Soganli range; the river follows the base of these spurs to the town, but here cuts through a rent in the mountain and forms a precipitous ravine several hundred feet deep. On the west, north, and northeast of the town are, therefore, high, rocky, and almost inaccessible hills; on the southeast is an open rocky plain. The fortifications, as they existed in eighteen hundred and seventy-seven, had almost all been built since the Crimean war, under the direction, it is said, of Prussian engineers. They consisted of a citadel in masonry, built on a perpendicular rock overhanging the gorge just north of the town, and of twelve detached forts." The garrison consisted of about twenty-three thousand men, and there were upwards of two hundred Krupp guns.

On the twenty-eighth of October General Loris-Melikof summoned Hussein Pasha to surrender; but the Turks were determined to defend themselves to the last. They were now so closely surrounded that no one could go in or out without the permission of the Russians. On the fifth of November ten Turkish battalions issued from Fort Hafiz Pasha and tried to prevent the erection of new batteries on Vizinkioi. They were repulsed, however, and driven out of their fort, leaving the guns spiked.

The Grand Duke Mikhaïl, knowing that the garrison of Kars had sufficient provisions to last them half a year, and that it would be a difficult operation to keep up the investment through a severe winter for a line of nearly fifteen kilometers, determined to strike a quick and sudden blow. The assault was fixed for the night of the fifteenth of November; but, in consequence of the bad weather and the obscurity of the moon, it was postponed until the night of the seventeenth.

The Grand Duke thus describes the action: —

"On the evening of the seventeenth all the troops assembled at the points indicated, and at half past eight the columns moved forward. A perfectly clear sky and the full moon which had just risen gave promise of a clear and calm night; the temperature, which had fallen below the freezing point during the morning, was growing colder and colder. A solemn and cold silence reigned in the air, and the most attentive ear could not have distinguished any noise in the least alarming. The line of our skirmishers, dimly seen, was advancing prudently, step by step, followed by the troops for the assault, which at first marched in compact columns, then, as they approached the line of attack, formed in deployed order in company column.

"About nine o'clock some shots were heard at the Turkish

outposts, and then, as ours did not reply, they ceased. Only our batteries at Djavra as a signal opened a cannonade against the heights of Tekmas, attracting the attention and forces of the enemy toward this point. But not a half-hour elapsed before a musketry fire of the Turks burst forth along the whole line of attack, and after a few minutes the works and the trenches of the forts which had been attacked began a continuous firing."

The three columns pressed forward against the positions which they had been assigned to storm. Fort Suvari was taken in half an hour. General Grabbe was shot dead in front of Fort Kanly; at four o'clock the Pasha surrendered, but only three hundred men were left of its garrison. At Fort Hafiz Pasha a terrible struggle ensued, but at last, as the Grand Duke said, "the garrison was crushed to pieces and annihilated." At daybreak the Russians had possession of all the fortifications on the right bank of the Kars River. Two hours later the rest of the garrison, thoroughly demoralized, were flying toward Erzerum, pursued and cut down by the Cossacks. Hussein Pasha managed to escape. Lieutenant Greene says: "It was a good night's work, — a fortified place of the first order captured in open assault, with seventeen thousand prisoners, three hundred and three guns of various calibre, twenty-five thousand or more small arms, and an immense quantity of provisions and material of all kinds." The Russians lost in this battle only seventy-seven officers and two thousand one hundred and ninety-six men. Thus, for the third time within fifty years the Russians had possession of Kars.

In the following month one division was sent to aid in the investment of Erzerum; but the severity of the winter and the difficulty of establishing the siege batteries caused so much delay that it was only on the twelfth of January that Mukhtar Pasha was finally shut off from communication with Trebizond. General Heimann had already summoned him to surrender, so as to spare the city the horrors of a bombardment, but the offer was declined. One of the conditions of the armistice of January thirty-first was the evacuation of the city, and on the tenth of February the garrison marched out and embarked for Constantinople. Thus ended the campaign of Armenia, to the glory of the Russian arms.

PASSAGE OF THE BALKANS. — ADVANCE UPON CONSTANTINOPLE.

The Grand Duke Nikolaï, against the advice of all his generals, except Gurko and Skobelef, resolved to continue the campaign through the winter, and to cross the Balkans before the Turks had time to recuperate. Todleben and the other officers advised " the prudent military course " of putting the troops into winter-quarters, of investing Rustchuk, and waiting until spring for the passage of the mountains. The plan of the winter campaign was for Gurko " to defeat the army in his front at the Araba-Konak Pass, capture Sofia, and then advance by the old Roman road leading from Sofia past Philippolis to Adrianople; Radetski was to defeat the Turks at Shipka, advance over that pass, and join Gurko in front of Adrianople; while the Tsesarévitch, commanding all the troops left on the north of the Balkans, was to protect the communications from any attack from the direction of the Quadrilateral and prosecute the siege of Rustchuk, with the assistance of Todleben as his chief engineer."

General Gurko had an army of sixty-five thousand infantry and six thousand cavalry, with two hundred and eighty guns. The winter had set in with great severity. The roads were slippery, and the horses were useless in dragging the guns, each of which had to be hauled and pushed by more than a hundred men up over a mountain crest nearly five hundred and fifty meters above the valley. The men subsisted the while on less than a ration of black biscuit, and slept in the snow. On the thirtieth of December all the guns were in the Kuriak valley, and the Turkish position was turned. On the first day of January the Turks abandoned all their fortifications at Araba-Konak, and two days later left Sofia in the hands of the Russians, with enough provisions to last Gurko's army a month. Had it not been that one of the detachments sent as a second turning column had been overwhelmed by a snow-storm and obliged to give up the undertaking, the Turkish force would in all probability have been captured or destroyed. Gurko then advanced from Sofia to Philippolis, completely destroying Suleiman Pasha's army, which amounted to fifty or sixty thousand men.

Meantime, during the first week of January, General Kartsof succeeded in crossing the Balkans by the Trojan Pass, with a loss of only a hundred men out of four thousand five hundred. The passage at Shipka Pass, which had been in the hands of the Russians for five months, was considered a remarkably brilliant feat. General Radetski had at his disposal a force of fifty-six thousand infantry, of which more than six thousand men were sick from frost-bites and exposure. Radetski, remaining in the works at the summit of the pass, sent General Skobelef and Prince Mirski to cross the mountain on both flanks of the enemy and attack the pass at the south, while he entered simultaneously with his own forces from the north. Although the snow was in places over three meters in depth, both columns succeeded in getting into the valley; Prince Mirski met with no opposition in the descent, but had a hard fight on the eighth and ninth, near the village of Shipka, which he carried; Skobelef, on the other hand, was much delayed on his march by the Turks, who occupied a ridge northeast of the village of Imetli and outflanked him. On the ninth occurred the most brilliant assault of the whole war. Skobelef, who had been obliged to leave all his artillery, attacked the Shenovo redoubts and carried them, causing Vesil Pasha, who commanded the Turkish army, to surrender his whole force.

Twelve thousand laid down their arms at Shenovo, besides the twenty-four thousand posted on the mountains. The Russian loss was one hundred and thirty-five officers and five thousand three hundred and forty-nine men, or twenty-two per cent of those who were brought under fire.

"The capture of this Shipka army," says Lieutenant Greene, "surpasses in boldness and brilliancy the advance of Gurko over the Balkans at Araba-Konak. Although Radetski's attack in front caused him terrible losses, and apparently gained no result, yet without this it is possible that the Turks might have withdrawn from the mountains under cover of the fog, and, concentrating about Shipka village, have broken through between Mirski and Skobelef, and escaped to the south; and although Mirski may be blamed for opening his attack before he had established communication with Skobelef, according to the plan of battle, yet it is possible that, had he remained idle at Gusevo during the eighth, the Turks might have discovered him and begun to retreat. Finally Skobelef's energetic attack, as soon as he had got all his men together in the valley, was one of the most splendid assaults ever made."

After the capture of Shipka and the battle of Philippolis the Turkish troops blew up the powder-magazines and abandoned Adrianople. On the twentieth of January the Russians entered the city. The Turkish inhabitants of all the region fled in panic at the approach of the victorious army. The Russian troops fell in with one immense train of refugees, numbering two hundred thousand people, who were deserted by their escort after a sharp skirmish, and then plundered by the Bulgarians of the neighboring villages. Thousands of helpless women and children perished in the snow or were massacred by their cruel plunderers.

On the twenty-ninth of January the last shot of the war was fired at Tchorlu. Two days later, two hundred and eighty-two days after the declaration of war, the Turkish commissioners signed the armistice which served as a basis for peace.

The conditions were these: The erection of Bulgaria into an autonomous tributary principality, with a native Christian government and a native militia; the independence of Montenegro, Rumania, and Servia, with additions of territory; the introduction of administrative reforms into Bosnia and the Herzegovina; the surrender of Viddin, Rustchuk, and Silistria on the Danube; the evacuation of Bielgradjok, Rasgrad, Bazardjok, and the fortifications of the line of Buïuk-Tchekmedje; and, lastly, the payment of a war indemnity to Russia.

On the twelfth of February the British fleet passed through the Dardanelles and anchored near Constantinople, while the Russians advanced to San Stefano on the Sea of Marmora.

END OF THE WAR.

On the third of March the Treaty of San Stefano was signed by Ignatief and Nelidof on the part of Russia, and Savfet and Sadullah on the part of Turkey. It seemed as if Russia had reached the goal of its ambition. Turkey was completely in its hands. A part of the war indemnity, amounting to eleven hundred million rubles, was to be exchanged for territory in Bessarabia and Armenia; and the rest, or three hundred and ten millions, was to be paid in money. But the Great Powers, having allowed Turkey to be reduced to this extremity, now suddenly determined to block Russia's plans. They refused to consent to a separate treaty between Turkey and Russia. England began to make extensive military preparations, and at the same time obliged Greece, which on the first of February had declared war, to withdraw its troops from the Turkish provinces. It was proposed to hold a congress at Berlin and discuss the Treaty of San Stefano. Russia at first declined to submit to this project; but, seeing that England was in earnest, at last it yielded. On the thirteenth of June Lord Beaconsfield, Gortchakof, Shuvalof, Andrassy, and Bismarck, together with the other plenipotentiaries, met at Berlin;

the congress lasted a month, and in the twenty sessions which took place the Treaty of San Stefano was amended by subtractions and additions. The Turkish Empire was again put in a position of comparative stability and independence. Bulgaria was divided into three unequal parts: Bulgaria proper was to be autonomous; Southeastern Bulgaria, now called Rumelia, was to have a Christian governor-general under the control of the Porte; and the country stretching westward from the Rhodope to Mount Pindus, with one million five hundred thousand inhabitants, was handed back to the Sultan. Bosnia and the Herzegovina were to be occupied by Austria; Montenegro and Serbia were recognized as independent, and their boundaries were regulated; Rumania was enlarged south of the Danube, as a compensation for the loss of part of Bessarabia, which was ceded to Russia. Batum, Ardahan, and Kars, together with the adjacent territory, were also given to Russia. Batum, however, was to be a free commercial port. Lord Salisbury, in his despatch to the English Government announcing the conclusion of the Treaty of Berlin, thus summed up the results: "The Sultan's dominions have been provided with a defensible frontier, far removed from his capital. The interposition of the Austrian power between the two independent Slav States, while it withdraws from him no territory of strategical or financial value, offers him a security against renewed aggression on their part which no other possible arrangement could have furnished. Rich and extensive provinces have been restored to his rule at the same time that careful provision against future misgovernment has been made, which will, it may be hoped, assure their loyalty and prevent a recurrence of the calamities which have brought the Ottoman Power to the verge of ruin. Arrangements of a different kind, but having the same end in view, have provided for the Asiatic dominions of the Sultan security for the present and the hope of prosperity and stability in the future. Whether use will be made of this — probably the last — opportunity which has been thus obtained for Turkey by the interposition of the powers of Europe, and of England in particular, or whether it is to be thrown away, will depend upon the sincerity with which Turkish statesmen now address themselves to the duties of good government and the task of reform."

If England found cause for self-congratulation upon the result of the Berlin congress and the acquisition of Cyprus, Russia, whose immense sacrifices in blood and treasure were scarcely requited, might well complain. Aksákof, who was intimate with the Tsesarévitch, expressed the general discontent when at a session of the Moscow Slav Committee he declared that the congress was a colossal absurdity, a blundering failure, and an impudent outrage upon Russian sensibilities; that Russia had been mocked with a fool's cap and bells, and that Russian diplomacy was more destructive than nihilism; that the honor of Russia had been trampled under foot and made a mockery. Aksákof, as a punishment for his outspoken denunciations, was banished to his estates. For the same reasons the sale of the *Golos* was for weeks forbidden upon the streets.

The Emperor, in order to clear away the distrust with which England and Germany regarded the delay of the Russian troops on Turkish territory, publicly declared that the strict fulfilment of the Berlin Treaty was his policy, and on the eighth of February, eighteen hundred and seventy-nine, the supplementary convention between Russia and Turkey was signed at Constantinople. The war indemnity was fixed, after deducting the value of the territory ceded to Russia, at eight hundred and two million five hundred thousand francs. Soon after the troops began to leave the principalities. By the tenth of March Reuf Pasha re-entered Adrianople; but it was estimated that twenty thousand of the inhabitants, fearing the violence of the Turks, left the land with the Russians. The new province of East Rumelia was evacuated in July. The governor-general, Aleko Pasha, under the nominal suzerainty of the Sultan, won immediate popularity by discarding the fez and wearing the Bulgarian national dress, by causing the Bulgarian flag to be raised instead of the Turkish, and by selecting the members of his council from the natives. Bulgaria was also reorganized; the first national parliament met at Trnova on February twenty-third, under the presidency of the Russian governor-general, and proceeded to discuss the constitution, which was finally accepted on the twenty-eighth of April. On the following day Prince Von Battenberg, a nephew of the Russian Emperor, was chosen as the first hereditary prince under the title of Alexander the First. A deputation of Bulgarians expressed to the Emperor the thanks of the nation for his assistance in accomplishing their freedom. By the third of August the Balkan Peninsula was completely evacuated.

CHAPTER XVI.

ASSASSINATION OF THE EMPEROR.

1881.

POPULAR DISCONTENT. — ASSASSINATION OF THE EMPEROR.

TURKEY, which during the two previous years had passed through many serious ministerial crises, which was vanquished in the war, bankrupt, and dismembered, seemed to be in a desperate condition; but victorious Russia was scarcely better off. It was said that if Constantinople fell into the hands of the Russians it would prove the Achilles' heel of the empire; nevertheless, the popular discontent that not one foot of land had been gained beyond the Danube, emphasized by the financial depression, by the taxes and the paper currency, began to express itself in revolutionary measures. In April, eighteen hundred and seventy-eight, Viera Sasulitch shot General Trepof, but was acquitted at the trial. In August General Mezentsof, chief of the hated "Third Section," was assassinated, and the arrests from Arkhangelsk to Kholmogorui showed how widespread the disaffection was. The university students of Saint Petersburg, Moscow, and Kief, and the assembly of Kharkof, demanded a constitution, and were rudely arrested and sent to Siberia. In April, eighteen hundred and seventy-nine, Solovief shot at the Emperor, who, in order to quiet the panic, called Valuïef to form a special commission, with extreme powers, to crush these nihilistic proceedings. In spite of all such arbitrary proceedings, revolutionary pamphlets were everywhere circulated. Among other things, they demanded that the people should be delivered from the espionage of the police, that the press and speech should be free, that professors should be allowed to teach unrestricted, and that amnesty should be granted to political offenders. To the arbitrary measures of General Miliutin the revolutionary committees called upon the army to respond, saying : " Despotism must fall sooner or later, but still the crisis may not come for years, to the cost of many lives. It therefore depends on all honorable and thoughtful men in the army to hasten this result." In April, eighteen hundred and seventy-nine, the excitement was still further increased by General Gurko's order compelling every householder in Saint Petersburg to keep a watchman at his door day and night to prevent the posting of seditious placards and the spreading of revolutionary pamphlets. The cities of Saint Petersburg, Moscow, Kief, Kharkof, and Odessa were declared to be in a state of siege, and the police were authorized to expel all persons considered dangerous. Throughout the summer fires of incendiary origin broke out in all the larger cities of the empire ; during May there were seventeen thousand three hundred conflagrations, causing a loss of upwards of two million rubles. The life of the Tsar was attempted, now by blowing up a railroad, now by boldly undermining the Winter Palace. Alexander was publicly declared to be the personification of a cursed despotism, and of everything mean and bloodthirsty ; his reign was denounced as a curse from beginning to end, the liberation of the serfs a delusion and a lie.

A slight reaction set in when the enlightened Armenian, General Loris-Melikof, was called to the assistance of the Tsar and immediately established a certain measure of freedom in place of the absurd repressionary measures of the "Third Section ; " this part of the police was abolished.

The nihilistic committees, however, still continued their activity, and the Emperor was frequently threatened with assassination unless he should give the country a constitution.

On the thirteenth of March, eighteen hundred and eighty-one, Alexander attended a review, and afterwards took coffee at the Mikhailovski Palace with his sister, the Princess Alexandra. On his return, as he was driving along the Iekaterinovski Canal, an Orsini bomb was thrown, which exploded and tore off a part of the carriage. The Emperor alighted unhurt and approached the assassin, who had been seized by two marines and the chief of police, Colonel Dvorzhetski. At this instant another bomb was thrown by an accomplice. It burst, and shattered the Emperor's legs, killed the man who threw it and a small boy who was passing, and injured a large number of bystanders. Colonel Dvorzhetski was wounded in sixty places. The Emperor, exclaiming "Help me!" fell to the ground and was immediately driven to the Winter Palace, where he died in the middle of the afternoon. The excitement was intense, and was by no means diminished by the discovery of a mine on Little Garden Street containing more than thirty-two kilograms of dynamite, connected with a basement leading from an ostensible milk and cheese shop. The editors of all the Saint Petersburg newspapers were summoned, and commanded to write guardedly.

In spite of the care of the police, a proclamation by the Executive Committee of the Nihilists was posted in a conspicuous place. It read as follows:—

"The Executive Committee consider it necessary once more to announce to all the world that it repeatedly warned the tyrant now assassinated, repeatedly advised him to put an end to his homicidal obstinacy and to restore to Russia its natural rights. Every one knows that the tyrant paid no attention to these warnings and pursued his former policy. Reprisals continued. The Executive Committee never drop their weapons. They resolved to execute the despot at whatever cost. On the first of March this was done.

"We address ourselves to the newly crowned Alexander the Third, reminding him that he must be just. Russia, exhausted by famine, worn out by the arbitrary proceedings of the administration, continually losing its sons on the gallows, in the mines, in exile, or in wearisome inactivity caused by the present régime, — Russia cannot longer live thus. She demands liberty. She must live in conformity with her demands, her wishes, and her will. We remind Alexander the Third that every violator of the will of the people is the nation's enemy and tyrant. The death of Alexander the Second shows the vengeance which follows such acts."

That this was not the universal feeling, however, is shown by the naïve account of a deputation of persons who came to bring their votive wreaths to put upon the Emperor's bier as he lay in state in the Petropavlovski Cathedral.

"The nearer we approached the cathedral," said the speaker, "the more our hearts sank. At last we were inside the church. There were many generals assembled, — thirty, if not more. They made way for us. We all dropped on our knees and sobbed aloud. We bowed our heads to the ground, nor could we restrain our tears; they kept flowing like a stream. O, what grief! We rose from our knees. Again we knelt and again we sobbed. This we did three times. What we felt all this time, how our hearts were aching beside the coffin of our father and benefactor, there are no words to express. And what honor was done us! Many wreaths were lying on the coffin. General Rilaief took our wreath and placed it straightway on the breast of our Little Father. The other wreaths were moved aside. Our peasants' wreath was laid on his heart. As during his whole life we were nearest his heart, so after his death our offering of thanks was laid on his martyr breast. This idea so affected us that we burst into tears. The general allowed us to take leave of the Tsar. We kissed his hand, — and there he lay, our Tsar-martyr, with a calm and loving expression on his face, as if he, our Little Father, had fallen asleep."

The funeral procession, on the nineteenth of March, was

most imposing. The route led from the Winter Palace to the Petropavlovski Cathedral by the Admiralty and the English Quay, across the Nikolaievski bridge into the fortress by the Ivanskaia gate. The procession had thirteen sections, divided into one hundred and seventy-two groups. The representatives of provincial assemblies, trade guilds, and the courts of justice, of economic and philanthropic societies, were in full regalia. The "bright and spotless character" of the late Emperor was represented by a knight in golden armor on a superb steed and carrying a drawn sword. The standards of the various districts of the empire and the imperial emblems were carried by pages, — the crowns of the kingdoms, the imperial globe and sceptre, the four swords of the empire reversed, the fifty-seven foreign orders and decorations, and the seventeen Russian orders and medals, borne on velvet cushions. The funeral car was of gilt, drawn by eight horses. At each corner sat one of the late Tsar's aides, and the cords of the pall were held by sixteen generals. Sixty liveried pages followed with burning torches. Then came on foot the new Emperor in the full uniform of the Preobrazhenski guard, and the other members of the imperial family.

On the day of the funeral mass, March twenty-seven, it snowed. The scene in the cathedral was impressive in the extreme. The cathedral was dimly lighted. The silence was broken only by the howling of the storm. The heralds, dressed in black velvet trimmed with silver braid and tassels, the imperial escutcheon picked out in dark embroidery, with the crown emblazoned in gold on their breasts, and holding in their hands their tabards surmounted with the double-headed eagle in gold, stood waiting for the mass to begin. The Emperor, wrapped in an ermine robe with a sacred picture on his breast, lay in state under a baldachin of gold and silver cloth lined with ermine. The canopy reached to the top of the dome, and was surmounted by alternate rows of ostrich feathers and the imperial arms. Among the mourners were the Prince and Princess of Wales, Archduke Rudolf of Austria, Crown Prince of Germany, Prince Alexander of Bulgaria, the imperial family, and a host of famous princes and generals. First, the High Mass was celebrated, with beautiful soft music by the choir; then came masses for the dead, and the Protodeacon intoned a prayer for the sins, voluntary and involuntary, of the Emperor, while all the mourners held lighted candles in their hands. Afterwards the last farewells were said, the silk standard was removed, and the Emperor was laid beside his wronged and unhappy Empress. Then the guns of the fortress sounded, and the mourning flag was taken down and replaced by the imperial standard.

Alexander the Third was Tsar of all the Russias.

The new Emperor began his reign under gloomy auspices. Five of the conspirators who had accomplished the death of his father were discovered and condemned to death by a court of trial comprising five senators, the marshal of the nobility, the mayors of Saint Petersburg and Moscow, and a representative of the peasants. One of them, a woman of rank, Sofia Perovska, the daughter of a councillor of the Ministry of Domains, and granddaughter of a Minister of the Interior under Nicholas the First, asked to suffer the same fate as the others. It was she who gave the signal to Hartmann for exploding the mine under the imperial train on the nineteenth of November; she also waved a handkerchief to Ruisakof when the Emperor's carriage drove into the Canal Street. She and the others were hung in spite of the threats of assassination which the Nihilist society, "the Will of the People," expressed.

The policy of Alexander the Third, whose reign began with the first public execution of a woman for half a century, was immediately marked by signs of retrogression and reaction, and hence was a disappointment to the true friends of Russia, who hoped to see a liberal and wise administration follow an administration of weakness and vacillation.

Russia, whose first glory began with Rurik and Igor, — Russia, dispersed after Iaroslof the Great, reunited by the Dynasty of Moscow, Europeanized by Peter the Great and Catherine the Second, freed from serfage by Alexander the Second guided by the enlightened wisdom of his mistress the Princess Dolgorukaïa, — ought now to enter into a new phase of its history. Hitherto the foreign policy of this great country has been turned to three aims, — the ending of the duel with the Polo-Lithuanian State for the leadership of the Slav world, the struggle with its Western neighbors to gain the freedom of the Baltic and Black Seas, and the revenge for the Tatar yoke, whether taken on the Turanians of Central Asia or those of Constantinople. Having conquered a place among the European States, it must secure also a place among free nations. When Russia displays boldness, resolution, and wisdom in following out a system of liberal schemes, then will begin the true history, not of the Russian State, but of the Russian People.

INDEX.

A.

ABDUL AZIZ, Sultan, becomes unpopular, iii. 337; forcibly dethroned, 338; dies by unknown violence, 338.
ABDUL HAMID succeeds to throne of Turkey, iii. 339.
ABO, treaty of, cedes South Finland to Russia, ii. 159.
ACADEMY, Russian, undertakes dictionary, ii. 216; incorporates with Academy of Sciences, 216.
ACHMET III. seeks to retake Azof, ii. 107.
ADDRESS from Poles to Alexander II., iii. 236.
ADOLPH, Friedrich, made Prince of Sweden, ii. 159.
ADRIAN, patriarch, death of, ii. 92.
ADRIANOPLE entered by Russians, iii. 41; abandoned by Turks, 377.
AGRICULTURE followed by early tribes, i. 58.
AIX LA CHAPELLE, Congress of, ii. 370.
AKKERMAN, treaty of, made with Turkey, iii. 38.
AKSAKOF complains of Berlin Congress, iii. 380.
ALADJA-DAGH, battle of, won by Russians, iii. 372.
ALASKA sold to United States, iii. 307; transferred formally, 308.
ALBERT, Bishop of Livonia, builds Riga, i. 144.
ALEKO PASHA wins popularity in Rumelia, iii. 381.
ALEXANDER NEVSKI, Prince of Novgorod, i. 159; wins battle of Neva, 160; submits to Batui, 162; dies near Vladimir, 164.
―――― of Tver flies from Pskof, i. 192; pardoned by Uzbek, 192; finally executed, 193.
―――― of Lithuania marries Helena, i. 228.
―――― I. comes to the throne, ii. 271; reconciles George III. of England, 272; seeks peace with France, 272; makes alliance with England, 277; visits tomb of Frederick, 278; decides to continue war, 285; quarrels with Novosiltsof, 296; discontent runs high against, 300; disturbed by action of Napoleon, 320; prohibits French goods, 321; debate over his policy, 326; retires to his capital, 329; seeks alliance against Napoleon, 345; firm policy of, against Napoleon, 349; proclamation of, at Freiburg, 354; confers with Deputies of Paris, 359; takes Poland and cedes Saxony, 361; modifies his Polish plan, 361; relations of, to restored France, 364; policy of, as to Poland, 366; regards Greek cause with indifference, 373; early promise of his reign, 374; becomes harsh in latter years, 384; takes Empress to Taganrog, 397; dies at Taganrog, 398; character and services of, 399.
―――― II., early life and education of, iii. 174; succeeds to the throne, 175; manifesto of, to Russian people, 176; resolves of, as to Crimean War, 177; manifesto after Sevastopol, 201; same, after close of war, 207; initiates valuable reforms, 209; speech of, to Deputies at Moscow, 209; coronation of, 210; moves to abolish serfage, 221; offers amnesty to Poles, 241; amity of, with William I., 314; speech of, to the Cossacks, 320; denounced by Revolutionists, 383; killed by explosive bombs, 384; affection of peasantry for, 385; splendid funeral of, 386.
―――― III. succeeds to throne, iii. 387.
ALEXANDRA, Princess, executed, i. 265.
ALEXIS makes humane war on Poland, i. 381; treats with Poland against Sweden, 382; confines English to Arkhangel, 399.
―――― Mikhailovitch, character of, i. 370.
―――― , Prince, marries Charlotte of Brunswick, ii. 120; gives Peter great trouble, 120; hides in Germany and Italy, 121; brought home and renounces crown, 121; proved a traitor and put to death, 122.

390 INDEX.

ALFRED of England served by Other, i. 40.
ALLIANCE, efforts to strengthen, ii. 290.
———, French, prospects of, ii. 298.
——— " of Four Powers " quells the Khedive, iii. 76.
——— " of Three Emperors " formed, iii. 319.
ALLIED Army lands at Eupatoria, iii. 154.
ALLIES, movements of, in Southern Europe, ii. 256; capture Dutch fleet in the Texel, 261; conditions of, offered to Napoleon, 348; three great armies of, in the field, 349; decide to march on Paris, 358; financial preparations of, iii. 143; despatch troops to Turkey, 145; move on the Chersonesus, 162; intrench before Sevastopol, 168; gain by naval attacks, 184; ask for truce at Sevastopol, 188; sickness in armies of, 188; movements of, in pursuit of Russians, 198.
ALMA, Heights of, fortified by Russians, iii. 154; forced by Allies, 155.
———, Ravine of, desperate fight in, iii. 156.
———, battle of, its effect in Russia, iii. 157.
ALMANAC, change made in, in 1700, iL 78.
ALPHABET, Slavonic, first invented, i. 69; abandoned, ii. 100.
———, Russian, contrived to admit printing, ii. 100.
AMBASSADORS, how received and entertained, i. 291.
AMIENS, Peace of, rupture of, ii. 275.
AMOROSI, Bishop, killed by mob, ii. 198.
AMUR River, Russian acquisitions on, iii. 305.
AMUSEMENTS, prohibited in Old Russia, i. 297; instituted by Peter, ii. 84.
ANASTASIA, Tsaritsa, dies, perhaps by poison, i. 260.
ANDRASSY, Count, declarations of, iii. 313; note of, for pacification, 329.
ANDREI reigns in Suzdal, i. 159.
ANNA IVANOVNA, Council treats with, ii. 135; accepts proposal of Council, 136; enters Moscow as capital, 136; summons High Council, 137.
——— I., character and person of, ii. 138; oppressive style of her government, 138; court costume and etiquette of, 140; habits and methods of government, 141; becomes unpopular, 152.
——— Leopoldovna becomes Regent, ii. 154; weakness and incapacity of, 154; condemned, with her party, 156.
——— Paulovna, marriage with Napoleon stopped, ii. 318.
ANTIQUITIES, Russian writers upon, iii. 270.
APRAXIN invades Eastern Prussia, ii. 164.

ARAKTCHEEF made Minister of War, ii. 297; made Prime Minister, 382; opposed by peasantry, 386.
ARAL, Sea of, navigation begun upon, iii. 45.
ARCIS, battle of, victory doubtful, ii. 358.
ARDAHAN, fortress, taken by Russians, iii. 370.
ARKHANGEL, effort to suppress trade at, ii. 95.
"ARMED Neutrality," proclaimed against England, ii. 222; Act of, revived by Paul I., 263; given up by Alexander I., 272.
ARMIES collected by France and Russia, ii. 321.
ARMY, Russian, general constitution of, i. 288; equipments and divisions of, 289.
———, Heavy, of Alexander and Russia, ii. 325.
——— of Russia, reinforced continually, ii. 335.
ARNAUD, St., letter to French Minister, iii. 151; criticises Russian tactics, 156.
ARTISANS, foreign, invited to Russia, i. 356.
ARTISTS, Italian, at Court of Moscow, i. 232.
ARTS, rise of, in Russia, i. 310; useful, promoted by Peter, ii. 97.
ASIA, Central, dubious place of Russia in, iii. 286; Russian boundaries in, 287; details of geography of, 291–293.
ASIATIC tribes, how regarded by Russia, iii. 283.
ASKOLD, first Christian Prince of Russia, i. 69; and Dir, besiege Byzantium, i. 66.
ASSEMBLIES, International, held in Russia, iii. 280.
ASSUMPTION, Church of, in the Kreml, i. 307.
ASTRAKHAN subdued by Ivan IV., i. 255.
AUGUSTUS of Poland, submits to Charles XII., ii. 64; reconciled with Peter, 106.
AUSTRIA, policy of, suspected by Russia, ii. 262; soldiers of, charged with treachery, 283; attempts negotiations with Russia, iii. 116; persists in seeking pacification, 124; real interest of, in Turkish War, 131; and Prussia support the Alliance, 143; supplanted by Russia, 309; and Hungary disturbed by Russian action, 313.
AUTHORS, Western, popular in Russia, ii. 393.
AZOF, offered to Russia by Cossacks, i. 355; destroyed by Cossacks, 355; Peter decides to march upon, ii. 28; second expedition against, 30; capitulates to Russians, 30.

INDEX.   391

B.

BADER, Franz, originates Holy Alliance, ii. 368.
BAGRATION, Gen., covers retreat of Kutuzof, ii. 280; overrules Barclay de Tolley, 329.
BALAKLAVA, intrenchments of Allies at, iii. 163; battle of, 165.
BALKANS, crossed by Russian army, iii. 354; final evacuation of, 381.
BALTIC, Peter seeks to secure passage of, ii. 51; provinces of, saved from insurrection, iii. 246.
BANKS, agricultural, founded in Russia, ii. 167.
BAR, Confederation of, violent spirit of, ii. 189.
BASMANOF, his treason to the sons of Boris, i. 325.
BATUI, Tatar Chief, makes second invasion, i. 153.
BATUM, expedition of Russians against, iii. 369.
BELGRADE, Peace of, ends Turco-Russian War, ii. 148.
BELL, famous "Tsar-kolokol," at Moscow, i. 310.
BELLES-LETTRES, advance of, in Russia, ii. 392.
BENNINGSEN, prominent in conspiracy, ii. 269; attacks Paul I. in chamber, 269; makes advance at Osterode, 287; opens campaign of 1807, 291.
BEREZINA, French force passage at, ii. 343.
BERLIN, entered and pillaged by Russians, ii. 166; Congress of, meets to discuss treaty, iii. 378.
BERNADOTTE chosen King of Sweden, ii. 308.
BESTUZHEF, Alexander, revolutionary acts of, iii. 16.
BESTUZHEF-RIUMIN, opinion on Greek Church, i. 90; as to writings of Novgorod, 138; succeeds against Lestocq, ii. 161; made Vice-Chancellor, 159; disgraced and removed, 164; concerned in insurrection, iii. 19.
BEZBORODKO rewarded for services, ii. 224.
BIBIKOF defeats Pugatchef, ii. 200.
BIBLE Societies established, ii. 383.
BIELINSKI, eminent critical writer, iii. 27.
BILLAULT, French Minister, speaks for Poland, iii. 244.
BIREN, nominated Regent, ii. 152; deposed and exiled, ii. 153.
BIRGER, of Sweden, defeated on the Ijora, i. 160.
BISMARCK gains advantage from Russia, iii. 311.

BLACK Sea, Russians not to cruise in, iii. 135; entered by Allied Fleet, 136; navigation of, debated, 178; made neutral ground, 205; neutrality of, set aside, 319.
"BLACK Tomb" opened by Samokvasof, i. 62.
BLÜCHER, steadily opposes Napoleon, ii. 356; makes trouble in Paris, 363.
BOGDANOVITCH, as to policy of Russia, ii. 352.
BOGOLIUBSKI, besieges Kief, i. 111; founds Tsars of Moscow, 113; movements of, after fall of Kief, 114; attacks Novgorod, 114; efforts of, for new capital, 116; slain by boyars, 118.
BOLOTNIKOF, marches on Moscow, i. 332; retires to Tula, 333.
BOMARSUND taken by Allies, iii. 151.
BONAPARTE, wins at Marengo, ii. 262; returns all Russian prisoners, 262; makes overtures to Paul I., 263; questions the India scheme, 267; angry at murder of Paul I., 270; displeased by Russian policy, 272; threatens England, 277.
"BOOK of Instructions" of Catherine II., ii. 205.
BORIS and Gleb, Russian demigods, i. 160.
BORIS GODUNOF, aspires to throne, i. 312; removes all other regents, 312; becomes virtual Tsar, 313; retires to monastery, 318; obtains the throne, 319; encourages learning, 321; wife and child of, put to death, 326.
BORODINO, battle-field of, described, ii. 332; details of battle of, 333; fruitless carnage at, 334.
BOSQUET, Gen., displaced from command, iii. 186.
BOURDON, Mad., describes Shah Indeh, iii. 292.
BRIBES and corruption denounced by Catherine, iii. 207.
BRIDES, capture of, at marriage, i. 56.
BRIDGES, splendid, in Russia, iii. 276.
BRIGADE, Light, at Balaklava, iii. 165.
"BRIGAND of Tushino" approaches Moscow, i. 334.
BRUNE, Gen., reduces Zyp, ii. 261.
BUFFOONERY, Anna I. encourages, ii. 142.
BUILDINGS, Russian, mostly wood, i. 23.
BUKAREST, Congress of, ii. 312.
BULGARIA, ravaged by Bashi-Bazouks, iii. 333; welcomes the Russians, 354.
BURNET, Bishop, his opinion of Peter, ii. 39.
BURROUGHS, Stephen, voyage to North Sea, i. 274.
"BUSY BEE," first Russian Review, ii. 170.
BUTURLIN, sent to Cossacks, i. 380.
BYZANTIUM preserved by miracle, i. 66.

C.

"CADETS, Corps of," founded by Münnich, ii. 144.
CANALS, important, projected by Peter, ii. 96.
CANROBERT, Marshal, relieved in Crimea, iii. 183.
CAPEFIQUE, his story of Peter's assassination, ii. 180.
CARDIGAN, Earl of, famous charge of, iii. 166.
CARLSBAD, Congress of, excitement about, ii. 370.
CATHERINE, "Maid of Marienburg," story of, ii. 59 – 123; acknowledged by Peter, 108; described by Margravine of Baireuth, 124; crowned as Empress Catherine I., 124; becomes absolute sovereign, 128; continues plans of Peter, 129; nominates Peter II. to succeed, 129.
——— II., usurps the throne, ii. 179; procures death of Peter III., 180; notice of her dramatic works, 216; her designs on Turkey, 226; terrified by French Revolution, 245; her complicated diplomacy, 246.
CAUCASUS, doubtful war with tribes of, iii. 42; Russian occupation of, 283; rapid improvements in, 286.
CENSUS and tribute laid on Novgorod, i. 162.
CHANCELLOR, discovers White Sea, i. 273; second voyage to White Sea, 273; shipwrecked on return to England, 274.
CHARLES X., of Sweden, invades Poland, i. 382.
——— X., of France, Nicholas disturbed by flight of, iii. 46.
——— XII. of Sweden, comes to Little Russia, ii. 48; makes resumption of land, 52; congratulated by European Powers, 56; operations of, in Poland, 60; enters Russia to subdue Augustus, 62; character of, by Guerrier and others, 67; makes rapid march into Russia, 69; approaches Moscow from Berezina, 70; winter sufferings of his army, 71; routed and broken up at Poltava, 73.
CHATILLON-SUR-SEINE, congress opened at, ii. 356.
"CHIEF Citizens," class founded by Nicholas, iii. 23.
CHINA, treaty with, by Iaguzhinski, ii. 133; relations with, under Nicholas I., iii. 42; position of Russia towards, 304; Russia finally settles with, 306.
CHOLERA, peasants revolt on account of, iii. 45; ravages Polish and Russian armies, 67; breaks out in French army, 149.
CHRISTIANS, slain by Vladimir, i. 78; institutions of, respected by Tatars, 172; in Turkey, Russia claims to protect, iii. 110; revolt against Turkey, 325; last appeal of, to Consuls, 326; encouraged by financial pressure, 328; insurgent, difficulty of appeasing, 330.
CHURCH, peculiar form of, in Novgorod, i. 137; slow increase of power of, 173; revenues and management of, 237; of Vasili the Blessed, curious style of, 309; reorganized by Peter, ii. 92.
CIVIL state, idea of, from Greece, i. 94.
——— liberty, narrowness of, under Vasili, i. 246; advanced under Ivan IV., 278.
CIVILIZATION, extinct, signs of, in Turkestan, iii. 288.
CLARENDON, Earl, becomes English Minister, iii. 96; his note as to state of Turkey, 97.
CLEMENT VIII., Pope, bishops submit to, i. 364.
CLIMATE, severe in winter, i. 30.
COALITION, disposition of, against France, ii. 255; overcome by Napoleon, 284; renewed by Northern Powers, 284.
COAST line, great share of, in Western Europe, i. 17; small amount of, in Russia, 18.
COINS, ancient, discovery of, i. 58.
"COLLEGES" of Government, created by Peter, ii. 85; of Mines, etc., suppressed, 209.
COLONIES, military, founded by Araktcheef, ii. 385.
COLONIZATION of immigrants favored, ii. 210.
"COMMISSION for the Code," influence of, ii. 206.
COMMUNISTS publish principles at Krakov, iii. 78.
CONFEDERATES, Polish, capture the King, ii. 191.
CONFERENCE, Berlin, attempts help for Turkey, iii. 335.
CONFRATERNITIES formed against Jesuits, i. 361.
CONSCRIPTION, Polish, serious effect of, iii. 240.
CONSTANTINE, Emperor, as to Russian names, i. 60.
CONSTANTINOPLE, taken by Mahomet II., i. 215; blockaded by England, ii. 312; results of conference at, iii. 344.
CONSTITUTION, liberal, attempt for, checked, ii. 137; refused to the nobles, iii. 229.
CONSULS, French and German, killed by Turks, iii. 332.
COSSACKS, intractable character of, i. 367; defeated at Berestitchko, 379; again defeated at Ivaneto, 380; definitely annexed to Russia, 381; difficulty of

union with, 386; revolt at Hadiatch, 387; of Don, revolt against Russia, ii. 45; last earl of their power, 202; to march against India, 264; full instructions to, 265; march of, stopped by death of Paul I., 266.
COSTUMES, curious, of native women, i. 41; ridiculous, at Court of Anna I., ii. 143.
COUNCIL of Regents appointed for Feodor, i. 311.
COURTS, form of improved, iii. 230.
CRIMEA, Khan of, marches on Moscow, i. 252; and Livonia, war against both, 258; second expedition against, fails, ii. 21; Turks finally driven from, 193; disturbances in, 223; geography of, iii. 152; war of, great loss of life in, 206.
CRIMINALS, State, pardoned by Alexander II., iii. 212.
CYPRUS, given to England by Berlin Congress, iii. 380.

D.

DALL, Wm. H., statements as to Alaska, iii. 308.
DANIEL, succeeds to throne of Galitch, i. 124; efforts of, for freedom of Galitch, 126; first Prince of Moscow, 187.
DANTZIG, taken by the Russians, ii. 146.
DANUBE, crossed by Russians, iii. 146–350; operations of Russians upon, 352.
DAYS, great variation in length of, i. 22.
DEATH, penalty of, abolished by Elizabeth, ii. 168.
DEBTS, rigorous laws for collection of, i. 286.
DEITIES, worshipped by certain tribes, i. 42; greater and lesser, of early authors, i. 52.
DE LA GARDIE, invades Russia with Swedes, i. 271; drives Brigand from Tushino, 335; takes Baltic ports, 341.
DEMIDOF, family founded by means of Peter, ii. 96.
"DEMON, The," great poem by Lermontof, iii. 30.
D'ENGHIEN, Duc, seized and executed, ii. 276.
DENMARK, fleet of, seized by English, ii. 267; forced to give up Schleswig-Holstein, iii. 311.
DERBY, Lord, criticises Russian action, iii. 349.
DERZHAVIN, greatest lyric poet in Russia, ii. 219.
DEVLET-GHIREI, Khan, invades Moscow, i. 268.
DIBITCH, Count, enters Poland with Russians, iii. 65.
DIET of Grodno, sad spectacle of, ii. 237.
DIMSDALE, Dr., inoculates Catherine II., ii. 212.
DIPLOMACY, methods and manner of, i. 290.
DMITRI IVANOVITCH claims Moscow, i. 197.
—— Donskoi, military movements of, i. 198; defeats Tatars on the Voja, 200; threatened by Mamai, 201.
——, brother of Feodor, killed by Uglitch, i. 317.
—— the False, his appearance, i. 332.
—— ——, the second, assassinated, i. 339.
—— ——, the fourth, executed, i. 374.
—— Pojavski commands popular army, i. 342.
DNIEPER River, influence of, i. 26.
DOBRUDSHA Wilderness, Russians attacked in, iii. 148.
DOKTUROF, sent to Charles I. of England, i. 397; brought before Parliament, 398.
DOLGORUKI, becomes powerful, ii. 131; incites revolt, but is detected, 150; sent to Napoleon, 280.
DOMESTIC establishments include slavery, i. 295.
DOROSHENKO defeated in Little Russia, i. 397.
DOROSTOL, battle of, i. 73.
DRAMATISTS and satirists, various Russian, iii. 261.
DRESDEN, battle of, won by French, i. 350.
DRESS, harsh notions of, in Old Russia, i. 297.
DREVONINSKI, as to religious state of Russia, i. 366.
DRINKING, suppressed by Anna I., ii. 142.
DRUJINNIKI, or Guards, their influence, i. 87.
DRUNKENNESS, universal in Old Russia, i. 298.
DUBIENKA, battle of, under Kosciuzko, ii. 236.
DUCKWORTH, Admiral, blockades Constantinople, ii. 312.
DUEL, judicial, employed in Russia, i. 286.
DUROC, his plan for restoring Poland, ii. 319.

E.

ECKHARDT, Julius, on female education, iii. 254.
EDIGER, the Tatar, invades Russia, i. 208; raises siege of Moscow, i. 208.
EDUCATION, made compulsory by Peter, ii. 97; promoted by Catherine II., 213; restricted and regulated by Nicholas, iii. 25; public, state of, in Russia, 253; female, efforts toward, 254.

"ELECT of Whole Muscovite Empire," title, i. 342.

ELIZABETH of England, Ivan IV. corresponds with, i. 266; makes treaty with Ivan IV., 276; embassy to, from Boris, 320; receives Russian envoys, 320.

——— Petrovna, intrigues against Anna II., ii. 155; seizes the government, 156; sudden death of, 166; fanatical zeal of, 166; results of her reign, 172.

EMANCIPATION of serfs, early discussed, ii. 206; begun in Northern Russia, 376; slightly favored by Nicholas, iii. 23; preparation for, 218; begun in Lithuania, 222; gradual progress of, 224; final conditions of, 225; influential promoters of, 228.

EMIGRANTS, Greek, to Moscow, i. 231.

EMIGRATION, as affecting local names, i. 47; consequences of, 49.

EMS, Conference held at, iii. 312.

ENGLAND, and Holland offer to mediate, i. 347; seeks to open Oriental trade, 352; accepts alliance against Napoleon, ii. 278; curious changes in Cabinet of, iii. 86; refuses to anticipate fall of Turkey, 91; further conference as to Turkey, 95; learns action of Russia, 105; acts with France on Eastern Question, 106; ministers of, reach Turkey, 108; awakens to designs of Russia, 113; and France will occupy Black Sea, 135; declares war upon China, 304; disturbed by Gortchakof, 319; great feeling in, for Bulgaria, 334; objects to Berlin Conference, 336; strong action of, against Turkey, 343; fleet of, passes Dardanelles, 378.

ENGLISH form exploring company under Cabot, i. 272.

——— army, occupy Balaklava, iii. 163; repulsed from Redan, 187; repulsed again, 196.

ENTAIL, law of, abolished by Anna I., ii. 144.

ERASMUS HANDELIUS mediates for Poland, i. 347.

ERFURT, Conference of, by Napoleon and Alexander, ii. 303.

ERZERUM, Russians move toward, iii. 374; finally taken by Russians, 375.

EUGENIUS IV., Pope, seeks union with Greek Church, i. 214.

EUPATORIA, occupied by Turks, iii. 168; Russians repulsed before, 169.

EUROPE, eastern and western divisions, i. 17; sovereigns of, roused against Tatars, 157; military relations of, with Charles XII., ii. 63; attitude of, on Eastern Question, iii. 115.

EVDOKIA, wife of Peter, sent to convent, ii. 44; full story of, 119.

"EXPLOSIVE Bullet Treaty," universally signed, iii. 324.

EYLAU, battle of, account of, ii. 287; Russians retire from field of, 288.

EYRE, Gen., bravery of, at Sevastopol, iii. 187.

F.

FALCONET, sculptor of statue of Peter I., ii. 215.

FAMINE, great in all Russia, i. 321.

FEAST, commemorative, at Vladimir, i. 117.

FEODOR, Ivanovitch, succeeds to throne, i. 311; dies, ending his dynasty, 317.

——— Alexiovitch, succeeds to crown, i. 399; state of royal family at his death, ii. 13.

FERMOR makes second invasion of Prussia, ii. 164.

FILY, Russians hold council at, ii. 334.

FINANCE, condition of public, iii. 233.

FISH, heavy, found in Volga, i. 27.

FORBES, Archibald, censures Russian action, iii. 358.

FORCED marriage, abolished by Peter, ii. 83.

FOREST, Zone of, defined, i. 28.

FORSTER, George, as to fall of Poland, ii. 238.

FOUR Powers, indignant at Turkey, iii. 121.

FRANCE, negotiates for Oriental trade, i. 352; amity of, with Peter, ii. 117; assists Russia in Sweden, &c., 149; joins Russia against Germany, 158; civilization of, carried to Russia, 171; language of, popular under Elizabeth, 172; institutions of, favored by Catherine, 214; relations to Italian States, 253; expels Turks from Greece, iii. 40; sympathizes with Poland, 72; shut out of Convention of London, 75; returns to place in Convention, 77; answers circular of Nesselrode, 117.

FRANCIS JOSEPH, his cruelty toward Hungary, iii. 84.

"FRANKFORT, Basis of," Napoleon insists on, ii. 357.

FREDERICK II., his letter to Western Powers, i. 157.

——— of Prussia, Elizabeth jealous of, ii. 162; stirs up Polish affairs, ii. 194.

FRENCH actors dismissed by Peter III., ii. 176; troops, plan of sending, to India, 266; army, painful march of, to Kustendje, iii. 149; army, sufferings of, at Varna, 150; batteries silenced by Russians, 164; capture Mamelon and White Works, 185; repulsed from Malakof, 187; hurt by explosion in Brancion Redoubt, 192.

G.

GALITCH governed by boyars, i. 122.
GALITSUIN, fails in movement against Turks, ii. 21; driven into exile, 25.
GALLICIA, principality of, located, i. 100.
GALLIPOLIS fortified by Allies, iii. 146.
GAMBLING encouraged by Anna I., ii. 141.
GAZETTE, Moscow, its great influence, iii. 249–272.
GEDIMIN, establishes power of Lithuania, i. 176; appeals to Pope for protection, 177.
GENEVA, Convention of, Russia adheres to, iii. 324.
GEOGRAPHY, and history, promotion of, ii. 100; Russian, investigations in, iii. 277.
GEOLOGY, successful explorations in, iii. 278.
"GEORGE the Black" killed by Milosh, ii. 313.
GERMANS, invasion and domination by, i. 145.
GERSTENZWEIG, Gen., suicide of, iii. 238.
GILBERT of Lannoy, his account of Novgorod, i. 128.
GLINKA, political editor, ii. 391.
GOGOL-IVANOVSKI, eminent writer, iii. 31.
"GOLOS," daily journal, character of, iii. 272; remarks of, on Prussian affairs, 317.
GONTCHAROF, novelist, style of his work, iii. 258.
GORGEY, Gen., betrays Hungarians at Vilagos, iii. 82.
GORTCHAKOF, ordered to leave Turkey, iii. 125; declines to evacuate Turkey, 127.
———, Prince, takes command of army, 169; holds important councils of war, 189; his loose policy as to defence, 194; conciliates Poles, 236; circular of, to European Powers, 282; made Chancellor of Russia, 309; circular of, to the Six Powers, 318; his summary of Eastern Situation, 345.
GOVERNMENT, Russian, extortions of, i. 285.
GOVERNMENTS, provincial and municipal, iii. 232.
"GRAND Army" of Napoleon, formed, ii. 324; broken up by desertion, 352.
GREECE, invaded by Iaroslaf, i. 83; independence of, recognized, iii. 41.
GREEK Church, benefits and difficulties of, i. 91; Emperor, ideal character of, 93; war of 1827, outline of, iii. 39.
"GREEK Project" for dismembering Turkey, ii. 225.
GREEKS, early settlement of, i. 32; and Serbians, effect of revolt of, ii. 372; massacred by Turks, ii. 373.

GREENE, Lieut., as to defence of Plevna, iii. 367; as to passage of Shipka, 377.
GREGORY XIII., Pope, mediates for Poland, i. 271.
GRIBOIEDOF, eminent dramatist, iii. 31.
GRIGORIEF, Prof., on Russian policy, iii. 287.
GROKHOF, battle of, Poles repulsed at, iii. 65.
GUERILLAS, French attacked by, ii. 340.
GURKO, Gen., gains much at Plevna, iii. 366; moves toward Balkans, 367; severe service of, 375; offensive orders of, 383.
GUSTAVUS ADOLPHUS, treaty of, with Russia, i. 349; seeks alliance with Russia, 351.
——— III. makes great revolution, ii. 197; invades Russia, 227; makes Peace of Verela, 228.
——— IV. treats Alexander rudely, ii. 307; makes treaty with England, 307; nearly driven from Finland, 307; arrested and expelled, 308; succeeded by Charles XII., 308.

H.

HAIDUKI rise against Janissaries, ii. 311.
HANSE League has monopoly in Russia, i. 137.
HAZRET IASAVI, his mosque described, iii. 290.
HELENA GLINSKI, widow of Vasili, noticed, i. 247.
HENRY IV. intercedes with Sviatoslaf, i. 103.
——— of Anjou made King of Poland, i. 270.
——— III. of France sends merchants to Russia, i. 276.
HERETICS and fanatics oppose Nikon, i. 391.
HERMAN DE BALK, Landmeister of Livonia, i. 146.
HERODOTUS, his account of Finnish tribes, i. 44.
HERRMANN, writer, his judgment of Four Sovereigns, ii. 68.
HERZEN, Alexander, remarks on insurrection, iii. 19.
———, publisher in London, iii. 217; champion of Nihilists, iii. 263.
HIGH Council, members condemned by Anna I., ii. 138.
HISTORIANS, Russian, works of, noticed, iii. 268.
HOLLAND and Hanse Towns, united to France, ii. 319.
HOLY Alliance, formed by Alexander I., ii. 369; hated in Europe, 396.

"HOLY SITES," question of, stirred by Louis Napoleon, iii. 86.
HOLY Synod founded by Peter, ii. 92.
HORDE, Great, broken down by Khan of Crimea, i. 230.
HUSSEIN AVNI and others, killed by Hassan, iii. 338.
———, Pasha, routed and driven from Kars, iii. 374.

I.

IAGELLO, successor of Olgerd, i. 178; marries Hedviga of Hungary, 179; removes capital to Cracow, 179.
IAGUZHINSKI laments over tomb of Peter, ii. 128.
IAKOB KHAN, notice of life of, iii. 294; obstinate resistance of, 302.
IAN KASIMIR succeeds Vladislas, i. 377.
"IARLUIK," or Patent issued by Khan, i. 168.
IAROSLAF, troubles of, with the princes, i. 82; distresses Novgorod, 120; and Vladimir, reign in Galitch, 122; of Suzdal confirmed by Tatars, 159.
IASSY, or Jassy, Peace of, ends Turkish War, ii. 231.
IBN-DOST, Arab writer, as to Russian justice, i. 87.
IBN-FOSZLAN, Arab writer, as to funerals, i. 53.
IBRAHIM of Egypt revolts against Turks, iii. 74.
IBRAÏLA, first shot fired at, iii. 350.
ICE, battle of the, won by Alexander Nevski, i. 161.
IEZIERSKI questioned by insurgents, iii. 64.
IGOR, third Variag prince, i. 67; subdues the Emperor Lecapenus, 68; death of, according to Leo the Deacon, 68; slain by the Drevliané, 88.
IMPERIAL Council replaces the Senate, ii. 378.
INDIA, English rule in, scheme to destroy, ii. 264.
INDUSTRIES, internal, encouraged by Peter, ii. 96.
INKERMANN, Russians attack Allies at, iii. 166; battle of, lost by Russians, 167.
INNOCENT III., Pope, answered by Roman, i. 124; denounces Livonians, 144.
——— IV., crowns Daniel king, i. 125; letter of, to Alexander Nevski, 161; orders Mindvog baptized, 175.
INOCULATION, Catherine II. promotes, ii. 212.
INSURRECTION breaks out in Herzegovina, iii. 325.
INVASIONS, barbaric, in early times, i. 36.

IONIAN Islands taken by Russians and Turks, ii. 252.
IRMUK, Timofeivitch, invades Siberia, i. 277.
IRON-CLAD vessels added to Russian navy, iii. 323.
ISIASLAF, deposed by Sviatoslaf, i. 103; defeated by Iuri, 109; puts Viatebeslaf on throne, 109; defeats Iuri on the Rut, i. 110.
ISMAIL assaulted and taken by Suvarof, ii. 231.
ISTOMIN, Admiral, killed at Sevastopol, iii. 180.
ITALY, political relations of, with Russia, iii. 310.
IURI DOLGORUKI, disputes throne of Kief, i. 108; finally obtains throne, 110; defeated by Mstislaf the Bold, 120.
———, called Second, founds Nijni Novgorod, i. 121.
——— II. of Suzdal, defeated at Kolomna, i. 154; slain at battle of the Sit, i. 155.
——— of Moscow, quarrels with Mikhail of Tver, i. 188; marries sister of Uzbek, 189; invades country of Tver, 189; slain by Dmitri, 191.
IVAN KALITA, marches against Tver, i. 191; denounces Alexander, 193.
——— II., weak government of, i. 193.
——— III., or "Great," prophecy at birth of, i. 217; character of, by Stephen of Moldavia, 217; marches on Novgorod, 219; holds court in Novgorod, 220; arrests Hanse merchants, 221; extends Russian power to Asia, 221; absorbs Tver and other provinces, 222; called Binder of Russian Land, 223; rebels against Akhmet the Tatar, 225; manages Tatar envoys, 227; lays plans against Lithuania, 228; operates against Livonian Germans, 230; marries Sophia Paleologus, 231; compared with Louis XI. of France, 233; difficulty of fixing successor, 234.
——— IV., or "Terrible," asserts authority at thirteen, i. 249; crowned with title of "Tsar," 250; marries Anastasia Romanof, 250; besieges Kazan with difficulty, 252; invades Knights of Livonia, 257; sickness of, and mutiny against, 259; replies to Kurbski, and leaves Moscow, 262; reconstructs government, 264; begins to punish mutineers, 264; prays for souls of his victims, 266; calls council as to Poland, 267; plans of, against Poland, 269; speech of, to Polish envoys, 270; founds Strelitz, or National Guard, 278; tolerates Reformed Faith, 279; causes death of his son Ivan, 279.
——— Sossanin saves life of Mikhail, i. 344.

IVAN VI. imprisoned by Catherine II., ii. 181.
IVANOVSKI, discoveries of, in Russian tombs, i. 54.

J.

JAPAN, history of commercial efforts in, iii. 306.
JENA and Auerstädt, battles of, ii. 284.
JENKINSON, English Ambassador to Russia, i. 274; enterprise of, in quest of trade, 275.
JESTERS employed among early Russians, i. 298.
JESUITS, meddling habits of, i. 359; expelled by Stephan Batory, 360; encouraged by Sigismond III., 360; seek to subdue Russia to Rome, 360; finally expelled from Russia, ii. 94; terrible barbarities charged to, 188.
JEWS and foreigners invited to Galitch, i. 125.
JOB, Archbishop, made Patriarch, i. 317; proclaims falsity of Otrepief, 324.
JOHN ZIMISCES expels Russians from Greece, i. 74.
JONAS of Moscow censures priests, i. 142.
JOSEPH II. of Austria, movements of, ii. 229.
JOUBERT, Gen., defeated at Novi, ii. 257.
JUDICIAL proceedings, improvement in, iii. 229.
JURIES established in Russia, iii. 230.
"JUSTICE, Song of," sung by minstrels, i. 369.
JUSTICES of Peace, system of, iii. 231.

K.

KADLUBEK, Bishop, as to acts of Roman, i. 123.
"KALEVY-POEG," national poem of Esthonia, i. 147.
KALKA, battle of, Russians defeated at, i. 152.
KALMUIKS return to Chinese territory, ii. 199.
KANTEMIR of Moldavia joins Peter, ii. 108.
KARAKOZOF attempts life of Alexander II., iii. 250.
KARAMSIN, writer, as to condition of women, i. 56; censure of, as to sack of Kief, 111; remark of, on Tatar invasion, 156; as to Tatar influence, 169; remarks on Ivan III., 217, opposes Speranski, ii. 382; eminent as literary editor, ii. 391.
KARS, city of, taken by Gen. Muravief,
iii. 202; again besieged, 370; new movement against, 371; fortifications of, described, 372; stormed by Russians, 373.
KARTSOF, Gen., crosses Balkans by Trojan Pass, iii. 376.
KATKOF, Mikhail, powerful appeal of, iii. 242; stirs Russia against Poland, 243; demands against Swedes and Germans, 246; stirs up Russian feeling, 249.
KATTNER, Herr, dedicates book to German army, iii. 317.
KAZAN, Tatar capital, taken by Ivan III., i. 226; determined against by Ivan IV., 252; walls of, undermined, 254.
KAZI-MOLLA preaches in the Caucasus, iii. 284.
KHAZARUI, native tribe like Jews, i. 43.
KHEMNITZER, first Russian fabulist, ii. 218.
KHIVA, unsuccessful march against, iii. 44; expedition to, history of, 300; subdued by Kaufmann, 301.
KHLOPITSKI, action of, in Polish revolt, iii. 57; made Dictator of Poland, 58; resigns dictatorship, 62.
KHMELNITSKI, Bogdan, head of Cossacks, i. 375; takes field against Poles, 376; victor at Khersun, and "Yellow Waters," 376; sends memorial to Vladislaus, 377; treats with Polish envoys, 378; troubles after his death, 383.
KHODJENT, great city of Turkestan, iii. 289.
KHOVANSKI checks revolt in Pskof, i. 374.
———, chief of Streltsui, put to death, ii. 19.
KHRULEF, Gen., fails at Eupatoria, iii. 169.
KIEF, city of, early importance of, i. 26; greatness of, under Iaroslaf, 85; principality of, located, 98; taken by princes of Smolensk, 115; taken and pillaged by Tatars, 156; becomes subject to Gedimin, 176.
——— Prince of, made Head of Empire, 102.
KIRGHIZ and Kalmuiks, region of, i. 29; Tatars troublesome to Russia, iii. 295; and Kokandians yield to Russia, 296.
KLAPKA, Gen., continues against Austria, iii. 83.
KOKANDIANS, fresh troubles with, iii. 297.
"KOLOKOL," paper issued by Herzen, iii. 217; of Herzen, great power of, 271.
KOLTSOF, eminent poet, iii. 31.
KÖNIGSBERG surrenders to Lestocq, ii. 292.
KONISSKI, Bishop, petitions for help, ii. 187.

KONSTANTIN defeats Russians at Orsha, i. 239.
——— Paulovitch renounces crown, iii. 13.
———, Duke, threatened, iii. 50; flees from Warsaw, 53; retires from Poland, 54.
———, Prince, made high admiral, iii. 178.
———, Duke, made viceroy of Poland, iii. 238.
KORNILOF, Admiral, his plan against Allies, iii. 161; killed at Malakof, 164.
KOROSTIN, city, burned by Olga, i. 68.
KOSCIUZKO, becomes Hero of Poland, ii. 239; makes insurrection at Krakof, 239; efforts to consolidate parties, 241; defeated at Matsiovitsai, 243; set at liberty by Paul I., 250.
KOTCHUBEY, and Iskra executed, ii. 48; advises Alexander I., 271; and Stroganof dismissed, 296.
KOTOSHIKIN, Gregory, writes against boyars, i. 394.
KOTZEBUE tries "Northwest Passage," ii. 394.
KRAKOF, retaken by Prussians, ii. 241; insurrection at, against Austria, iii. 78; insurrection at, quelled by Nicholas, 79.
KREML, or Kremlin, its grandeur and importance, i. 306.
KRIJANITCH, Iuri, elevator of Russian letters, i. 394.
KROPOTOF, editor, noticed, ii. 391.
KRÜDENER, Mad., her mystical counsels, ii. 368; her influence upon Alexander I., 383.
KRUKOVIETSKI made Dictator, iii. 68.
KRUSENSTERN makes first Russian voyage round the world, ii. 394.
KÜCHELBECKER remarks on Russian people, ii. 388.
KULEN, Vandamme defeated at, ii. 350.
KULIKOVO, battle of, won by Dmitri, i. 202.
KULISH, as to Poles and Russians, i. 37.
KÜNERSDORFF, Prussians routed at, ii. 165.
KURBATOF, eloquent letter of, to Peter, ii. 74.
KURBSKI, Andrei, abandons Ivan IV., i. 261; writes letter to same, 262; elegant and powerful writings of, 302.
KUTUZOF, fights his way out of Austria, ii. 279; takes command of Russians, 331; reinforces himself on retreat, 331; retreats from Borodino, 333; retires beyond Moscow, 335; beats Murat at Vinkovo, 340; his pleasant ways with the army, 342.

L.

LAKES, Northern, deep valley of, i. 21.
LAMBERT, Count, succeeds Gortchakof, iii. 237; recalled from Poland, 238.
LAND, Black, extent and nature of, i. 28; productive, in Russia, 38.
LAPUHKIN, Mad., arrested and condemned, ii. 160.
LAW, maritime, new principles sustained, ii. 222.
LAWS, Byzantine and Slavic, conflict of, i. 103; of Russia, as affected by Mongols, 170; improvement in structure of, 233; of civil justice, administration of, 285; provision for administering, ii. 208.
LAZZARONI, terrible riot of, in Naples, ii. 254; second riot of, in Naples, 257.
LEARNING, favor for, under Mikhail, i. 356.
LEIBNITZ advises with Peter as to reforms, ii. 85.
LEIPSIG, battle of, Napoleon beaten at, ii. 351.
LELEVEL, revolutionist, character of, iii. 61.
LEO VI. submits to Oleg, i. 67.
——— X., Pope, mediates for Moscow and Poland, i. 240.
——— the Deacon, as to early Russians, i. 62.
LERMONTOF, Mikhail, eminent poet, iii. 29.
LESTOCQ, Court Physician, his intrigues, ii. 159; disgraced and exiled, 161.
"LETTER of Justice," or Laws of Novgorod, i. 135.
LEWENHAUPT, Swedish general, defeated, ii. 71.
LIAPUNOF abandons insurgents, i. 333.
LIBERALISM, advance of, in Russia, ii. 388.
LIBERATORS, monument erected for, i. 343.
LIBERTY, civil, remarkable principles of, ii. 205; ideas of, demanded by insurgents, iii. 20.
LITERATURE, encouraged by Iaroslaf, i. 86; rapid growth of, under Christianity, 95; peculiar, of Novgorod, 138; rise of, in Russia, 300; and science, great advance of, ii. 169; great men of, under Catherine II., 218; leaders of, further noticed, 220; active advancement of, 391; difficulties of, under Nicholas, iii. 33; real advance of, in Russia, 35; turned in favor of reform, 216; development of, in Russia, 257; for and against Nihilism, 264; Russian, as affected by European ideas, 265.
LITHUANIA, decline and absorption of, i. 184; condition of, under Ivan III.,

INDEX. 399

227; new quarrels of Ivan with, 229; forces of, defeated at Vedrosha, 229; Alexander of, makes truce with Ivan, 230; people of, robbed by Russian law, iii. 246.
LITHUANIAN tribes, notice of, i. 174.
LITHUANIANS, wholesale baptism of, i. 179.
LIVONIA and Crimea, war against both, i. 258; and Poland, forces defeated by Russia, 267.
LIVONIAN Knights, defeated at Dorpat, i. 163; intercept German workmen, 257; make alliance with Poland, 257; order of, broken up, 267.
LIVONIANS revolt and abjure Christianity, i. 144.
LOMONOSOF, works and character of, ii. 170.
LONDON, Conference of, makes Luxembourg neutral, iii. 312.
LORD STRATFORD overlooks Protocol, iii. 132.
LORIS-MELIKOF, Gen., retires from Kars, iii. 370; improves popular feeling, 383.
LOUIS XVIII., expelled from Mitava, ii. 264; enters Louvre, and meets Alexander, 360.
—— Napoleon, his rise and prospects, iii. 85; visits Victoria, 179.
"LOVE and Fidelity," order of, founded, ii. 123.
LOVTCHA, village, captured by Russians, iii. 363.
LUBLIN, Diet of, results in Act of Union, i. 358.
LÜDERS, Count, enters Transylvania, iii. 82; made Viceroy of Poland, 238.
LUITPRAND, remark on Russian names, i. 60.
LÜTZEN and Bautzen, battles won by French, ii. 347.
LUXEMBOURG, France asks evacuation of, iii. 312.

M.

MACK, Gen., operations of, at Naples, ii. 253; army of, broken up at Ulm, 279.
MAGNUS, Danish prince, made King of Livonia, i. 268.
MAINTENON, Mad., visited by Peter, ii. 116.
MAKAROF, editor, notice of, ii. 391.
MAKHMET-GHIREI slain by Mawai, i. 241.
MALAKOF, tower of, built by Russians, iii. 160; great strength of works at, 192; taken by French by assault, 195.
MAMELON, captured by French troops, iii. 185; re-named after Col. de Brancion, 185.

MANGU KHAN, audacious demand of, on France, i. 165.
MANNSTEIN describes Anna's court, ii. 142.
MARFA, seeks to save Novgorod, i. 218; defeated at Korostuin and the Shelona, 219.
MARK, Bishop of Ephesus, defeats union with Rome, i. 214.
MARKOF, Russian minister, unpleasant ways of, ii. 276.
MARLBOROUGH visits camp of Charles XII., ii. 63.
MARRIAGE, ridiculous, of Galitsuin, ii. 143.
——, forced, abolished by Peter, ii. 83.
MARRIAGES between Russians and Tatars, i. 168; royal, how managed in Russia, 283.
MASSENA, operations of, against Allies, ii. 258.
MATHEMATICIANS, eminent Russian, iii. 280.
MATVIEF, introduces European refinements, i. 396; accused and deposed, 399.
MAURICE, Emperor, as to ancient tribes, i. 59.
—— of Saxony seeks to get Kurland, ii. 132.
MAXIMILIAN of Austria mediates for Moscow and Poland, i. 239.
MAXIMUS the Greek, at Court of Moscow, i. 242; banished to monastery, 243.
MAYRAN, Gen., killed before the Malakof, iii. 187.
MAZEPPA, real story of his adoption by Cossacks, ii. 45; gains confidence of Peter, 46; tampers with Polish agents, 46; joins the Swedes, 49; denounced by Peter and driven into Turkey, 49.
MEDICINE, jealousy toward such as practised, i. 299; and surgery, encouraged by Peter, ii. 100; readiness of women to study, iii. 255.
MEHEMET ALI fails to drive out Russians, iii. 363.
MEINHARD made Bishop of Livonia, i. 144.
MELIKOF, Prince, wisdom of, as to public press, iii. 273.
MENGLI-GHIREI of Crimea, ally of Ivan III., i. 224.
MENSHIKOF, acquires superior power, ii. 128; his ambition and greed of authority, 130; opposed by Peter II. and Elisabeth, 130; arrested and disgraced, 131.
——, Prince, sent to Constantinople, iii. 101; his pompous entry into Turkey, 102; insults Fuad Effendi, 103; makes further trouble in Turkish Cabinet, 112; commands at Sevastopol, 153; resigns command, 169.

MERCHANTS, oppressed by nobles, i. 294.
MERRICK, John, ambassador from James I., i. 348.
METTERNICH gets influence over Alexander, ii. 371.
―――, Prince, as to Eastern Question, iii. 131.
MEZENTSOF, Gen., assassinated, iii. 382.
MICHAEL, Saint, Cathedral of, etc., i. 308.
MICHELSON, captures Pugatchef, ii. 201; invades Moldavia, 311.
MIDHAT PASHA gets control in Turkey, iii. 339.
MIKHAIL, charged with poisoning Kontchaka, i. 189; set in pillory by Uzbek, 189; slain by agents of Iuri, 190.
―――, of Tver, subdued by Dmitri, i. 199.
―――― Vorotinski defeats Tatars, i. 269.
―――― Romanof, chosen Tsar at fifteen, i. 344; opens new Polish War, 354.
―――, Grand Duke, heads Russian army, iii. 369; describes storming of Kars, 373.
MILAN, Prince of Serbia, strong movements of, iii. 340.
MILITARY art, Western, brought into Russia, i. 353.
MILORADOVITCH killed by insurgents, iii. 17.
MILOSH successfully rebels in Serbia, ii. 313.
MINDVOG, becomes Prince of Lithuania, i. 175; invades Russia, 175; defeats Livonian Knights, 175; slain by Dovmont, 176.
MINES, Peter arouses interest in, ii. 96.
MININ and Pojarski, honors accorded to, i. 343.
MINING, Russian, results of, iii. 252.
MINISTRY founded to replace "Colleges," ii. 377.
MIROVITCH, seeks to deliver Ivan VI., ii. 181; executed for treason, 182.
MOHILA, Peter, promotes religious learning, i. 365.
MONARCHY, Russian, nature and peculiarity of, i. 282.
MONASTERIES and monks restrained, ii. 93.
MONGOLS, invade and ruin Galitch, i. 125; power of, weakened, 223; power of, begins to decline, 254.
MONKS of St. Cyril rebuked by Ivan, i. 287.
MONTENEGRO forbidden to join Turks, iii. 326.
MORALS, public, sad condition of, ii. 168.
MORDINOF, letter of, to Alexander I., ii. 300.
MOROZOF, minister of Alexis, movements of, i. 371; driven into convent of St. Cyril, 372.

MOSCOW, princes of, subjected to Khans, i. 171; becomes centre of Eastern Russia, 185; princes of, methods of their ambition, 186; first built by Iuri Dolgoruki, 187; greatness of, increases under Ivan, 194; advanced and improved under Dmitri, 205; gains over Suzdal and Nijni, 206; besieged by Shemiaka, 212; with Poland, many alliances of, 239; ravaged by feuds among boyars, 248; suffers great conflagration, 251; architectural glory of, 305; great liability of, to fire, 306; joins the usurpation of Otrepief, 326; almost all burned by Poles, 340; great revolt in, against Miloslavski, 372; riot at, on account of Polish War, 384; Academy of, founded by Feodor, 399; riot and tumult in, ii. 16; great triumph in, 30; complaints at, against Peter, 40; scourged by the plague, 197; treasures of, removed, 338; brandy and spirits burned in, 338; conflagration of, 339; French distressed in, 339.
MOUND-DWELLINGS of ancient people, i. 57.
MOUNTAINS of Russia and other countries, i. 19.
MOZAFFAR, revolts against Russia, iii. 299; defeated at Zera-Bulak, 299.
MSTISLAF the Brave, bold message of, i. 116.
―――― the Bold leaves Novgorod, i. 131.
MUKHTAR PASHA defeated by insurgents, iii. 331.
MUNICIPALITIES, privileges of, regulated, ii. 209.
MÜNNICH, seeks to develop cavalry, ii. 147; and Lascy penetrate Crimea, 148.
MURAD V., becomes Sultan, iii. 338; deposed and retired, 339.
MURAT the Tatar supports Dmitri, i. 198.
―――, Marshal, enters Königsberg, ii. 292.
MURAVIEF, Gen., made Governor of Poland, iii. 243; great cruelty of, in Poland, 244.
MURIDISM, or fanatical faith of the Caucasus, iii. 284.
MYTHOLOGY of ancient Russian poets, i. 51; Russian writers upon, iii. 270.

N.

NAPLES and Hanover important to Alexander I., ii. 275.
NAPOLEON, wins at Eylau, but gains nothing, ii. 289; seeks to negotiate with the Powers, 289; stirs Turkey and Prussia against Russia, 290; attacks Benningsen at Friedland, 291; pride of, displayed

at Erfürt, 304; decides to repudiate Josephine, 305; joins Fifth Coalition against Austria, 308; differs with Alexander I., 314; plan of, for reconstructing Poland, 315; gives Poland his Civil Code, 316; joins his army at Dresden, 323; surprises Vilna, 326; parleys with Alexander I., 328; enticed by Russian retreat, 330; orders forward his reserves, 331; enters Moscow with army, 338; evacuates Moscow, and retreats, 341; leaves army with Murat, 343; masses his new army on the Elbe, 346; quarrels with Metternich, 348; pressed by the Allies, 351; offers the "Conditions of Frankfort," 353; makes vigorous defence of French posts, 355; dethroned by the senate, 360; returns to Paris, 362.

NAPOLEON III., slow action of, in Eastern Question, iii. 123; imperial letter of, to the Tsar, 140.

NARVA, battle of, between Peter I. and Charles XII., ii. 54; retaken by Peter I., 59.

NASHTCHOKIN, Aphanasi, great services of, i. 395; builds first Russian vessel, 395; founds the press in Russia, 395.

NASTASIA ZIMA tortured for Lutheranism, ii. 94.

NATALIA NARUISHKIN marries Alexis, i. 396.

NAVARINO, Turkish fleet destroyed at, iii. 39.

NAVIGATION, steam, development of, iii. 251.

NAVY, rapid growth of, under Peter I., ii. 94.

———, Russian, becomes active on Black Sea, iii. 133; great improvement of, 323.

———, Turkish, inactivity of, iii. 351.

NAWTINGALL, envoy to Alexis from Charles I., i. 398.

NAZIMOF, Rescript of, begins emancipation, iii. 222.

NESSELRODE, Count, his services, iii. 19; his diplomacy with England, 98; his last demand on Turkey, 114; succeeded by Gortchakof, 309.

NESTOR, the Chronicler, as to Russian slaves, i. 36; as to funeral pyres, 54; as to barbarous customs, 55.

NEVA, Dnieper, and Volga, influence of, i. 28; posts upon, taken by Peter, ii. 58; great inundation from, 395.

NEW CODE, Commission formed to draw, ii. 204.

NEWSPAPERS, first one in Russia, ii. 100; increase of, 391.

NEY saves his division, ii. 342.

NICEPHORUS brings Sviatoslaf against Peter, i. 72.

NICHOLAS I., succession given to, iii. 14; disperses insurgents, 16-18; becomes despotic and illiberal, 21; makes demands on Turkey, 38; invades Turkey on the north, 40; attends Diet of Warsaw, 48; proclamation against Polish revolt, 61; unfortunate jealousy of, for France, 73; seeks to annoy France, 77; undertakes against revolution, 80; complains of Turkey, 87; seeks favor with England, 87; sentiments of, to English minister, 89; seeks to partition Turkey with England, 90; his policy penetrated by England, 92; seeks alliance with Austria and Prussia, 137; rejects proposition of Napoleon III., 141; death of, and notes of character, 170; despair of, after Eupatoria, 172.

NIHILISM, beginning of, in Russia, iii. 263; its literary friends and enemies, 264.

NIHILISTS, proclamation issued by, iii. 384; arrested and executed, 387.

NIKOLAI, Fort, taken by Turks, iii. 128; destruction described by Langlois, 200.

———, Grand Duke, seeks to cross Balkans, iii. 375.

NIKOLAIEF, arsenal of, saved by treaty, iii. 203.

NIKON, or Nitika, religious seclusion of, i. 389; becomes Patriarch of Moscow, 390; overcomes monks of White Sea, 391; resigns as Patriarch, 392; imprisoned by Council of Moscow, 392.

NIKOPOLIS, captured by Gen. Krüdener, iii. 356.

NOBILITY, titles of, abrogated by Feodor, ii. 81.

NOBLES, freed by Peter, ii. 111-175; ask privileges on account of emancipation, iii. 228.

NOLAN, Capt., carries order at Balaklava, iii. 165.

NOVELISTS, various, eminent in Russia, iii. 259.

NOVGOROD, early name of St. Petersburg, i. 25; first building of, 65; principality of, located, 98; Bogoliubski defeated at, 115; city, ancient, importance of, 127; republican government of, 129; throne of, offered to Sviatoslaf, 131; various troubles in, 132; political structure of, 133; methods of justice in, 134; works and industries of, 136; punished by Dmitri, 204; fully annexed to Moscow, 206; reduced by Vasili, 213; moved against by Ivan III., 218; ceded to Kasimir IV. of Poland, 219; taken by Ivan, and republic ended, 220; punished by Ivan, and fifteen hundred slain, 266; disturbance at, headed by Wolk, 373.

O.

OATH, Vasili Shuiski made to take, i. 331.
ODESSA, bombarded by Allies, iii. 147; escapes bombardment, 198.
ODYSSEY translated by Zhukovski, iii. 33.
OLEG, second Variag prince, i. 66; invades Tsargrad, 66; killed by a serpent, 67.
OLEG SVIATOSLAVITCH makes civil war, i. 104.
OLGA, Princess, story of, i. 56; avenges death of Igor, 68; converted to Christianity, 69.
———, Saint, said to be native of Pskof, i. 140.
OLGERD, succeeds Gedimin, i. 177; reduces Novgorod, 177; quarrels with Poland, 178; expels Mongols from Crimea, 178.
OMER PASHA, name for Michael Lattas, iii. 128; plans campaign on Danube, 128; beats Russians at Oltenitsa, 129; fortifies Kalafat, 129.
ORLOF, and Elphinstone, naval expedition of, ii. 193; family of great influence, 203.
———, Count, obtains treaty with Turkey, iii. 75; despatched to Vienna, 137; fails in effort at Vienna, 138.
OSIP NEPIA, Russian envoy to England, i. 274.
OSMAN PASHA loses naval battle at Sinope, iii. 134; repulses Russians at Plevna, 357; surrenders at Plevna, 367.
OTHER, Norwegian navigator, visits England, i. 41.
OTREPIEF, Gregory, character of, by Ustrialof, i. 320; imposture of, 322; affiliates with Sigismund, 323; defeated by Vasili Shuiski, 325.
———, the False Tsar, indiscretion of, i. 327; slain in the Kreml, 329.
OXUS River, alterations in its channel, iii. 288.

P.

PAGANISM, modern existence of, i. 42.
PAHLEN, Count, chief conspirator against Paul I., ii. 268; disgraced and dismissed from service, 271.
PAINTERS, eminent, belonging to Russia, iii. 275; historical and *genre*, 276.
PAINTING not affected in Russia by Renaissance, i. 304.
PALACE, Imperial, remaining buildings of, i. 308.
PALMERSTON, Lord, protests against fall of Krakov, iii. 79.
PAMPHLETS, bold tone of, issued in Russia, iii. 171.
PAPER, Russian, decline in value of, ii. 321.
PARIS, Peter visits and inspects, ii. 114; Allies reach, and reduce city of, 358; last treaty made at, 365; embassies present at treaty of, iii. 203; matters settled by treaty of, 204; peace with Russia gained by treaty of, 205.
PASKIEVITCH, Gen., besieges Warsaw, iii. 67; marches into Hungary, 82.
PASSOSHKOF writes on "Poverty and Riches," ii. 99.
PATKUL, his movements against King of Sweden, ii. 52; position of, in Poland, 64; arrested by Secret Council, 65; delivered to Charles XII., and executed, 65.
PATRIARCH system recognized in Russia, i. 55.
PATRIARCHATE established at Moscow, i. 316.
PATRIOTS, various, views of, as to Poland, iii. 242.
PAUL I., his curious and frivolous character, ii. 249; secures alliance with various powers, 252; exasperated with Austria and England, 262; his orders to the Don Cossacks, 264; conspiracy formed against, 268; dies, strangled by conspirators, 270.
PAVEL (or Paul I.) succeeds Catherine II., ii. 248.
PEACE of Tilsit, enthusiasm over, ii. 295.
PEASANTRY, and lower classes, condition of, i. 292; made to be attached to the soil, 315; attachment of, to soil, effects of, 316; uneasy condition of, under Boris, 323; question of freeing in Poland, iii. 235.
PEASANTS, free, forced to become serfs, ii. 207.
PELISSIER, Gen., takes command of French, iii. 183; his recall attempted, 188.
PEROVSKA, Sophia, executed with conspirators, iii. 387.
PERSIA, provinces of, given up by Anna, ii. 145; invades Russian Georgia, 247; Russia still at war with, 314; recommences war with Russia, iii. 36; and adjacent regions, troubles in, 43.
PESTEL, Col., promotes regicide movement, ii. 390; his plans noticed, iii. 14; and others, executed for rebellion, 20.
PETCHENEGI, barbarous tribes conquered by, i. 44; repressed by Vladimir, 81; defeated by Iaroslaf, 83.
PETER the False taken and hanged, i. 333.
——— I. (the Great), made Tsar at nine years old, ii. 14; and Ivan, both declared Tsars, 18; taught by Zotof, 22; youthful habits of, 23; gets the better

of Sophia and her friends, 25; noted for irregular life, 26; goes to Arkhangel, 27; nearly perishes at sea, 27; fails to take Azof at first, 28; takes Azof by intrenchment, 30; meets great popular prejudices, 31; takes supper with conspirators, 32; journeys to the West, 33; singular behavior of, 34; splendidly received in Holland, 36; writes to Adrian as to his plans, 36; leaves Holland, and goes to England, 37; engages many workmen, 38; returns by way of Germany, 38; employs Patkul against Sweden, 53; new preparations of, after Narva, 57; lays foundation of St. Petersburg, 58; captures Swedish vessels, 59; speech of, to army before Poltava, 73; treats Swedish prisoners kindly, 74; proposes a peculiar despotism, 77; fidelity of, to Russian interests, 78; founds the State Inquisition, 90; seeks to divert trade to the Baltic, 95; stimulates literary service, 98; acknowledges his wife, Catherine, 108; reaches the Pruth, but retreats, 109; invades Sweden with fleet, 112; political relations of, with Europe, 113; journeys to Paris, 114; visits Parisian workshops, 115; calls on Mad. de Maintenon, 116; subdues Sweden by Peace of Nystad, 118; becomes broken down, and soon dies, 124; fierce and impetuous nature of, 125; great equestrian statue of, 215.

PETER, the Archimandrite, seeks death of Tsar, ii. 121.

———— II., proposed under regency, ii. 127; crowned at Moscow, 131; dies of small-pox, 132; doubt as to successor of, 134.

———— III., accession of, to throne, ii. 174; unexpected policy of, 174; ill conduct of, in private, 176; friend of Frederic of Prussia, 177; foolish devotion of, to Frederic, 178; abdicates in favor of wife, as Catherine II., 180; killed by Alexis Orlof, 181.

PETROF, Anton, insurrection under, iii. 227.

PHILARET set free, and made Patriarch, i. 350.

PHILIP, Archbishop, executed by Ivan IV., i. 265.

PHILIPPSON, Curator, quits body of students, iii. 248.

PHYSICIANS, danger attending their profession, i. 299; female, Russian ladies preparing for, iii. 255.

PISEMSKI, novelist, his work sketched, iii. 260.

PLAINS, vast, found in Russia, i. 19; of Russia, political unity of, 31.

PLANUS CARPINUS describes Grand Horde, i. 165.

PLATEAU, great, of Alaun, i. 20.

PLAYS become frequent in Russia, ii. 99.

PLEISCHWITZ, armistice signed at, ii. 347.

PLEVNA, second battle of, lost by Russians, iii. 359; third battle at, lost by Russians, 364; at last completely invested, 366.

POEMS, heroic and romantic, frequency of, i. 304.

POETRY and Drama of Russia noticed, iii. 267.

POLAND, united to Lithuania, i. 179; and Lithuania, old jealousies of, i. 358; Augustus of, joins Russia against Sweden, ii. 53; war recommenced in, 146; causes of its final ruin, 185; national weakness of, 186; religious difficulties of, 188; agonized by religious war, 190; finally dismembered by Three Powers, 195; progress of reforms in, 233; second partition of, by Russia and Prussia, 235; fall of, caused by aristocracy, 238; last dismemberment and ruin of, 244; territory of, entered by French, 286; and Russia, hatred between soldiers of, 309; flourishes awhile under Napoleon, 317; great enthusiasm in, for Napoleon, 327; fourth partition of, 362; reconstruction of, 367; condition of, under Nicholas, iii. 47; revolt in, makes progress, 49; conspiracy in, ready to strike, 50; outbreak of insurrection in, 51; insurrection in, fails at first, 52; sudden increase of insurrection in, 53; efforts to stay revolt in, 55; insurgents in, mutual distrust of, 56; trifling spirit of the people, 60; deprived of all nationality, 70; religious results of depression of, 71; early visit of Alexander II. to, 210; hopes for improvement of, 234; insurrection in, gets desperate, 239; fighting by insurgents throughout, 240; end of last revolt in, 245.

POLATSKI, Simeon, the Poet of Reform, i. 393.

POLES, in Moscow, collide with Russians, i. 339; defeated before Moscow by Poyarski, 343; Russians make treaty with, 350; defeated at Zbarosh, 378; make treaty with Khmelnitski, 379; have fresh success against Russians, 384.

POLEVOI, Nikolai, eminent editor, iii. 27.

POLIANKA, Congress of, makes peace with Poland, i. 354.

POLICE, secret court of, harsh doings of, ii. 90; abolished, 175.

POLISH Succession, diplomacy as to, ii. 145; fresh agitation of, 184.

POLOTSK, principality of, located, i. 100.

POLTAVA, or Pultowa, Charles XII. besieges, ii. 72; Charles wounded before, 72; moral effects of victory of, 75.

POLYKARPOF writes history of Russia, ii. 101.
PONIATOVSKI becomes King of Poland, ii. 185.
———, Joseph, commands Polish army, ii. 316.
POPOF, Admiral, invents "Circular Monitor," iii. 323.
POPULATION of different parts of Russia, i. 46.
POSSEVINS, Antonio, Pope's legate to Russia, i. 271.
POTEMKIN, great success and influence of, ii. 204; honors to, after Treaty of Constantinople, 224; encouraged by Catherine II., 227; captures city of Otchakof, 230; moves against Selim III., 230.
POTOTSKI, Gen., to lead Polish revolt, iii. 51.
POWERS, Great, check plans of Russia, iii. 378.
——— of the West, embassies sent to, i. 399.
PRAGA, captured by assault, ii. 243; battle of, Poles repulsed at, iii. 65.
PRAGUE, Congress of, agreed to, ii. 348.
PRATZEN, desperate fight on plateau of, ii. 282.
PRESS, state of censorship of, iii. 233; daily, development of, 271; interdicted by police, 273; humorous, different sheets noticed, 274.
PRINTING patronized by Ivan IV., i. 302.
PRODUCTIONS, found in Russian commerce, i. 293; agricultural, facts of, iii. 252.
PROKOPI LIAPUNOF joins insurrection, i. 332.
PROTOKOL, London, signed and submitted, iii. 345; rejected by Turkey, 346.
PROVINCES, benefits to, by new treaty, iii. 378.
PRUSSIA, treaty with, by Peter II., ii. 133; Russia becomes jealous of, 162; dismembered by Napoleon, 293; arrangements with, against Napoleon, 346; great discouragements for, 347; joins Russia against Poland, iii. 245.
PRUTH, Russians repulsed from the, ii. 110; Treaty of the, made with Baltazhi-Mahomet, 110.
PSKOF, city, present state of, described, i. 140; independence of, recognized by Novgorod, 141; city, taken by "Sword Bearers," 160; poetic lament over fall of, 237; sedition spreads to people of, 373.
PUBLIC Opinion, as affecting diplomacy, iii. 115.
PUGATCHEF revolts under name of Peter III., ii. 199.
PUNISHMENTS, severe and terrible, used, i. 286; corporal, modified, iii. 232.

PUSHKIN, writer, his opinion of Charles XII., ii. 68.
———, Alexander, greatest Russian poet, iii. 28.
PUTIATIN, Count, oppresses students, iii. 247; appealed to by them, 248.

Q.

QUAKERS, deputation of, visit Alexander I., ii. 383.
QUARANTINE Battery, severe fight before, iii. 182.

R.

RADITSKI, Gen., carries Shipka Pass, iii. 376.
RAGLAN, Lord, dies of cholera, iii. 188.
RAILROADS, Russian system of, iii. 250.
RAILWAYS first introduced under Nicholas, iii. 24.
RAINFALL small in Russia, i. 22.
RASKOLNIKI, terrible fanaticism of, ii. 167; lenient treatment of, 175; fanatically oppose government, 198; mildly treated by Alexander I., 377.
READ, Gen., attacks French at Traktir, iii. 191.
REDAN, English repulsed from, iii. 196.
"RED PLACE," great execution in, i. 266.
REFORMS of Peter, opposition to, ii. 76; not to cause social changes, 77; as to peasantry and slaves, 80; as to titles of nobility, 82; as to seclusion of women, 83; as to public amusements, 84; as to forms of government, 85; as to minor political affairs, 86; as to extortion in office, 87; as to civil law, 88; as to police and hospitals, 89; Dolgorukis react against, 131.
———, in Poland proposed by Diet of 1791, ii. 234; begun and furthered by Alexander I., 375; liberal, reaction against, 384; promised by Alexander II., iii. 211; create remarkable liberalism, 213.
RELIGION of the Russian Slavs, i. 51; largely tolerated by Peter I., ii. 94.
"RETRIBUTION," English frigate visits Sevastopol, iii. 136.
REVENGE, singular mode of, i. 42.
REVENUE, public, statistics of, iii. 233.
REVENUES and living of royal family, i. 284.
REVIEWS, Russian, prominent ones noticed, iii. 273.
REVOLTS in many States, Alexander meddles with, ii. 371.
REVOLUTION of 1741, significance of, ii. 157; of 1762, beginnings of, 179; ideas of, become prevalent, 389; French, of 1848, consequences of, iii. 80.

RHEDEDIA, giant, slain by Iaroslaf, i. 83.
RIAZAN, and Murom, principality of, located, i. 93; battle of, and great defeat of Russians, 154; and Novgorod-Severski joined to Moscow, 237.
RICHELIEU succeeds Talleyrand, ii. 365.
RIESENKAMPF remarks on Russian trade, i. 137.
RITTICH, views of, as to native tribes, i. 35.
RIVERS, found in Russia, i. 23; great importance of, 24; and lakes, system of, 25.
ROMAN, of Volhynia, conquers Galitch, i. 123.
ROSEN, Gen., defeated by Poles at Igani, iii. 66.
ROSTOPTCHIN reviles the French, ii. 300.
———, Governor of Moscow, his character, ii. 335; contrives to inspirit the people, 336; proclamation of, after Borodino, 336.
ROUSSET, writer, describes fall of Sevastopol, iii. 193.
RUILEEF and Pestel, republican leaders, ii. 390.
RUMANIA, joins Russia against Turkey, iii. 349; troops of, reinforce Russians, 361.
RUMIANTSOF defeats Turks at Kahul, ii. 193.
RURIC, first Variag prince, i. 65.
"RUSKAIA PRAVDA," or Code of Iaroslaf, i. 84.
RUSSELL, W. H., remarks on fall of Sevastopol, iii. 197; describes powder explosion, 199.
RUSSIA, compared with rest of Europe, i. 17; numerous seas of, 18; mountains and surface of, 19; White, limits defined, 45; Great, Little, Red, and Black defined, 46; distributed into principalities, 96; early unity of race and language, 101; capital centre of, changed, 112; invaded by Mongols in 13th century, 149; intestine troubles in, 167; laws of, as affected by Mongols, 170; religious heads of, at Moscow and Kief, 183; Eastern, gathered round Moscow, 185; condition of, at death of Vasili, 216; historians of, estimate of Ivan IV., 244; condition of, at accession of Ivan IV., 245; rapid extension of power of, 256; diplomatic position of, under Feodor, 313; and Poland, with Sweden, all at war, 314; and Poland, mutual attitude after Mikhail, 357; general ignorance and superstition in, 324; provinces of, troubled and demoralized, 331; condition of, at end of Polish war, 345; implores help from England, 348; repudiates union with Rome, 364; Little, its oppressed people look to Tsar, 369; greatness of, in service of Peter, ii. 79; divided by parties after Peter's death, 127; virtually ruled by Germans, 139; makes treaty with Poland, 189; withdraws troops from Warsaw, 189; progress of, under Catherine II., 211; and France, difficulties between, 251; and France operate in European affairs, 274; immense army raised by, 286; debate as to policy of, 344; and England, understanding between, 363; meets contempt at Madrid, 372; new plans for government of, 380; laws of, codified by Nicholas I., iii. 22; history of, by Ustrialof, 26; troops of, enter Austria, 81; interferes in favor of Denmark, 84; publishes secret correspondence, 99; seeks to divide France and England, 107; fresh diplomatic efforts to conciliate, 118; betrays real design on Turkey, 122; declines mediation of Austria, 133; questions France and England, 136; fails of alliance with Prussia, 139; receives ultimatum of Allies, 142; popular feeling in, after death of Nicholas, 171; serious losses of, by Treaty of Paris, 206; foreign ships admitted to ports of, 208; popular call for improvement in, 214; territorial policy of, 282; facile character of soldiers of, 303; keeps Italy and Denmark from Franco-Prussian War, 313; feeling of, after above war, 314; popular voice of, against Prussia, 315; jealousy of, toward Prussia, 316; demands truce for Serbia, 342; moves for correcting Turkish misrule, 342; threatening attitude of, toward Turkey, 343; prepares to march upon Turkey, 347; popular discontent in, 382; disappointed in her new ruler, 387; reflections on destiny of, 388.
RUSSIA, army of, Swedes defeat at Narva, ii. 55; defeated at Friedland, 292; enters Turkey, iii. 117; force and position of, 153; commanders of, noticed, 161; great sortie of, fails, 180; modern plan of recruiting, 321; first draft to recruit, 322.
———, fleet of, destroyed by storm, i. 66; defeats Turkish vessels, ii. 229; taken by Admiral Cotton, 306.
———, people of, combine to stop civil war, i. 341; terrible ignorance of, ii. 198; incline to liberal ideas, 387; aptness of, to learn, iii. 252.
RUSSIAN, character, energy of, i. 48; capital upon Danube proposed, 72; warriors disguised as merchants, 89; Christianity, sources and influence of, 90; Christianity, moral effects of, 92.
RUSSIANS proper, proportion to other

tribes, i. 45; drive Asiatic Turks into Kars, iii. 128; attacked by Turks at Tchetat, 130; gain something at Balaklava, 166; prepare to attack Allies, 190; defeated at Traktir Bridge, 191.

S.

SAARDAM, Peter works at boat-building in, ii. 35.
SACRIFICES, human, tribes charged with, i. 42.
SADKO, merchant of Novgorod, story of, i. 139.
SAINT-MARTIN, views of, as to native tribes, i. 35.
SAINT-SIMON, gives character of Peter, ii. 114; remarks on Russian alliance, 116.
SAINTS made by Russian Church from old gods, i. 53.
SALISBURY, Lord, as to new treaty provisions, iii. 379.
SALONICA, consuls murdered at, iii. 332.
SAMARCAND, city of, noticed, iii. 292.
SAMOKVASOF, ancient dwellings found by, i. 57.
SAN STEFANO, Treaty of, amended at Berlin, iii. 379.
SCHLITTE, the Saxon, sent to Germany, i. 257.
SCHÖNBRUNN, Treaty of, makes fresh war, ii. 284; Congress of, its results, 310.
SCHOOLS, first founded by Vladimir, i. 81; technical, established by Peter, ii. 98; system of, undertaken by Alexander, 378.
SCHUYLER, EUGENE, remarks on Central Asia, iii. 286; as to Russian attitude, 315.
SCIENCE, retrograde fortune of, in Russia, ii. 385.
SCRIPTURES, Slavonic, revised by Nikon, i. 390.
SCULPTORS, eminent, belonging to Russia, iii. 275.
SCYTHIANS, ancient barbarous habits of, i. 33.
SEA-FIGHTS, several, won against Swedes, ii. 58.
SEAS, numerous, found in Russia, i. 18.
"SECRET Convention," by France and Russia, ii. 273; signed at Erfurt, 305.
SELIM III. deposed by Janissaries, ii. 312.
SENATE, founded by Peter, ii. 85; re-established as at first, 167; made Court of Revision, iii. 231.
SERAPHIM and Evgeni abused by insurgents, iii. 18.
SERBIA, massacre of Christians in, ii. 311; threatening movements of, iii. 340; forces of, defeated by Turks, 341.

SERFDOM, great men working to destroy, iii. 34.
SERFS, intolerable condition of, i. 366; emancipation of, Speranski favors, ii. 381; debate on emancipation of, iii. 218; numbers and situation of, 219; their own estimate of their condition, 220; approaching freedom of, 221; how organized after emancipation, 226; some of, refuse terms of freedom, 227.
SERGIUS, St., patron of Muscovite princes, i. 204.
SEVASTOPOL, visited by Alexander I., ii. 398; Allies proceed to, iii. 151; topography of, 157; account of city of, 158; fortifications of, 159; landward defences of, finished, 162; bombarded a second time, 181; a third time bombarded, 185; fourth bombardment of, 186; bridge built in harbor of, 189; fifth and last bombardment of, 193; evacuated by Russians, 196; final destruction of works at, 200.
SEYMOUR, English minister, his interview with Nicholas, iii. 88.
SHAGAN, Joseph, his account of the Khazarui, i. 43.
SHAH INDEH, mosque in memory of, iii. 292.
SHAKHAVSKOI proclaims a new Pretender, i. 332.
SHAMYL, leader of mountain tribes, iii. 42; becomes leader of the Murids, 284; wonderful escapes and final capture of, 284; dies a captive at Kaluga, 285.
SHEMIAKA, attacks Moscow, i. 212; evacuates same, 213.
SHEREMETIEF, made Field Marshal, ii. 57; defeats Swedes at Errestfer, 57; again defeats them at Hummelsdorff, 58; quells revolt at Astrakhan, 60.
SHIPKA PASS, evacuated by Turks, iii. 355; Turks fail to recapture, 362.
SHIPS, Peter builds, on the Don, ii. 29; foreign, admitted to Russian ports, iii. 208.
SHUVALOF, IVAN, promotes literature, ii. 168; sent with Napoleon to Elba, 360.
SIBER, Siberian capital, taken by Irmak, i. 277.
SIERAVSKI, Gen., defeated by Russians, iii. 66.
SIGISMOND, prevented from crowning Vitovt, i. 183; threatens English trade, 281.
——— of Poland, besieges Smolensk, 336; plans treachery against Russia, 338; invited to enter Moscow, 339; captures Smolensk and takes Vasili, 340.
SILISTRIA unsuccessfully besieged by Russians, iii. 147.
SILVESTER, priest, minister of Ivan IV.,

i. 251; and Adashef, quarrel with Ivan IV., 258; banished from court, 260; his "Domostroi," or Rules of Society, 301.

SIMEON the Proud, succeeds Ivan Kalita, i. 195; styled "Grand Prince of all the Russians," 196; encourages arts and manufactures, 196.

SIMPSON, Gen. James, succeeds Lord Raglan, iii. 188.

SINEUS and Truvor, Variag princes, i. 65.

SINOPE, battle of, causes general indignation, iii. 134.

SISTOVA, passage forced and captured by Russians, iii. 353.

SIT, battle of, and Iuri II. slain, i. 155.

SKOBELEF, Gen., saves Russians at Plevna, iii. 360; hardships of, at Plevna, 365; brilliant assault of, at Shenovo, 376.

SKOROPADSKI, last hetman of Ukraina, ii. 50.

SKRZYNETSKI, Gen., succeeds to Polish command, iii. 65; repulsed at Ostrolenka, 66.

SLAVES held by most Russians, i. 89.

SMOLENSK, principality of, located, i. 97; attacked and taken by Vasili, 238; and Krasnoé, hard fighting at, ii. 330; evacuated by the French, 341.

SOBIESKI becomes King of Poland, i. 387.

SOCIETIES and Orders, increase of, in Russia, ii. 389.

SOCIETY, in Novgorod, constitution of, i. 135; minor relations of, 293; of the North, action of, iii. 15; agricultural, of Poland, 235; agricultural, broken up, 237.

SOFTAS, revolt of, at Constantinople, iii. 337.

SOKOVNIM and other conspirators subdued, ii. 32.

SOLDIERY opposed to Christianity, i. 70.

SOLINTKOF defeats Prussians, ii. 165.

SOLOVIEF attempts life of Emperor, iii. 382.

SOLOVIOF, opinion of, as to Ivan III., i. 234.

SONGS, ancient Tchud, deploring slavery, i. 146.

SOPHIA, determines to become Regent, ii. 14; flattered by writers, 15; triumphs and becomes Regent, 17; has her seat behind the throne, 18; quarrels with Peter, 22; seeks to supplant Peter, 24; banished to a monastery, 26; conspires against Peter, 32; stirs up trouble with Streltsui, 41; imprisoned in convent, 44.

——— of Anhalt becomes Catherine II., ii. 178.

——— NARUISHKIN, death of, ii. 396.

SPERANSKI, Mikhail, notice of, ii. 297; made Secretary of State, 298; suddenly disgraced, 323; advancement and influence of, 379; plans for constitutional changes, 380; reforms of, meet opposition, 381.

ST. PETERSBURG, decided foundation of, ii. 101; built on islands, 102; inundated by Neva, 104; more progressive than Moscow, 104; joy in, for victory over Swedes, 118; return to, obtained by Ostermann, 143; terrible flood covers, 395.

STATES-GENERAL convened to elect Tsar, i. 318.

STATISTICS, eminent students of, in Russia, iii. 280.

STEIN, German patriot, advanced by Alexander, ii. 323; and Anslett, obtain Treaty of Kalish, 345.

STENKO RAZIN ravages Eastern Russia, i. 388; finally defeated by Boriatinski, 388.

STEPHEN BATORY made King of Poland, i. 270.

STEPPES, of Kirghiz, i. 20; arable, zone of, 29; barren, region of, 29.

STOLBOVO, Peace of, by Russia and Sweden, i. 349.

STONE, houses of, forbidden save in St. Petersburg, ii. 103.

STONES, every boat forced to bring to St. Petersburg, ii. 103.

STRATFORD, Lord, seeks to restrain Menshikof, iii. 111.

STRELTSUI, revolt of, against Matveef, ii. 16; surrender to Sophia, 19; arrested by Romodanovski, 42; executed at wholesale by Peter, 43.

STROGONOFF, Gregory, gets lands on the Kama, i. 277.

STUDENTS, Turkish, urge Sultan to war, iii. 124; Russian, trouble excited with, 247.

SUFFRAGE first promoted by Nicholas I., iii. 23.

SULEIMAN PASHA attacks Shipka Pass, iii. 361.

SUPERSTITIONS indulged in all Russia, i. 299.

SUVAROF, Prince, replaces Count Putiatin, 249.

SUVOROF, or Suwarrow, relieves Prince of Koburg, ii. 230; takes Praga by assault, 243; his contempt of Prussian styles, 250; recalled from retirement, 254; his action as Marshal of Austria, 255; his famous passage through the Alps, 260; story of his wonderful retreat, 260.

SUZDAL, principality of, located, i. 99.

SVIATOSLAF, important reign of, i. 70; wages Bulgarian War, 71; takes tribute from Greeks, 71; declines duel with Zimisces, 75; evacuates Greek frontier,

75; slain by Petchenegi, 76; portrait of, by Leo the Deacon, 76.
SWEDEN, movements of Patkul in, ii. 52; urges war with Russia, 117; affairs with, get complicated, 158; threatened by Russia and Prussia, 196; fleet of, repulsed at Hogland, 228.
SWORD-BEARERS, Order of, founded, i. 144.
SWORDS, ancient, story of, from Nestor, i. 58.
"SYSTEM of the North," of Catherine II., ii. 183; abandoned by Russia, 221.

T.

TALITSKI writes against Peter, ii. 93.
TALLEYRAND, plan of, to break Coalition, ii. 319.
TAMERLANE becomes chief of Mongols, i. 203; attempts to invade Russia, 207.
TASHKENT, great city of Turkestan, iii. 289; city of, taken by Abramof, 298.
TATAR Hordes, dissensions among, i. 224; broken up by strategy, 226.
TATARS, or Tartars, characters of, by Chinese, i. 150; retire from Russia, 153; invasions of, results to Russia, 158; take census of Novgorod, 163; imposts of, resisted by Russians, 163; hold complete rule in Russia, 168; tolerate all religions, 172; further trouble with, 240; ravage open country, 241; and Turks, besiege Astrakhan, 268; and other nations, relations to Russia, 319; invade Nova Serbia, ii. 191.
TAXES, system of assessing and collecting, i. 293; management of, under Peter, ii. 91.
TCHARTORIUSKI, memorial to Alexander I., ii. 285.
TCHERNICHEF, envoy to Napoleon, ii. 322.
TCHERNIGOF, principality located, i. 98.
"TCHIN," or Order of Rank, fixed by Peter, ii. 82; table of, 400.
TCHORLU, last battle of the war at, iii. 377.
TELEGRAPH, extension of, outlined, iii. 251.
TEMPERATURE, great range of, i. 22.
TEMPLES and priests not in early history, i. 52.
TEMUTCHIN, or Ghenghis Khan, conquests of, i. 151.
TERLETSKI, Bishop, made Deputy Patriarch, i. 362; intrigues with Sigismond, 363.
TEUTONIC Knights, Order of, founded, i. 146; attacked by Vitovt, 182.
THEATRE, first, founded by Volkof, ii. 171.

THIERS, M., his fruitless mission to Russia, iii. 314.
THIEVES and extortioners punished by Peter, ii. 87.
"THREE Emperors," battle of, described, ii. 281; conference of, at Berlin, iii. 320.
TILSIT, remarkable conference at, ii. 293; treaty of, general terms of, 294.
TIMMERMANN teaches Peter use of boats, ii. 23.
TIMUR defeats Vitovt on the Vorskla, i. 181.
TODLEBEN, Gen., ordered to invest Plevna, iii. 365.
TOKHTAMUISH, puts Mamai to death, i. 203; sacks and burns Moscow, 203.
TOLSTOI, Count Alexis, dramatist, iii. 266.
———, Leof, writer of romance, iii. 266.
TOWNS, new, many founded by Catherine II., ii. 210.
TRADITION as to subjection of Mordva, i. 121.
TRADITIONARY literature, abundance of, i. 303.
TRAVEL, excellent Russian works upon, iii. 279.
TRAVELLERS in Russia, older, noticed, i. 300.
TREBIA, Macdonald repulsed at, ii. 257.
TREDIAKOVSKI, works and troubles of, ii. 170.
TREES found in Northern Russia, i. 28.
TREPOF, Gen., shot by Sasulitch, iii. 382.
TRIBES, ancient, according to Herodotus, i. 35; ancient, compared with modern, 35; outlying, on Russian frontier, 143.
TRIBUTES, mode of exacting and collecting, i. 88.
TROITSA, Convent of, besieged, i. 334.
TUNDRAS, region of, i. 21.
TURGENIEF, writes against serfdom, iii. 34; novelist, his character noted, 258; attacks Socialism, 263.
TURKESTAN, government of, re-created, iii. 299; Eastern, recovered by Chinese, 303.
TURKEY declares war against Poland, i. 353; declares war with Russia, ii. 107, 192, 227; fleet of, defeated at Chios and Tchesmi, 193; makes hasty peace with Russia, 196; war with, freshly urged, 229; seeks favor with Napoleon, 310; finally reduces Serbia, 313; shelters Hungarian refugees, iii. 83; relations of, discussed by Russia and England, 93; proposal of Nicholas I. to partition, 94; state of, at Menshikof's visit, 104; progress of diplomacy in, 109; asks changes in "Vienna Expedient," 120; wisdom of its Cabinet made plain, 122;

INDEX.   409

Great Council of, again reject "Vienna Expedient," 125; integrity of, maintained by Treaty of Paris, 204; attractive reforms offered by, 327; finances of, embarrassed state of, 328; increasing difficulties of, with insurgents, 331; indorses atrocities in Bulgaria, 334; rejects proposals of Conference, 344; replies to manifesto of Russia, 348.
TURKISH Army occupies Eupatoria, iii. 168.
TURKMANTCHAI, Peace of, ends Persian War, iii. 37.
TURKOMANS, doubtful status of, iii. 302.
TURKS, movements of the Powers against, ii. 20; wanton barbarity of, at Plevna, iii. 364; agree to armistice and basis of peace, 377.
TUSHINO, insurgents of, join Sigismond, i. 336.
TVER, insurrection at, against Mongols, i. 191; House of, new struggle with, 199.
TVERDILLO betrays Pskof to Livonians, i. 140.

U.

UKRAINA, hardy and free people of, i. 367; ceded to Russia, 399; Charles XII. approaches Russia by way of, ii. 70; Jews and Catholics persecuted in, 190.
UNION of Lublin, consequences of, i. 359.
UNITED STATES brings home Kossuth, iii. 83; continued friendliness with Russia, 307; purchases Territory of Alaska, 307.
USSUM HASSAN allies with Ivan III., i. 224.
USTRIALOF, writer, his opinion of Feodor, i. 311; writes History of Russia, iii. 26.

V.

VALDAI, plateau of, great river source, i. 24.
VALLEY of the Dwina, noticed, i. 20.
VANKA KAIN, notorious robber, ii. 168.
VARIAGI, tribe of, traced and defined, i. 60; further defined, 61; habits and dispositions of, 63; name of Russia given by, 64.
VARNA, allied camp at, broken up, iii. 150.
VASES, ancient, of silver and gold, i. 34.
VASILI, combat of, at Novgorod, i. 139; succeeds Dmitri in Moscow, 205; makes treaty with Vitovt, 209.
———, the Blind, succeeds to throne in Moscow, i. 210; troubles of, with Iuri, 211; returns to Moscow, 212; denounces union with Rome, 215.

VASILI GALITSUIN, minister for Sophia, ii. 20.
——— IVANOVITCH, arrests magistrates of Pskof, i. 235; humbles Pskof and ends republic, 235; quarrels with Sigismond, 238; establishes fair at Makarief, 241; strengthens himself as Autocrat, 242.
——— SHUISKI, denounces the False Dmitri, i. 327; conspires against Otrepief, 329; succeeds to throne, 330; makes alliance with Sweden, 335; abdicates throne of Russia, 337.
VENGROV, battle of, fought with insurgent Poles, iii. 241.
VENICE, negotiations with, by Ivan III., i. 232.
VERONA, Congress of, assembled, ii. 372.
VIASMA, battle of, won by Ney and Eugene, ii. 341.
VIATKA, new colony formed from Novgorod, i. 141.
VICTOR EMANUEL, made King of Italy, iii. 310; recognized by Russia, 310.
VICTORIA of England visits with Louis Napoleon, iii. 179.
VIENNA, Conference of, contrives pacific expedient, iii. 119; attempts mediation, 132.
———, Great Conference of, iii. 178; fails, 179.
———, Peace of, ends Polish War, ii. 147.
VIKULOF becomes hermit author, ii. 93.
VILLAGES and Communes, nature of, i. 56.
VILNA, terror and destruction at, ii. 344.
VINNO DE RÖHRBACH, Grand Master, i. 144.
VITOVT, besieges Castle of Vilna, i. 180; betrays Iuri and pillages Smolensk, 180; brings great force against Tatars, 181; gains battle of Tannenberg, 182.
VLADIMIR, early character of, i. 77; marries Rogneda, 78; examines all religions, 79; besieges Kherson, 79; is baptized and marries Anna, 80; destroys idols and baptizes people, 80.
——— and Evfrosinia executed, i. 205.
——— MONOMAKH succeeds to throne, i. 106; advice of, to his sons, 107; people of, subdue Suzdal, 119.
VLADISLAUS of Poland, proposes for throne, i. 337; invades Moscow, 350.
VOLGA, River and branches, i. 26; early civilization upon, 27; Dnieper, and Neva, influence of, 28.
VOLHYNIA, principality located, i. 100.
VOLKOF, minister of Peter III., humanity of, ii. 175.
VOLTAIRE, as to Catherine II., ii. 182; close correspondent of Catherine II., 215.

VOLUINSKI, character of, by Solovief, ii. 150; famous jest upon, by Kurakin, 151; convicted of conspiracy, 151; executed for same, 152.
VORONTSCHOF, predictions of, as to Prussia, ii. 163.
VSEVOLOD, ambitious reign of, i. 119.
———, Gabriel, exiled from Novgorod, i. 130; first ruler of Pskof, 140.

W.

WALLACE, English traveller, observations of, i. 50; remarks on the Tsars, 172.
———, Mackenzie, remarks on serfage, iii. 223.
WAR, civil, of Oleg, ended by peace, i. 105; of David of Volhynia, 105; triple, arising from Peace of Tilsit, ii. 306; opened by Turkey at Isaktcha, iii. 127.
WARSAW, Polish insurrection reaches, ii. 240; terrible riots in, iii. 68, 236, 237; invested by Paskievitch, 68; finally entered and subdued, 69.
———, Diet of, seeks to amend Constitution, ii. 233; action of, as to revolt, iii. 59; ruled by insurgents, 63.
WIDOWS, burning of, for dead husbands, i. 53.
WILLOUGHBY, and Chancellor, sail for North Sea, i. 272; lost with his two vessels, 273.

WILMOT, Miss, ridicules French and Russians, ii. 302.
WILSON, English envoy, denounces Peace of Tilsit, ii. 295.
WINDS, great influence of, in Russia, i. 21.
WOMEN, treatment of, in ancient times, i. 55; secluded and tyrannized over, 295; abject condition of, in Russia, 296; freed from seclusion by Peter, ii. 83.

Y.

YPSILANTI defeated by Turks, ii. 373.

Z.

ZALIVSKI, revolutionist leader in Poland, iii. 48.
ZAPOROSHTSUI, wild tribes of the Dnieper, i. 368; tribe of, extinguished, ii. 201.
ZARUTSKI captured and executed, i. 346.
ZHERKIEVITCH, writer, as to Kutusof, ii. 342.
ZHUKOVSKI, eminent Russian translator, iii. 32.
ZIELENTSE, battle of, fought by Poniatowski, ii. 236.
ZIMISCES, John, gains fight at Dorostol, i. 75; challenges Sviatoslaf to duel, 75.
ZORNDORFF, Russians beaten at, ii. 165.
ZUBOF sent against Mohammed, ii. 247.
ZÜRICH, Massena wins victory at, ii. 259.

From the sentence "Toward the end of the year," on page 86, unto the end of Chapter V., page 126, in Volume III., is mainly a paraphrase from Camille Rousset's admirable history of the Crimean War.

www.ingramcontent.com/pod-product-compliance
Lightning Source LLC
Chambersburg PA
CBHW051742300426
44115CB00007B/661